Acclaim for Kati Marton's

HIDDEN POWER

"What are the secrets of the successes or the failures of our best known first ladies? How have they affected the course of America's history? Kati Marton knows, and she shares this very personal and acute knowledge with us. This is that rare book that is both dishy and informative."
—Barbara Walters

"A deft survey of a dozen First Couples."
—*Time*

"Entertaining. . . . *Hidden Power* gets and keeps the reader's attention."
—*Los Angeles Times*

"A smart, insightful look at how these singular marriages have shaped presidential history."
—*The Atlanta Journal-Constitution*

"Proof that there's a genius to synthesis. Marton weaves through the relationships of presidential couples from the Wilsons to the present occupants of the White House as if she knew them all personally."
—*The Austin Chronicle*

"[A] smart examination of a woman's r~~ol~~ ~~·ly~~

"Compelling. . . . Illumina~~t~~ ~~·l-~~ paced."
~~·~~ (Raleigh)

"An intelligent, entertaining lo~~ok~~ ~~·~~ecent presidential marriages and how they have affected the country."
—*Rocky Mountain News*

KATI MARTON

HIDDEN POWER

Kati Marton is the author of three previous works of non-fiction—*Wallenberg*, *A Death in Jerusalem*, and *The Polk Conspiracy*—and a novel, *An American Woman*. She has written for *The New Yorker*, *The New York Times*, *The Atlantic Monthly*, *Vanity Fair*, and *The New Republic*. A former correspondent for National Public Radio and ABC News, Marton received a George Foster Peabody Award for broadcast journalism. She lives in New York City with her husband and her son and daughter.

Also by Kati Marton

HIDDEN POWER

HIDDEN POWER

PRESIDENTIAL MARRIAGES THAT
SHAPED OUR HISTORY

**Scripps Miramar Ranch
Library Center**

KATI MARTON

ANCHOR BOOKS
A DIVISION OF RANDOM HOUSE, INC.   NEW YORK

FIRST ANCHOR BOOKS EDITION, JULY 2002

Copyright © 2001 by Kati Marton

All rights reserved under International and Pan-American Copyright Conventions. Published in the United States by Anchor Books, a division of Random House, Inc., New York, and simultaneously in Canada by Random House of Canada Limited, Toronto. Originally published in hardcover with an epilogue in slightly different form in the United States by Pantheon Books, a division of Random House, Inc., New York, in 2001.

Anchor Books and colophon are registered trademarks of Random House, Inc.

The Library of Congress has cataloged the Pantheon edition as follows:
Marton, Kati.
Hidden power : presidential marriages that shaped our recent history / Kati Marton.
p. cm.
Includes index.
ISBN 0-375-40106-7
1. Presidents—United States—Biography. 2. Presidents' spouses—United States—Biography.
3. Presidents' spouses—United States—Political activity. 4. Married people—United States—
Biography. 5. Power (Social sciences)—United States—Case studies. 6. United States—
Politics and government—Case studies. I. Title.
E176.1 .M368 2001   973'.09'9—dc21   [B]   2001021351

Anchor ISBN: 0-385-72188-9

Author photograph © Jade Albert
Book design by Fritz Metsch

www.anchorbooks.com

Printed in the United States of America
10 9 8 7 6 5 4 3 2 1

FOR

RICHARD, ELIZABETH AND CHRISTOPHER—

the three who make all else possible

CONTENTS

HIDDEN
POWER

INTRODUCTION

I never wanted your advice and assistance more in my life. The times are critical and I must have you here to assist me. . . . I can do nothing without you.

—JOHN ADAMS TO HIS WIFE, ABIGAIL

I hope some day somebody will take time to evaluate the true role of wife of a President and to assess the many burdens she has to bear and the contributions she makes.

—PRESIDENT HARRY S. TRUMAN

IT IS MORE THAN STYLE, MORE THAN HAIRDOS AND WHITE HOUSE DECOR AND inaugural gowns and controversies over china and guest lists. The role of presidential spouses (so far only women, hence the ubiquitous unofficial title "first lady") is vital to a full understanding of their husbands' administrations and the presidency itself. It is time to take up President Truman's challenge.

What is most private in most lives—marriage—inevitably has a huge public impact once a couple reaches the White House. At the same time, the public pressures of the presidency reshape the private marital relationship, strengthening some marriages, deadening others, reshaping still others. Some first ladies crumble, like Mary Todd Lincoln; others take over in crisis, like the second Mrs. Woodrow Wilson, without doubt the most powerful first lady in history. For some first ladies, like Pat Nixon, one can only feel immensely sorry, as they seem to wither away from neglect. Others, like Eleanor Roosevelt, Nancy Reagan and Hillary Rodham Clinton, become highly controversial in their own right. And some, like Betty Ford and Lady Bird Johnson, emerge as nationally admired women who seem to transcend their husbands' difficulties.

Inevitably, presidential marriages are different from all others. To get elected to America's pinnacle of power requires absolute commitment not only from the candidate but from his spouse as well. Presidential couples must surrender most of their privacy and many aspects of family life for their dream. What sort of marriages have as their central purpose the fulfillment of a single burning ambition? What sort of wives are willing to share the exhausting, sometimes humiliating journey? And what happens when they reach the promised land at 1600 Pennsylvania Avenue?

The most confident presidents generally have been those with the healthiest respect for their wives, men who sought and listened to their wives' personal and political advice. Whatever Americans may fear about the "hidden power" of presidential wives, it is unrealistic and unreasonable to expect the president to do without a full partner, both public and private.

A politician needs more than ambition and stamina to succeed. Ideally, he needs a partner who will be a trusted sounding board, a link to the real world from which his power and position isolate him. He needs someone completely trustworthy to whom he can confide his deepest fears and insecurities, a person to whom he can reveal his full appetite for power. "I am so devoured by egoism," wrote Winston Churchill, whose marriage was among the happiest and most productive of any world leader in the last century, to his wife, Clementine, in 1916. He continued: ". . . I would like to have another soul in another world and meet you in another setting and pay you all the love and honour of the great romances." Unfortunately, devouring egos are rarely capable of paying their partners that sort of romantic attention.

It is as difficult to stop a politician obsessed by power as it is to stop a fast-moving train. The human sacrifice is enormous, but the reward great. The presidential couple instantly becomes two of the most famous people in the world. They are surrounded by sycophants and ceremony. Their arrival is accompanied by the sound of "Hail to the Chief"; their first view in the morning is of the Washington Monument; their backyard is the Rose Garden; his office, the Oval; their transportation, *Air Force One.* Loved or reviled, their names forever evoke a time in our lives.

This volume is not another anthology of the lives of first ladies. Rather, it is a study of husbands and wives at the precarious intersection of power, love and marriage. How did both the inner life and public face of White House marriages shape presidential history?

I focus only on the twentieth century, as this is a study of both marriage and the presidency as we have come to know them in the recent past. Still, earlier presidential marriages carry similarly dramatic stories, from John and Abigail Adams's astonishingly tender and productive partnership to the tragic collapse of Mary Todd Lincoln. They are worthy of equal study. While each couple's story is of course unique, they all illustrate that the effect of marriage on the presidency (and presidency on the marriage) is far deeper and more profound than commonly realized.

If the present account is sometimes tipped to the women's side of the story, this is deliberate. Too little attention has been paid to the role of first ladies in relation to the policies and administrations of their husbands. A successful presidential candidate identifies the pulse of his time, the issues that most concern people, whereas a first lady's success depends on her grasp of the essence of her times. Lady Bird Johnson, for example, embodied the Ideal Woman of her era: modest but fearless, supportive but smart. During the greatest crisis since the Civil War, she stood by her man without losing her own identity, and in so doing won admiration even from those who disliked her embattled husband. On the other hand, Pat Nixon, withdrawn and self-effacing, seemed out of step with the nation, and her decision to disengage from her marriage and the resulting lack of involvement in her husband's struggle to survive the Watergate fiasco hurt him.

Ironically, while women have been breaking down the last remaining barriers toward full equality, the first lady's political role remains circumscribed, as the backlash to Hillary Clinton's effort to make radical changes in the role of first lady clearly demonstrated. It was no accident that both Tipper Gore and Laura Bush presented themselves in the 2000 campaign as "anti-Hillarys," more traditional wives.

But the institution's outer face has never been the primary source of the first lady's power. The quality of her relationship with her husband has been the key factor in determining the extent of her influence. For any real understanding of presidents, knowing the inner life of presidential couples—the human chemistry behind the formality of the office—is essential. Measuring the indirect and subtle role of a wife on a husband is the quicksilver part of the historian's task. In studying the way a president relies on his wife, we learn something profound about that commander in chief.

∞

WHEN WE ELECT a president we are electing more than a man or—eventually—a woman. Presidential couples rise together, serve together and, sometimes, fall together. Although Hillary Clinton set new standards for the public role of a first lady, the Clintons were not the only presidential couple who blended the political and the personal in their marriage. In fact, the intense mingling of the public and private has been more the rule than the exception among presidential couples. His career is their career. As careful as the wives are about hiding this fact, they sometimes slip. "When we were President . . ." Barbara Bush has said more than once; every first lady thinks and sometimes talks the same way.

Most politicians are, almost by definition, performers. They are nearly always "on," aiming to please whatever audience they are addressing. It is not easy to have an intimate relationship with anyone sustained by love of not one person but the many. Is it possible for the most famous person on the planet to have a "normal" marriage? Can anyone—even a spouse—speak frankly to someone the world flatters and fears? In healthy marriages, power is distributed evenly. One-sided adulation, self-pity, intense scrutiny and loss of privacy all mitigate against such a union. A public show of distress or disapproval by a wife can be fatal for the politician. Yet there have been some very strong presidential marriages in which husband and wife shared almost equally in rewards and sacrifices. The nation benefited from such solid partnerships. But in part because of a squeamishness about unelected power, Americans tend to undervalue or deride the role of the president's spouse, even while subjecting her to the most relentless scrutiny and occasional adulation. Yet all but two of the first ladies discussed in this volume played a positive and consequential role in the presidency. And two saved their husband's administrations.

Presidents need to be married. (Only one, James Buchanan, was not.) The public expects it. Even today, in our cynical, media-intense age, the country looks at the president and first lady as role models. Beyond public expectations, it is a fact that no man needs a strong partner more than the president, isolated and cocooned as he is in what Truman called the Great White Prison. With the exception of Woodrow Wilson and his second wife, the presidential couples of the last century began their political ascent together. No one knew these presidents or understood their obsession better than their wives. "He might live longer if he didn't run for president, and if he did [live longer], would it be worth it?" Lady Bird Johnson wrote in her diary in May 1964.

The quality of presidential marriages differs widely, of course, but they do have some things in common. The couples tend to be solid and middle-aged. (The most obvious exception was the Kennedys, whose youth was one of the animating factors of their special aura.) The extraordinary pressures and the sheer invasiveness of the modern presidency tend to draw couples closer. No divorces have followed tenure in the White House. If the relationship between the politician and his wife is inherently unequal, the presidency tends to balance it. "One thing that happens to a president is that his ties with the outside world are cut," Jacqueline Kennedy noted, "and the people you really have are each other. . . ." Lady Bird agreed: "If you weren't close before, you'd sure better get close now." Kennedy, Johnson and Clinton, famous philanderers, leaned on their wives more in the White House than before, whether or not they still misbehaved. "The White House has been good for us," Bill Clinton said near the end of his second term, and this despite the most sordid scandal in presidential history.

The presidency does not strengthen all couples. The White House did nothing for the Lincolns. At times during the Roosevelt years, the presidential home was divided into almost openly hostile "Franklin" and "Eleanor" camps. Eleanor Roosevelt may cast a shadow over her successors, but her marriage was dysfunctional. The saddest modern presidential story may well be that of the Nixons. Richard Nixon married the girl he thought he loved and then abandoned her for his real passion: politics. A strong, honest, clear-eyed partner who could have calmed his anger and given him the love he missed as the child of a cold, withholding mother would have benefited him enormously. Instead, he turned his back on Pat, and they both suffered from incurable loneliness and self-fulfilling paranoia.

First ladies form part of our national folklore. They conjure up a specific time in our country's life. Whether as soul mates, helpmates or those who are essential to their husbands' political survival, all first ladies have played a part in history. Yet we often see them though a prism that oversimplifies the complexity of their roles. Bess Truman and Jacqueline Kennedy played more substantial roles in their husbands' administrations than is usually recognized. For all her grumbling about being a prisoner of the White House, Bess kept her husband steady and anchored to their small-town values. Jackie put an indelible stamp on the Kennedys' thousand days by inventing Camelot as a preemptive strike against historians only a few days after the assassination. John F. Kennedy, the supreme ironist, "would have been derisive of such a romantic idea," according to Arthur Schlesinger, Jr., but Jackie's image of a magic time and place endured. Nancy Reagan's image as couture-obsessed would-be royalty obscured her generally constructive role in the Reagan presidency. In fact, Reagan could not have been elected without Nancy (she tried to set the record straight in a bitter memoir, reveal-ingly entitled *My Turn*). Barbara Bush's chosen image of herself as a mild, white-haired grandmother was deceptive; a sharper politician than her husband, she was his tart-tongued sounding board and his first line of defense in private and public. As controversial as any first lady, Hillary Clinton, at a critical moment, saved her husband's presidency, then rewrote American political history by running and winning a Senate seat while still first lady—and evoking dreams for some of another Clinton in the White House.

CLEMENTINE CHURCHILL MIGHT HAVE SPOKEN for many presidential spouses when she wrote Winston, without irony, "You took me from the straitened little by-path I was treading and took me with you into the life of color and jostle of the highway." Lady Bird, wife to perhaps the most "devouring ego" of the American presidency, made a similar point. "Lyndon stretched me to the last limit of my capacity. . . . I did enjoy the opportunity of living in that House . . . with that man."

Most men who win the presidency nurture that dream from an early age. Franklin Roosevelt, Kennedy, Johnson and Clinton, for example, chose their partners with the final prize already somewhere in their minds. The wisest chose partners who could tell them bad news when no one else dared. "There is a danger of your being generally disliked by your colleagues and subordinates," Clementine wrote her husband on June 27, 1940, "because of your rough and sarcastic and overbearing manner . . . and you are not so kind as you used to be." On another occasion, she wrote, "I beg you not to do anything without telling me first, and giving me time to give you my valuable opinion on it." Many first ladies spoke in similar terms to their husbands. Roosevelt, Johnson, Jimmy Carter, George Bush and Clinton married such partners. While their choice of wives did not guarantee success, it gave them an advantage over those presidents, such as Wilson and Nixon, whose wives could not deliver hard news. The less streamlined the politician—Carter and George Bush père come to mind—the more important his spouse's ability to compensate for his shortcomings.

Presidents and first ladies are not always the best sources for their own history. Rarely departing from their "story line," they fix their eyes firmly on their legacy, as well as on the day's headlines. They are seldom interested in the confessional culture. From the second Mrs. Wilson's sorry attempts to justify her bad judgment, to Nancy Reagan's view of herself as "Ronnie's lightning rod," first ladies hold to their predetermined roles. For the story behind the image, aides, friends and Cabinet members are often more revealing than first couples.

Ironically, those presidential couples most cautious about revealing themselves—who have given the fewest interviews and have not published correspondence or diaries—have missed a chance to present their own version of themselves. The greatest love story of the modern presidency, that of Woodrow and Edith Wilson, is revealed in their extraordinary letters, which show clearly a passionate man underneath the stern Presbyterian moralist of the history books. Eleanor Roosevelt's deeply moving expression of her need of intimacy, and her anguish at her husband's inability to provide it, are both revealed in her letters. FDR, not a self-revealing man, left no such correspondence. When Harry Truman caught his wife burning their letters and protested, "Bess, think of history," she replied dryly, "I am." But in fact, she was wrong. Harry's surviving letters to his wife reveal a human and vulnerable man, fearless about expressing his need for the gruff Bess. How endearing to read Truman's letter to his wife, written during the historic meetings with Stalin and Churchill in Potsdam. "No, your taste in hats is not screwy," he reassures Bess, then apologizes for his inability to shop during the meetings: "I can't get Chanel N° 5 . . . not even on the black market. . . ." The senior George Bush also offered a moving self-portrait in his collection of letters to family and friends; he reveals a sweet nature that his politics often masked. The Clintons, probably the most scrutinized presidential couple in history, may never reveal themselves in letters or truly candid memoirs. However sound their reasons for discretion, their search for privacy will leave others to define this polarizing political couple.

The partnerships described in this book are both personally compelling and important for our time. Woodrow and Edith Wilson represent a stunning parable of the danger of true romance in the White House. Successful first ladies enlarge the president's world. Edith, who embodied the hypocrisies of Victorian society, power veiled by the parasol and pearls of the antebellum South, shrank her husband's world even before his stroke. With the Twenty-Fifth Amendment, no first lady today could behave as she did once Wilson was bedridden and isolated.

∽

DESPITE EDITH WILSON'S ANTI-FEMINISM, however, the Great War changed the role of women in American society. From munitions factories to universities, girls and women found their way into male bastions. Jeannette Rankin, a Republican from Montana, was now a member of Congress. In 1920, she helped the House pass the Nineteenth Amendment—for female suffrage—by a single vote.

After a taste of global engagement and social upheaval, the country's conservatism reasserted itself. Between the two world wars, the United States turned toward a selfish insularity. There was a general fatigue with sacrificing for war, with Woodrow Wilson's moral rebukes and with Europe's blood feuds. While the Old World lay prostrate, America's business was business. The booming new field of advertising targeted women not as citizens but as consumers. They were now bombarded with messages telling them that their home was the temple where they could best fulfill themselves. Women's suffrage was cleverly translated into the right to shop. A 1930 ad for household products in the *Chicago*

Tribune cleverly merged the two, foreshadowing many later ad campaigns. "Today's woman gets what she wants. The vote. Slim sheaths of silk to replace voluminous petticoats. Glassware in sapphire blue or glowing amber. The right to a career. Soap to match her bathroom's color scheme." The march toward full equality for women would take many more twists and turns.

THIS BOOK DOES NOT DEAL with every twentieth-century presidential couple. The stories of Warren and Florence Harding, Calvin and Grace Coolidge and Herbert and Lou Hoover simply do not resonate today. They were not figures who, by force of their personalities or their actions, shifted historic currents. The long shadows cast by their predecessors, the Wilsons, and their successors, the Roosevelts, eclipse them.

All presidential couples since the Roosevelts, save one, are included because each has something to teach us about the intersection of power and marriage and about the evolving role of women in society. The exception is Dwight and Mamie Eisenhower. Like the Hardings, Coolidges and Hoovers, the Eisenhowers did not leave a deep, historic imprint as a couple. Mamie's role in the presidency was a simple extension of her many years as a dutiful army wife. She played no significant role in her husband's administration. As a couple, the Eisenhowers were a nostalgic throwback and suited America's postwar age of conformity.

This is a work of history and interpretation, and wherever possible I have used primary sources: extensive interviews with participants and eyewitnesses to the presidential events, oral histories and correspondence. I have also relied to a considerable extent on presidential studies by Michael Beschloss, Alan Brinkley, Robert Caro, Robert Dallek, Doris Kearns Goodwin, Henry Graff, David Maraniss, Arthur Schlesinger, Jr., Carl Anthony Sferraza, Jr. and others. They are listed, with my thanks, in the notes that follow the text.

The lights of public scrutiny turn ever brighter on the occupants of the modern White House. The twenty-four-hour news cycle, the constant need to fill the airwaves, leaves them ever less privacy. Leadership needs a certain aura to thrive, but mystery is no longer available to the president. We live in peaceful, prosperous times, but we do not yet know the long-term consequences of stripping our leaders to their under-shorts.

Our system endows the presidency with the powers of both the chief of state and the head of government. The president can rise to great heights, but to do so he needs a strong relationship with the people, a relationship based on more than competence. For this reason, and perhaps a residual nostalgia for the monarchy that once ruled the colonies, there has always been a regal tint to the office. Paradoxically, the most decent presidents, and best husbands, have not always excelled in the office; Carter, Ford and the senior Bush come to mind. Thus, one can argue, as Arthur Schlesinger, Jr., has, that a public obsession with the private lives of presidents is not healthy for the nation. No less a figure that the nation's most revered ex-first lady shared this view recently. In January 1998, observing the White House sex scandal and the nation's addiction to it, Lady Bird Johnson expressed concern. "We will all lose," she told me. "We are narrowing the number of people who will be willing to run." But there will always be those "consumed whole" by the temptation to claim a place in history. May they choose their partners carefully and well. Like it or not, the state of presidential marriages matters to us all. As we shall see.

Chapter 1

Edith and Woodrow Wilson

Fools for Love

I am absolutely dependent on intimate love for the right and free and most effective use of my powers and I know by experience . . . what it costs my work to do without it.
—WOODROW WILSON TO EDITH GALT, *August 16, 1915*

The dear face opposite me was drawn and lined; and as I sat there watching the dawn break slowly I felt that life would never be the same; that something had broken inside me; and from that hour on I would have to wear a mask—not only to the public but to the one I loved best in the world; for he must never know how ill he was, and I must carry on.
—EDITH WILSON, *My Memoir*

ON JANUARY 1, 1900, TWO THOUSAND WASHINGTONIANS BRAVED THE BITTER cold and falling snow and patiently waited for the White House doors to open for the traditional New Year's reception. They came by trolley and in elegant carriages to mark the dawn of a new century and with it, as the presence of dozens of diplomats in the queue signaled, America's emergence as one of the world's most powerful nations.

The day also marked the hundredth anniversary of the death of George Washington, but America was now an altogether different country than the fledgling republic bequeathed by Virginia's "First Gentle-man." In the past twenty years, seven million Americans had abandoned roots and rural traditions and joined the great urban migration. "Amer-ica fever" was sweeping the muddy villages and mining towns of Central and Eastern Europe. An entire Italian family could buy steerage tickets from Naples for as little as $15. Half a million immigrants were expected to arrive in New York that year. The combination of the rich land, a fearless, mobile population and breathtaking new technology—from the combine to alternating-current electricity—was allowing America to challenge the rest of the world.

Inside the White House resided a Victorian man and his withdrawn, sickly wife. William and Ida McKinley, good-natured, well liked and unchallenging, had little interest in the new age. While the country had stretched and grown, the White House had not. It had been built as the home of the president of a small republic. The presidential offices were a rabbit warren of jumbled rooms, alongside the First Family's private quarters. A handful of men in formal morning attire, black cutaway coats, gray-and-black-striped trousers and silk ties jockeyed for space in the overcrowded, ill-lit offices. Down the hall in the presidential bed-room, Ida spent much of her time crocheting. She neither had, nor wished for, her own staff or an office of her own. But the American peo-ple felt close to their president, who was still accessible to citizens. When he was in residence in the White House, hundreds of them arrived every weekday, expecting to meet him.

It would take another year and an assassin's bullet to bring to power the first twentieth-century president, Theodore Roosevelt. Roosevelt was not content for the United States to be the world's economic giant; his sights were set on global military and diplomatic might. Colorful and ebullient, he and his coolly confident second wife, Edith, were the first modern presidential couple. They and their six children filled the mansion with the boisterousness associated with the family. Roosevelt decreed that henceforth the Executive Mansion would be called the White House, a name he considered less stuffy and more in line with the democratic image he intended to convey. Edith, meanwhile, began to institutionalize the office of first lady. She persuaded Congress to finance the mansion's modernization, adding the West Wing and—for the first time—allocating space for the first lady's offices. She hired the first full-time White House social secretary. Edith ran the White House with the ease and detachment of a born chatelaine, though she treated the public and political aspects of the role with aristocratic disinterest. Nevertheless, in both style and substance, Edith and Theodore Roosevelt virtually initiated the ascendancy of an imperial presidency. Though Edith did not personally make use of the first lady's own pulpit, she helped lay the foundation for her successors. Another Roosevelt would take it into territory Edith never could have imagined.

Helen Herron Taft, the wife of President William Howard Taft, who succeeded Roosevelt, achieved a number of breakthroughs as first lady between 1909 and 1913. She was the first woman to be allowed a seat within the bar of the Supreme Court, the first to publish her memoirs and the first to be buried at Arlington National Cemetery. But her historic role is overshadowed by the second Mrs. Woodrow Wilson, Edith Bolling Galt Wilson, with whom this narrative of marriage and power truly begins.

Edith Wilson became first lady during a period when the inherent inequality between men and women—society's patriarchal nature—was beginning to be questioned. Since the 1890s American women made up one-third of college students and more than one-third of professional workers. Edith, however, seemed content with the crumbs of education reserved for a Victorian woman. She wanted no part of the generation of college-educated women who were forming local suffrage associations and going door-to-door to enlist support. She would have found repellent Theodore Dreiser's *Sister Carrie,* which sparked a national scandal. So great was the uproar caused by this story of a country girl who uses sex to climb out of poverty that the publisher was forced to withdraw the book after selling only 456 copies. Another book, *What a Young Husband Ought to Know,* fared better. The book advised men that "the sexual impulse in the male . . . marches like a mighty conqueror, arousing and marshaling the mightiest human forces [leading to] the attainment of the world's greatest and grandest achievement in art, in letters, in inventions, in philosophy, in philanthropy, and in every effort that is to secure the universal blessing of mankind." The book went on to assure readers that with patience and self-control, husbands could teach their wives to accept sex as a necessary hardship on the road to motherhood.

Edith willingly accepted the role her nineteenth-century southern upbringing assigned to her. She embraced the Victorian feminine ideal of the virtuous, compliant and passive child/woman. She proudly proclaimed both her disapproval of women she called "devils in the workhouse" and her adherence to women's subservience to men. She called Woodrow Wilson "My Lord and Master" and he called her "Little Girl"—not for her the nascent female solidarity movement. Yet no presidential wife ever wielded more real power than she did, the first lady who said she wished only to be a good wife.

The Wilsons' story is perhaps the most poignant in the chronicles of presidential marriages, and among the most controversial. In rapid succession it encompassed death, bereavement, unexpected bliss and sudden physical decline. It is also the story of an astonishing White House cover-up in which the first lady was the main perpetrator. At a time when American women still could not vote, rarely held jobs beyond that of a domestic or a grade-school teacher, a woman ran the White House and the executive branch. Woodrow and Edith embody the White House's greatest love story, one that had the most tragic outcome for the nation and the world.

⌦

NO CEMENT BARRIERS or electric fences imprisoned the White House's residents in the early years of the century. At first glance, it was just a very large house in the heart of a medium-sized city. Until the 1860s, Washington had remained a winter outpost where politicians converged to debate a handful of subjects not controlled by the states. Humidity drove residents away for the summer. New York was the country's financial capital, Boston its cultural mecca. But the Civil War had changed Washington, as it became the hub of wartime operations. "Slowly," historian Henry Adams wrote, "a certain society had built itself up about the Government. Houses had been opened and there was much dining; much calling; much leaving of cards."

In the waning years of this era, Woodrow Wilson, a man past his middle age, and Edith Bolling Galt, a woman well into hers, fell in love and carried on an ardent affair in the White House.

The fifty-nine-year-old president was widowed in 1914, during the second year of his first term. Ellen Axson Wilson's sudden death coincided almost exactly with the outbreak of World War I, and the convergence of the two events shattered Wilson's well-ordered world. His famously stern demeanor masked a passionate and emotionally needy man. It is hard to imagine an isolation greater than the one that fell over him, suddenly alone in that house. Wilson had always preferred the company of women to that of politicians. His daughter Nell recalled, "Father enjoyed the society of women, especially if they were what he called 'charming and conversable.' " His first wife and daughters had been the core of his existence. "My heart has somehow been stricken dumb . . . ," Wilson wrote at the time of Ellen's death. "She was beyond comparison the deepest, truest, noblest lover I ever knew." The following year he would marry again.

In March 1915, Edith Galt recalled later, "I turned a corner and met my fate." Invited to tea at the White House by a cousin of the president, she stepped off an elevator and ran into Wilson. Edith would later revealingly recall the encounter primarily in sartorial terms. How fortunate, she wrote, that she had "worn a smart black tailored suit which Worth had made for me in Paris and a tricot hat which I thought completed a very good looking ensemble."

Wilson was immediately smitten. Invitations to dinner and hand-delivered letters from the White House to her town house soon crossed Washington almost daily. So did shipments of Edith's favorite flower, orchids. "The orchids carried a certain significance," White House chief usher Irwin Hoover recalled, "and when she appeared it would always be with just one of them, worn high on the left shoulder."

Two hundred and fifty surviving letters chronicle their love affair in remarkable detail. They form an indispensable window into the passionate courtship and the simultaneous entry of the United States into world affairs. "My dear Mrs. Galt," Wilson wrote on April 28, 1915, "I have ordered a copy of Hamerton's *Round My House. . . .* I hope it will give you pleasure—you have given me so much! If it rains this evening would it be any pleasure for you to come around and have a little reading—and if it does not rain, are you game for another ride?"

On the surface, they seemed almost bizarrely unsuited. At forty-two, she was tall and buxom. Wilson was ramrod straight and thin as a rake. His face was long, his features sharply chiseled and lined. Her face was smooth, her cheeks full. Where she was impulsive, he was logical and loved elaborate argument. Where he was rational and careful, she was jealous, self-indulgent, intuitive, judgmental and seemingly fearless. He was a scholar who loved the company of books and, at the same time, a deeply moral man who believed America must be an example to other nations. Edith was interested primarily in travel and fashion. A substantial portion of her memoirs is devoted to descriptions of what she wore to which historic event. Politics, she thought, was a bore.

But deeper ties pulled Woodrow and Edith together. Both were Virginians, Edith the granddaughter of a slaveowner, the child of once prosperous gentry. Both were enthralled by the romance and the mythology of the Old South. As a little boy, Wilson had seen Robert E. Lee pass through Atlanta after the surrender. Though he had no southern ancestry, Wilson once said that the South was the one place on earth where nothing had to be explained to him. Edith shared this powerful connection to land and place and spoke with a soft southern lilt that Woodrow admired. Left financially independent by her first husband, she combined traditional southern charm with the surface worldliness of a well-traveled woman. With neither a husband nor children to look after, Edith was a free spirit, with the seductive air of a much younger woman.

Events in Europe intensified the courtship. Wilson was under tremendous pressure during those early months of 1915. The Kaiser's army had launched gas warfare against the French and British. Germany warned American travelers that if they sailed on British ships, they did so "at their own risk." In his letters to Edith, Wilson shared his innermost thoughts. "Here stands your friend, a longing man, in the midst of a world's affairs—a world that knows nothing of the heart he has shown you. . . . Will you come to him sometime without reserve and make his strength complete?"

On May 4, 1915, Wilson took Edith onto the south portico of the White House and, drawing his chair close to hers in the chilly air, told her he loved her and asked for her hand in marriage. Feigning shock, as her nineteenth-century upbringing prescribed for such a sudden proposal, Edith turned him down. "You cannot love me," she wrote him that same night, "for you really don't know me, and it is less than a year since your wife died."

But she kept the courtship going, adding, "I am a woman—and the thought that you have need of me is sweet!" Still, she seemed to shun her suitor's more explicit physical advances. She told him that her first marriage had been "incomplete." Her reserve only enhanced his zeal. "For God's sakes," he wrote her, "try to find out whether you really love me or not."

The presidency was a powerful courtship tool for Wilson. He made Edith feel that she shared the burden of the office. During the very week Woodrow first proposed marriage, on May 7, 1915, German submarines torpedoed the great British liner *Lusitania,* killing 1,200 civilians, including 128 Americans. "I need you," the president wrote two days later, "as a boy needs his sweetheart and a strong man his helpmate and heart's comrade. . . . Do you think that it is an accident that we found one another at this time of my special need and that it meant nothing that we recognized one another so immediately and so joyously? . . . I hope you will think of me tonight. I shall be working on my speech of tomorrow evening and on our note to Germany. Every sentence of both would be freighted with greater force and meaning if I could feel that your mind and heart were keeping me company." That night, in what some historians have called "a state of ecstasy," the president gave one of his most powerful speeches.

On May 10, Edith wrote Woodrow that his "wonderful love can quicken that which has lain dead so long within me." As American neutrality hung in the balance, the president personally typed a letter of protest to the German government. The same day he wrote his beloved. "And, oh, I have needed you tonight, my sweet Edith! What a touch of your hand and a look into your eyes would have meant to me of strength and steadfastness as I made the final decision as to what I should say to Germany."

In another letter he wrote her the same day, Woodrow's mind was not on Germany but on his overwhelming physical desire, which he made clear was not yet "complete." Referring to himself in the third person, Wilson wrote her the very next day, virtually announcing his intention to consummate their relationship. "He has been permitted a sacred enterprise: there is a heart to be rescued from itself—which has never known that final divine act of self surrender which is a woman's way to love and happiness. If she cannot be taken—taken away from herself by siege, *she must be taken by storm*—and she shall be!"

How seductive it must have been to have this austere, powerful man want her. "The clock is striking midnight and I must go to bed. I have on my wrapper and am by the window," she replied. "I also have on one pair of the lovely white silk stockings [a gift from Wilson] and they are a joy—and make me feel so very rich. . . . A fond and very tender kiss my precious Woodrow before we put out the light—and I feel your dear arms fold around me."

While their personal drama continued, Wilson wanted her involved in affairs of state. He described his troubles with Secretary of State William Jennings Bryan, who opposed the president's hard line with Germany. And Edith offered her opinions without reserve or much understanding. "I think it will be a blessing to get rid of him [Bryan]," she wrote on May 5, "and might as well frankly say I would like to be appointed in his place—then I should have to have daily conferences with you—and I faithfully promise not to interfere in any way with your continuing to do all the work!" The tone was playful, but this letter marks her entry into affairs of state—with ultimately historic consequences.

"And how you can hate too!" Wilson replied. "Whew! I fancy this very sheet lying before me on which you have written about Mr. Bryan is hot under my hand. . . . And yet Sweetheart, I must add that in my secret heart (which is never secret from you) I love you for that too. For he is a traitor, though I can say so as yet only to you."

All the untapped sensuality and the strength of character that until then Edith had masked behind a southern belle's veil of frivolity had found a focus. "He came in from the Blue Room," she wrote later, "looking so distinguished in his evening clothes and with both hands held out to welcome me. When I put mine in them and looked into those eyes— unlike any others in the world—something broke down inside me, and I knew I could and would go to the end of the world with or for him."

Theodore Roosevelt had scoffed that Woodrow Wilson possessed all the passion of "an apothecary clerk." But Wilson's women knew better. During his first marriage, Woodrow had written about the temptations he felt when he was away from his wife. He dared not stay overnight in New York on his own, given "the imperious passions" that fired him. At least at home, he wrote her, he "must stay out of mischief." His temptations, he told Ellen, meant "not one wit of real infidelity to you—it is anatomical and not of the heart." Ellen Wilson's reaction to this astonishing missive is not recorded.

By the end of May 1915, Woodrow's "siege" must have been successful, for he wrote, "I venture to say, my Lady, my Queen, that never in your life have you looked so wonderfully beautiful as I have seen you look when the love tide was running in your heart without check. . . . I have seen a transfiguration, and it has filled me with as much awe as ecstasy! I can't think this morning, I can only feel and only realize the exquisite thing that happened to me, the beautiful love I have won. . . . the sweet woman who has given it to me."

The American people scarcely would have recognized their stern Presbyterian leader. But in those pretelevision days, politicians could present almost any image of themselves. Wilson conveyed the image of a church elder who read Thucydides in his free time. With his soaring oratory—tinged with a faint Scottish burr—invoking the blessing of God, his speeches often sounded like sermons. His idealism and his morality were the qualities that Americans associated with him. Few people saw the man Edith fell in love with.

His personal happiness was in stark contrast to the turmoil around him. Though Edith rejoiced when Secretary of State Bryan resigned, much of the country was shocked. Americans were divided over the prospect of engagement in a European conflict. While they wanted the president to defend their right to travel safely on the seas, they did not necessarily want to go to war over it. In 1915, Wilson shared that view.

As the European conflict grew daily closer, the president had a secret source of strength. "My love for you," he wrote Edith, "has come to me in these days when I seem to be put to the supreme test of my life, like a new youth. . . . You are oh so fit for a mate for a strong man!"

Though not yet married, the president wanted Edith by his side. He invited her to the summer White House in Cornish, New Hampshire, where, away from the prying eyes of the capital, the couple spent lazy days picnicking and reading to each other. "When we walked, we would try to forget that lurking behind every tree was a Secret Service man," Edith wrote later. By mid-August, they were secretly engaged. Wilson began in earnest to prepare her for the role of full presidential partner. Statecraft, he assured her, was not so very intellectually taxing. "Don't you see," he told Edith, "how comparatively easy it is to keep . . . a very complicated public matter in your head when a dispatch or memorandum about it turns up every day?"

Wilson's daily love letters to Edith were now accompanied by packets of state papers, with his handwritten marginal notes. He expected her not just read them but also to comment on them. There was only one other person on whom the president relied for both political and emotional support, Colonel Edward Mandel House, a transplanted southerner, his most trusted unofficial adviser. "Mr. House," Wilson said in 1913, "is my second personality. He is my independent self. . . . If anyone thinks he is reflecting my opinion by whatever action he takes, they are welcome to the conclusion." Allies since the early days of Wilson's political ascent, Wilson and House had an intense melding of personalities, hopes and ambitions. "Talking to him," Wilson said, "is like talking to myself."

Wilson was anxious that Edith and the shadowy Texan become friends. "I feel about your character and the disinterested loyalty of your friendship," Wilson wrote Edith, "just as I have so often told you I felt about House." But Wilson would soon learn how fierce she was in her judgments—and how possessive of him. "I know what a comfort and a staff [House] is to you . . . but he does look like a weak vessel and I think he writes like one. . . ."

House was not her only target among the president's inner circle.

She also went after Joseph Tumulty, the president's loyal secretary, a fixture since Wilson's days as governor of New Jersey. Edith found Tumulty entirely too Irish Catholic and middle-class. "My idea [regarding Tumulty]," she observed, "may be colored by his commonness." With foreboding, Wilson replied, "You are a little hard on some of my friends . . . you Dear . . . House and Tumulty for example; but I understand and am able to see them, with your mind as well as with my own." The president was hopeful that Edith would come to appreciate his aides.

> You do not know them and have not been faithfully served by them, and therefore your heart is not involved in the judgment as mine is. Take Tumulty. You know that he was not brought up as we were; you feel his lack of breeding; and you do not like to have me represented by any one less fine than you conceive me to be. . . . To your fastidious taste and nice instinct for what is refined, he is common. . . . I share your judgment up to a certain point and feel it as perfectly as if it were my own—though there are fine natural instincts in Tumulty and nice perceptions, which you have not yet had a chance to observe. . . . He is absolutely devoted and loyal to me. . . .

Edith's continued hostility toward Colonel House began to shake Wilson's own confidence in him. Still, he tried to bring her around, while yielding a bit. "About him you are no doubt partly right. You have too keen an insight and too discerning a judgment to be wholly wrong, *even in a snap judgment of a man you do not know.* . . . His very devotion to me, his ardent desire that I should play the part in the field of international politics that he has desired and foreseen for me, makes him take sometimes the short and personal view when he ought to be taking the big and impersonal one. . . . You are going to love House someday. . . . You must remember, dear little critic," he wrote, pleading for her to soften toward House, "that Sweetness and power do not often happen together."

As he agonized about whether to declare war against Germany, Woodrow's dependence on Edith deepened. "These are very solemn thoughts, my precious one, my little partner, and they seem to draw me nearer to you than ever," he wrote her on August 22. "As things thicken about me I more and more realize what you mean to me and more and more feel my dependence upon you to keep the darkness off. . . ." When Edith protested mildly that she did not have the background to be his adviser, he told her that even if he weren't in love with her, he'd seek her "clear sighted counsel" above that of anyone else in the world, including House.

The president installed a direct phone line between her home and his office to circumvent the White House switchboard. He taught her how to use the secret code in which he communicated with his emissaries abroad. Edith soon learned to use the simple cipher that consisted of numbers based on a master key. From then on, like two children sharing a secret, the president would write secret messages in longhand and Edith would encode them in her own handwriting. Wilson would then type the code numbers out on his typewriter. She also decoded incoming messages for him. Edith was privy not only to the secret presidential code but to the personal code between Wilson and House. As she later noted proudly, "In this way I followed day by day every phase of the mosaic which he was shaping into a pattern of statecraft, and we continued this partnership of thought and comradeship unbroken to the last day of his life. It was a rare privilege, and except for formal interviews with officials, I always 'sat in' when one or two people we knew came to discuss policies. In that way I was never a stranger to any subject, and often able in small ways to be of help."

Each day Edith awaited the arrival of his "big envelope" of state documents. "I am afraid this has been another wretchedly busy day for you," she wrote on August 13, 1915, "for I know from the manifold things I found in my big envelope today—how thoroughly you are going into things. You are a dear person to take the time to write little sentences on each of the papers you send me. . . . I felt so queer this afternoon reading all these reports from the different theaters of war, sitting here in my quiet room. . . . I, an unknown person, one who had lived a sheltered, inconspicuous existence now having all the threads in the tangled fabric of the world's history laid in my hands—for a few minutes—while the stronger hand that guides the shuttle stops long enough in its work to press my fingers in token of the great love and trust with which you crown and bless my life." She may have felt "queer" about all this statecraft dropping in her lap, but she eagerly awaited more. "Is it true that you have asked the Secretaries of War and Navy to give you suggestions for preparedness for war?" she asked him.

By now she was as enthralled by the political partnership as the emotional. "Much as I enjoy your delicious love letters," she told him, "I enjoy even more the ones in which you tell me . . . of what you are working on . . . then I feel I am sharing your work and being taken into partnership as it were." In one of her more revealing passages she wrote, "I love the way you put your dear hand on mine while with the other you turn the pages of history."

The Washington press corps of the time respected the president's privacy. It now seems remarkable, but no photographs of the president leaving Edith's home near Dupont Circle were ever taken. But the capital's rumor mill was active, passing on stories of the commander in chief in love. The salons savored each new morsel, but Wilson's political allies were troubled. In September 1915, House, along with a handful of Wilson's Cabinet members including Secretary of the Treasury William McAdoo—Wilson's son-in-law—and Secretary of the Navy Josephus Daniels, agonized over the potential political cost of Wilson's infatuation. Daniels, Wilson's oldest friend in the Cabinet, was chosen to warn Wilson against a too early remarriage. Less than a year after his wife's death and one year before the presidential elections of 1916, his friends feared the affair could be politically damaging. When Daniels said that he could not perform as "Minister Plenipotentiary and Envoy Extraordinary to the Court of Cupid," McAdoo was dispatched with a clumsy blackmail conspiracy based on an event that had taken place years earlier, and had caused the only real crisis in Wilson's first marriage.

In 1907, during a Bermuda holiday recommended by his doctor, Woodrow, unaccompanied by Ellen, began what was delicately called "an intimate friendship" with another vacationer, Mary Peck Hulbert. What actually transpired between them is a matter of some dispute, but clearly something happened—enough to lead Wilson into a continued correspondence with Mrs. Hulbert, and even to send her $7,500, a huge sum in those days. McAdoo tried to use the old affair to derail his father-in-law's wedding plans. He told Wilson that Hulbert planned to sell the president's incriminating letters, which was not true.

Wilson reacted swiftly. Rushing to Edith's house, he told her of "a folly long ago loathed and repented of" and said he stood before her "stained and unworthy." As he had hoped, Edith did not break off the engagement. "I will stand by you—not for duty, not for pity . . . but for love." The president was overheard singing "Oh, you beautiful doll, you great big beautiful doll!" as he left Edith's house.

Both lovers showed their mettle: Wilson for resisting blackmail, Edith for standing by her suitor, now revealed as imperfect. Edith soon learned of the role House and McAdoo played in the plot to thwart her wedding plans. Now she had real cause to attack her husband's advisers. Fortified by adversity, Edith and Woodrow emerged stronger and more committed to each other than before.

The Cabinet's fear of a public outcry at his sudden remarriage was unjustified. Nothing, however, stopped the Washington chatterers from chattering. A popular joke of the day was: "What did Mrs. Galt do when the president asked her to marry him?" The answer: "She fell out of bed." That bit of sophomoric humor would have long-term consequences for Anglo-American relations and the wit to whom it was ascribed, British diplomat Charles Crauford-Stuart.

The lovers quietly wed on December 18, 1915, in the front parlor of Edith's small town house, and immediately set off for Hot Springs, Virginia. "Nothing," the president informed the press, "need[ed] to be described" of his two-week honeymoon. The press duly respected his wish to be left alone, but history did not. On January 4, 1916, the British steamship *Persia* was torpedoed by a German submarine. Two Americans were among those killed, forcing Mr. and Mrs. Wilson to cut short their idyll and return to Washington.

∽

FEW FIRST LADIES HAVE SO RELISHED the pomp and the attention, or dressing up for the part, as Edith did. "My first public appearance as the wife of the President," she wrote later, "was at a reception to the diplomatic corps. . . . I wore a white gown brocaded in silver with long white tulle drapery, then known as 'angel sleeves.' It was thrilling the first time to greet all the Cabinet in the Oval Room upstairs and then with the President precede them down the long stairway with the naval and military aides forming an escort, the Marine Band playing 'Hail to the Chief,' and the waiting mass of guests bowing a welcome as we passed into the Blue Room."

Edith did not like to be called first lady, however, for that implied a public responsibility. Mrs. Woodrow Wilson was her title of choice. In her mind, she served her husband, not the country. She was intrigued by politics and diplomacy, but only as an activity she and Woodrow could share. As the country mobilized for war, Edith could legitimately finesse many of the traditional functions of the White House's chatelaine. She could devote herself full-time to her true passion: the role of first wife, as opposed to the more public role of first lady.

As they began their marriage, Wilson attempted to mediate among the countries at war. He dispatched Colonel House on a peace mission to London, Paris and Berlin. Simultaneously, Wilson began laying the foundation for a new postwar order, based on principles that would forever be associated with his name: open diplomacy, the preservation of the right to neutrality and the right to self-determination. Later, these would form the spine of his famous Fourteen Points. At the same time, Wilson floated a proposal for an association of nations to replace aggression with mediation. Wilson promised that the United States would abandon its long-standing policy of isolation in exchange for a peace without vengeance. The ruling powers nodded politely but disregarded Wilson's ideas.

With his "little partner" almost always by his side, Wilson's most productive year as chief executive was perhaps 1916. "I helped Woodrow in the study until nearly twelve," Edith wrote in her diary on November 25, 1916. "He was writing what he says may prove the greatest piece of work of his life and oh, if it is only so, for it will mean so much." When the president summoned his ambassador to Berlin to help him draft his message to the belligerents, the envoy noted, "Mrs. Wilson was present . . . and at times asked pertinent questions showing her deep knowledge of foreign affairs. . . ."

An invigorated Wilson now reached beyond the usual Democratic Party base to pass progressive legislation that would transform the nation's social fabric. Workmen's compensation, child labor laws and the eight-hour day were part of his daring leadership. "Mr. Wilson has done what high statesmanship in a democracy must do," the *New Republic* wrote. "In a very real and accurate sense the President has made himself the spokesman of a whole people."

Nineteen hundred sixteen was also a presidential election year. Wilson's slogan was increasingly fragile: "He kept us out of war." On Election Day Wilson eked out a narrow victory against Republican Charles Evans Hughes, winning 277 of 531 electoral votes. A few months later, Edith became the first first lady to ride with the president to and from his swearing-in.

∽

THE WOMAN WHO CONSIDERED HERSELF the president's full partner vehemently opposed granting women the right to vote. Edith was offended by the growing momentum of the women's suffrage movement. The suffragettes' way was not her way. Her diary makes references to "those disgusting creatures" and their "unladylike" conduct. Much to Edith's annoyance, suffragettes positioned themselves at the White House gate. "Woodrow decided to pardon those devils in the workhouse," she wrote of the women who had displayed a banner "so outrageous that the police arrested them."

While still maintaining a wary alliance with Colonel House, Edith continued to pressure the president to dump Tumulty and Josephus Daniels. Wilson held his ground. Edith was willing to bide her time. But since she sat in on all but Cabinet meetings, his once close advisers had lost their direct channel to him. "The little circle close to the President," House wrote, "seems to have dwindled down to the two of us, Mrs. Wilson and myself."

On a fine Saturday in the spring of 1917, Woodrow and Edith strolled the quiet streets of the capital and unintentionally made a little history. On the way back to the White House, they stopped first at the home of the secretary of war and then at the home of the secretary of the navy. "I think this is the first time in American history," a member of the White House staff noted, "that a President's wife has accompanied the President in a purely business call on a Cabinet officer."

At 8 P.M. on April 2, 1917, flanked by cavalry troops, Edith and Woodrow drove up Pennsylvania Avenue to the Capitol ablaze with its first night lights, the Stars and Stripes snapping atop the cupola. Wilson had summoned a historic joint session of Congress. "When we reached the Capitol," Edith recalled, "the crowd outside was almost as dense as Inauguration Day, but perfectly orderly. Troops were stationed on guard round the entire building which stood out white and majestic. . . . When my husband came in and all rose to their feet my very heart seemed to stop its beating."

Though Wilson hated war, he cast America's declaration of war as a moral crusade: to make the world safe for democracy. "We will not choose the path of submission," the president proclaimed, his words almost drowned out by the applause that punctuated nearly every sentence. He called for war without hatred against the German people, a war "to vindicate the principles of peace and justice in the life of the world."

"Through the cheering multitudes we drove slowly home in silence," Edith wrote. "The step had been taken. We were both overwhelmed." Though she could not then foresee it, her husband's long agony had begun. Wilson himself understood what he had unleashed: "Think what it meant," Wilson said to Tumulty, "the applause of the people in the Capitol and the people lining the avenue as we returned. My message tonight was a message of death to our young men. How strange to applaud that!" Thereupon, Tumulty recalled later, Wilson dropped his head on his desk and "sobbed like a child."

Edith and Woodrow, closer than ever, began the day at 5 A.M. and ended it at midnight. Theirs would now become a wartime presidency. Edith canceled all White House social functions. "The khaki of our Army and the blue of our Navy uniforms began to give color to the streets of Washington," she wrote. The president led a united country in the gigantic business of turning from a peacetime to a wartime economy.

Early in 1918, Wilson again summoned a joint session of Congress to lay down the terms for peace, and to outline his plan for the League of Nations. He fervently believed he could bring the Allies around, if he could only meet them face-to-face. When, on November 11, 1918, an exhausted and humbled Germany signed the Armistice, Wilson proposed a peace conference to be held in Paris.

But at the height of his fame, Wilson had begun to lose touch with his own people. He had turned the peace process partisan, urging voters in the 1918 congressional elections to reelect a Democratic majority, so he could be "your unembarrassed spokesman at home and abroad. . . . A Republican majority," he warned, "would be interpreted by the other side of the water as a repudiation of my leadership." The move backfired, as the country sent a Republican majority to both houses. Without consulting the Republican leadership, Wilson now prepared to go to Europe. He chose only one Republican for the Paris delegation, a gentle retired diplomat named Henry White.

On December 4, 1918, Edith and Woodrow stood on the bridge of the *George Washington,* watching the New York skyline and the thousands of people who lined the waterfront slowly disappear from view. He was the first sitting president to leave the United States. Eleven battleships escorted the presidential party on its crossing. Among those accompanying the president were Wilson's doctor, Cary Grayson, and Edith's secretary, Edith Benham. Observing the Wilsons' closeness, Benham wrote, "The more I am with the Wilsons, the more I am struck with their unrivaled home life. I have never dreamed such sweetness and love could be."

Europe, scorched by the worst war in its history, awaited not an American president but the Second Coming. Nearly the entire population of the French city of Brest crowded the quay, bearing banners that read "Hail the Champion of the Rights of Man" and "Honor to the Founder of the Society of Nations." From their Paris-bound train the Wilsons glimpsed men, women and small children solemnly saluting as the train sped by. Two million Parisians thronged the streets of the capital to hail the president. Deafening cheers of *"Vive Vil-son"* and bouquets of violets rained on Woodrow and Edith's open carriage. "I saw General Foch pass, Clemenceau pass, Lloyd George, generals, returning troops," an American reporter wrote, "but what Wilson heard from his carriage was something different, inhuman—superhuman."

For the first time in half a century, the chain that traditionally bars the great Arc de Triomphe was removed so the Wilsons could ride under the arch all the way to the Concorde. Long columns of French soldiers stood sentry on either side of the president's procession. Edith was overwhelmed. "Roofs were filled," she wrote, "windows overflowed, until one grew giddy trying to greet the bursts of welcome that came like the surging of untamed waters." On their black mounts, the gold-helmeted Garde Républicain escorted the Wilsons through the gates of the Murat Palace, their home for the duration of the peace conference. "The world and his wife were there," Edith recalled, "all in their smartest attire with uniforms and medals conspicuous in the foreground. . . . I was towed along through room after room, and being a head taller than [the President of France], I felt like a big liner with a tiny tug pushing her out from her moorings."

The British repeated this ecstatic welcome. The Wilsons became the first commoners ever to stay in Buckingham Palace, the guests of King George V and Queen Mary. In Rome, the Wilsons' reception had an almost religious fervor. Woodrow was hailed as "the god of peace," bells rang out and people lit candles next to his photograph in churches and in shops.

With the pomp that accompanies both war and peace in the Old World, the Paris peace conference convened on January 12, 1919. There was no cheering inside the richly paneled and tapestried conference rooms of the Quai d'Orsay. Hard men, unimpressed by the austere American, gathered around long tables to press their claims. All Wilson wanted from the conference was a "just peace" and a world organization to maintain it. Against nationalistic arguments, he managed to force acceptance of several key points, at great cost to his psyche and health. "Seeing him growing grimmer and graver, day by day," Edith wrote later, "how I longed to be a man so I could be of more help to him. All I could do was to try to soothe him with a finer fancy, touch him with a lighter thought." Wilson was able to prevent the French from dismembering Germany, and blocked much of Italy's attempt to seize territory along the Adriatic, which he deemed essential for the survival of the new state that would become Yugoslavia. But he was forced to yield to France and Britain on punitive war reparations from Germany. Remarkably, however, most of his Fourteen Points survived. Wilson's proudest achievement, the League of Nations, became part of the covenant of the Treaty of Versailles.

AN OCEAN AWAY, the political currents were shifting. The United States was once again turning inward, losing interest in Wilson's dream of a new international order. The president had been absent for three months, a political lifetime. Tumulty, left behind, now urged his chief's return to Washington. When Wilson did return, he found a changed capital. The war was over, and the Republicans were on the attack. Senator Henry Cabot Lodge, Wilson's longtime foe, declared the League of Nations unacceptable. More moderate Republicans asked that Wilson dilute the language regarding America's responsibility in future European conflicts.

Physically and emotionally drained by the peace conference, Wilson, who had a history of frail health, was not up to the horse trading. The once nimble politician came home the rigid prophet. Instead of working to win them over, Wilson dismissed enemies of the League as "blind and little provincial people . . . the littlest and the most contemptible." The battle between Lodge and Wilson turned intensely personal, polarizing Congress and, soon, the country. Wilson argued that peace without the League was ridiculous to contemplate. Peace *with* the League would sacrifice America's sovereignty, Lodge shot back. Edith noticed a weariness in her husband that sleep could not cure, and signs of paranoia. She tried as best she could to shelter him from stress.

Back in Paris in late March 1919 for the second phase of the peace conference, Wilson saw his dream slipping away. He had left Colonel House in charge of interim negotiations at the conference. "House has given away everything I had won before we left Paris," Wilson confided to Edith. Indeed, contrary to the president's wishes, House, anxious for a compromise, had yielded on fundamental Wilsonian principles. Unwittingly playing into Lodge's hands, House agreed to separate the League of Nations from the peace treaty. Edith described her husband's shock. "He seemed to have aged ten years, and his jaw was set in that way he had when he was making superhuman effort to control himself. Silently he held out his hand, which I grasped."

Rather than giving House a chance to explain, Edith fueled her husband's anger at the colonel, whom she said she would never see again. The president was in the grip of a two-front war—the Republicans at home, the Allies in Paris. Wilson approached his toughest battle with Edith as his only confidante.

On April 3, 1919, Wilson ran a fever of 103 degrees. He was attended by Dr. Grayson, the White House physician who had been looking after the president since his first term. Grayson, a debonair young naval officer, had a distinct advantage over Wilson's other aides: the doctor and Mrs. Wilson had a prior history; she had first met him in 1903 when she had suffered a miscarriage during her first marriage. In fact, Grayson was indirectly responsible for her meeting the president. He did not pose a threat to Edith.

Edith, more fiercely protective of Woodrow than ever, almost never left his side. She described his heartbreaking decline during a trip to a cemetery for fallen American soldiers in France:

> His head bared—and how white the hair had grown those last months—his tall, slight form tense with emotion, as he spoke to the living and for the dead in a passionate plea to end all war and never again make such sacrifice necessary. . . . I couldn't speak for the tears. We drove home in silence, for my husband's control had also broken and only by supreme effort had he been able to finish his speech. . . . How many times I have thought of that May day in that city of the dead and wondered if men like Mr. Henry Cabot Lodge and his supporters in the Senate could have been there for just that hour would they have dared vote against any instrument, such as the League of Nations, to stop war! I wonder!

In late April, Wilson suffered a mild "cerebral incident." The once unfailingly courteous Wilson now snapped at servants in his official Paris residence, accusing them of being spies for the French government. He sat mute during meals and exhibited wild mood swings, from euphoria to depression. His emotions burst through unchecked. "Mr. Prime Minister," he exploded at Lloyd George, "you make me sick!"

Years before, when Wilson first decided to give up academia for politics, his first wife had had a premonition. In a letter to her brother, Ellen voiced an agony familiar to wives of politically ambitious men. "Maybe these husbands ought not always to be encouraged to get the things to which their ambitions lead them, but how can wives who love them do anything except help them? . . . even when it is right, it may wear out their strength and health and spirits and yet they will never be happy unless they get it." Her prophecy seemed to be coming true.

Wilson's physical decline was accompanied by a shift in the power balance of his marriage. Until then, Woodrow had been the teacher, the wise counselor, the man showing the way to the untutored woman. Now Edith became the strong one, assuming more and more responsibility for them both.

Henceforth, Edith's decisions would increasingly have national consequence, as Wilson relied more than ever on her and, to a lesser extent, on Dr. Grayson. From such routine tasks as placing his calls, to the less routine one of trying to shore up his slipping memory, Edith was by his side. In large measure due to her distrust of House (not to mention his failures at the conference), the long and close relationship between Wilson and his adviser had frozen into formality. The two men who once professed to be brothers never saw each other again after the Paris conference. House never recovered from his loss. "My separation from Woodrow Wilson," he later wrote, "was and is to me a tragic mystery. . . . While our friendship was not of long duration it was as close as human friendships grow to be. . . . Until a shadow fell between us I never had a more considerate friend."

⌦

ON JUNE 28, 1919, the sound of cannon fire reverberated through Versailles' Great Hall of Mirrors as Wilson, Clemenceau, Lloyd George and the others signed the treaty that officially ended World War I. "I love to think of my husband as he looked that day," Edith recalled. "I felt a curious tightening of my throat as I looked at this dear figure, grown more slender in those months, but alert and alive." For Wilson, the greatest achievement of the peace conference was the League of Nations, which he hoped would keep the new countries free and the old imperial powers in check. Now, in late June, the architect of the Versailles Treaty sailed home. "Already the sense of freedom from that unremitting labor was relaxing the look of strain," Edith noted, "and the happy thought of going home made him radiate content."

But the battle over America's participation in the League of Nations had now grown fierce. Two of American's titanic political figures were engaged—Wilson and Henry Cabot Lodge, who despised everything Wilson stood for. "We shall make reservation after reservation," Lodge vowed, "amend and amend, until there is nothing left." Though the Massachusetts senator had himself preached international cooperation, politics were his chief motive for destroying the League. "If Wilson gets his League," he told Undersecretary of State William Phillips, "the Republican Party will be done for fifty years."

For Wilson, the League was a way "to cut out the heart of war," or else "that heart is going to live and beat and grow stronger." But in 1919, he was no longer up to a bare-knuckled fight. At a time when he most needed to be resilient, flexible and shrewd, he was dominated by his worst qualities—stubborn self-righteousness and intolerance of others' views. He turned the battle for the League into an all-or-nothing national referendum about himself. If Congress was too blind to do his bidding, he would take his message directly to the people.

Edith was horrified at the notion of a long, transcontinental train trip, fearing that her husband was not up to it. But even she could not stop him from a mission he saw as a holy obligation. "I promised our soldiers," he told her, "when I asked them to take up arms, that it was a war to end war; and if I do not do all in my power to put the Treaty in effect, I will be a slacker and never able to look those boys in the eye. I must go." "Neither Dr. Grayson nor I," Edith wrote, "could find an answer [to this]."

As the presidential train sped across the hot, dusty land, the president "grew thinner and the headaches increased in duration and in intensity until he was almost blind during the attacks," Edith wrote. "Only rest, complete rest, and an escape from the maddening crowds could restore my husband. But I was trapped." The crowds grew bigger and noisier, and Wilson more fervent. Speaking through a fog of pain, he pressed on. "Never a moment to relax and rest," Edith recalled. "And so on across the continent. From one city to the next, a small local committee would accompany us, which meant constant entertaining even on the train. . . . Dr. Grayson's disregarded warnings against attempting the tour haunted my sleep."

Eight thousand two hundred miles and forty speeches into his tour, in the baking, dry heat of Pueblo, Colorado, Wilson exhorted the assembled crowd, "France [is] free and the world [is] free because America had come. . . ." As the train rattled on toward Wichita, Kansas, that night, Woodrow cried out to his wife, "I'm terribly sick." Edith called it the most heartbreaking night of her life. The president had suffered a stroke that temporarily paralyzed his left side. "Nothing the doctor could do gave relief." Edith ordered the train to head back to Washington.

During the long homeward journey Edith made up her mind. "The dear face opposite me was drawn and lined; and as I sat there watching the dawn break slowly I felt that life would never be the same; that something had broken inside me; and from that hour on I would have to wear a mask—not only to the public but to the one I loved best in the world; for he must never know how ill he was, and I must carry on." In this, the most astonishing passage of her memoir, she revealed her determination to cover up her husband's condition, both from the country and from him.

"President Suffers Nervous Breakdown," screamed the *New York Times* banner headline on September 27, 1919. "Tour Canceled. Speeding Back to Washington for a Needed Rest." At Edith's instruction, Dr. Grayson issued a calming, deliberately misleading statement from aboard the train: "President Wilson's condition is due to overwork. The trouble dates back to an attack of influenza last April in Paris, from which he has never entirely recovered. The President's activities on this trip have overtaxed his strength and he is suffering from nervous exhaustion. His condition is not alarming but it will be necessary for his recovery that he have rest and quiet for a considerable time."

Shortly after the president returned to the White House, he suffered another stroke, which permanently paralyzed his left side and blurred his vision. Soon, this condition was complicated by a urinary obstruction. He was so weak that Edith would not allow doctors to operate. Even after the urinary problem cleared up, Wilson only faintly resembled the dynamic figure of just weeks before. His once resonant voice was now an old man's croak. He could neither read nor stand on his own. He grew a beard and mustache to disguise his slack jaw.

Determined to keep the tragedy from the country, Edith closed down the White House. Overnight, she converted the Executive Mansion into an infirmary, and the presidency itself into a form of therapy, incentive for a very sick man to get better. In those more trusting times, the very fact that the president was in residence seemed enough to reassure people. The press were easily manipulated. "Fortunately," the *Times* concluded in an editorial, "there is every reason to accept the official assurance that it is not serious and that the tour was interrupted only because a continuation of the great strain to which it subjected the President might have led to serious illness thereafter."

Behind the tightly drawn draperies, Edith and Grayson had assumed the powers of the presidency. Much later, and without a trace of irony, Edith explained that "The only decision that was mine was what was important and what was not." Not the country, not Congress, not even his Cabinet knew the president's real condition. The government was in a state of suspended animation. No bills were signed, no proclamations were issued, no appointments made, no posts filled. No leader led. Papers were shuffled and the wheels of the bureaucracy turned aimlessly. Edith governed by default, deciding the national agenda on her own. "It was my habit to acquaint myself with the context of each matter and put the papers in convenient stacks before carrying them to him for signature. We would prop him up in bed, and he would sign as many as he could before growing exhausted."

The White House's official line continued to be "He shows signs of improvement," without further details or explanations. "I had been in and out of the room many times during this period," Chief Usher Irwin Hoover recalled, "and I saw very little progress. . . . All his natural functions had to be artificially assisted and he appeared just as helpless as one could possibly be and live."

Edith was sustained by a blinding optimism. "For days [his] life hung in the balance. Then the will to live, to recover and fight for his League of Nations, almost imperceptively at first began to gain ascendancy over the forces of disease, and the President got a little better." Hoover had a different memory. "He lived on; but oh what a wreck of his former self! He did grow better, but that is not saying much. I was with him at some time every day and saw him, even up to the end. . . . There was never a moment during all that time when he was more than a shadow of his former self. . . . It was so sad that those of us about him who almost without exception admired him, would turn our heads away when he came along or we went near him."

In her own mind, Edith had assumed her "stewardship" not from personal ambition but solely to serve her husband. "I studied every paper, sent from the different Secretaries or Senators, and tried to digest and present in tabloid form the things that, despite my vigilance, had to go to the President," she recalled. The president's attention span ran to no more than a few minutes a day. Edith thought she could handle the job. Her husband had made statecraft seem easy. She was under the illusion that she could fill in for him by reading all the cables, decoding secret messages and putting off things she deemed unimportant. But this was fantasy, not statesmanship. In fact, by protecting and "serving" her husband, she was—there is no other way to put it—undermining the national interest.

Edith admitted much later that she had subordinated the country to her husband's recovery. "Woodrow Wilson was first my beloved husband whose life I was trying to save, fighting with my back to the wall— after that he was the President of the United States." Her most potent weapon was her control of all access to him. "One night," Grayson recalled, "[the president] summoned me to his room, and, asking the nurse to leave us, he said, 'I have been thinking over this matter of resigning and letting the Vice President take my place. It is clear that I should do this if I have not the strength to fill the office. . . ." But Wilson never "broached this topic again."

Later, Edith tried to justify her actions. She claimed that Dr. Francis X. Dercum, a Philadelphia nerve specialist, had advised her to "have everything come to you; weigh the importance of each matter, and see if it is possible by consultations with the respective heads of the departments to solve them without the guidance of your husband." She wrote that Dercum had warned her, "every time you take him a new anxiety or problem to excite him, you are turning a knife in an open wound." Edith further claimed that when she suggested Wilson might resign, Dercum replied, "For Mr. Wilson to resign would have a bad effect on the country, and a serious effect on our patient." This, then, was Edith's rationale for taking over the presidency and for keeping the rest of the country in the dark. Historians and doctors have since questioned whether any physician would give advice that struck at the heart of the Constitution.

Edith did not allow House's letters to reach her husband. She blocked Tumulty from entering her husband's sickroom. Vice President Thomas Marshall, held in contempt by Wilson ("A small caliber man," Wilson had called him), was neither qualified nor particularly interested in assuming power and is best remembered for his bon mot, "What this country needs is a good five-cent cigar." (The Twenty-fifth Amendment, ceding power to the vice president during presidential infirmity or death, was not enacted until after the assassination of John F. Kennedy.) Wilson had an uneasy relationship with his secretary of state, Robert Lansing, whose loyalty he always questioned. When, in desperation, Lansing called a Cabinet meeting to deal with the accumulated business, Edith called it a "betrayal" and reported it to her husband. Lansing resigned following the president's censure. "In our case," Edith wrote, "to have good nurses was almost as important as to have good Cabinet officers."

The only other person aiding in Edith's cover-up was Dr. Grayson, who later said he had advised the first lady to make a full public disclosure of her husband's condition, and for the president to resign. Grayson claimed Edith overruled him on both counts. "She stood like a stone wall," the doctor recalled, between the sickroom and the officials who insisted that their business was so important that they must see him.

" 'The welfare of the country depends upon our presenting this case to him in person,' " Grayson recalled one delegate's assertion. "I am not thinking of the country now," Edith answered, "I am thinking of my husband."

As carefully as Edith and Grayson controlled news about the president's health, wild rumors circulated about his condition. Some said he'd gone mad, pointing to the bars on the upstairs windows (installed earlier to keep Theodore Roosevelt's young children from falling out). By December 1919, Edith could no longer prevent a congressional delegation from calling on her husband. "The Smelling Committee," as Wilson dubbed it, consisted of Senator Albert Fall of New Mexico, an outspoken opponent of the League, and Senator Gilbert Hitchcock of Nebraska, a staunch Wilson supporter. In a dark, windowless corner of the first-floor sickroom, Edith propped up her husband with pillows. His limp left side was well covered, while his good right arm was exposed. "Never was a conspiracy so pointedly or artistically formed," Irwin Hoover recalled of the staged interview. Edith stood at the foot of her husband's bed with pencil and pad in hand, "so I would not have to shake hands with [Fall]."

"Well, Mr. President," Fall, a hearty westerner with a handlebar mustache, greeted Wilson, "we have all been praying for you." "Which way, Senator?" the sick man asked. The Republican senator, later convicted for bribery in the Teapot Dome scandal, turned to Edith. "You seem very much engaged, Madam," he said. "I thought it wise to record this interview," she replied, "so there may be no misunderstanding or misstatements made."

The charade worked. Fall told waiting reporters, hungry for any scrap of real news about the president, that Wilson was mentally fit and physically on the mend. The *Times* reported that the senators' visit "[silenced] for good the many wild and often unfriendly rumors of Presidential disability." Edith had won a critical round. There was nothing she could do, however, to save her husband's doomed crusade for the League of Nations.

Though by mid-December Wilson was hobbling around, his mind never fully recovered. He grew ever more uncompromising about the League. Let the Republicans bear full responsibility for the fate of the treaty, he thundered. He would not compromise one letter. Tragically out of touch, Wilson was still counting on public support to force Republicans to accept his terms. But the country's mood had shifted since his tour. The war was over. There was money to be made, lives to be rebuilt. Wilson's own party feared his obstinacy and Lodge's growing strength.

Even the British tried to reason with their former ally. London dispatched former foreign minister Lord Edward Grey, nearly blind and ailing himself, on his final diplomatic mission. But Grey was carrying more than official freight. In his entourage was the man who Edith thought had entertained the capital in 1915 with his quip about her falling out of bed when the president proposed marriage. Crauford-Stuart had always denied having been the source of the joke, but Edith was unforgiving. Wilson demanded Grey send the diplomat home. Grey politely declined and waited for weeks for the freeze to thaw. Finally, he returned to London without ever seeing Wilson.

Woodrow Wilson, partially paralyzed by a stroke, and his wife,
Edith, motor through Washington, March 21, 1920.

Edith was the last hope of those still determined to save the treaty and the League. Senator Hitchcock implored Edith to ask her husband to accept the Lodge reservations limiting American participation in the League. She agreed to try. "Woodrow, for my sake," she pleaded, according to her own memoirs, "won't you accept these reservations and get this awful thing settled?" The tired, sick president shook his head. "Little girl," he pleaded, "don't you desert me now. That I cannot stand. Can't you see that I have no moral right to accept any change in a paper I have signed without giving every other signatory, even the Germans, the right to do the same thing?" Fearful for his health, Edith vowed never again to "ask my husband to do anything dishonorable."

Wilson's unyielding position on the League pushed his supporters on the Hill into a corner. The choice was between democracy and imperialism, Wilson insisted. The upcoming presidential elections should be a "great and solemn referendum" on the treaty. He commanded his supporters to vote for ratification of the Versailles Treaty with no reservations and reject all compromise. Had Wilson still been in full command of his once powerful political and verbal skills, he probably would have found enough common ground between the isolationists and his supporters to bridge the gap. But he no longer had the strength to try.

On March 19, 1920, the treaty meant to end the war that would end all future wars was rejected by the Senate. "I feel like going to bed and staying there," the architect of the peace sighed. During the sleepless night that followed the defeat, he told Grayson, "If I were not a Christian, I think I should go mad, but my faith in God holds me to the belief that He is in some way working out His own plans through human perversities and mistakes."

America retreated into isolationism. One by one, the vanquished and the victorious mocked Wilson's vision of a just peace. Without the support of the most powerful country, the League of Nations was powerless to stop Germany, Italy and Japan as they moved toward another world war.

So effectively had Edith nurtured the illusion that Wilson was on the mend that he refused to designate his successor. Sometime during the spring of 1920, in his feeble scrawl, Wilson even started a file entitled "3d Inaugural."

On March 4, 1921, a pale, withered Wilson rode from the White House to the Capitol with Warren G. Harding, the Republican who had won a landslide victory over Democrat James M. Cox. Out of office, Wilson had planned to write a book summarizing his political philosophy. He produced a single page, "A Dedication: to E.B.W., I dedicate this book because it is a book in which I have tried to interpret life, the life of a nation, and she has shown me the full meaning of life. Her heart is not only true but wise; her thoughts are not only free but touched with vision; she teaches and guides by being what she is; her unconscious interpretation of faith and duty makes all the way clear; her power to comprehend makes work and thought alike easier and more near to what it seeks. [Signed,] Woodrow Wilson." He never wrote another line. Wilson died at his home in Washington on February 3, 1924. The last word he uttered was "Edith."

But Edith's fierce devotion did not end with her husband's passing. When told that Senator Lodge had been named as an official delegate to her husband's funeral, she fired off a note to him: "As the funeral is private and not official and realizing that your presence would be embarrassing to you and unwelcome to me I write to request that you do not attend." Lodge had no choice but to honor her wish.

SO ENDED THE WHITE HOUSE'S GREATEST LOVE STORY, with a tragic outcome. Edith lived for four more decades, long enough to see her husband's vision vindicated by the creation of the United Nations. She had shared but nine of her eighty-nine years with him, four of them more as nurse than wife. Until her last breath, she was convinced she had done the right thing, enabling her husband to hold on to the presidency.

In retrospect, it is astonishing to realize how great her powers were in the last eighteen months of Wilson's presidency. A woman with two years of formal education, bred for the drawing room, opposed to women's suffrage, had not only assumed most presidential powers but the control of the flow of information to the country. It was an unprecedented situation for this or any other democracy.

It is doubtful any first lady will ever again wield the power Edith did. The Twenty-fifth Amendment assures a smooth succession in case of presidential illness or incapacity. Moreover, one of the benefits of modern media scrutiny is that it forces the government to be open, even in times of crisis. Woodrow Wilson's gaunt White House portrait has continued to remind succeeding residents of the sometimes high cost of the presidency, and the potential risk of a commander in chief who falls in love while in office. It is supremely ironic that the man forever associated with open diplomacy clung to power through a cover-up.

CHAPTER 2

ELEANOR AND FRANKLIN ROOSEVELT

THE PARTNERSHIP THAT CHANGED THE WORLD

No one who ever saw Eleanor Roosevelt sit down facing her husband, holding his eyes firmly and saying to him, "Franklin, I think you should . . . Franklin, surely you will not . . ." will ever forget the experience. . . . It would be impossible to say how often and to what extent American government processes have been turned in a new direction because of her determination.

—REXFORD TUGWELL, *member of Franklin Roosevelt's brain trust*

He might have been happier with a wife who was completely uncritical. That I was never able to be, and he had to find it in some other people. Nevertheless, I think I sometimes acted as a spur, even though the spurring was not always wanted or welcome. I was one of those who served his purposes.

—ELEANOR ROOSEVELT

THOUGH LESS THAN A DECADE AND A HALF SEPARATES THE WILSONS AND the Roosevelts, the journey takes us from the most private couple to occupy the White House in the twentieth century to one of the most public. Franklin and Eleanor Roosevelt redefined the roles of president and first lady; he with his buoyant, expansive, imaginative leadership, she with the power of her moral force. Through their example, their leadership and FDR's legislative record, it is no exaggeration to say that together they transformed the nation. All their successors have been measured against them.

Franklin and Eleanor constructed brave and rich lives for themselves and, in the process, touched millions of people. Each redefined the office they held and left it permanently altered. Franklin transformed the Democratic Party and the country's political culture. This High Church Episcopalian saw that the tradition of self-reliance did not work when too many were hungry and unemployed. He acted on his belief that the government of a modern industrial state must provide food for the hungry and jobs for those who want to work. It is impossible to measure the exact impact of Eleanor's compassionate spirit and obstinate prodding on the New Deal. No one, however, can doubt her role in Franklin's personal and political evolution.

More has been written about this couple than any other in presidential history. Every facet of their lives has been documented, analyzed and held up for public scrutiny. Yet succeeding generations must study the Roosevelts to test their own notions regarding the intersection of marriage and power. By contemporary standards, theirs was not a "good" marriage. Still, for most of their tenure, they thrived in the White House—and the nation was enriched by the presence there of these two singular personalities. In fact, Eleanor and Franklin's identities and contributions were vastly more separate and distinct than Bill and Hillary Clinton's. But then the freedom and the creativity with which the Roosevelts were allowed to manage their affairs over a half century ago is beyond the reach of present-day presidential couples.

Unlike Hillary, Eleanor did not have to plead with the public and the media for a "zone of privacy." The culture of the time deemed it her right. Leading separate lives enabled the Roosevelts to preserve their marriage without the American people knowing the emotional cost of the effort. But the White House has sheltered other imperfect marriages that did not produce such an activist first lady. Imbued with extraordinary stamina and idealism, Eleanor was a born reformer who, in a different time, might have become a missionary. She took full advantage of her position as first lady to do her heart's bidding. If her husband gave her full rein to do so, it was because it suited both his personal and political needs. Ultimately, the country benefited from the Roosevelts' unconventional union. They were, in many ways, the first modern couple to occupy the White House.

⸻

THE PARTNERSHIP DID NOT START OUT THAT WAY. Eleanor and Franklin were born into the most privileged of nineteenth-century New York society, a world to which one either did or did not belong. Both sets of parents possessed money, land, connections and a strong sense of entitlement. The Roosevelts on both sides emulated the values, tastes and pretensions of the British aristocracy. Like the rest of their social class, their parents' energy and focus was spent in the ritual migrations of the East Coast privileged class: from New York to Long Island, Newport or Maine, and the yearly tours of the Continent. Their calendars were marked with metronomic precision: the opening of the Opera, the coming-out parties, high teas and regattas. Everyone within their circle knew his or her place, knew the rules and certainly knew the other players within the circle.

Franklin, the only child of an elderly Hudson River squire and his much younger wife, was the center of his parents' universe. His childhood was spent in Hyde Park, New York, in one of the great river houses on a large forested estate. Until he left for boarding school at Groton, the household revolved around this extraordinarily handsome and good-natured little boy. Franklin's struggle as an only child was to snare a bit of freedom from his excessively loving, overly protective mother, Sara Delano Roosevelt. She wanted too much from her child, so he learned to keep his own counsel. Dissembling became a key to Franklin's survival. No one—not his wife, not his children, not the women he loved—ever pierced the protective shell he began to construct during those early years. The fact that his nearest friend lived a mile and a half away reinforced the boy's self-reliance and isolation from his peers. What Franklin was prepared for, first at Hyde Park and later at Groton and Harvard, was a life of ease among those of his own class. He set off for the world a breathtakingly secure man, skillful at keeping his emotional distance with charm and good manners.

Eleanor's childhood is the story of a chain of losses. She was the solemn child of frivolous, beautiful parents. Her mother was a society belle who did not hide her disappointment that her daughter was plain. You have no looks, she told the child she called "Granny," see to it that you have manners. "Attention and admiration," Eleanor later said, were the two things she longed for in her childhood. She never had a chance to win either from her mother, who died when Eleanor was eight. Her father, who made up for her mother's constricted love with effusive out-pourings, was not a steady presence in the little girl's life. Eleanor nonetheless adored the man who called her his "little Nell." When, two years after her mother's death, her father died of alcoholism, she and her two younger brothers were left the wards of their grandmother.

Eleanor's salvation came when, at fifteen, she was sent to the Allenswood Academy, a progressive boarding school near London. She arrived in England a bundle of fears and insecurities. The headmistress of Allenswood was the first to perceive that the shy girl had an extraordi-nary quality. Despite Eleanor's pedigree, she was seen to have an open mind, avid to learn and hungry for every new idea. And she had some-thing else: a humanity that set her apart. When she returned home after three years at Allenswood, Eleanor had a stronger sense of herself. She had been encouraged to use her mind, and she had shone. "For the first time in all my life," she said, "all my fears left me."

When Franklin accidentally encountered his fifth cousin Eleanor on a train, he saw a more self-assured young woman, no longer trying quite so hard to bend to society's expectations of who she should be. She was tall and graceful, with beautiful eyes, thick, fair hair and a lively curiosity Franklin had not encountered in a girl of his set. "E. is an angel," he wrote in code in his diary, to keep his mother in the dark. A year later, the two Roosevelts were engaged. Sara Roosevelt, not yet ready to share her adored son, tried and failed to keep them apart. Eleanor was given away in marriage by her uncle, President Theodore Roosevelt, on March 17, 1905.

Despite such similar backgrounds, and even a blood tie, the couple's differences were clear. Franklin, tall and conventionally handsome, used his all-is-well smile to keep the world at arm's length. "If something was unpleasant," Eleanor later said of her husband, "he didn't want to know about it; he just ignored it. . . . I think he always thought that if you ignored a thing long enough, it would settle itself." Relentlessly charming, he could talk for forty minutes at a stretch on any subject, so long as it was not personal. He liked sending people away happy.

Eleanor, intense and still somewhat insecure, inept at small talk, impatient to "be useful," longed to connect more than socially. Moreover, deprived in childhood of the focused devotion which Franklin had had in excess, she hungered for intimacy. "You could not find two such different people as Mother and Father," their daughter, Anna, noted. But neither Roosevelt knew nor cared much about their differences. Photographs show a secret joy, almost a look of relief, on their faces during this period. Franklin was declaring his independence from his mother. Eleanor, who had never had a steady, loving presence in her life, thought she had found it in Franklin. "Everything is changed for me now," she wrote him. "I am so happy. Oh! so happy and I love you so dearly. I cannot begin to write you all I should like to say, but you know it all I am sure and I hope that you, too, dearest are very very happy." For the first time in her nineteen years, she dared drop her reserve and entrust someone with her deepest feelings. "Dearest Honey," she wrote him when they were apart, "I miss you dreadfully and feel very lonely, but please don't think it is because I am alone, having other people wouldn't do any good for I just want you!"

The young lovers tried to placate Franklin's mother, who still tried her best to keep them apart. "Not only I but you are the luckiest and will always be the happiest people in the world," Franklin wrote Sara, "in gaining anyone like E. to love and be loved by." But Sara would not cede her preeminent position in her son's life. Nor was it in his nature to confront her directly. How much pain Franklin might have spared Eleanor had he been willing to draw clearer boundaries.

No doubt Franklin and Eleanor saw in each other their own missing qualities. He was drawn to her serious, high-minded side and the generous empathy he did not yet possess. She already bristled at their overprivileged lives. "One thing I am glad of every minute I stay here," she wrote her fiancé from a Long Island mansion, "is that we won't ever have to have a house half so beautiful or half so overwhelming! I'm afraid I wasn't born to be a high life lady, dear, so you'll just have to be content with a simple existence, unless you teach me how to change!" She saw how much Franklin enjoyed being Franklin, and wished for some of that lighthearted sense of well-being for herself. Cynical observers who saw only their surface differences said that in marrying Eleanor, Franklin was trying to get close to her "Uncle Teddy," the politician he most admired. That is at odds with their evident and powerful feelings for each other.

A poem she sent him—part admonishment, part solemn vow— reveals how momentous their bond was to Eleanor. She kept a copy of the Elizabeth Barrett Browning poem, and its lofty standard for love, all her life.

> *Unless you can think, when the song is done,*
> *No other is soft in the rhythm;*
> *Unless you can feel, when left by one,*
> *That all men else go with him;*
> *Unless you can know, when unpraised by his breath,*
> *That your beauty itself wants proving;*
> *Unless you can swear "For life, for death!"—*
> *Oh, fear to call it loving!*

"I wondered," she wrote Franklin, "if it meant 'for life, for death' to you at first, but I know it does now. I do not know what to write. I cannot write what I want. I can only wait and long for Sunday when I shall tell you all I feel I cannot write."

Their first child, Anna, was born on May 3, 1906, followed in rapid succession by James, Franklin (who died soon after birth), Elliott, Franklin and John. "For ten years I was always just getting over having a baby or about to have one," Eleanor wrote.

But her husband never did leave his mother. Through her control of the family finances, Sara still largely determined where and how they lived and even how they raised their children. Five years into their marriage, Sara bought them a town house in New York City adjacent to her own with a connecting door between the two on each floor. At the dining table at Hyde Park, Franklin sat at one end and Sara the other, Eleanor along the side. To this day, two enormous armchairs flank the fireplace of the cavernous Hyde Park living room. The hearth belonged to mother and son; Eleanor was the visitor. Until she built her own house nearby, she had no place that was hers.

Eleanor could have borne all this had Franklin been the partner she longed for. But once their courtship was over, he could not share his emotional life with his wife and was puzzled by her need to do so. "In the autumn of 1908," Eleanor wrote,

> I did not know what was the matter with me, but I remember that a few weeks after we moved into the new house on East 65th St. I sat in front of my dressing table and wept, and when my bewildered young husband asked me what on earth was the matter with me, I said I did not like to live in a house which was not in any way mine, one that I had done nothing about and which did not represent the way I wanted to live. Being an eminently reasonable person, he thought I was quite mad and told me so gently and said I would feel different in a little while and left me alone until I should become calmer.

It was more than her emotional life that was unfulfilled. The high-necked frocks and tight corsets she wore were only the outward manifestation of the constricted lives of women of Eleanor's class. While her husband enjoyed his man-about-town status, her hungry mind was undernourished. Eleanor was searching for a way out of her confinement.

Escape came once Franklin launched the political career he patterned after Uncle Teddy's. Moving to Albany when Franklin became a New York state senator, then Washington when he was appointed undersecretary of the navy in the Wilson administration, finally freed Eleanor from Sara's yoke. Organizing her children's and husband's lives, she discovered she was a natural administrator. Always motivated more by duty than pleasure, she was now scrupulous about fulfilling her duty as the helpmate of a rising political star. "I was perfectly certain that I had nothing to offer of an individual nature and that my only chance of doing my duty as the wife of a public official was to do exactly as the majority of women were doing." Doing as the majority of political wives were doing—though surely most did not have five toddlers at home— meant a round of ten to thirty social calls each afternoon. But she did not enjoy the Washington matrons' minuet of luncheon parties, the leaving of calling cards, the prescribed good works. Eleanor liked what she called real talk, conversation with a purpose. She yearned for the deeper rewards of real service.

The differences between Franklin and Eleanor continued to assert themselves. Where he was devious, she was straightforward. He loved playing games with people, she was incapable of manipulation. Where he fled hard personal truths, she embraced them. Where he was patient, she was impatient. Where he was practical, she was uncompromising. Franklin was the sort of man who was familiar to all yet intimate with none. Exuding a surface openness—he invariably called people by their first names in an age when it was unusual to do so—he never really dropped his guard with anyone.

Eleanor's overactive conscience precluded fun for its own sake— something as essential as oxygen for Franklin. Her husband was a flirt who thrived in lighthearted female company. He almost always had a good time, even at formal events that simultaneously bored her and made her anxious. Nor could he join Eleanor in soul-searching conversation. She had come up against what some called his little "black box," that place no one penetrated, where he stored his most private thoughts. Her husband was discovering that his greatest love was politics. "It is a little like a drug habit," Franklin wrote, "almost impossible to stop definitively." At some level, he surely sensed he could never make Eleanor happy for long. "I am sometimes a little selfish," he wrote a friend, ". . . and make life a trifle dull for her really brilliant mind and spirit." He wrote her in 1913, "I know it's hard for both of us to lead this kind of life," aware that it was hard only for Eleanor.

In 1918, when she was thirty-four years old, "the bottom dropped out" of Eleanor's world when she discovered she was sharing her husband with another woman. She had had her suspicions for some time. Franklin seemed too eager to pack her off with "the chicks" for their summer retreat in Campobello, New Brunswick. "You goosy girl," her husband had chided her for impugning his motives. The packet of love letters Eleanor found in his suitcase when he came home ill from a European mission broke her heart and forever shattered her love for Franklin. That they had been written by her social secretary, Lucy Mercer, deepened the pain. Lucy was of Eleanor's social class and breeding; she was a younger, more beautiful and more lighthearted version of Eleanor. Lucy and Franklin had fallen in love in her house, under her nose. The man who had given Eleanor confidence as a woman and had provided her a secure place in the world suddenly snatched them away. It was a reprise of her worst childhood trauma: the loss of her beloved father. Those she most loved seemed always to desert her. She never again allowed herself to love freely. Unlike her prior losses, however, this heartbreak transformed her.

Eleanor agreed to stay with Franklin for the sake of their five children and for his political future, which a divorce would have ended. FDR pledged never to see Lucy again. No doubt Eleanor was also motivated by more complex emotions: a powerful bond of affection, respect, a common history and shared goals. But for a woman as absolutist in her judgments as Eleanor, her husband's betrayal was beyond redemption. "How could she forgive him," one of her grandchildren later asked, "after her childhood experiences?" Two years later, on February 14, 1920, Eleanor wrote her mother-in-law, "Did you know Lucy Mercer married Mr. Wintie Rutherfurd two days ago?" Rutherfurd, a wealthy widower with six children, was more than twice Lucy's age.

In a conventional sense, Eleanor and Franklin's marriage ended in 1918. She abandoned her dream of a union based on perfect understanding and a complicity that would keep the rest of the world at bay. "After that, father and mother had an armed truce," their son James wrote, "that endured to the day he died, despite several occasions I was to observe in which he in one way or another held out his arms to mother and she flatly refused to enter his embrace. [But] there was always an affection between them. . . ." Like the Clintons a half century later, the Roosevelts were embattled but permanently bound to each other.

Eleanor had idealized her husband as much as she had her mercurial father. She was disappointed by both men. But rather than allowing that disappointment to crush her, gradually and through great pain, she made it work for her. No longer burdened by trying to be the perfect wife or the perfect daughter-in-law, she declared her independence. At a time when women did not even have the right to vote, much less participate in the male-dominated civic or professional world—when, in fact, Edith Wilson more than Eleanor represented the "ideal woman"—she began the personal journey from which she never retreated. Rather than withdrawing into herself, her pain spurred growth, made her even more compassionate. She now stopped playing by the rules of her social class and plunged into political life.

BOTH FRANKLIN AND ELEANOR SUFFERED excruciating pain during those early months and years following his betrayal. She was let down beyond imagination; he was unmasked for the first time in his life. He had to face the disappointment of the two women who were at the core of his existence: his wife and his mother. One photograph captures the family's dark mood during a period of forced togetherness. Taken in 1920 on

In one of the last photos taken before he contracted polio, Franklin Delano Roosevelt sits confidently between the two warring women in his life, his mother and Eleanor. Eleanor, whose discomfort is palpable, had recently learned of her husband's affair with Lucy Mercer.

the front steps of their summer home on Campobello Island, Franklin and Eleanor flank Sara Delano Roosevelt. Eleanor is looking down, an expression of unbearable sadness on her face. For once Franklin is not masking distress with his winner's smile. His five children and his mother all seem to have caught the contagion of the couple's anguish. The Roosevelts' agony, however, stayed private.

Eleanor and Franklin found a common and safe language in politics. Eleanor started small, building up her confidence in groups like the League of Women Voters and Democratic women's organizations. At this stage, she wrote better than she spoke, but her prodigious energy and lack of ego or vanity were great gifts. Her full focus was on issues: housing, child labor laws, voter registration and birth control. Along the way she earned her husband's respect, admiration and, though rarely expressed, gratitude. The two forged a new relationship based not on passion or intimacy but on shared values, mutual need and, eventually, affection.

One of the people who first recognized and nurtured Eleanor's political skills was Louis Howe. A former Associated Press reporter, Howe grasped Franklin's enormous gift and potential. "Beloved and Revered Future President," Howe called him. He was also the first to see the Roosevelts' formidable potential as a political couple. He worked with Eleanor to improve her shrill, nervous speaking voice. He also told her to "say what you need to say and sit down." With Howe's guidance, she began to develop her own style, as different from Franklin's as she was from him herself, but effective in its way.

With lowered expectations of her marriage and suppressed rage at her husband, she invested her emotions in friends. "Out of a long experience I have decided that to me lasting friendships and intimate contacts with people mean more than any other things in life," she wrote. She sought out people who needed her. "In all our contacts," she later wrote, "it is probably the sense of being really needed which gives us the greatest satisfaction and creates the most lasting bond."

In the early years after their trauma, reserve, good manners and familiarity eased her relations with Franklin. Hesitantly at first, they began to weave a new pattern for their union. "Dearest Honey," Eleanor wrote Franklin from a League of Women Voters Convention in Cleveland, "I've had a very interesting day and heard some really good women speakers. Mrs. [Carrie Chapman] Catt is clear, cold reason. . . . I listened to Child Welfare all the morning and Direct Primaries all the afternoon . . . attended a N.Y. delegate's meeting and am about to go to bed, quite weary. Meetings begin tomorrow at ten. . . . Much much love dear and I prefer doing my politics with you!"

The story of how everything changed for Franklin and Eleanor in the summer of 1921 never loses its power. Franklin had taken his children sailing at Campobello. After an icy ocean dip, he caught what seemed at first to be merely a summer chill. He took to his bed—and never walked again. Due to his polio, Eleanor became the strong one, Franklin the dependent one. It was only then that the Roosevelts discovered who they really were and how dependent they were on each other. For weeks after Franklin was stricken, Eleanor slept on a couch in his room and nursed him day and night. She did not weep in front of him. She said later that Franklin with his collapsed legs reminded her of Michelangelo's *Pieta*. It helped that Franklin was not given to introspection and that Eleanor lacked the time for it. "To tell the truth," Eleanor wrote, "I do not think I ever stopped to analyze my feelings [regarding Franklin's illness]. There was so much to do to manage the household and the children and to try to keep things running smoothly that I never had any time to think of my own reactions. I simply lived from day to day and got through the best I could."

Franklin's courage matched Eleanor's as he submitted to his wife's total care with a stoicism that no one could have predicted. Several times a day, Eleanor and Louis Howe raised and lowered his large frame, bathed him, rubbed him, ministered to his every need. Whether he would ever walk again was at best uncertain, but from that uncertainty, Eleanor and Franklin gleaned hope and strength. He made up his mind he would walk again. She knew that his only chance to escape the invalid's half-life was by returning to the political arena.

"He was still pretty sick and pretty weak," FDR's future Cabinet member, Frances Perkins, recalled of his early return to politics. "It wasn't just a question of rousing his interest. It was a question of his actually being able to bear the burden that came with more responsibility. I heard [Eleanor] say, 'I do hope that he'll keep in political life. I want to keep him interested in politics. This is what he cares for more than anything else. I don't want him forgotten. I want him to have a voice in various things. . . . It's *good* for him.' "

But first she had to face down her mother-in-law. "Mama made up her mind that Franklin was going to be an invalid for the rest of his life and that he would retire to Hyde Park and live there," Eleanor wrote. "I hated the arguments, but they had to happen. I had to make a stand." She had come far from the shy girl who could only say, "Yes, Mama." In their shared determination to return him to public life, Eleanor and Franklin drew close together again. "My mother-in-law thought we were tiring my husband and that he should be kept completely quiet," Eleanor recalled. "She always thought that she understood what was best, particularly where her child was concerned." Sara lost the war for her son's soul. "[Politics] was a growing bond between Mother and Father," Eleanor and Franklin's daughter, Anna, recalled. "[Mother] was very much more realistic than Granny ever would have been capable of being, because of [Granny's] background which didn't have any of these social and political interests which Mother did have. . . . The polio was very instrumental in bringing them much closer into a very real partnership . . . their overall goals were the same." Ultimately, their son James noted, "[Franklin] came to admire his wife more than he did his mother."

The next several years changed them both. Franklin learned lessons about pain, loss and vulnerability that were already familiar to Eleanor. She now saw as a strength his ability to mask despair with a smile. The fact that they were almost never alone—for Franklin needed almost constant help—no doubt eased them through the crucible of those years. And Eleanor, who loved to feel needed, was now desperately needed.

Franklin was the strategist as Eleanor began her role as his "eyes, ears and legs," at first to keep his name alive. His future depended largely on her good political instincts. The qualities that first drew Franklin to her—her modesty, her self-effacement and her seriousness of purpose—now inspired admiration from a wider public. Her high-pitched voice was becoming familiar on the stump and on the airwaves as she crisscrossed New York State, preparing for Franklin's return to politics. I'm only being active until you can be again, she constantly reassured him. She was still very much the traditional wife at this stage, encouraging and bolstering, but never acknowledging her own ambitions or passions. A wife's job, she told an interviewer, was to be a partner, mother, homemaker, in that order. Earlier, she had placed the mother's role at the top of the list. "But today," she noted revealingly, "we understand that everything else depends upon the success of the wife and husband in their personal relationship."

At times, the combination of her crushed hopes for personal happiness and the burden of restoring her husband and raising five children overwhelmed her. "I was trying to read to the two youngest boys," Eleanor remembered. "I suddenly found myself sobbing as I read. I could not think why I was sobbing, nor could I stop. . . . Mr. Howe came in and tried to find out what the matter was. . . . The two little boys went off to bed and I sat on the sofa in the sitting room and sobbed and sobbed."

Politics proved therapeutic for her as well. "I was beginning to find the political contacts Louis [Howe] wanted," Eleanor wrote. "I drove a car on election day and brought people to the polls. I began to learn a good deal about party politics in a small place. It was rather sordid in spots. . . . I saw how people took money or its equivalent on election day for their votes and how much of the party machinery was geared to crooked business. . . . I learned again that human beings are seldom all good or all bad and that few human beings are incapable of rising to the heights now and then."

∞

"I AM BACK," Franklin Delano Roosevelt proclaimed, having hauled his crippled legs up to the Madison Square Garden stage in the tumult of the 1924 Democratic convention. He was there to nominate Al Smith, "the Happy Warrior," for president, but it was his own comeback that the crowd cheered. "All the delegates to the national convention remembered . . . this beautiful, athletic, handsome young man," Frances Perkins recalled. "Then they heard he had polio and he was dead, so far as they knew. . . . He came to life and there he was. He looked so well that day . . . and his voice was strong. The man on the street just assumed . . . this fine fellow we thought was dead still lives."

Franklin applied himself to forcing his lifeless legs to walk again, seeking relief on a houseboat and in the soothing waters of Warm Springs, Georgia. Eleanor encouraged him to take his time, freeing him of any guilt about his long absences from the family. "Don't worry about being selfish," she wrote him. "It is more important that you have all you need and wish than anything else and you always give the chicks more than they need and you know I always do just what I want!"

With a surge of energy, she formalized her independence from both Franklin and Sara. She moved into her own house. Val Kill Cottage was a modest stone house two miles from the Roosevelt mansion. Building it was Franklin's idea, a sign that he was reconciled to her need for autonomy. "My Missus and some of her female political friends want to build a shack on a stream in the back woods . . . ," Franklin wrote to Elliot Brown, a friend whose help he enlisted on the building project. Privately, he referred to Val Kill as "Honeymoon Cottage" or "the love nest." Indeed, Eleanor's circle of politically active women—Nan Cook, Marion Dickerman, Elizabeth Read and Esther Lape—were lesbians. Next door to her new home, Eleanor built the Val Kill Shop, a furniture factory employing locals. She was putting into practice a theory dear to both Roosevelts: creating small industries in agricultural areas would keep farmers busy in the off-season and keep them on the land. But this was only the embryo of her expanding activism. Released from her old insecurities and inhibitions, it seemed there was nothing she would not try. She and her friend Dickerman bought the Todhunter School, a New York City private school for girls. Eleanor taught literature, drama and American history there.

By 1928, after seven years of physical therapy and Eleanor's tireless activism, Franklin was ready to accept the call from New York State Democrats to run for governor. "The demand for Mr. Roosevelt," Walter Lippmann wrote, "came from every part of the state. It could not be quelled. It could not be denied. The office has sought the man." Eleanor shrewdly deflected rumors that she was responsible for her long-absent husband's candidacy. "I never did a thing to ask him to run. . . . My husband always makes his own decisions. We always discuss things together, and sometimes I take the opposite side for the fun of the thing, but he always makes his own decisions."

Instinctively, she understood the public's limited tolerance for a high-profile political spouse. Once the Roosevelts moved into the Albany Governor's Mansion, Eleanor declared her political days behind her. "Now that my husband is actually back in active politics, it is wise for me not to be identified with any of the party committees," she wrote in her letter resigning from the Democratic State Committee. It was not the last time Eleanor would underestimate both her love of politics or her husband's need for her to stay in it.

For a politician who was a prisoner of his wheelchair, particularly one determined that his infirmity go unnoticed, a trusted partner was essential. A politician must get out and listen to the people, letting them take his measure; Franklin could do this only in the most limited way. And thus his wife became his indispensable partner. "Walking was so difficult for him," Eleanor wrote,

> that he could not go inside an institution and get a real idea of how it was being run. . . . I would tell him what was on the menu for the day. . . . I learned to look into the cooking pots on the stove and to find out if the contents corresponded to the menu; I learned to notice whether the beds were too close together. . . . I learned to watch patients' attitude toward the staff; and before the end of our years in Albany I had become a fairly expert reporter on state institutions. . . . From [FDR] I learned how to observe from train windows: he would watch the crops, notice how people dressed, how many cars there were and in what condition, and even look at the wash on the clothesline. . . . Franklin saw geography clearly. . . .

More and more, Franklin Delano Roosevelt and his "Missus" were accepted as partners.

Roosevelt was a man who knew what he wanted and who, within obvious limitations, lived his life exactly as he saw fit. He despised being alone, and his paralysis only reinforced that. Forced to part with Lucy

Mercer, he found someone else to fill the role that Eleanor did not. From 1921 until 1941 his secretary, Missy LeHand, was his unofficial "wife." Pretty, adoring and devoted entirely to the man she alone called "F.R.," Missy had virtually no other life but to serve him as secretary, companion and hostess during his wife's absences. She was with him on his houseboat, the *Larooco,* and in Warm Springs when Eleanor was not. Unlike Eleanor, Missy shared his love of nonsense, never tired of hearing his stories, never interrupted. Missy, and not his wife, shared the dark days of his early physical rehabilitation, when it was noon before he could bear to face the world. Though she hated the water, she swam with him and accompanied him on long drives around the Georgia countryside. She fussed and clucked over him and worshipped him in a way that was alien to Eleanor's personality.

There is little agreement among historians and family members as to whether the Missy-Franklin relationship was ever consummated. Some "experts" as well as members of his own family feel FDR would have been "too embarrassed" to have sex in his condition. But, unlike with Lucy, Franklin was quite open about this relationship, not its emotional or romantic content, but his need of Missy and their obvious rapport. "Everyone in the closely knit inner circle of father's friends accepted it as a matter of course," Elliott Roosevelt recalled. "I remember being only mildly stirred to see him with Missy on his lap as he sat in a wicker chair in the main stateroom [of the *Larooco*] holding her in his sun-browned arms, whose clasp we children knew so well. . . . He made no attempt to conceal his feeling about Missy."

ELEANOR SEEMS NOT TO HAVE BEEN BLIND to Missy's role in her husband's life. Shortly after William Bullitt, a wealthy businessman and diplomat, began dating Missy, FDR appointed him ambassador to Russia. Eleanor wrote her friend Lorena Hickock, "I wonder if that is why FDR has been so content to let Missy play with [Bullitt]!" "I once asked Mrs. Roosevelt," Eleanor's friend Trude Lash remembered, "if she thought her husband and Missy had an affair. She did not say no. She said she didn't *think* he did." Eleanor's feelings for her husband were different now than they had been when she discovered his love affair with Lucy. But still she was a proud woman, and Missy took pains not to arouse her. She made it seem as if her devotion was to both Roosevelts, rather than only to the man she loved. Outwardly, Eleanor embraced Missy, while at the same time she deftly put her in her place. "Missy was young and pretty and loved a good time," Eleanor wrote, "and occasionally her social contacts got mixed with her work and made it hard for her and others. To me she was always kind and helpful and when I had to be away she took up without complaint the additional social responsibilities thrust upon her." Eleanor was able to save face by treating Missy as a family retainer. "In the early days of Warm Springs," Eleanor wrote, "Miss LeHand spent a good deal more time there than I could. I still had four children at home during the school year. . . . Also I was carrying on a certain amount of political activity. . . ."

Franklin and Eleanor turned a domestic situation that might have defeated less resilient souls to their mutual advantage. Eleanor was as free as he was to find her own happiness, within the boundaries of their marriage. "Somehow I wish that we could live in the same town these days," she wrote Joseph Lash, her young friend from the antifascist student movement, "so if you wanted me at any time I could be available. As it is I just want you to know that having you near makes me happy and I hope it helps you." In another letter advising Joe on his marriage, Eleanor is clear about what she herself had sought in love. "When you do come home and get engulfed in work, will you stop long enough now and then even if T. is working with you to make her feel she is first in your life, even more important than saving the world? *Every woman wants to be first to someone sometime in her life and the desire is the explanation for many strange things women do, if only men understood it!*" How modest and how *ordinary* this woman's dream—and yet how far from the reality of her own marriage.

Franklin never actually admitted he could not walk. The press cooperated in his "splendid deception." He made it a rule during his first campaign for governor that he was not to be photographed looking crippled. "No pictures of me getting out of the machine, boys," he instructed newsmen who observed him being lifted in and out of his car. The request was honored and took on the weight of an executive order. During his presidency, if a newcomer violated the unwritten understanding, the Secret Service moved in. The public was never to know of the effort it cost FDR to appear a healthy man. The years of saltwater baths, ultraviolet light, electric currents, walking with twenty-pound weights, parallel bars at waist height, the agonizing effort to strengthen his withered muscles were all masked by the jaunty smile and the triumphant tilt of his head. Polio and politics only reinforced Franklin's natural talent for camouflaging his feelings.

When Eleanor was asked if her husband's illness affected his "mentality," she answered, "Yes," without evasion or embellishment. "Though he learned to bear it, I am afraid [his polio] was always a tragedy." Still she deftly turned the question in his favor. "Anyone who has gone through great suffering is bound to have a greater sympathy and understanding. . . ."

By the time they reached the White House in 1933, the Roosevelts' pattern of mutual dependence and independence was fixed. But the White House alters every marriage. Partners who previously saw little of each other are now thrown in daily contact, as they share their living and work space, as well as ceremonial duties. They are together and yet—under the blazing light of public attention—they are almost never alone together. Suddenly, they are the most famous couple in the world, and their every movement is subject to scrutiny, comment and criticism. The marriage has to become a partnership, with both partners willing to participate in the office they have fought so hard to attain. For a man like Roosevelt, whose freedom of movement was already severely limited, the White House was not Harry Truman's "Great White Prison." For FDR, the White House was compensation for his punishing fate. Now the world came to him.

With the notable exception of Bess Truman, no other modern-day first lady was as unenthusiastic about her role as Eleanor was in 1933. She was "happy for my husband, because I knew that in many ways it would make up for the blow that fate had dealt him when he was stricken," she wrote. But as she saw it, "This meant the end of any personal life of my own. . . . I had watched [my aunt] Mrs. Theodore Roosevelt and had seen what it meant to be the wife of a president." She feared the end of her hard-won independence, her ability to earn her own income, to live life as she liked. "The turmoil in my heart and mind was rather great. . . ." Once again, Eleanor was about to demonstrate she could take a situation and bend it to suit her needs without betraying her sense of duty. Hoping to shed the ceremonial aspects of her new position, she told reporters there would be no first lady, just plain old Mrs. Roosevelt.

Franklin's way of dealing with his wife's fears was characteristic. He made light of them and penned this verse:

> *Did my Eleanor relate*
> *all the sad and awful fate*
> *of the miserable lives*
> *lived by Washington wives. . . .*

The Roosevelts succeeded three undistinguished, unremarkable presidential couples who broke little social or political ground and are primarily remembered as the bridge between their predecessors and successors. The brief tenure of Warren and Florence Harding was notable for its mediocrity and corruption. Harding, best remembered as a reckless philanderer, called his cold, imperious wife "the Duchess." They were a loveless, childless couple. "Silent Cal" Coolidge and his wife, Grace Ann, followed, without leaving much of a social or political imprint. The third of this transitional trio were the Hoovers, Herbert and Lou. Lou, a graduate of Stanford University, was both intelligent and independent, but her husband's rigid, insensitive response to the economic and humanitarian crisis of the Depression determined their legacy.

Sometime between FDR's election and his first inauguration, Eleanor reached out to him, in her way. She asked her husband for a specific responsibility in his office, one that included handling part of his mail. Missy would consider that interference, Franklin told her. "I knew he was right," Eleanor wrote, "but it was a last effort to keep in close touch, and to feel I had a real job to do."

Eleanor found emotional sustenance elsewhere. Lorena Hickock, a short, feisty woman, was assigned by the Associated Press to cover the first lady. During an overnight train ride, Eleanor shared with Hickock the story of her lonely childhood and her disappointing marriage. Hick, as Eleanor would soon call her, revealed her own traumatic history, which included being raped by her father. The reporter and the first lady formed a relationship of need and trust. It was Hick, who eventually left her job to work for the Roosevelt administration, who persuaded Eleanor to hold weekly news conferences for women reporters. Hick also suggested that Eleanor write a daily newspaper column about her activities. Her writing and speaking and her growing self-assurance transformed the role Eleanor dreaded into something substantial. Hick acted as Eleanor's public relations adviser, editor and confidante. The streetwise reporter provided the first lady a safe outlet for her exasperation with her husband. "I know I've got to stick," she wrote Hick, "I know I'll never make an open break and I never tell FDR how I feel . . . I blow off to you, but never to F!"

The intensity of the Lorena-Eleanor correspondence has fueled rumors of a relationship deeper than friendship between the two women. "Hick darling," Eleanor wrote her friend following the first inauguration, "I want to put my arms around you . . . to hold you close. Your ring is a great comfort. I look at it and I think she does love me." Eleanor expressed feelings she withheld from her husband. "Remember one thing," Eleanor wrote Hick during her first week in the White House. "No one is just what you are to me. I'd rather be with you this minute than anyone else. . . ." Eleanor's intense need to connect was expressed through her correspondence. This was a passionate friendship, but how far their embraces went seems beside the point. They loved each other, and for a few years, Hickock played a vital role in Eleanor's life. The dynamic of the relationship shifted once Eleanor gained self-confidence and the love of thousands of people whose lives she touched. Then Hick became the needy one and something of a burden for the first lady.

∞

FROM THE MINUTE Eleanor crossed the threshold of the White House, it was apparent that things were about to change. As is customary, her predecessor, Mrs. Herbert Hoover, greeted Eleanor and proceeded to relate the many improvements she had made in the management and the decor of the mansion. "Mrs. Roosevelt listened attentively," Chief Usher Hoover later wrote, "but it was obvious that it was not what she wished to know." Following a quick tour, Eleanor declined the offer of a limousine and quickly hailed a passing cab.

"My first act," Eleanor remembered, "was to insist on running the [White House] elevator myself without waiting for one of the doormen to run it for me. That just wasn't done by the President's wife." With a respectful press corps rarely transgressing beyond strict boundaries, the American people knew little about how the new first lady abdicated her role as traditional wife in exchange for the freedom to travel, to write and to speak out. Eleanor and Franklin rarely dined alone or shared intimacies. Franklin's placement of a chest of drawers in front of the sliding doors that connected his wife's study to his bedroom was only the physical manifestation of their separate lives in the White House.

Eleanor and Franklin soon discovered that the big old house suited their lives and their relationship remarkably well. They turned the White House into an informal place of high energy and spontaneity. In those days, anyone could walk through the gates and stroll the grounds without ever having to show any identification. To compensate for the absence of real warmth in their marriage, the Roosevelts needed the stimulation and companionship of others. Among the dozens of people invited to reside for a time in the White House was a young writer named Martha Gellhorn (not yet married to her future husband Ernest Hemingway), recently fired from her government job. "It was just a great big house . . . always full of chums and funny people, and it was one of the most pleasing and easygoing amusing places you could possibly be in. And there was absolutely no sign of imperial nonsense." Gellhorn soon discovered that things could turn serious as well, especially at mealtime. "I was seated next to him [FDR] and Mrs. R. at the far end of the table at a given moment rose up the way she did and said, 'Franklin, talk to that child at your left. She says that all the people in the South have pellagra or syphilis.' "

Eleanor gave the shortest shrift to both the ceremonial and housekeeping aspects of her role. "People just came to dinner," Gellhorn recalled, "took off their coats and went into whatever room downstairs. Mrs. R. was waiting for them to serve them some rotten wine. They always had terrible food and terrible wine. She didn't know anything about food, or care about it. I don't suppose he [FDR] did; he cared about his martinis, which he mixed upstairs. And they just sat about and chattered and then they went into the dining room, which I don't remember as being in any way overpowering, except that there were a lot of people at table, because it was a combination of people who were supposed to be fun and amuse the President, or chums, and people that they had to have."

It is clear from their choice of companions how different were the Roosevelts' needs and expectations in relationships. Eleanor won people over with intensity and idealism, Franklin with ebullience. "If Father became friendly with a princess or a secretary," their daughter, Anna, recalled, "he'd reach out and give a pat to her fanny and laugh like hell and was probably telling a funny story at the same time, whereas to Mother that was terrible. He loved to outrage Granny, to tease her. He could never do that with Mother. She was much too serious. Mother was inhibiting to him. She would never go along. That's why he turned elsewhere."

Franklin had his entourage, many of whom not only worked in the White House but composed part of the First Family. Missy occupied a suite of rooms on the third floor. But there were others who were frequent, long-term guests, including Crown Princess Martha of Norway and FDR's cousins Daisy Suckley and Laura Delano. These women provided him with diversion and unquestioning loyalty. Franklin, of course, was not a stranger to strong women. His mother had been mistress of all that transpired at Hyde Park. But Sara's identity was drawn entirely from her husband, her son, her domestic empire. Typical for a man of his generation, FDR was not especially comfortable with women who challenged him intellectually. The Eleanor he married was not the assertive, competent, self-confident woman she would become.

FDR liked his women pliant and seductive. Once, when his wife told him that he was to dine alone with Madame Chiang, the tough-minded wife of Chinese president Chiang Kai-shek, the president replied heatedly, "Indeed I shan't! I am going to bed early!" Eleanor later remarked, "I don't think that Franklin likes women who think they are as good as he is." His daughter, Anna, was also hurt by this. "Pa seems to take for granted that all females should be quite content to 'keep the home fires burning,' and that their efforts outside of this are merely rather amusing and to be aided by a patronizing male world only as a last resort to keep some individually troublesome female momentarily appeased," she wrote her husband, John Boettiger, noting that her mother "goes along very strongly with me in our feeling that OM [Old Man] is a stinker in his treatment of the female members of his family."

Though FDR admired Eleanor's single-mindedness and her moral absolutism, he could take them only in limited doses. Presidential adviser Harry Hopkins, a close friend of both Roosevelts, recalled one such occasion. Eleanor had been relentlessly trying to reach her husband, to plead for a stay of execution for a convicted black sharecropper. FDR was equally determined to avoid his wife's calls. "Mrs. Roosevelt," Hopkins remembered, "would not take no for an answer. The president finally got on the phone himself and told Mrs. Roosevelt, that under no circumstances would he intervene. . . ." It may have been awkward at times for Hopkins to navigate between the two Roosevelts, but, Hopkins once admitted, "I never cease to admire Eleanor's burning determination to see that justice is done."

"FDR sometimes was impatient because he was tired and Mrs. Roosevelt had something important she wanted to tell him," Trude Lash recalled. "She wanted him to do something right away. The people around him very often didn't tell him the truth. It is so tempting to only say agreeable things to the president. And they would tell him how wonderful things were, either because they were involved or they didn't want to get hurt by it or they didn't want him to get upset. But she would tell him. She had the courage not to get discouraged. And the president knew this."

Eleanor also had her "court." Earl Miller, a former state trooper who became Eleanor's driver, bodyguard and companion, was a key member of her entourage. A physically powerful man, Miller taught her to shoot, drive and ride. He encouraged her to overcome her fear of sports and the outdoors. When, much later, Lash asked Earl if the rumor of an affair between him and the first lady were true, Miller answered, "You don't sleep with someone you call Mrs. Roosevelt." Still, Earl clearly filled the need for masculine presence in Eleanor's life. In all her homes, there was always a room for Earl.

Joe Lash, the melancholy young man who became her biographer, was also a fixture in her life. Eleanor loved Joe with an almost adolescent intensity. She frequently signed off her letters to him, "I love you," a formulation she almost never used with her husband. Later, Lash's wife, Trude, also joined Eleanor's inner circle. Eleanor loved giving the young couple advice on their troubled relationship and seemed to savor vicariously their passion and commitment to each other. All the emotions missing from her marriage she channeled into these friendships. But sex with any of these intimates remained largely unexplored territory for a woman whose roots were firmly Victorian. "She loved deeply," Joe Lash maintained, "but she was unable to let herself go."

Eleanor was shy and slow to open up, but her friendships were deep, authentic and lifelong. How different her approach was to those she truly loved and trusted from the surface warmth she extended Franklin. "A little bit of my heart seems to be with you always Joe," Eleanor wrote Joe Lash. "You'll carry it round wherever you go and in its place the thought of you will be with me wherever I go. . . ." Eleanor often said, "If I have a weakness, it is the need for approbation from those I love." Trude remembered: "She was wonderful about keeping in touch. She wrote sometimes twice a day. Very often the letters were just greetings or 'I am thinking of you' and nothing else. . . . She was a lonely person and needed a lot of friendship and affection and she gave herself so completely that she was always in danger of being hurt. The way you are if you give too much, too exposed. . . . She was very honest about herself. She knew that she got easily hurt. She would not show hurt, except she would get very quiet."

Eleanor's respect for Franklin was part compensation for the absence of intimacy. "I realize more and more that FDR is a great man," she wrote Joe Lash, "and he is nice to me, but as a person I'm a stranger, and I don't want to be anything else!" Her once consuming love for "Dearest Honey" had cooled. "Last night," she wrote Hick in September 1939, "I . . . was asked if I loved my husband, which I did not answer!"

Franklin also gave her that which he gave so many Americans: "I've never known a man," Eleanor wrote, "who gave one a greater sense of security. I never heard him say there was a problem that he thought it was impossible for human beings to solve. . . . I never knew him to face life or any problem that came up with fear."

Franklin also taught his wife not to take criticism personally. She was deeply hurt when conservative Hearst columnist Westbrook Pegler accused her of social activism only to satisfy her own ego. "Don't upset yourself," her husband advised. "Remember, never enter into a contest with a skunk. All you can do about creatures like him is ignore them. You don't need such people. You should be proud they're not on your side." And in time she accepted the criticism as part of the territory.

She thrived as first lady. During her first year in the White House, she traveled forty thousand miles, reporting back to Franklin about the fledgling New Deal's progress. The *Washington Star* was only mildly tongue in cheek when it printed the headline, "Mrs. Roosevelt Spends Night at White House." By 1935, she was earning almost as much money from her radio shows as was the president. The times served her well. The Depression and then the war loosened conventions regarding both marriage and women's role in society. More and more women had to look for work outside the home to help support their families. Attitudes were slowly changing regarding what was a "suitable" role for a woman, and Eleanor's example no doubt encouraged that shift. When a 1938 Gallup Poll queried the public, "Do you think that the president's wife should engage in any business activity which interests her if she doesn't do it for a profit?" Seventy-three percent of those polled replied "Yes."

It is striking how each of the Roosevelts managed to be productive and personally fulfilled in their first term. Franklin understood Eleanor's need to be "useful" and the consequences for both of them if she were not. Eleanor could be a dark presence in the White House when she fell into what she called her "Griselda" mood, sulky and uncommunicative. Franklin, who needed cheeriness around him, found her silences intolerable. She was not above using this passive-aggressive weapon to get her way in matters of policy. During the summer of 1935, every time Eleanor raised the subject of the four million unemployed young men and women, her husband put her off. But through a combination of persuasion and calculated aloofness, she wore him down. Eleanor described how she got Franklin to launch the National Youth Administration. "I waited until my usual time for discussing questions with him," she wrote in her memoir, "and went into his room just before he went to sleep. I described the whole idea. . . . He looked at me and said, 'Do you think it is right to do this?' I said . . . it might be a great help to the young people . . . but it might be unwise politically. Then Franklin said: 'If it is the right thing to do for the young people, then it should be done. I guess we can stand the criticism. . . .' "

The bond of their shared history was strong. A part of Franklin still saw Eleanor as the slim and shy nineteen-year-old girl he once referred to as "an angel" in his diary. "That's just the way Eleanor looks, you know," Franklin once said to Frances Perkins, pointing to his wife's youthful portrait. "Lovely hair, pretty eyes. And she always looks magnificent in evening clothes, doesn't she?" Part of FDR's strength was his ability to see what he wanted to see in others and in himself. At times he may even have convinced himself that theirs was a conventional marriage. "Dearest Babs," he wrote her from Rio de Janeiro, "Your radio [wire] was welcome this morning, but I'm sorry about F's sinus. . . . Another year, let's cut out and take a trip to Hawaii and Samoa instead."

∞

ROOSEVELT, LIKE JOHN F. KENNEDY, was a master of compartmentalization, revealing different parts of himself to different people. Though, as his son James noted, "Of what was inside him, of what really drove him, Father talked with no one."

Part of his strength as a leader was his fundamental self-sufficiency. Since he left neither memoirs nor much personal correspondence, it is hard to know precisely how Franklin viewed his marriage. No doubt he admired Eleanor's courage in standing up to him when so few others did.

Like other wives of charismatic leaders, "she got used to the fact that women adored him," Trude Lash recalled. "He was very handsome and charming. Plus he had power." Sometimes this acceptance required tremendous self-control. "Princess Martha got on Eleanor's nerves a little . . . she was really very flirtatious, in an obvious way, almost like a young girl, but she was too old to be a young girl. She wanted to literally sit at the president's feet. And there were others who adored him and sometimes FDR got tired of it and asked Eleanor to deal with them. Like [newspaper heiress] Dorothy Schiff, who bought a house close to the Hyde Park house. So the president asked Eleanor to take care of her. When Missy got sick, it was Mrs. Roosevelt who took care of her, who went to Massachusetts to see her."

An important part of "his" White House was the cocktail hour, when FDR would mix strong drinks for his friends. It was a time for unwinding and storytelling. For a man confined to his wheelchair, who could not indulge in other presidential pastimes such as golf, horseback riding or even a brisk walk, the cocktail hour was an essential escape from the day's cares. Eleanor, whose father, brother and two uncles had died of alcoholism, and who had no gift for banter, could not share in this pastime. Hearing her husband's rolling laughter mingled with peals of female mirth wafting from his study tapped into her old insecurities. She knew her presence would instantly alter the chemistry of the room. Occasionally, Eleanor would force herself to breach his world, but these efforts were awkward for both of them. She would quickly knock back a drink, as if taking medicine. Her zeal for not wasting time sometimes clouded her judgment. "Now just leave me alone," Franklin sometimes chided Eleanor if she became too serious. "It'll get done as fast as I can

Eleanor and Franklin, circa 1933.

get it done." Once, when she pushed too hard, he flung her pile of papers at Anna and commanded her, "Sis, you see about this." Like a chastened child, Eleanor retreated.

As first lady, Eleanor's top priority was not her husband. Other roles and obligations consumed her. If, as she later wrote, she was "one of those who served his purposes," he, too, served hers. The platform he provided her was powerful, and she was adept at using it. Returning from trips to Appalachia or the Dust Bowl, she flooded Franklin with so many memos that he imposed a three-memo-a-night limit. Just as her husband used his Fireside Chats to reach into American homes, Eleanor's column, "My Day," erased the distance between the White House and ordinary people. With her artless, unpolished prose, she made the First Family seem like just an average household facing average problems, with perhaps an above-average head of household.

On the eve of FDR's first Fireside Chat, on March 12, 1933, when he explained his plan for turning the economy around, his wife wrote in "My Day":

> There is a certain amount of tension in the house before an important speech. Last Thursday a message had to go to Congress and the radio speech had to be ready for the evening, so there was considerable work for everybody connected with the President. When the time actually came, the President was as calm as a May morning. The household went down in the elevator to the diplomatic Reception Room. The President took his seat behind the desk which is specially wired. . . . I was agreeably surprised that we had chairs, for whenever the speech is short we all stand up. I sat beside Miss Perkins [Secretary of Labor] and had an opportunity for a nice little talk.

"To the prisoners of newspapers where wars are always raging," the *Nation* observed, "[Eleanor Roosevelt's column] is like a sunny square where children and aunts and grandmothers go about their trivial but absorbing pursuits and security reigns. In the sense of security it generates lies the deepest appeal of 'My Day.' " Long before CNN and the networks wired the country into an electronic village, Eleanor's deft use of the press catapulted her to national, then global, fame. With her unthreatening, low-key style, she embraced causes as controversial as civil rights, then absorbed the brunt of the criticism and kept the president at one remove from the heat. But they were working toward the same ends. In part as a result of Eleanor's relentless agitation, by the end of World War II, African Americans were in the workforce and integrated into the armed forces. Partly because of her own feelings of being an "outsider" to her own society, this highborn woman identified with the deprived and the disenfranchised, not as Lady Bountiful, but as one of *them.* "The unemployed are not a strange race," she wrote to a sympathetic audience. "They are like we would be if we had not had a fortunate chance at life."

FDR and his wife often differed over how far and how fast social reforms should proceed. In some respects Franklin was still the prisoner of his class, age and, above all, of politics. Thurgood Marshall, the first African American appointed to the Supreme Court, bore witness to their differences. Marshall had called on Attorney General Francis Biddle to plead the case of a black man accused of shooting a sheriff in Virginia. During the meeting, Biddle phoned the president and asked Marshall to pick up an extension so he could hear what Roosevelt had to say. "I warned you not to call me again about any of Eleanor's niggers," FDR threatened Biddle, oblivious to the black lawyer's presence on the line. "Call me one more time and you are fired."

Part of the secret of Eleanor's success as first lady was that she was remarkably free of self-importance or a sense of entitlement. "Almost any woman in the White House during these years of need would have done what I have done," she wrote. In appearance she was the most unthreatening woman imaginable. Her hair was always slightly unkempt and her clothes were bought off the rack in seven-minute shopping expeditions. She looked like Everywoman. She wanted attention focused on causes, not on her. She was incapable of being anything other than who she was. On that point, her detractors and her husband agreed.

In July 1940, Eleanor and Franklin shattered two ironclad traditions of American politics and demonstrated the depth of their interdependence. The occasion was the Chicago Democratic Convention. The Roosevelts were far away at Hyde Park, each in a separate house on the estate, listening to the reports from Chicago. The president wanted the convention to nominate him by acclamation for an unprecedented third term. With neither Roosevelt in attendance, the mood in the hall had turned sour. FDR was the party's choice, but not without certain misgivings. Where was the president? Why hadn't he declared himself if he wanted a third term? An insurrection was in the making.

FDR had the solution to the impasse. "Send Eleanor," the president told Frances Perkins, on the line from Chicago. "She always makes people feel right." Perkins called Eleanor. "Things look black here," she told the first lady. "I think you should come." Eleanor was reluctant. She felt her appearance would smack of "petticoat government." It would harm the president to have his wife seem to be making up his mind for him. Besides, her husband had not asked her directly. Persuaded he must, FDR finally called her. "Would you like to go?" he asked, reluctant to admit he needed her. "No, I would not," she replied. "Do you really want me to go?" she asked. "Perhaps it would be a good idea," her husband said at last, completing their awkward dance. So she went, and became the first wife of a president to address a national political convention.

The audience rose to its feet in a rousing cheer at the familiar sight of Eleanor. But the floor erupted in a wild chorus of shouts and boos when FDR's choice of running mate, Henry Wallace, was presented for confirmation. It took Eleanor's intervention to soothe the delegates. When she reached the rostrum, the floor fell quiet. She spoke without a text. "This," she told the delegates, was "no ordinary nomination in an ordinary time, no time for weighing anything except what we can best do for the country as a whole. . . . No man who is a candidate or who is President can carry this situation alone." In times like these, she cautioned the delegates, the candidate must be allowed to choose his own running mate. With those simple words, Eleanor altered the chemistry of the convention, turning hostility into pride at the party's choice. Like her husband, Eleanor knew how to reach people by speaking to them directly, and they followed her because they sensed these were *her* words.

FDR finally spoke to the delegates via radio from Hyde Park. "Like most men of my age," FDR told the delegates, "I had made plans for myself, plans for a private life of my own choice and my own satisfactions to begin in January 1941. These plans like so many other plans, had been made in a world which now seems as distant as another planet." His wife sprang to her feet along with thousands of others when Franklin's last words came across the convention's loudspeaker. The band played "Hail to the Chief" as Eleanor slipped out of the hall to catch her flight back to Hyde Park.

∞

IN 1940, when German paratroopers surprised neutral Holland, and Nazi forces targeted Belgium, Eleanor embarked on a new role: preparing the country for war. She wrote in her column, "Much has been said in this country about not wanting to participate in foreign wars. . . . But when force not only rules in certain countries, but is as menacing to all the world as it is today, one cannot live in a Utopia which prays for different conditions and ignores those which exist. . . ."

The war changed Eleanor and Franklin's partnership yet again. The New Deal had brought them closer: their goals were the same; they were in the trenches together. The war shifted FDR's focus to mobilizing and winning, and away from the New Deal. Eleanor's insecurity about not being "useful" surfaced, along with the fear that the war effort would weaken the bond she and Franklin had forged. This insecurity led Eleanor to make one of her rare mistakes as first lady. She took an official position in her husband's administration.

As a member of the Office of Civilian Defense, Eleanor worked with New York mayor Fiorello La Guardia to prepare the civilian population for war. *Time* magazine dubbed her the "OCDiva." Eleanor, who had learned to brush off criticism, was unprepared for the intensity of the barrage. After five months of criticism, Eleanor discovered that there was simply no way the wife of a president could ever be treated as anything else. She resigned, ruefully noting in her column,

> I was interested yesterday to find that my resignation from the Office of Civilian Defense rated front page stories in the *New York Herald Tribune* and the *New York Times* and an editorial in both papers. I am beginning to feel puffed up with importance! . . . They both point out that the wife of any president cannot be looked upon as an individual by other people in the government. . . . I hoped that this was

not true, but I have found out that it was. . . . People can gradually be brought to understand that an individual, even if she is a President's wife, may have independent views and must be allowed the expression of an opinion. But actual participation in the work of the government we are not yet able to accept.

More than half a century later, Hillary Rodham Clinton would come under similar fire when she, too, assumed a formal position in her husband's first administration.

With FDR's total focus on the war, Eleanor felt sidelined. There were now many things Franklin could not share with his wife. Eleanor did not even know when her husband was about to meet Winston Churchill to discuss the shape of postwar Europe in the historic Atlantic Conference. Franklin had told her only that he was going "fishing in the Cape Cod Canal." Eleanor's activism also took its toll on their partnership. "I was conscious of the fact that because I saw a great many people I might let slip something that should not be told, so I used to beg my husband not to tell me any secrets," she wrote in "My Day."

Churchill was struck by the distance between the two Roosevelts. "Mrs. Roosevelt . . . was away practically all the time," Churchill wrote his wife during one of his extended White House visits. "I think she was offended at the President not telling her until a few hours before I arrived of what was pouring down on her. He does not tell her secrets because she is always making speeches and writing articles and he is afraid she might forget what was secret and what was not. . . ."

Their son James claimed that around 1942, Franklin approached Eleanor about spending more time as husband and wife. Sara Delano Roosevelt had recently died, and Missy had suffered a disabling stroke, and the president was lonely. Eleanor, meanwhile, had lost her close bond to Harry Hopkins, and Lorena Hickock had become too fiercely possessive of her and had been delicately put off. But for Eleanor the painful memory of Lucy Mercer had never quite faded. She would not leave herself open to another hurt. It is unlikely that Franklin and Eleanor ever articulated these things to each other. Fearlessness and imperviousness to any foe—the qualities with which FDR fought polio and that he conveyed to the country at war—blocked deep emotional connections. So much of his presidential aura was based on performance rather than intimacy.

Eleanor had long ago given up on intimacy with her husband. What she sought was a more meaningful contribution to the war effort. "I'm rather tired," she wrote her daughter, "because I have nothing to do these days, so I asked Pa tonight if I could do anything but it appears I can't so I guess I go to HP [Hyde Park] the 13th and enjoy my leisure!" Enjoying leisure, of course, was something Eleanor was not equipped to do. As was typical, FDR met her needs while serving his own purposes. In 1942 he dispatched his wife on a morale-raising trip to war-battered England.

All of Eleanor's remarkable personal qualities surfaced during this trip. A guest of the British royal family, she stayed in bomb-scarred Buckingham Palace and experienced the nightly pounding of Hitler's carpet bombs. Those who followed her journey were struck by the degree to which she managed to be the same Eleanor dining with the king and queen as in the G.I. chow line. Her astonishing energy left reporters out of breath as they tried to keep up. "Hustle did you say?" a British reporter later wrote. "She walked fifty miles through factories, clubs, and hospitals." She saw her real role as stand-in for the absent mothers of the "boys" at the front. "The boys are very upset over the mail situation," she wrote her husband. "Some have been here for two months and not a line from home. Also their pay in many cases is very late and they buy bonds and don't get them." Never passing up the chance to strike a blow for a good cause, she urged her husband, "Someone ought to get on top of this situation and while they are about it they might look into the question of how promptly the families are getting allotments." American reporter Chalmers Roberts wrote, "Mrs. Roosevelt has done more to bring a real understanding of the spirit of the United States to the people of Britain than any other single American who has ever visited these islands."

The president was waiting for her on the tarmac when she landed in Washington. "I really think Franklin was glad to see me back," she wrote in her diary, "and I gave a detailed account of such things as I could tell quickly and answered his questions. Later, I think he even read this diary and to my surprise he had also read my columns."

A classic Eleanor-Franklin clash, pitting her idealism against his pragmatism, erupted during this period. For the first time, information began to trickle out of Nazi-occupied areas that something unimaginable was happening to the Jews. Eleanor embraced their cause, while Franklin maintained that large-scale rescue of refugees would be a diversion from winning the war. A mark of Eleanor's personal growth was that the woman who once referred to Justice Felix Frankfurter as "an interesting little man but very jew" now wrote in her column, "The Jews are like all the other people of the world. There are able people among them, there are courageous people among them, there are people of extraordinary intellectual ability . . . integrity and people of great beauty and great charm. . . . I do not know what we can do to save the Jews in Europe and to find them homes, but I know that we will be the sufferers if we let great wrongs occur without exerting ourselves to correct them."

As early as 1940, Eleanor collided with the State Department's policy of obstructing Jewish immigration from Europe. The man in charge of refugees for the department was an old FDR friend and former ambassador to Italy, Breckenridge Long. Long was a well-known anti-Semite. Eleanor pleaded with her husband to meet with the chairman of his own Advisory Committee regarding Long's obstructionism. "I am thinking about these poor people who may die at any time and who are asking only to come here on transit visas and I do hope you can get this cleared up quickly." But Long persuaded FDR that the refugees would pose a wartime security problem. "Something does seem wrong," Eleanor wrote her husband, when nothing changed and America's doors remained firmly bolted against thousands of desperate refugees. "*What* does seem wrong?" her irritated husband challenged.

"Franklin, you know [Long] is a fascist!" Eleanor erupted over lunch one day. "I've told you, Eleanor, you must not say that," he warned. "Well, maybe I shouldn't say it," his wife countered, "but he is!" On October 25, 1941, Eleanor wrote in her column, "I have been reading . . . of the removal of the Jewish people from Germany to Poland and Russia. . . . It is a leavetaking which savors somewhat of death." When she eventually learned the full consequences of the missed opportunity to save lives, it was her most bitter disappointment.

AFTER FORTY YEARS of shared love, loss, recovery and accommodation, during their final year Franklin and Eleanor were physically and emotionally more apart than they were together. Franklin was a very sick man, but his wife was unable or unwilling to acknowledge that fact. It is striking that a woman as compassionate as Eleanor would respond so indifferently to her husband's declining health in the final year of his life. Eleanor, blessed with an iron constitution, felt good health was a matter of mind over matter. Together, she and Franklin had overcome so many of the effects of his paralysis. Now, in 1944, she refused to face what was apparent to others: that FDR's health was rapidly failing.

His cousin Daisy Suckley observed something else that Eleanor refused to acknowledge: the president was also lonely. "We went in to dinner [in the White House] behind the P[resident] in his little wheel chair—One almost forgets that it is not normal to have to be wheeled in a chair. He doesn't let you think of it, and you just see his cheerful fine face, so full of character. . . . He gets lonely when left alone. . . . He said he hated to drive alone. . . . It is so different when one can walk about, get things for oneself, *do* something. . . ." The unmarried Daisy, who, like Franklin, was raised along the Hudson, a product of the same sheltered, affluent world, loved him uncritically and considered looking after him the greatest privilege of her life. "With you I don't have to perform," Franklin once confided to his cousin. Daisy was content to bask in his presence, awake or asleep. She watched over him during his final months. She was alert to his every change of mood or expression. "As soon as the door was closed," Daisy noted in her journal, "he relaxed completely, yawned and yawned. He said it was the greatest possible rest to be able to just be as he felt and not to have to talk and be the host. . . . It has apparently become the habit not to relax but to force himself to keep up the outward appearance of energy and force."

Though unwilling to face up to her husband's real condition, Eleanor was not without feelings of guilt. "Maybe I'd do the most useful job if I just became a 'good wife' and waited on FDR," she wrote her friend Esther Lape in November 1944. "Anna has been doing all of it that Margaret [Daisy] does not do, but she can't go on doing it." At this late stage, however, Eleanor could not transform herself or her relationship with her husband. For her, it was a matter of "waiting on" Franklin, not spending companionable time with him. Even with his declining health, Eleanor still saw her role as primarily his conscience, not his wife.

Anna noticed a change in her father when he returned from the December 1943 Teheran Conference. His fatigue was now chronic, and the usual remedies—trips home to his beloved Hyde Park, long drives in the company of charming women, his ritual martinis—no longer restored his spirits. His legendary ebullience gave way to an ashen complexion and hollow cheeks; his shirt collar suddenly seemed outsized, and his appetite for food and much else was gone.

There was an unappealing puritanical streak in Eleanor's dismissal of Anna's concern. I'm not interested in "physiology," she sniffed. She maintained her rigorous travel schedule uninterrupted. When Daisy suggested that a daily drive with his wife might be therapeutic, Franklin laughed and said, "I would have to make an appointment a week ahead!" Anna brought in Dr. Howard Bruenn, who confirmed that FDR was suffering from heart failure and prescribed digitalis and bed rest. Franklin showed little interest in his own condition and treated it as he did other unpleasant truths, with studied indifference. But the great performer could no longer act the part of the vigorous man. "I cannot live out a normal lifespan," the sixty-three-year-old Roosevelt told his daughter. "I can't even walk across the room to get my circulation going." It was the first time he had acknowledged the magnitude of his struggle to his daughter.

Franklin had not kept his long-ago pledge to Eleanor. He had seen Lucy Mercer Rutherfurd a number of times, even before she was widowed in 1941. He had made sure she attended all four of his inaugurations, unobserved. She had first visited the White House in August 1941, signing in as Mrs. Paul Johnson. FDR's secretaries knew to put her calls through immediately. The couple spoke French during those private conversations. "How would you feel," Franklin asked Anna in the spring of 1944, "about our inviting an old friend of mine to a few dinners at the White House?" His daughter understood he was referring to Lucy. Her

mother had shared with her the story of the affair. "It was a terrible decision," Anna recalled. "I realized that Mother wasn't going to be
there . . . and I was sure she didn't know about it but my quick decision
was that the private lives of these people were not my business. Who was
I to say you can or cannot? . . . I never said anything to Mother." It was a
cruel burden for a father to inflict on his daughter.

Lucy visited in the summer of 1944 and continued to be a presence
in FDR's life for the final year. Anna shepherded Lucy through the back
door of the White House and kept her name off the official logs. Only
the president's butler, Alonzo Fields, waited on them during dinner. The
visit buoyed the tired man's spirits. Then the president turned suitor to
the fifty-one-year-old widow, calling on her in his car, driving with her
through Washington's quiet streets just as they had three decades earlier.
He continued to see Lucy at her estate in northern New Jersey, and at his
Warm Springs sanctuary.

Daisy, FDR's frequent companion in Warm Springs, was also privy
to their secret. She described the newly widowed Lucy Rutherfurd as

> a perfectly lovely person, in every way one can think of and a wonder-
> ful friend to him. [Lucy] worries a lot about him, as I do. . . . We
> understand each other perfectly . . . and [have] felt for years that he
> has been terribly lonely. Harry Hopkins told a friend of hers that
> when he was living in the White House there were evenings after
> evenings when Franklin was left entirely alone, but for HH. [Lucy
> and I] got to the point of literally weeping on each other's shoulders
> and we kissed each other, I think just because we each felt thankful
> that the other understood and wants to help Franklin!

Lucy shared FDR's cottage in Warm Springs and wrote Daisy, "You
can imagine how very wonderful it was for me to feel myself under the
same roof and within the sound of the voice we all love after so many,
many years." Returning home to Aiken, South Carolina, after seeing
Franklin, Lucy wrote Daisy, "It is only a week ago that we left you but to
me it seems months—or years. I have been hoping for word from
F[ranklin]. You who live within the radius of the arc lights do not know
how hard it can be when one is beyond their rays."

Lucy cared for the ailing president in a way Eleanor never could. His need of her reveals much about what he missed in his marriage. With Lucy, Franklin could be lighthearted, indulge his love of conversation for the sheer pleasure of it. One moment in 1944 serves to crystallize all that was missing between Eleanor and Franklin, while at the same time illuminates Lucy's role in his life. On December 2, FDR drove Lucy to his favorite hill in Georgia. Looking out on the lush sweep of Pine Mountain Valley, he spoke for an hour about his hopes for the postwar world, mingled with tales of the countryside around them. Lucy merely smiled and listened, happy to be in his company. Eleanor, for whom the day was never long enough, was constitutionally incapable of sitting and listening to her husband for that long.

Eleanor seemed to fear more for his administration than she did for his health. Appalled to learn that his newly appointed secretary of state, Edward Stettinius, had appointed a group of right-wing businessmen as assistant secretaries, she promptly called her husband in Warm Springs. "Franklin, this is a terrible thing you are about to do," she erupted. FDR no longer had the energy to do battle with his wife. Quick to sense when her husband was about to hang up on her, Eleanor retreated. "All right, Franklin, I've got to go downtown. I'll call you tomorrow." But she could not contain herself that long, and instead fired off a letter. "I realize very well that I do not know the reasons why certain things may be necessary," she wrote her husband. "I suppose I should trust blindly when I can't know and be neither worried nor scared and yet I am both. . . . I hate to irritate you and I won't speak of any of this again, but I wouldn't feel honest if I didn't tell you now." Eleanor had not changed; what she failed to notice was that FDR was no longer the same man.

Franklin must have shared his annoyance with Lucy, for she wrote Daisy, "These State Department . . . episodes must be exhausting . . . and how can one help worrying, especially when one does not know what goes on from day to day?"

Edith Wilson, who knew something about presidential illness, was shocked when she saw Franklin Delano Roosevelt on his fourth Inauguration Day. "Did you get a good look at the president?" she asked Frances Perkins. "Oh, it frightened me. He looks exactly as my husband looked when he went into his decline."

Franklin had a final historic journey to make. The first lady was desperate to go along for the secret meeting with Stalin and Churchill. FDR asked Anna, however, not Eleanor, to accompany him to the Yalta Conference. He was a very sick man; his daughter could do things for him that his wife could not. He needed looking after, not prodding. For Eleanor, it was one more injury, one more rejection.

FDR spent his sixty-third birthday at sea and received a surprise package from Lucy and Daisy. It was full of sentimental knickknacks recalling their long history with him. From Eleanor, he received an irritated letter sent several days earlier chiding him for his nominee for secretary of commerce. She also sent a birthday message, but it never got through. FDR's ship was under radio silence due to the proximity of two German submarines. The missed communication was emblematic of their final months.

Franklin returned from the long journey bone-tired and obviously unwell. On March 1, 1945, he addressed Congress for the very first time from his wheelchair. "I hope you will pardon me for the unusual posture," he said, "but I know that you will realize that it makes it a lot easier for me not having to carry about ten pounds of steel around on the bottom of my legs, and also because I have just completed a fourteen-thousand-mile trip." Those who knew the fiercely proud man now understood, possibly for the first time, how sick he was. Much of the country was stunned to hear the president admit he was a cripple. He had trained people not to notice his polio, few ever mentioned it and many were unaware of it altogether. Very few people knew how exhausting it was for him to stand even briefly. In one stroke, he declared the deception over. Just as he had lost the energy to spar with Eleanor, he no longer had the strength to disguise his handicap.

The Roosevelts, always faithful in observing rituals, celebrated their fortieth wedding anniversary shortly after his meeting with Lucy. En route home for a weekend at Hyde Park, Franklin and Eleanor made plans for the future. He wanted Eleanor to go with him to the opening session of the United Nations, and then, in early summer, to London, Holland and the front. "The war in Europe," he told Perkins, "will be over by May." He wanted to drive through London and bask in the warm glow of victory.

In April, he went to Warm Springs, accompanied by Lucy, Daisy and another cousin, Laura Delano. He had drawn particularly close to his daughter and called her every night he was there. "But there was a funny little thing there," Anna remembered, "just to show that he never discussed his real personal life with anyone. He never once mentioned Lucy Mercer. His private life was his private life." Franklin's final act was to sit for a portrait intended for Lucy. On April 12, he looked up suddenly and said, "I have a terrific pain in the back of my head." Lucy, Daisy and Laura carried him to his bed, where he died of a cerebral hemorrhage.

Eleanor arrived quickly from Washington. Laura compounded the first lady's loss by telling her about Lucy's presence. The old wound was reopened and was made sharper when she learned of her daughter's role in the reunion. Surely this would explain the "impersonal feeling" Eleanor described at the news of her husband's death. Self-imposed detachment was her way of coping with the fresh wave of anguish.

Perhaps it was that much further back I had had to face certain difficulties until I decided to accept the fact that a man must be what he is, life must be lived as it is. . . . All human beings have failings, all human beings have needs and temptations and stresses. Men and women who live together through long years get to know one another's failings; but they also come to know what is worthy of respect and admiration in those they live with and in themselves. If at the end one can say, "This man used to the limit the powers that God granted him; he was worthy of love and respect and the sacrifices of many people, made in order that he might achieve what he deemed to be his task," then that life has been lived well and there are no regrets.

"He might have been happier with a wife who was completely uncritical," she wrote. "That I was never able to be, and he had to find it in some other people. Nevertheless, I think I sometimes acted as a spur, even though the spurring was not always wanted or welcome. I was one of those who served his purposes.

"I think I lived those years very impersonally. It was almost as though I had erected someone a little outside of myself who was the President's wife. I was lost somewhere deep down inside myself. That is the way I felt and worked until I left the White House." Many other presidential wives survive by the same means, but none achieved what Eleanor did.

FROM HER CORRESPONDENCE, we know much more about Eleanor's inner life than we do about Franklin's. Did he open to anyone that "black box" containing his innermost thoughts? Lucy's family continues to treat her relationship with the president as private. Winthrop Rutherfurd III, grandson of Lucy's husband, first learned of the affair in 1967 when he read about it. "We never talked about this in the family," he said in 1999. "It was not our business. It was theirs."

Among her bedside papers when Eleanor died was a poem entitled "Psyche" by Virginia Moore, which Eleanor had clipped out of a newspaper and marked "1918," the year she discovered her husband's love affair. The poem is not only a testament to her lifelong pain but to her indomitable spirit as well.

The soul that has believed / And is deceived / Thinks nothing for a while /
    All thoughts are vile.
And then because the sun / Is mute persuasion, / And hope in Spring
    and Fall / Most natural,
The soul grows calm and mild / A little child
Finding the pull of breath / Better than death . . . The soul that had
believed . . .
And was deceived / Ends by believing more / Than ever before. . . .

No present-day couple could live as the Roosevelts did during their twelve years in the White House. Eleanor and Franklin's traits—his love of martinis and the company of charming women, and her prolonged absences and intense friendships—might well be politically damaging in today's climate. Unable to forge a conventional marriage, Eleanor and Franklin turned their personal differences into a strong political partnership. The most gifted politician of the last century, FDR relied on his wife, the indomitable idealist, to be his moral compass. A marriage that might well have collapsed under the weight of two such powerfully divergent personalities survived, and enriched the country. The Roosevelts were inexhaustible. His expansive, reassuring spirit and her blend of humility and energy guided the nation through the twin crises of the Depression and World War II. All succeeding presidents and first ladies have measured themselves against the Roosevelt standard.

"The story is over," Eleanor declared the day she left the White House. Their story had come to an end, though a new chapter of hers was just beginning. For the next seventeen years, until her death on November 7, 1962, she continued to be a principled voice for the New Deal ideals of justice, civil and human rights. The world became her stage.

CHAPTER 3

BESS AND HARRY TRUMAN

THE GOOD HUSBAND

I never saw a human being so taken up by another as Harry Truman was by Bess.
—CLARK CLIFFORD

You are still on the pedestal where I placed you that day in Sunday school in 1890. What an old fool I am.
—HARRY TRUMAN *in a letter to his wife from the White House*

THE PASSAGE FROM ELEANOR AND FRANKLIN'S ROCKY RELATIONSHIP TO BESS and Harry's solid union was akin to traveling from the Hudson Valley with its mountains and twisting rivers to the flat, open plains of the Midwest. The Roosevelts were authentic American aristocrats, landed, widely traveled and confident of their birthright. The Trumans were authentic Middle Americans, neither rich nor glamorous, products of small towns and neat farms in the heartland described by Mark Twain and painted by Thomas Hart Benton. Much has been written about the inner strength that enabled Truman to manage one crisis after the next without losing his balance, but historians have paid scant attention to one of his greatest personal resources: his rock-solid marriage.

Because Bess Truman was neither glamorous nor in pursuit of an independent agenda, she has often been underestimated by historians. This is a serious error, one Harry himself never made. While he navigated the nation through some of the roughest waters of the American century, Bess was there as both his constant sounding board and as a reminder of who they were and where they had come from. Loyal, blunt, unpretentious and self-reliant, she was the solid embodiment of the country he loved. She was also difficult, stubborn and unaccommodating.

But he adored her and always looked up to her. Until the end of their days, when he looked at his short, stout, gray-haired wife, he still saw a spirited, athletic girl with long blond hair and blue eyes, the Bess Wallace whom Truman started courting almost in their childhood. Success, with all its traps and trappings, in no way diminished Harry's devotion. No matter where high office propelled him, no matter the company he kept, he never stopped courting his wife. His adviser Clark Clifford said that the Trumans were the only couple he had seen unchanged by the presidency. The man who surprised the country with his supple performance always remained a very good husband.

∞

HARRY TRUMAN ASSUMED OFFICE under traumatic circumstances during a critical moment in our nation's life. He lacked FDR's charisma. His flat, nasal tones were no match for his predecessor's rich baritone; nor did Truman possess Roosevelt's great wit or raconteur's charm. Truman was a farmer, not a gentleman farmer like Roosevelt. Harry's mother often boasted that no one could plow a straighter furrow than her son.

Truman had a great deal to prove in assuming FDR's mantle; his wife also faced a great burden. The day the country bade farewell to its most public first lady, it welcomed one of its most private. Bess had little love for the White House and hated what she called "the rigmarole" of official duties. No first lady today could get away with what Bess did: her long absences in Missouri, her snubbing of the press, her lack of support of "good causes." As first lady, Bess was Eleanor's opposite. She despised being in the public eye. Harry was her business, history was her enemy.

She was terrified of the spotlight. Aboard FDR's special funeral train from Hyde Park to Washington, Frances Perkins caught the insecurity Bess generally masked with gruffness. "I don't know what I'm going to do," Bess confessed. "I don't know how I'm going to handle my part of it. It's bad enough for Harry, but what am I going to do? I'm not used to this awful public life." In a voice Perkins described as "plaintive and emotional," Bess asked if she would have to hold regular press conferences the way Mrs. Roosevelt had. Eleanor was unique, Perkins told her. "I have nothing to say," Bess said, "I don't even think about public affairs."

In fact, Bess thought a great deal about public affairs, but she was not going to share that with Perkins or anybody but her husband. She loved politics. "I've been in politics for twenty-five years," she once proclaimed to a reporter. She had always been Harry's full political partner and did not intend to change now. As for her husband, however his wife chose to play her new role suited him, just as long as Bess was close by. It was Bess who enabled Harry to write in his diary the day FDR died, "Went to bed, went to sleep, and did not worry any more."

Harry Truman, who had spent his boyhood on a farm without running water, found the courage to spend billions of dollars to reconstruct ravaged Europe. He authorized the use of the atomic bomb against Japan—his most momentous decision. He established NATO and, with the famous Truman Doctrine, drew the line on Soviet aggression. He saved Berlin with the airlift and sent troops to South Korea in response to North Korea's surprise attack in June 1950. He raced to ensure that the United States would be the first nation to recognize the new State of Israel, and laid the foundations for American foreign policy for the half century that would follow. Truman transmitted a contagious vitality to the American people. In the French phrase, he was "comfortable in his skin." Bess, "the only person in the world whose approval and good opinion" he needed, had much to do with that.

Her views on marriage and on the role of political wives were far from her predecessor's. "A woman's place in public," Bess declared, "is to sit beside her husband and be silent and be sure her hat is on straight."

As freshly demobilized G.I.'s reclaimed places filled by women during the war, Bess's reticence meshed with the times. It was a time when ladies wore white gloves and gentlemen tipped their hats when they passed them. Bess's *ordinariness* reassured the country that normalcy had returned. She drove the American dream car—a Chevrolet—around Washington and shopped like any suburban matron at Woodward and Lothrop's department store.

The Roosevelts played the part of a close couple in public and lived something different in private. By contrast, the Trumans kept a low public profile and were intensely connected in private. As with most good marriages, they essentially agreed on the rules governing their partnership. Both were raised to believe it was a man's role to provide for his wife and family. The wife was there to stand beside him, support him, never upstage him, never embarrass him, never get in front of him. The Trumans projected the image of a secure, loving, but undemonstrative couple to the country. It was the way post–World War II Americans searching for normalcy wished to be.

They met when he was six and she was five. He fell in love and stayed in love. Years later, Harry still saw in the dowdy matron a young girl who could beat any boy in Independence, Missouri, in tennis and outrun most of them around the baseball diamond. In his own mind, he was still the boy who was too nearsighted to play ball and spent much of his time pushing a plow or reading great tomes of history. She was all Harry ever wanted. No other woman would interest him, which may make him unique in the annals of politics. His voluminous letters provide a moving record of his love for his wife.

Truman never went to college—there wasn't enough money and his family could not spare him from the farm. But unlike Richard Nixon, another twentieth-century president from humble beginnings, Harry was not grudging or angry. He was determined, and determined to win Bess. She was a town girl, from a place where everybody knew who their neighbors were and what they were up to. In the Independence social hierarchy, the Wallaces were near the top. Daughter of a "good" family, Bess lived in a big house and was courted by the "right" suitors. Decades later, their daughter, Margaret, found among her mother's effects letters from other suitors. Harry's character, not his promise of escape and adventure, won Bess, who waited for him to return from the Great War to marry him at the alarmingly old-maidish age of thirty-four.

The power balance between Bess and Harry was made possible in part by Elizabeth Wallace Truman's advantage of birth and social position. As he rose steadily—from farmer to haberdasher, army captain to judge, United States senator to vice president and finally president—Bess remained who she had always been, unimpressed and unintimidated by her husband. She was already who she wanted to be. She hoped only to end her days in the same white clapboard house on Independence's leafy North Delaware Street where she was born. Unlike in most political marriages, Bess was the one who did most of the leave-taking, while Harry suffered and missed her. "It was quite a wrench to see you go away," Truman wrote Bess during the summer of 1941, when he was a senator. "I watched the train pull out as I walked up the platform and I felt most decidedly lonesome." It was a familiar feeling for Truman.

Though Bess usually got her way, Margaret Truman remembered that her mother made her father happy. The undemonstrative, steady Bess played the stabilizing, maternal role for both husband and daughter. "What she could say with a look! Make you feel so small. But they were well matched," Margaret observed fifty years later. "They had the same upbringing, they came from the same region. They both went through hard times. Mom's father killed himself. . . . They were both stubborn and had definite ideas about right and wrong. And neither of them had social aspirations." They also agreed on a wife's proper role and appearance. Harry liked to point out with pride that his wife—5 feet 4 inches tall and 140 pounds—"Looks just like a woman ought to look who's been happily married for a quarter of a century."

To many outsiders, Bess seemed to take her husband entirely for granted. She frequently took off for six weeks at a time to spend time in Independence with her mother and her bridge club. Bess never aspired to live in the White House, and she hated it. It seemed to her that she was giving up more than she was getting. She was forced to sit in the back of a big black limousine, while pesky "news hens" claimed the right to know what she was up to. Most of all, she feared that the presidency would diminish the only role she cared about, being Harry's wife.

In the White House, they were no longer able to share politics the way they had previously. Over her husband's entire political life, Bess had played the role of his first sounding board. She had enjoyed ten years in the clubby world of the Senate. She had been his political partner, had even worked in his office during part of his term. When he was in the Senate, she had urged him to undertake the investigation of defense contracts that led to the Truman Committee. His effort saved the taxpayers millions of dollars and gave him a national profile. Senator Truman always brought home a stuffed briefcase that the two of them would tackle together after clearing the dinner table. But in the White House, an army of aides, agents, reporters and servants formed a wedge between Bess and Harry. Bess felt superfluous.

As her husband agonized about dropping the atomic bombs on Japan, his wife, who could be selfish and singularly unhelpful, smoldered at being a spectator rather than a participant in his new life. Unlike Harry, who frequently poured his heart out or vented his anger in letters, his wife's way had always been to disengage and leave him miserably alone. "I was ever so lonesome when you all left," Harry wrote Bess on December 21, 1946, upon her departure for Christmas with her mother in Independence. The refrain was their theme song. Was this her way of keeping the upper hand she had always had in the relationship?

How much his wife's attitude had to do with Truman's essential humility, how much their different social status, is a matter of conjecture. What is undeniable is that Harry had a partner who treated him the same way at the end of their life as at the beginning. Truman took the presidency, but never himself, seriously. Bess always saw Harry as a man, not as a position. She never gave him what he called the "bump of ego" that so many politicians get from those who shelter them from reality. When, as a result of a snowstorm, Harry arrived late for Christmas in Independence, his irate wife greeted him with "I guess you couldn't think of any more reasons to stay away. As far as I'm concerned, you might as well have stayed in Washington." Back in the White House, Harry wrote a letter that surely has no equal for humility and misery from a sitting president. "You can never appreciate what it means to come home as I did the other evening after doing at least one hundred things I didn't want to do and have the only person in the world whose approval and good opinion I value look at me like I'm something the cat dragged in. . . . I won-

Harry and "the Boss" at home, April 15, 1942. What is remarkable
about this picture, staged to boost Senator Truman's chances for
the vice presidential nomination, is the state of the kitchen,
utterly ordinary and even sloppy.

der why we are made so that what we really think and feel we cover up?"
he asked plaintively.

If Harry impressed his countrymen as salt of the earth, Bess helped
to keep him that way. A steadying presence amid the turbulence, Bess
embodied their remarkable shared journey and anchored him to the values they shared growing up. On their wedding anniversary on June 28,
1948, he wrote Bess, "Twenty-nine years! It seems like twenty-nine days.
Detroit, Port Huron, a farm sale, the Blackstone Hotel, a shirt store,
County Judge, a defeat. Margie, Automobile Club membership drive,
Presiding Judge, Senator, V.P. and now!" But they were not together that
day, and he needed her. When she wasn't around, Harry was apt to drink
too much and his temper would flare. Who but a wife can tell a president
to take a deep breath and count to ten? With Truman, the temper often
took epistolary form. In a famous incident, he sent a scalding note to
Washington Post music critic Paul Hume for an unflattering review of a
concert performance by Margaret, who had embarked on a singing
career. The outraged father wrote: "I have just read your lousy review.
You sound like a frustrated man that never made a success, an eight ulcer

man on a four ulcer job, and all four ulcers working. I have never met you but if I do you'll need a new nose and plenty of beefsteak and perhaps a new supporter below. . . ." When Bess saw the letter in the *Washington Post,* she erupted at her husband. "I don't think I ever saw her so angry," Truman recalled.

And then she would take off again. "He was very lonely in the White House," Secret Service agent (and future chief usher) Rex Scouten remembered, "with nothing much to do. We were an outlet for him. On his daily walks he enjoyed the talking as much as the walking. On weekends we'd drive out to General Marshall's place in Leesburg to get away from that big, empty house." During her many absences, a letter from Bess would immediately alter the day's mood for the president. Clark Clifford recalled, "Once he went to the mail room after a few days without a letter from Bess and announced, 'If you don't get me a letter from Mrs. Truman I'm gonna fire all of you!' "

Holidays without Bess could be particularly lonely for him. One New Year's Eve, it occurred to Clifford that the president, alone again, may have had no plans. Clifford asked his boss to join him and his wife, Marny, at a black-tie dinner dance at the home of Washington socialite Mrs. Dwight Davis. Clifford was surprised by how quickly the president accepted. In keeping with the strict protocol of the times regarding presidential appearances, the party was changed from black to white tie. "The president had a spectacular time," Clifford said. "He drank bourbon and branch water and stayed late into the night." It is hard to imagine Truman having such a carefree time in the company of his wife.

Truman enjoyed the role of lifelong suitor. "You know there is no busier person than your old man," he wrote to his wife in July 1946, "but he's never too busy or too rushed to let his lady love, the only one he ever had, hear from him every day no matter what portends." To her he could show a sentimental side few others saw. "You are still on the pedestal where I placed you that day in Sunday school in 1890. What an old fool I am." He also felt he owed Bess his political success. "Suppose Miss Lizzie [Harry's nickname for Bess] had gone off with Mr. Young, Julian Harvey or Harris," Truman wrote a cousin from the White House, listing some of Bess's suitors from their school days, "what would have been the result? For Harry I mean. He probably would have been either a prominent farmer in Jackson County or a Major General in the regular army. . . ." He wrote Bess with the same ardor in his sixties as in his twenties. "I'm happier when I can see you—even when you give me hell." It is hard to avoid concluding that she took advantage of his need, sometimes giving too little back. But those were the roles they had chosen for themselves many years before. Both seemed comfortable playing them.

Bess continued to refuse to acknowledge that she was a public figure. At times her insensitivity to her husband's position was stunning. She was even willing to embarrass him to make a point. If the country needed reminding that Eleanor Roosevelt was no longer in the White House, they were reminded on October 12, 1945, when Bess was invited to be the guest of honor at a tea given by the Daughters of the American Revolution. Mrs. Roosevelt had resigned from the D.A.R. to protest its discriminatory practices. Now New York congressman Adam Clayton Powell pleaded with Bess to follow her predecessor's lead. (The D.A.R. had banned Powell's wife, pianist Hazel Scott, from performing at Constitution Hall because she was black.) But nobody was going to tell Bess whom she could or could not have tea with. Even Bess's childhood friend Mary Keeley wrote her urging that she cancel the D.A.R. tea; Bess's answer: "I agree with you that the D.A.R. is dynamite at present but I'm not 'having any' just now. But I was plenty burned up with the wire I had from that ——— from New York." Powell quickly dubbed Bess "the Last Lady."

Bess was unmatched in her lack of interest in being first lady and her minimalist approach to that role. She could not altogether disregard the public role of first lady, but she certainly tried. She even got rid of her Secret Service detail, though she accepted the services of a seventy-five-year-old driver. When one of a score of frustrated reporters assigned to cover the new first lady submitted the question "What will Mrs. Truman wear to the tea for the United Council of Church Women?," Bess answered, "Tell her it's none of her damn business." She gave no direct interviews under any circumstances. "But Mrs. Truman, how are we ever going to get to know you?" a reporter asked her. "You don't need to know me," she replied. "I'm only the President's wife and the mother of his daughter." She got away with it because the American people agreed with her. In the late forties, there was no public discussion of "relation-ships" or self-realization or intimacy or women's rights. In fact, talking about anything unpleasant or personal was deemed bad manners. The press respected those rules and rarely asked personal questions of the White House's occupants.

It was more than just midwestern reserve that made Bess hate public life and fear exposure. Bess considered the suicide of her father, David Wallace, who had been depressed over financial losses, in 1903 when she was eighteen to be a dark secret. So deep was the family's shame that Bess never told her only child, Margaret, about it. Bess was determined that the press would not publish the details of what the family regarded as an embarrassing and painful personal incident while her husband was in high office. The president understood her reticence about publicity and protected her. When an aunt told Margaret how her grandfather had died, "Dad was furious," Margaret recalled decades later, and he told her, "Don't you say anything to your mother about it." Margaret never did, nor did the press mention the suicide in her mother's lifetime.

Sometimes Harry needed Bess to keep him on an even keel. When the Russian ambassador Nicolai V. Novikov declined an invitation for dinner, the president ordered Secretary of State Dean Acheson to have him thrown out of the country. But on what grounds? asked the stunned Acheson. "He insulted Mrs. Truman by turning down that invitation at the last second," the president said. "I'm not going to let anyone in the world do that." Acheson reached for the telephone and asked Bess to reason with the president. She was practiced in this business. "Tell [the president] you can't do anything until tomorrow, something like that. By that time," she advised Acheson, "he'll be ready to laugh about it." Harry backed off, saying, "When you gang up on me, I know I'm licked. Let's forget all about it." Then he reached inside his jacket for the photo-graph Bess had given him when he left to fight in Europe. "I guess you think I'm an old fool," Truman growled, "and I probably am. But look at the back." On the back of the sepia photograph of the blond girl with the penetrating gaze was written, "Dear Harry, May this photograph bring you safely home again from France, Bess." In an era when men were supposed to be strong and silent, Truman was fearless about letting her—and even those in his inner circle—know he needed her.

Bess did not even try to mask her boredom with the ceremonial aspects of her role. Future New Jersey congresswoman Millicent Fenwick, invited to a reception at Blair House, the official guest house across the street from the White House, recalled a conversation with a fellow guest, an AFL-CIO delegate, who had been to the White House every year for the last twelve. The delegate said that she'd "Never been treated like this," adding, "I'm never coming back." The first lady simply ignored her guests, spending the entire time talking to two old friends from Independence.

Once, when Harry found Bess burning some of their letters, he tried to stop her. "Bess, think of history!" She replied tersely, "I am." She wanted no part of history, so there is only her husband's correspondence and the memories of their daughter and a few close associates to provide insight into their union. As with every marriage, there are things about the Trumans that are impenetrable, which leave unanswered questions. If they loved each other so, why was Bess always leaving him? And why did she choose her mother over her husband so often during their White House years, spending six weeks at a time in Independence looking after her? (She even brought her to live in the White House with the son-in-law her mother called "Mr. Truman," when she spoke to him at all.)

Madge Gates Wallace was a woman of overweening self-importance and nothing, not even the presidency, was going to change her view that Harry was not well-bred enough for her daughter. "Mrs. Truman was caught between her mother and her husband," Scouten remembered. "Mrs. Wallace simply did not acknowledge his presence, barely even talked to him in the White House. But the President was always polite to her. She did not approve of his poker playing or his drinking."

During the summer of 1945 when Truman was preparing to meet Stalin at Potsdam, he was lonely for his absent wife. He wrote her: "I sit here in this old house and work on foreign affairs, read reports, and . . . speeches—all the while listening to ghosts walk up and down the hallway. . . . Write me when you can—I hope every day. . . ." But she did not write to him every day. And she could bring him down. "Just two months ago today, I was a reasonably happy and contented Vice President," he wrote on June 12, 1945. "Maybe you can remember that far back too. But things have changed so much it hardly seems real. . . . I am blue as indigo about going [to Potsdam]. You didn't seem at all happy when we talked. I'm sorry if I've done something to make you unhappy. All I've ever tried to do is make you pleased with me and the world. I'm very much afraid I've failed miserably. But there is not much I can do now to remedy the situation. . . ."

Whatever Bess was engaged in—invariably family or household matters—was as important to her husband as matters of state. One cannot imagine Stalin or Churchill or for that matter FDR writing this letter home from Potsdam: "[Your] letter came last night while I was at Joe's [Stalin's] dinner. Was I glad to get it!" he wrote her on July 22, 1945. "I can't get Chanel N° 5 . . . there is none to be had—not even on the black market. But I managed to get some other kind for six dollars an ounce at the American PX. They said it is equal to N° 5. . . . I bought you a Belgian lace luncheon set—the prettiest thing you ever saw. I'm not going to tell you what it cost—you'd probably have a receiver appointed for me and officially take over the strong box. . . . But I seem to have Joe and Winnie [Churchill] talking to themselves and both are being exceedingly careful with me. . . . The weather is perfect and I feel fine. The boys say there's never been a conference as well presided over," he writes with the pride of a son appealing for his mother's approval.

Because Harry so valued her, Bess was empowered to give him straight-from-the-shoulder advice. Though she burned her letters to her husband, and their real interaction took place behind closed doors, she was not entirely successful in hiding her influence. Philanthropist Mary Lasker, for example, discovered Bess's quiet role while lobbying the president for an increase in the budget for the National Mental Health Institute. She was getting nowhere until presidential aide Matthew Connelly gave her an essential piece of advice. The only one who can get anything done, if she really wants to, is Mrs. Truman." Lasker took the case to the first lady, who did indeed take it up with the president. Lasker got $10 million added to the budget for mental health research.

THOUGH BESS HATED LIFE in the "Great White Jail," she wanted the voters to return Harry there, for his sake. After two years in the White House, Truman was considered "a gone goose," in Clare Boothe Luce's memorable words. Late one night on the whistle-stop campaign for the 1948 election, Bess approached presidential counselor Clark Clifford. It was obvious to Clifford that she was "a very worried wife." "I want to talk to you about the President's chance of winning," Bess said. "What do you really think?" I just don't know, Clifford answered. "The party people don't think he can win." Well, Bess said, *he* seems to think he can. "She was looking for reassurance," Clifford recalled. "But, unlike her husband, she did not have the essential optimism which a politician needs to survive."

If the American people were unaware of the iron bond between Bess and Harry, the White House staff had daily proof. White House maid Lillian Parks recalled the president getting a call in the Oval Office, informing him that Bess felt faint. "He tore out of the White House and ran across Pennsylvania Avenue [to Blair House] with honking cars almost on top of him. How that man ran. The Secret Service were in hot pursuit, but they couldn't possibly catch him."

The Trumans' relationship was based on complete acceptance of each other. They held little back. "It was nice to talk to you last night," he wrote on September 16, 1946, "even if you did give me hell about making mistakes." He enjoyed being the "softie" in the couple and letting her play the tough one. "They always kept to those roles," their daughter recalled. "He never spanked me when I was little. She did. When my allowance was cut from fifty to twenty-five cents because times were hard, he slipped an extra quarter into my palm. As I ran out the door to catch *Maytime* with Nelson Eddy and Jeanette MacDonald, I heard Mother shriek, 'How're we ever going to teach that girl the value of money if you do that, Harry.' They never changed."

About a year and a half into Harry's first term, Bess's resentment at their new life seemed to ebb. Her husband managed to lure her back into the old partnership. From then on, each evening the couple retired behind the closed doors of the upstairs oval study and worked side by side until eleven. Truman claimed to have consulted Bess on every major political decision: "Her judgment was always good. She looks at things objectively, and I can't always." Margaret said her mother was a better judge of character than her father and made many personnel suggestions during his administration. She advised that he fire FDR's former vice president, Commerce Secretary Henry Wallace. She also suggested that he hire Charlie Ross, their old Independence schoolmate, as press secretary. "The three of us had been in school together," recalled Ross, then Washington editor of the *St. Louis Post Dispatch*. "Little did I think the girl with the long blonde hair who sat in an up-front desk would one day get me into the White House's inner sanctum."

"I know he talked to her about decisions," Clifford recalled. "The President relied on her antennae for phonies and self-promoters. Truman was proud of the fact that she was a better judge of people than he was. In the middle of a discussion regarding a personnel matter, the President would say, 'Well, Mrs. T. thinks well of him.' " "In policy matters," Truman wrote later with characteristic reticence, "I think First Ladies have always had a great deal of influence. . . ." Bess, he said, was "a full partner in all my transactions—politically and otherwise."

There was more to the Trumans' marriage than the bonds of politics or even companionship. J. B. West, the White House chief usher, describes the Trumans' reunion after a long absence. "After a light dinner in the President's library," West recalled, "they sent the maids downstairs. The next morning I was in Mrs. Truman's study at nine, as usual. She scanned the day's menu, then, in a rather small, uncomfortable voice she said: 'Mr. West, we have a little problem.' . . . She cleared her throat demurely. 'It's the President's bed. Do you think you can get it fixed today? . . . Two of the slats broke down during the night.' "

"Her wit was dry, laconic, incisive and very funny," West recalled. "It's difficult to capture in words because it was so often silent." Margaret agreed. "I called it her Great Stone Face. She had a wicked wit, sharper than Dad's, and he loved it." West called the Trumans the closest family to live in the mansion. He recalled that the Trumans "did everything together—read, listened to the radio, played the piano, and mostly talked to each other."

Bess Truman never held a single news conference, never gave a proper interview in seven years in the White House. If reporters wanted information, they had to submit a list of questions, which the "ladies" assigned to cover her finally did: "If it had been left to your own free choice, would you have gone into the White House in the first place?" they queried in writing. Answer: "Most definitely would not have." "Do you enjoy being First Lady?" Answer: "There are enjoyable spots . . . but they are in the minority." "Do you think there will be a woman president of the United States?" Answer: "No." "Has living in the White House changed any of your views on politics and people?" Answer: "No comment." It did not bother Bess when *Newsweek* ran an article entitled, "Behind Mrs. Truman's Social Curtain: No Comment." With her family, she was funny and warm, "and then, the minute the doors would open," her friend Congressman Hale Boggs's wife, Lindy, recalled, "and all those people would begin to come in, she would freeze, and she looked like old stoneface. Instead of being the outgoing, warm and lovely woman that she had been previously, the huge crowds simply made her sort of pull up into herself."

But Harry did not ask Bess to be an active or highly visible first lady. His need of Bess was entirely personal. His letters to Bess are endless one-way conversations in which he recounts all he is doing, including detailed accounts of personnel and policy. No husband can pay his wife a higher compliment than letters of such quality and substance. He kept her up-to-date on everything. "I still have a number of bills staring me in the face," he wrote her on August 10, 1946. "[Secretary of State James] Byrnes called me from Paris this morning asking me not to veto a State Department reorganization bill, which I'd told Clark Clifford I was sure is a striped pants boys' bill to sidetrack the Secretary of State. Jimmy told me it wasn't but I'm still not sure. . . . It sure is hell to be President."

Truman's efforts to keep his wife in Washington during the long, muggy summer resulted in a brilliant, permanent addition to the familiar shape of the White House. What the old house needed, Truman thought, was a back porch where he and Bess—and succeeding residents—could spend hot summer evenings. The result was the Truman Balcony, a graceful addition on the second floor behind the six columns of the south portico, much criticized at the time, yet today it seems like such an integral part of the famous silhouette as to have been there from the beginning.

Not surprisingly, given Bess's aversion to the White House, the First Family's happiest time was when they moved into Blair House, across Pennsylvania Avenue, while the great mansion was being rebuilt. Official entertaining was minimal in the much smaller house, and the Trumans lived a more or less normal life. "He was the same dad I always knew," Margaret recalled. "On Sundays at four he'd say, 'Let's go for a walk.' And we'd walk what he called a military mile. People would say, 'Isn't that . . . No, it can't be.' And I'd turn back and whisper, 'Yup, it sure is.' "

It takes more than good character to make a marriage work. For a man of his generation, Harry was unusually open about his feelings and exceptionally accommodating of his wife. His tenderness paid off. Though Bess did her best to erase from the record her own feelings about Harry, she did not entirely succeed. Their daughter remembered Bess sometimes called him "Old Sweetness," and late in life Bess told a friend, "Harry and I have been sweethearts and married more than forty years," acknowledging her proudest achievement. "No matter where I was, when I put out my hand, Harry's was there to grasp it."

CHAPTER 4

JACQUELINE AND JOHN F. KENNEDY

A MARRIAGE ALL THE SAME

I know my husband was devoted to me. I know he was proud of me. It took a very long time for us to work everything out, but we did, and we were about to have a real life together. . . . I know I held a very special place for him—a unique place.
—JACQUELINE KENNEDY, *January 1964*

JOHN AND JACQUELINE KENNEDY WERE WELL SERVED BY THE TIMES, AND BY their immediate predecessors. They followed eight years of Mamie and Dwight Eisenhower, the stolid, middle-class, Middle American couple that stood for prewar values, tastes and marital customs. Mamie seldom rose before noon and was more the general's lady than first lady. The country, rich and secure, was ready for change. And Washington was at the center of the global drama of the Cold War. Worldly and glamorous, the Kennedys were the perfect couple for a foreign policy presidency.

More has been written about the brief tenure of Jacqueline Bouvier Kennedy Onassis and John Fitzgerald Kennedy than about any other occupants of the White House, except the Roosevelts. But the biographies and hagiographies are almost always about Jack *or* Jackie, as two distinct solar systems, as if they didn't coexist under one roof. According to popular mythology, the couple connected only occasionally, usually amid great pomp. It is true that they were among the most independent-minded people ever to inhabit the White House. "Since Jack is such a violently independent person, and I, too, am so independent," Jackie predicted early in their marriage, "this . . . will take a lot of working out."

The Kennedys as partners in a shared enterprise remain more elusive than Jack and Jackie, the icons. Yet they were, or were becoming, good partners, complementing each other, filling in each other's weak spots, as good couples do, proud of the other's emerging gifts. Because they were young and because they lived through an incredibly intense three years, there was growth and evolution both in their characters and in their marriage. Jackie's substantial role in her husband's presidency is too often lost in the breathless romance of the invented Camelot. In fact, she was a serious person masquerading as a flighty ornament. She had a very clear understanding of the charismatic power that flows from being first lady.

In her own way, Jackie became a great first lady. Her impact on the country and the world startled both her and her husband. During official trips to Europe and the Indian subcontinent, she deepened connections begun in the White House. Her greatest contribution, however, was not as an activist but as an aesthete. Raised to appreciate fine things, she brought that sensibility to the White House, setting her sights on making it a repository of all that was best in American culture, furniture and the arts. She broke new ground for future first ladies interested in becoming arbiters of taste, culture and style. In the end, Jackie's role as well as Jack's put a permanent stamp on the Kennedy administration.

⬤

IT IS SOMETHING like awaking in a lost kingdom, overgrown with Spanish moss and a profusion of exotic undergrowth: Camelot. The beautiful queen in the white castle, wrapped in couture silk, bejeweled yet dignified on the arm of her handsome, graceful knight who beams with pride at his lady, and the little blond prince and princess, perfections of breeding and grooming. It was exactly how many Americans wanted to be. And while it lasted, many were happy to grant the Kennedys the license required to produce this fantasy.

Illusion was followed by disillusion, or at least revelation. Never again would Americans be quite so easily seduced by two people they hardly knew. Jack and Jackie were the nation's final fling before Vietnam and Watergate and Washington's prosecutorial culture soured Americans on politicians. Jackie's subsequent marriage to a rich rogue helped to cure Americans of their belief in fairy tales. Perhaps to make sure the country would never again fall quite so naively, Americans have since claimed the right to know every grim and grimy detail of life inside the White House, and what its residents were up to before they got there. So Jack and Jackie would not be possible today, at least not in the manner they were accepted in 1961. But for three years this couple were national pinups.

It is striking in retrospect how free John and Jacqueline were to create their own image, how willingly both the media and the public accepted their version of themselves, how much privacy was freely ceded them. They set the rules; almost everybody played by them.

Jackie preferred the company of artists, rich Mediterranean idlers, country squires in villas. John's preference ran to his Irish mafia, his large and noisy tribe—especially his brother Robert—and the cool, bright young men who filled his Cabinet and war rooms. Yet Jack and Jackie were much more alike than most people think. Both were consummate performers who seemed to love each other most when they could observe each other in full performance. The country also loved to watch them onstage; they were so good at it, putting America's best foot forward to the world. Style was central to their substance. Deep emotions made them both uneasy. They preferred detachment, irony. It was rare that either of them showed any emotion other than laughter. When, in their final year together, they did, they shocked their friends. She loved and needed money more than he did, mostly because, having been born to it, he never had to think about it. They both loved power, she in the traditional manner of a nineteenth-century woman, drawn to great men as a moth to flame. He wanted it for himself and for his family, the vital unit. They both used wit to amuse and to keep others at arm's length. Kennedy often turned it on himself, Jackie's had more bite. They had ample reasons for being guarded with the world and with each other. But near the end they had begun to reach for a deeper connection. In short, they were singularly well suited to each other and to their roles as First Couple.

They learned early to maintain a facade. Each had the ability to look past pain—death, parents' divorce, sickness, a retarded sibling—and not merely get on with life, but do so in high style. What little maternal warmth existed in the Kennedy home was spread among nine siblings, and not equally. As for Jackie, she was a pawn in the angry breakup between her parents, who made no attempt to spare her feelings. She learned to keep her emotions in check, to give away as little of herself as possible. As a child she was happiest on her own, in the company of horses or gazing out at the Atlantic. "I only care for the lonely sea . . . ," she wrote as a teenager, "and I always will, I know." They both loved the grand sweep of history and wanted to be part of it. Jack had spent much of his sickly childhood in bed, reading of great men and exploits. Jackie was smitten with beauty and spectacle. She identified with great, heroic men and their clever, gifted paramours. She drew, she wrote good verse and she imagined great exploits. Her stated goal in college was not to be a housewife. She was a snob, an elitist whose sensibility was more European than American.

The Roman Catholic Church that was their mother ship taught them much about the connection between pomp and power. Jack knew something about the uses of secular pomp—Hollywood—from his father, who spent time there and romanced a film star, Gloria Swanson. "Time to put on the B.P."—Big Personality—Jack would say, entering a room ripe for conquest. He projected youth and idealism, when in fact he was street-smart and tough. He learned cynicism early, from his father. Jack and Jackie were not people to dwell on the unpleasant. Jackie camouflaged her steely determination with breathless innocence. Neither seemed emotionally needy, and since neither was capable of giving too much, this worked out well.

"We're a couple of icebergs," Jackie famously said of herself and her husband, "with most of who we are submerged beneath the surface." Both of them liked it that way. Jack's friend Ben Bradlee once said that Jack and Jackie fell in love with each other's images—he with her camellia-like beauty, her worldly air and the aristocratic pedigree that Boston's Old Guard still withheld from the Irish Kennedys. Perhaps she was drawn to the whiff of danger about him (so like her father's), his fortune and his unlimited prospects. They both got more and less than they bargained for.

His heart was rarely engaged. The love stayed inside the family. Jack's adored sister Kathleen wrote her brother, "I really can't understand why I like Englishmen so much, as they treat one in quite an offhand manner and aren't really as nice to their women as Americans, but I suppose it's just that sort of treatment that women really like. That's your technique, isn't it?" she teased. Kennedy cast women in specific roles: sex partners, objects of beauty and charm, and mothers. At age thirty-six he knew he had to marry; political tradition required it of him. He thought he chose a woman who shared his view that men had all the power, and that philandering was encoded in their genes. He would discover only later that he had also married a woman who, in her way, was as tough and combative and as calculating as he himself.

Psychiatrists sometimes contend that in an attempt to "make right" our past, we marry the parent we had most trouble with. Jackie's father, "Black Jack" Bouvier, was a handsome scoundrel who shared tales of his bad behavior with his daughter, including stories of his philandering. She listened carefully to his admonishment never to reveal too much of herself. Preserve the mystery, he instructed her. Much as Eleanor Roosevelt felt closer to her alcoholic father than to her cold, beautiful, suffering mother, Jackie, too, was obsessed by her weak father. His erratic, unpredictable behavior—by turns too present, too demanding or altogether absent—left Jackie scarred and emotionally detached. Unlike Eleanor, whose absent father made her yearn for a real emotional connection, Jackie decided that sensitive, caring men were not for her.

Also in contrast to Eleanor, Jackie did not leave behind a great paper trail documenting her emotional life. She wrote no memoirs, and what there is of her correspondence reveals her intelligence and sophistication, not her heart. Like so many children of divorce, she learned to mask her feelings as she navigated between two bitter, disappointed parents. If sexual adventures were Jack's chosen form of escape, books, particularly on art and history, were Jackie's. Like her husband, she read voraciously, assimilating the lessons of self-possessed actors on the world stage.

"I took the choicest bachelor in the Senate," she wrote with pride. In an unusual reference to her ambivalence about marrying him, Jackie analyzed herself in the only way she could: in the third person. "She knew instantly that he would have a profound, perhaps disturbing influence on her life. In a flash of inner perception, she realized that here was a man who did not want to marry. She was frightened. Jacqueline in a revealing moment envisaged heartbreak, but just as swiftly determined that heartbreak would be worth the pain." She was prepared to pay a heavy price for the life he could provide. "Look," she confided to a friend, "it's a trade-off. There are positives and negatives to every situation in life. You endure the bad things, but you enjoy the good. And what incredible opportunities—the historic figures you meet and come to know, the witness to history you become, the places you would never have been able to see that now you can. One could never have such a life if one wasn't married to someone like that." If she had the normal illusions about changing her husband once they were married, Jack soon dispelled them. In a revealing comment regarding how trapped the thirty-six-year-old Jack was by his history, she said of him, "He found his true love too late in life."

One year into their marriage, spinal fusion surgery resulted in an infection that almost killed him. She was heroic by his bedside, tireless and imaginative at finding ways to divert him. But when he recovered, she was marginalized. When a reporter doing a magazine profile of Senator Kennedy asked to talk to his wife, he retorted, "What do you want to talk to my wife about? She's out of it. You're doing a piece on me." When it came to Jackie's needs, her husband could be breathtakingly callous. In 1956, her first child had been stillborn while Jack was cruising in the Mediterranean with his brother Ted and Senator George Smathers. It was Jack's brother Bobby, alerted by Rose Kennedy in the middle of the night, who rushed to Jackie's bedside to comfort her and to take care of the child's burial.

Emotionally Jack and Jackie were out of sync. "It was difficult," her husband later understated, "I was thirty-six, she was twenty-four. We didn't fully understand each other." Jack did not share Jackie's spiritual longings, which led her to seek out Benedictine priests for a time and reach into poetry and philosophy, back to the ancient Greeks. Jack's reckless womanizing continued, seemingly unabated. In 1958, Jack's father, Joseph Kennedy, summoned elder statesman Clark Clifford and asked him to help his son Jack out of a potentially career-derailing bind. Jack was being blackmailed for his extramarital relationship with Pam Turnure, a beautiful young Senate staffer who bore a striking resemblance to his wife. Clifford settled the matter with discretion and dispatch. But Jack's relationship with Turnure continued for several more years—along with others.

As a senator, Jack was away most weekends. Even when Jackie was with him, they seemed apart. Sometimes, while he gave his stump speeches, she stayed in the car or sat unnoticed in the shadows of a cavernous hall. But even then her wit and her exceptional literary bent occasionally pierced the political rituals. Her letters sparkled with her intelligence and flattery. "I could never describe to you how touched and appreciative Jack was at the message you sent him," she wrote Vice President Richard Nixon on December 5, 1954, during Jack's convalescence. "If you could only know the load you took off his mind. He has been feeling so much better since then—and I can never thank you enough for being so kind and generous and thoughtful. . . . I don't think there is anyone in the world he thinks more highly of than he does you." Sitting next to Protestant theologian Reinhold Niebuhr at a fund-raiser, she dazzled him with her command of the intersection of sociology and theology. "She's read every book I ever wrote," the astonished Niebuhr later remarked, and subsequently decided to support Kennedy to become the country's first Catholic president.

The most astonishing fact about Jackie was her youth. She was thirty-one years old when she became first lady. But she had a remarkable grasp of the historical role she inhabited. She instinctively understood what the times called for, and that this was her moment. From her hospital bed, convalescing after her son, John's, birth during Thanksgiving 1960, she penned a nine-page letter to designer Oleg Cassini, prescribing what she wanted to wear to the inaugural ball: clothes she would wear "if Jack were president of France—très Princesse de Rethy—mais jeune . . . pure and regal." She perceived that the White House was the greatest stage in the world and she became fearless about using it. The president instructed his chauffeur on the way to the inaugural ball to turn on the light, so people could see Jackie.

From the start, this was the image the American people wanted. But even during that first glittering night, Jack left his wife, sneaking out of the presidential box to join Frank Sinatra at another, less formal gathering. As always, there was a woman in the picture: this time starlet Angie Dickinson. The president rejoined his wife after a while, a folded copy of the *Washington Post* tucked under his arm. Did he really think his wife believed he had slipped out to pick up an early edition of the paper? Historian Arthur Schlesinger, Jr., said Jackie was not a woman to miss a single detail.

But they both seemed to keep his compulsive need for other women sealed off from their marriage, as if his philandering had nothing to do with them, as if it were a medical condition that couldn't be helped. In the middle of a working lunch on nuclear arms, Kennedy startled British prime minister Harold Macmillan by asking, "I wonder how it is with you, Harold? If I don't have a woman for three days, I get a terrible headache. . . ."

Jackie never expressed concern about her husband's philandering to outsiders. Rex Scouten could not recall any time Jackie was not composed. "I could not guess how she felt but she certainly never let on that it bothered her." To emphasize what different times the Kennedys lived in, Scouten recalled an incident in the White House press room where two reporters nearly came to blows. One of the two had been talking about Kennedy's womanizing, and the other turned on him, enraged. "How can you say things like that about the *President*?"

∞

IN THE WHITE HOUSE, Jack needed Jackie as much as she needed him. As first lady, she had an independent role for the first time in their marriage.

If politics and his womanizing had pulled them apart, the presidency brought the Kennedys closer. Their White House years would reveal unexpected qualities in each; they were at their best then. "The one thing that happens to the President," Jackie noted later, "is that his ties with the outside world are cut. And the people you really have are each other.... I should think that if people weren't happily married, the White House would really finish it."

Jackie may not have been the most energetic political wife on the campaign trail—she was too aloof, too reserved—but "sharing" the presidency provided the perfect showcase for her particular talents. Jack's victory was earned with the thinnest possible margin. He was not going to unite the Congress and the country behind his leadership through domestic programs. "Nobody gives a shit about the minimum wage," he told one of his aides, Ted Sorensen. Kennedy's mark would be made in foreign affairs. In his ringing inaugural address he articulated his view of the imperial presidency. The world he depicted was a dangerous place—Communism was gaining ground.

The Kennedys' one thousand days were a period of dizzying contrasts, the majestic side by side with the inglorious. A president who seemed the image of youth and health was often in pain and on crutches. A chain-smoking, snobbish first lady made the White House a showcase for American civilization. Some of the behavior defies explanation. At her husband's insistence Jackie hired Pam Turnure to be her press secretary. "I think you are rather like me," Jackie wrote Turnure, outlining her responsibilities, "and so will answer questions the way I would—which is such a great relief—I feel so strongly that publicity has gotten out of hand and you must really protect the privacy of me and my children—but not offend them all—you can invent some lady-like little title for yourself.... I hope you will be fairly anonymous—for nothing you say is taken as Pam Turnure saying it—You are speaking for me.... Also, in your own private life—when you go out in NY, etc., you just mustn't answer their questions about what it is like working for us—just smile and look evasive." Could Jackie have been oblivious to the relationship? "Jackie had a low sexual charge," Schlesinger noted years later. "And she was not unused to this sort of behavior. After all, her father had behaved in much the same way. I suppose she just averted her gaze. And rolled with the punches."

The punches never stopped. A Yale graduate student named Raymond Lamontagne attended a party at Kennedy brother-in-law Sargent Shriver's house. No sooner had the young man planted himself next to a beautiful blonde sitting alone on a sofa than a presidential aide signaled her that someone wished to see her in a back room. Lamontagne did not see the blonde again. Moving over to sit beside another elegant young woman, a second aide whispered a warning in the luckless man's ear, "She's executive material." The second woman was Pamela Turnure. The man in the "back room" turned out to be the president.

While it may be wrong to impose contemporary standards on the Kennedys' marriage, Jack's treatment of women often seems extraordinarily unsympathetic. "I don't think he understood women," Ben Bradlee maintained. "I don't think he saw equality of the sexes as a viable option. He didn't think about it. I suppose that's the ultimate statement. I don't think he could talk to women if he weren't thinking about 'it.' We didn't talk about our wives then. Jackie didn't give him a lot of shit about issues that a modern wife would. . . . Jack didn't like to talk about relationships, none of us did. It wasn't a topic until after the seventies." Besides, Bradlee noted, echoing Schlesinger, "I'm not convinced that Jackie was deeply interested in sex. She said one night to Jack, 'Ben doesn't think I'm sexy.' You know, she was right. I didn't. Very chic. But not sexy. I think I was reflecting her own lack of interest in sex."

Schlesinger also agreed with Bradlee's characterization of Jack's view of women. "He was raised in the Irish tradition where women had a strictly defined domestic role. . . . Jack and Jackie were both ultimately reserved. They kept their center shrouded." The women's movement was a decade away and Jackie had little interest in it at this stage. She did not identify with "career women." "I have the same feelings about career women that you do," she told journalist William Lawrence. "You told Jack you might sleep with those Washington newspaperwomen, but you'd be damned if you'd have lunch with them."

Jackie shaped the role of first lady to suit her terms. "I don't *have to* do anything," she told Chief of Protocol Angier Biddle Duke. She was ruthless in controlling her own and her children's lives. She had no interest in those aspects of the first-lady role she called "dreary," like lunching with the wives of visiting dignitaries or ladies on the Hill. She let one of the other, more energetic members of the Kennedy family, or the ever accommodating Lady Bird Johnson, fill in for her. I'm not going to go down in the coal mines like Mrs. Roosevelt, she announced.

Jackie knew where she could shine. She would turn the White House into a place of great beauty and serious culture, a place where the best minds and talents would dine and perform in the most exquisite setting. These were things she knew something about: literature, poetry, the performing arts and great homes. Jackie understood the value of scarcity. She made each public appearance count, carefully stage-managing her looks, saying little, allowing the mystery about herself to grow. She was soon on the covers of more movie magazines than Elizabeth Taylor.

As chatelaine, she was armed with the polish and assurance of her breeding. "I want to make this into a grand house," she told the White House chief usher. She had the confidence to jettison tradition and put her own stamp on the mansion. The now legendary dinner for cellist Pablo Casals sealed the young first lady's reputation as much more than a hostess. "You know I've never seen so many happy artists in my life," Leonard Bernstein recalled. "It was a joy to watch it. And the feeling of hospitality, of warmth, of welcome, the taste with which everything was done. . . . The guests were so interesting, and most of all the President and Mrs. Kennedy. It was like a different world, utterly like a different planet. I couldn't believe that this was the same White House that I had attended a year or so before and performed in." For Jackie, such evenings were about much more than "entertaining." They were meant to demonstrate that beauty mattered, that art mattered, that there was such a thing as an American intelligentsia, and that it was every bit as polished as its European counterpart. These evenings at the White House were meant to showcase American civilization.

She had a gift for getting people to do her bidding. A letter from Jackie to Kay Halle, a well-connected Cleveland heiress transplanted to Washington, reveals Jackie's perfect distillation of grace, flattery and determination. Halle helped to compile the list of literary and artistic notables invited to the inaugural festivities and then put together a private book commemorating the event. The letter also provides an early glimpse of Jackie's search for a role as something more than an ornamental first lady. "Dear Kay," Jackie wrote on July 31, 1961,

> I just had to tell you how absolutely overwhelmed we were by the book you did for Jack. . . . One thing I wish you could help me with—you have ideas for things like that and I don't—what can we do for all those people—or some of them. Is it enough to just keep doing things in a private way—as one would do if not President—go to theaters, symphonies etc. and try to have the entertainment at the White House be substantial—I can't go around being on committees and thumping for government subsidies for art—I hate committees! And in a quiet little way we do subsidize arts—at least we're doing better—Isaac Stern came for lunch and the State Department is following all his ideas for overseas tours, etc. But that is so little—Do you think we should have an enormous reception for artists? That seems rather treating them like freaks—I try to work some into every state dinner—but that's a tiny drop in the bucket. If you have a brainstorm do tell me. . . .

Her fragile beauty and the soft, breathless voice camouflaged a will of steel. On occasion, even Jack was intimidated by her. "If Jackie said he had to go," their friend William Walton recalled, "then he went." She was so different from other women, from his sisters. "My sisters are direct, energetic types," he once said, "[Jackie] is more sensitive. You might even call her fey. She's a more indirect sort." Jack, who had a remarkably detached, clear-eyed view of himself, knew he had married "class," a thoroughbred who would sometimes give him trouble. He was also a fatalist and a risk taker, not a man to choose the safe or the predictable option.

The Kennedys shared a love of high-level gossip and a fascination with other peoples' love lives. When journalist Laura Berquist returned from an assignment in Cuba, the president quizzed her about Castro. "Who does he sleep with?" he asked her. "I hear he doesn't even take his boots off. . . ."

Jackie would do wicked imitations of statesmen and their wives, members of his staff and, behind his back, of Jack. She knew how to cut her husband down to size. When the notoriously unmusical Kennedy asked an aide to relay to Jackie a request that the Marine Band play something livelier, she replied, "I chose the music, but if he insists, have them play 'Hail to the Chief' over and over."

The 1960s preceded the era of self-absorption and self-analysis. Jack Kennedy prided himself on not having an interior life. It was part of his deeply instilled macho ethos, which was reinforced by his frail health. There is no reason to believe that, when they were alone, Jack and Jackie's conversation delved much below the surface. When her feelings were hurt, horseback riding, shopping and travel were her outlets for tension. She would sulk, and that drove her husband mad. "Jack always did what he had to do to make sure she was happy," their close friend Walton recalled. "It made him crazy when she wasn't."

The beginning was inauspicious. The CIA-sponsored invasion of Cuba in April 1961 ended in the deaths of 114 Cuban exiles and the imprisonment of more than 1,100 others. For the new president, it was his first and most humiliating failure. Kennedy had trusted his military advisers and was swept along by the sheer bureaucratic momentum of a bad plan. When told of the unfolding catastrophe in the Bay of Pigs, he retreated to the White House family quarters. His wife had seen him cry only in frustration over his agonizing back pain. Now he put his head in his hands, and tears rolled down his cheeks. She held him in her arms. Shaken, they momentarily lost the sense that the sky was the limit for the new administration. What he knew intellectually before, he now understood in the most painful personal way: his was the loneliest job in the world. "Before the Bay of Pigs," his old friend Charles Spalding recalled, "everything was a glorious adventure, onward and upward. Afterward, it was a series of ups and downs, with terrible pitfalls . . . cautious of everything, questioning always."

On May 31, 1961, President and Mrs. Kennedy stepped from *Air Force One* to the accompaniment of a Garde Républicain drumroll and were greeted by President Charles de Gaulle. No one could tell Kennedy was a virtual cripple. For weeks following a tree-planting ceremony in Ottawa, Kennedy's back trouble had flared, forcing him to use crutches. De Gaulle, the last great figure of World War II still in power, was transfixed by Jackie, who spoke to him in excellent French. Fifty black Citroëns escorted the mounted, saber-armed Gardes, as millions of Parisians chanted "Kenn-a-dee!" and "Zhack-ee!" Not since the Wilsons had any foreign head of state been accorded such a tribute. At a sumptuous dinner for the Kennedys in the Hall of Mirrors at Versailles, de Gaulle turned to the president and said, "She knows more about French history than most French women." She charmed culture minister André Malraux into loaning the *Mona Lisa* to the National Gallery, as a personal gesture to her.

"From the moment of her smiling arrival at Orly Airport," *Time* magazine reported, "the radiant First Lady was the Kennedy who really mattered." Jackie knew the effect she wanted: an elegance so simple every other woman looked overdressed, fussy, as if trying too hard. In her white satin gown, she beat the French at their own game of hauteur. "Versailles at Last Has a Queen," ran a French headline. "She played the game very intelligently," de Gaulle said, "without mixing in politics. She gave her husband the prestige of a Maecenas." Kennedy credited his wife with easing his time with the difficult de Gaulle. "De Gaulle and I are hitting it off all right," he told aides, "probably because I have such a charming wife." Watching the general and Jackie locked in conversation at Versailles, he marveled, "God, she's really laying it on, isn't she?" Under the influence of Jackie's charm offensive, de Gaulle concluded his final meeting with Kennedy by saying, "I have more confidence in your country now." The trip ended with Kennedy's most famous public tribute to his wife. "I am the man," he told 540 reporters from all corners of the world, "who accompanied Jacqueline Kennedy to Paris." She had accomplished the metamorphosis from timid political spouse, who feared she was a liability to her husband's career, to regal and respected partner.

Secretly traveling with the Kennedys was the man known as "Dr. Feelgood," Dr. Max Jacobson. He called his special injections "vitamin shots," but they were really a potent and dangerous cocktail of amphetamines, steroids, hormones and animal organ cells that he administered to his many celebrity clients. He injected both the president and the first

Camelot at its height: the Kennedys entertain André Malraux,
the French minister of culture, May 11, 1962, while Lyndon
Johnson, flanked by Lady Bird, eyes the scene.

lady during this trip—Jack, to relieve his back pain, and Jackie, for a
quick surge of energy. It was another sign of how high a price these two
were willing to pay for stellar performances. "I don't care if it's horse
piss," Kennedy said when cautioned about the shots. "It works."

From Paris the Kennedys journeyed to Vienna for the Khrushchev summit. The talks between the short, feisty Soviet leader and the tall, elegant young president were uncompromising, with neither giving an inch on the major flashpoints: Cuba, Berlin, Laos, and the nuclear arms race. "Roughest thing in my life," Kennedy said of his talks. The Russian deliberately showed his most threatening, bullying side, to shake up and test the American. Again, it was Jackie who provided relief. During a banquet at the Schonbrun Palace, leaning in close to the first lady, Khrushchev launched into a series of comic anecdotes. When he boasted to her of the number of teachers in the Ukraine, she cut him off with "Oh, Mr. Chairman, don't bore me with statistics!" The Communist Party boss was beguiled. "She knew how to make jokes," he said. "As our people say, she was quick with her tongue. . . . Even in small talk she demonstrated her intelligence."

Jackie diverted attention away from her husband's lackluster performance at his first superpower summit. Images of Jackie mobbed by adoring Austrians and giggling behind her white gloved hand at Khrushchev's wit were beamed around the world. She would fix her deep gaze on other men of consequence, melting their reserve and suspicion about her husband. The chilly Indian prime minister Jawaharlal Nehru found Jack Kennedy highly resistible. During Nehru's November 1961 state visit, the chemistry between the two leaders was conspicuously poor. Kennedy was unable to mask his view that the Indian was smug and rude. Jackie, applying her most ethereal charm, her powerful blend of intelligence and beauty, connected with Nehru, who spontaneously threaded his arm through hers. She accepted his invitation to visit India.

Standing in the backseat of an open car at Udaipur, Jackie performed the Indian palms-together greeting. The crowds roared in delight, *"Jackie Ki Jai! Ameriki Ran!"* ("Hail Jackie! Queen of America!") Nehru introduced her to yoga, persuading her to try standing on her head. "What was accomplished," Ambassador John Kenneth Galbraith, who accompanied her, said, "was a sense of friendship between the Kennedy family and Prime Minister Nehru." India's flamboyance, the colors and the pomp, suited her, but the real audience for her bravura performance was far away. "Jack is always so proud of me when

I do something like this," she said, "but I have no desire to be a public personality on my own."

Following such performances, Jackie retreated to the sanctuary of her own world, her children, her horses, her clothes and her books. She was a self-indulgent woman who largely followed her own passions. She was clever enough and young and beautiful enough that she got away with a great deal. She treated the press with an elitist disdain, calling the ladies of the White House press corps "harpies." She once even suggested that they be restrained by bayonet-wielding presidential aides. The media loved the Kennedys and willingly played by their rules. No picture of Jackie the chain-smoker was ever printed. No article pointed out the number of days and nights she was not in residence in the White House. There were only the most playful references to her wardrobe budget (those expenses were in fact a source of great tension in her marriage).

Few people stayed immune to Jacqueline's blend of charm and manipulation. When you were on her radar, if you could be useful, there was nothing she would not do for you. When White House aide Gwendolyn King found a valuable eighteenth-century document Mrs. Kennedy had mislaid, "She was so grateful, you would have thought that I was her best friend, the way she was graciously thanking me. The next day, I passed her in the hall and she looked right through me. That was Jacqueline Kennedy."

If there was something Jackie was bred to understand and appreciate, it was power, how to acquire it—for women then, almost always through marriage—and how to keep it. "You know she had a marvelous facility for enlisting the help of all those whose help she wanted," Lady Bird recalled. "She was the most beguiling little girl and in need of help. And I think if I were a man I'd be rushing even faster to her side. But she had that effect on women too. I know I wanted to help her in any way I could." The whispery voice and the shy, demure, tentative tilt of her head were calculated to make her seem unthreatening, vulnerable. For Jackie was a young woman of her time and her class, constrained like strong women through the ages to camouflage her strength. Where Eleanor Roosevelt generally went straight for her goal, Jackie was indirect, oblique and used feminine wiles in a way Eleanor would have found intensely uncomfortable. But like Mrs. Roosevelt, she understood the power of her position and was unafraid to use it when she cared to.

When she learned that noted art collector Walter Annenberg of Philadelphia was in possession of a Benjamin Franklin portrait she thought belonged in the White House, she picked up the telephone. "Mr. Annenberg, today you are the first citizen of Philadelphia," she began, "and in his day Benjamin Franklin was the first citizen of Philadelphia. That is why, Mr. Annenberg, I thought of you. Do you think that a great Philadelphia citizen would give the White House a portrait of another great Philadelphia citizen?" In just a few days, the famous David Martin portrait of a scholarly, aging Franklin was hanging over the mantel of the Green Room. In much the same way, she persuaded Clark Clifford to join her cause. "You always come to the rescue . . . ," she wrote the famed Washington lawyer, "so I would be eternally gratified if you would keep me out of debtor's prison and make this work." And of course he did, establishing the Fine Arts Committee for the White House to locate art and antiques and to raise funds for their purchase.

On February 14, 1962, she unveiled her newly renovated White House to the nation. In a television special that broke viewing records, she walked CBS correspondent Charles Collingwood through a White House that seemed both transformed and very much hers. In her demure, highly cultured voice, she captivated the nation with her earnestness and her command of history. She seemed the perfect custodian for the nation's heritage. "We have such a great civilization," she said with seemingly childlike wonder. There was something arresting about this chic young woman displaying such understated authority. When, at the end of the tour, the president joined her, he seemed stiff and scripted by comparison.

Jack ceded decisions regarding the White House mostly to his wife. His interest in art and music was largely limited to drawings of sailboats, show tunes and jazz. He had no interest in classical music and was known to doze off at concerts. "Pablo Casals?" he asked a friend after the legendary cellist's White House concert. "I didn't know what the hell he played. Someone had to tell me." Jackie dressed not only the house but her husband as well. She turned the president from "a slob into a dude," in his friend Ben Bradlee's words.

Jackie donned what Arthur Schlesinger, Jr., calls her "veil of inconsequence" when she set her sights on a goal, almost always achieving what she sought. She had drive and focus and, when she wanted to apply it, incandescent charm. When she learned that historic Lafayette Square across Pennsylvania Avenue was about to be destroyed to make way for modern office buildings, she leaped into action. "The whole thing seemed to be going down the drain," William Walton recalled, "when Jackie stepped in and told us, 'You white-livered characters need some help and I'm going to get involved. The wreckers haven't started yet, and until they do, it can be saved.' Without her . . . we never would have saved the Square. . . ." She enlisted the help of eminent architect John Carl Warnecke to draw up a plan to provide the needed office space while still preserving the old homes on the lovely square. Warnecke proposed keeping the nineteenth-century facades but placing redbrick buildings behind the row house. "[Jackie's] focus was preserving that character that revealed the history of the beginning of our country," Warnecke said. "She had the gut instincts to know what to approve and what not to. The odds were against Jacqueline Kennedy, although she believed firmly that she could change not only the minds of the world's leading architects but the actual direction of architecture in the United States. . . . [At the] public presentation of the design . . . with Jackie's presence at the press conference . . . it received Fine Arts Commission approval."

But for all her success, Jackie prized her privacy and her freedom too much to get drawn too far into any cause. "We were always trying to get her to do things which she wouldn't do," August Heckscher, the administration's cultural adviser, noted. "I remember being disappointed, for example, when I finally did persuade Mrs. Kennedy to invite some poets who were gathering in Washington for a convocation at the Library of Congress to come to the White House . . . and she agreed to that. . . . And that fall just at the time of the Cuban [missile] crisis she canceled it. . . ." Her role as wife and mother always came first. "She was very affectionate in referring to the President and I was struck by it. We were discussing some dinner that was to be held and she said, 'Well we can do it almost any time but not in the early weeks of April, because that's going to be Jack's vacation and I want to keep that absolutely clear.' "

The first lady's willfulness was a fact of life in the White House. Jackie made it plain that she would be available for "kings and queens but not banana republic presidents." They were to be given "the PBO," the polite brush-off. When, pleading fatigue, she gave the president of Brazil the PBO and was photographed water-skiing with astronaut John Glenn, Robin Duke, the wife of Chief of Protocol Angier Biddle Duke, was left to explain. "The president [of Brazil] took me to task. 'Very interesting, your story about Mrs. Kennedy.' He just scoured the floor with me. Jackie was only interested in stars, and loved the trappings of royalty," Mrs. Duke recalled. "I remember one state dinner she was so busy having fun and talking to Ethiopian emperor Haile Selassie in French and ignoring the other guests. I tried to get her attention but she just ignored me until I was forced to grab her sleeve. She was very annoyed. And she was not nice to other women, the ones who were not chic, the decent human beings who bought their dresses at Lord and Taylor, not Givenchy. If that woman looked like a mud fence, that was the end of that woman for Jackie."

When the king of Saudi Arabia and the president of Ireland both presented her with horses, Angie Duke was again dispatched by the president to reason with her and explain that she could not accept gifts of such value from heads of state. "I understand what you're saying, Angie," Jackie answered demurely. "But there's a problem. I want the horses." She kept the horses.

∽

FOR JACK KENNEDY, boredom was an enemy, and with Jackie he was never bored. "He was very attentive, flirtatious [with women]," Walton recalled, "but if a woman bored him, he would drop her quicker than any known man. He often would talk across a very beautiful girl because she didn't have sense enough to come in out of the rain." Jackie knew how to keep his interest. She memorized poems like "John Brown's Body" and would recite them for his amusement. Her drawings were almost as sharp as her wit. On the occasion of their wedding anniversary, she drew one showing her putting on face cream at her dressing table while he growled from under the sheets, "I demand my marital rights!" When tensions ran high, she left cartoons and limericks for her husband in unexpected places. Upstairs in the White House, she created a sacrosanct refuge. "I think the best thing I could do was to be a distraction. Jack lived and breathed politics all day long. If he came home to more table thumping, how could he ever relax?"

Chief Usher J. B. West described the Kennedys' routine. "After lunch, the Kennedy children were bedded down, the maids and houseman scuttled away, silence reigned upstairs at the White House. During those hours, the Kennedy doors were closed. No telephone calls were allowed, no folders sent up, no interruptions from the staff." In the evening, Jackie summoned friends who amused Jack for cozy dinners full of gossip and humor and substance. There, she would do her latest impersonations—say, of the French ambassador doing his impersonation of de Gaulle—or dance the twist with Robert McNamara. "If you put busy men in an attractive atmosphere where the surroundings are comfortable," she recalled, "the food is good, you relax, you unwind, there's some stimulating conversation. You know, sometimes quite a lot can happen."

Jacqueline's social ease was important to her husband. Jack's parents had been frozen out of Boston's WASP establishment and had socialized mostly with other Irish Catholics. But Jack patterned his behavior after the Brahmins of Boston. Though he wanted to break out of his parents' Irish ghetto, he had no illusions about the Anglo-Saxon world he aspired to. When the *Boston Globe* revealed that his brother Teddy had cheated on a Spanish test at Harvard, the president told Bradlee, "It won't go over with the WASPs. They take a dim view of looking over your shoulder at someone else's exam paper. They go in more for stealing from stockholders and banks." Jackie referred to this attitude as her husband's "immigrant side."

He admired Jackie's effortless polish and her ability to snub the rich and famous at will. While touring India and Pakistan, she worried about her horse Sardar, the gift of the president of Pakistan. Jack cabled his wife playfully, "Dave [Powers], Kenny [O'Donnell], Ted [Sorensen], Taz [JFK's naval aide Tazewell Sheppard], Bob [McNamara], Dean

[Rusk] and Mac [Bundy] are doing nothing but taking care of Sardar—don't worry. All love, Jack."

He was not a man to say so, but his pride in her grew as he observed his wife's impact on the country. Jackie was changing the way American women dressed, entertained, spoke, the games they played and the books they read. Because she liked those small, intimate dinners, hostesses from New York to San Francisco began to favor cozy dinner parties around small, round tables, like hers. Waterskiing became a favorite middle-class sport after Jackie was pictured on water skis. The pillbox hat and the sleeveless sheath replaced the floral froufrou of Mamie's day. French, the first lady's second language and culture, became fashionable to learn and to speak. Just about anything Gallic was in. Sometimes Jack was even slightly envious of his wife's influence and certainly of her linguistic ability, which he did not share.

While Kennedy loved the elegant image she presented the world, he did not like paying for it. Bradlee recalled, "I remember a couple of nights, the two of them arguing about her bills. He had some guy come over and look at her books. He said she spent $40,000 on clothes. That stunned him. I don't think he ever bought anything."

They shared a romantic view of history. "You must think of him as this little boy," Jackie later told the journalist Theodore White, "sick so much of the time, reading in bed, reading history, reading [about] the Knights of the Round Table. . . . For Jack, history was full of heroes." When *Camelot* became a Broadway hit, Jackie used to play the show's music for him at night. Jack's favorite Shakespearean tragedy was *Henry V,* which his wife said "reminds me of him, though I don't think he knows that!" Kennedy's favorite verse from the play was the king's Saint Crispin's Day speech when Henry addresses his army on the morning of the great battle. The lines are revealing about the Kennedys' view of themselves and their role in history.

> *We few, we happy few, we band of brothers,*
> *For he that sheds his blood with me,*
> *Shall be my brother, be he ne'er so vile,*
> *This day shall gentle his condition.*
> *And gentlemen in England, now abed,*

Shall think themselves accursed they were not here;
And hold their manhood cheap whiles any speaks
That fought with us upon Saint Crispin's Day.

She wrote the actor Basil Rathbone asking him to recite the speech from *Henry V* at a state dinner, "for whatever lovely dreams of leading or being led on to victory lurk in his [JFK's] soul . . . of all the speeches that make you care and want to make the extra effort—sacrifice, fight or die—this is the one. The only person I would not wish you to say it in front of was Khrushchev, as we are not united in purpose."

Her obsession with style could blind her to other qualities. She once dismissed Chairman of the Joint Chiefs General Lyman Lemnitzer with a breezy "We all thought well of him until he made the mistake of coming into the White House one Saturday morning in a sport jacket." And the selfishness and self-indulgence would reemerge periodically. When, after the stressful Vienna summit, Kennedy's painful backaches left him using crutches, Jackie took off on a Greek vacation without him. Jack's aversion to the Virginia horse-and-hunting scene did not discourage the first lady from building a house there or retreating to it whenever she felt like it. When she missed her husband's forty-fifth birthday celebration at Madison Square Garden, at which the president was serenaded by Marilyn Monroe, wearing her now famous beaded and diaphanous dress, Jackie said it was because she had to attend a horse show.

∞

MOMENTS OF HIGH TENSION in the White House brought the Kennedys closer to each other. The president's personal physician, Dr. Janet Travell, was struck by a scene that preceded the gravest crisis of his presidency, the Cuban missile crisis. "I watched him walk briskly from the West Wing across the lawn to Chopper Number One. The usual retinue . . . trailed behind him. . . . They boarded the helicopter and waited to see the steps drawn up. . . . Instead the president reappeared in the doorway and descended the steps alone. How unusual, I thought. Then I saw why. Jackie, her hair wild in the gale of the rotors, was running from the South Portico across the grass. She almost met him at the helicopter steps and she reached up with her arms. They stood motionless in an embrace for many seconds. . . . Perhaps no one else noted that rare demonstration of affection." For a man as allergic to public displays of affection, who continually refused photographers' entreaties that he kiss his wife in public, the scene captured the growing intimacy between husband and wife.

Three days later, on October 22, 1962, at 7 P.M., President Kennedy faced the television cameras to make the most important speech of the Cold War. "Within the past weeks unmistakable evidence has established the fact that a series of offensive missile sites is now in preparation on [Cuba]," he said. Kennedy pledged that it would be his "unswerving objective" to remove the nuclear menace. A blockade would be the first step, to be followed by stronger measures, if necessary. "This is the first day of the world crisis," wrote Prime Minister Harold Macmillan in his diary the day after Kennedy's speech. The next thirteen days, with the world on the brink of nuclear war, were the most stressful that Kennedy and the country experienced since the end of World War II. "Now the Americans will realize what we in England have lived through for the past many years," Macmillan wrote. The president's nerves were being tested in the most dramatic way imaginable. Kennedy had recently read Barbara Tuchman's *The Guns of August,* in part about the misperceptions and missed communications that led to World War I. "The great danger and risk in all of this," he noted, "is a miscalculation, a mistake in judgment." "They're scared shitless," CIA director of operations Richard Helms said of the people in the White House. Before Jack relayed his ultimatum to Khrushchev, he telephoned Jackie at Glen Ora, their Virginia house, and asked her to come back to the White House with the children that evening so that they could be together. Later that week, the president suggested Jackie move out of Washington, to be closer to their assigned underground shelter in case of a sudden attack. She refused to leave the White House.

The hours and days of nuclear blackmail took their toll. Kennedy's aides had never seen him so tightly wound, so beleaguered, so dependent on his brother Robert. "At night after long hours of secret planning Kennedy would walk alone on the grounds of the White House trying to clear his mind," *Time* White House correspondent Hugh Sidey recalled. "Jackie would walk out to meet him and the two would go back inside for dinner where he would tell her everything that was happening." But, in Dean Rusk's famous words, "the other fellow blinked" first. On October 28, an announcer for Radio Moscow read the tenth message Khrushchev and Kennedy had exchanged since the beginning of the crisis. It was from the party chairman. "In order to eliminate as rapidly as possible the conflict which endangers the cause of peace . . . the Soviet Government, in addition to previously issued instructions to cease further work on weapons construction sites, has issued a new order to dismantle the weapons which you describe as offensive, and to crate and return them to the Soviet Union. . . ."

Kennedy, en route to 10 A.M. mass, turned to Dave Powers and said, "I feel like a new man. Do you realize that we had an air strike all arranged for Tuesday? Thank God it's over." Khrushchev had been in such a rush to resolve the crisis that Castro first heard about the settlement on the radio. When the president presented his key advisers silver calendars with the thirteen crucial days of October marked off, he gave his wife one too.

The new closeness did not translate into a diminution of Kennedy's appetite for other women. When planning a European tour in the summer of 1963, he asked his secretary of state if he knew of a quiet spot for a personal visit. The upright Dean Rusk suggested the Villa Serbelloni on Italy's Lake Como, owned by the Rockefeller Foundation, which Rusk had once headed. Kennedy instructed Rusk to clear the villa of all residents—staff, servants and even Secret Service. Even the caretakers who lived on the premises were evicted. Only the faithful Powers and Ken O'Donnell accompanied the president. When Rusk learned that Marella Agnelli, the wife of Fiat chairman Gianni Agnelli, was the lady for whom all the precautions were imposed, he was furious. Rusk never quite forgave Kennedy for putting him in such an uncomfortable situation. Kennedy reportedly savored his secretary of state's embarrassment.

Both Kennedys were game players, though Jack was a greater thrill seeker than his wife. Was it coincidence that when Jackie spent her vacation on the Amalfi coast, she was seen so often in the company of Gianni Agnelli that her husband telegraphed her, "A little less Agnelli, a little more Caroline"?

Of course his most dangerous liaison was the one with Judith Campbell Exner. She claimed to have visited him in the White House twenty times between May 1961 and April 1962, while at the same time seeing Mafia boss Sam Giancana. The president was thus leaving himself open to blackmail by two of the most dangerous people in the country, FBI director J. Edgar Hoover and Giancana. That he emerged unscathed was a function of the times, the different standards for what constituted fair journalism. "A journalist came into my office one day," Kennedy's press spokesman Pierre Salinger recalled, "and said, 'I hear Kennedy has mistresses.' I replied, 'Look, he's the president of the United States. He's busy running the country. He doesn't have time for a mistress.' He never mentioned it again, and neither did anyone else." But had someone chosen not to play by those rules, had the president's reckless behavior with a mobster's girlfriend come to light, Kennedy could have faced impeachment. What is bewildering is that an appetite for sex and thrills would so overpower this supremely rational man. But all his life, people had willingly covered for him, considering it a privilege to do so.

One of those who occasionally helped Kennedy out of potentially dangerous situations was Clark Clifford. "During the time he was a senator I was called in on incidents that looked quite delicate and sometimes I thought I was quite helpful. . . . I would say only that *he was bold beyond human belief,* impossibly bold, unbelievably bold and what the attitude of the family was, I do not know." Clifford refused to divulge the particulars of Kennedy's "boldness." But he did express some disappointment with Kennedy.

I would like to feel a man in the presidency would be willing if necessary to give up his friends, that he would be willing to make any sacrifice in order that he would give the very best that he can to this transcendent opportunity . . . the president represents everybody and he sets the moral tone of the country. . . . That is what I wanted John F. Kennedy to do. He was off to a magnificent start. The people took him into their arms. Here was this beautiful young wife who handled herself so exquisitely. Here was a whole new generation. Here was new hope for the country. Everybody thought, "What a marvelous time for America. We have this marvelous young couple. . . ." [But] I will not comment about his predilections in this regard. Once I start there is no limiting it.

With Kennedy it was more than just the aphrodisiac of power. Women found his combination of chiseled good looks, unself-conscious ease and laconic wit irresistible. All his life women had made themselves available to him, under almost any terms he set. They were often prepared to make fools of themselves—and of his wife. And she, who missed very little, could not have missed this. But she was willing to pay the price.

Their children pulled them closer together. Jack was in his forties when he became a father. He doted on his small son and daughter. Jackie's miscarriages and the stillborn birth of a daughter enhanced their joy in Caroline and John. The president loved showing off his appealing offspring, fixtures in the Oval Office who mixed with heads of state and lesser grandees of public life. He wanted more children. Bradlee recalled one time when his wife, Toni, and Jackie were on the lawn of the Kennedys' Virginia house, playing music on a portable record player when Jackie suddenly got up and said she had to go inside, her husband was waiting upstairs. "It was the day in the calendar when they were supposed to be trying for a baby. She was rushing in with anticipation, it seemed to us—whether for having the baby or the act itself, I do not know. It was definitely on her mind."

"He never wanted them all crowded together like Bobby and Ethel," Jackie recalled, "so small children in the middle were miserable and their parents harassed. But he always wanted a baby coming along when its predecessor was [growing] up. That is why he was so glad when he learned I was having Patrick."

On August 5, 1963, President Kennedy signed the proudest achievement of his presidency, the Nuclear Test Ban Treaty, banning atmospheric nuclear tests. It was the first arms control agreement between Washington and Moscow, a small step toward ending the Cold War, but

Kennedy liked to say that a great journey begins with small steps. His sense of triumph was short-lived.

Two days after the Moscow signing, Jackie, vacationing near Hyannis Port, Massachusetts, began labor five weeks prematurely. "Should I notify the President?" Dr. Travell asked Jackie. "Absolutely not," she replied. She told the doctor and the crew of the helicopter whisking her to the military hospital at Otis Air Force Base, "I don't want anything to happen to this baby." Minutes later Jackie gave birth by cesarean section to a four-pound-ten-ounce boy who was immediately placed in an incubator.

Despite her instructions that Jack not be alerted that she was in labor, he arrived forty minutes later. By then the base chaplain had baptized the baby Patrick Bouvier Kennedy, after Jack's grandfather and her father. Even before he reached his wife, JFK was told the child suffered from a severe respiratory problem involving the lung's hyaline membrane, which was common in premature infants. He wheeled Patrick into Jackie's room, where she held the baby for a few minutes, before father and son were sped to Boston's Children's Hospital. At the end of the awful day, in a bed two floors above where the infant was struggling to breathe, the president collapsed in exhaustion. At 5 A.M. on August 9, Patrick, aged forty hours, died. Kennedy returned to the room where he had spent the night, closed the door and wept. Returning to his wife's bedside, the two cried together. "There's only one thing I could not bear now," she told him. "If I ever lost you."

They wanted to put something in Patrick's coffin that was from both of them. Jack chose the Saint Christopher's medal that she had given him when they were married. Jack was reluctant to leave the small coffin. "Come on, Jack," Cardinal Cushing gently prodded, "let's go. God is good."

Jackie stayed in the hospital for another week. Her husband was worried about her. He asked Arthur Schlesinger, Jr., to get Adlai Stevenson, whom Jackie liked and admired, to write to her, to cheer her up. Their shared grief was greater than anything they had experienced before.

Jackie had seen him sick, seen him wracked by pain, seen him close to death. He had twice seen her devastated by the deaths of babies she

had carried nearly to full term. No one else—not his family, not his closest aides, surely not the women he slept with—had experienced what
they had together. The wall of reserve that shielded them even from each
other appeared to be crumbling. There was a different quality to their
marriage. Their friends noticed the new closeness. Less concerned about
the cool image than about helping each other through a rough time, they
were now willing to hold hands in public.

He wanted her to get better. He needed her. On September 12 they
celebrated their tenth wedding anniversary. He asked her to choose gifts
from a famous antique dealer's catalog. She gave him a Saint Christopher's medal to replace the one he had put in Patrick's coffin. He gave
her a gold ring with sapphire chips in memory of Patrick. Jackie's sister,
Lee, suggested a Greek cruise to lift her spirits. The flamboyant and
much investigated Greek shipping baron, Aristotle Onassis, offered
his yacht. Some of Kennedy's advisers cautioned against the first lady
accepting such potentially controversial hospitality. You have an election
year coming up, they told the president. Kennedy, knowing his wife's
love of luxury, put her recovery ahead of any potential image problem.

So she joined Onassis and feasted on hedonistic pleasures. And she
wrote unusually revealing letters to her husband, letters that expose her
complexity but also an authentic love. "I miss you very much, which is
nice, though it is a bit sad. But then I think of how lucky I am to be able
to miss you. I know I always exaggerate everything, but . . . I realize here
so much that I am having something you can never have—the absence of
tension. I wish so much that I could give you that—so I give you everyday . . . I have to give."

When he asked her to travel with him to Texas on his first campaign
trip for the upcoming presidential race, she agreed. Many were astonished that she would go to a place where Adlai Stevenson had been
pelted with eggs and spat upon weeks earlier. "You know how I hate that
sort of thing," she told friends, "but if he wants me there, that's what
matters." And so she went to Dallas.

⁂

UNTIL NOVEMBER 22, 1963, Americans of a certain age found common
ground by recalling where they were when the Japanese bombed Pearl

November 25, 1963. Jackie and her children wait for President
Kennedy's coffin to be placed on the caisson for the start
of the procession to the Capitol.

Harbor or when they heard FDR was dead. Now those dates were joined
by a third. And Jacqueline Kennedy's performance in the days that followed her husband's assassination is deeply etched in America's national
memory.

The country learned as much about her during the days after Dallas
as in the three and a half years she was first lady. She did not fall apart
after the unimaginable horror of witnessing her husband's assassination.
She took charge of his funeral and of his legacy. She lavished as much
care, showed as much respect for history in orchestrating the world's
mourning of him, as she had on any state dinner. Again she demonstrated her grasp of the power of symbols. The riderless horse, the great
men walking silently behind his coffin, her little boy's soldierly salute to

his father, her own ravaged, composed face—she knew the world would not soon forget these images.

Then she sat down and wrote her final letter from the White House. It was not to a friend or family. She was thinking of history. His legacy was now hers. She wrote Nikita Khrushchev.

> Dear Mr. Chairman President,
> So now, in one of the last nights I will spend in the White House, in one of the last letters I will write . . . at the White House, I would like to write you my message. I send it only because I know how much my husband cared about peace. . . . He used to quote your words in some of his speeches—"In the next war the survivors will envy the dead." You and he were adversaries, but you were allied in determination that the world shouldn't be blown up. You respected each other and could deal with each other. I know that President Johnson will make every effort to establish the same relationship with you. The danger which troubled my husband was that war might be started not so much by the big men as by the little ones. While big men know the needs for self control and restraint—little men are sometimes moved by fear and pride. If only in the future the big men can continue to make the little ones sit down and talk, before they start to fight. . . . I send this letter because I know so deeply of the importance of the relationship which existed between you and my husband, and also because of your kindness and that of Mrs. Khrushchev in Vienna. I read that she had tears in her eyes when she left the American Embassy in Moscow, after signing the book of mourning. Please thank her for that.
>
> Jacqueline Kennedy

One week later, Jackie summoned Theodore White to Hyannis Port, where she had gone to spend Thanksgiving. On a stormy night Jackie poured out her memory of Dallas to the stunned reporter, who scribbled down notes that would be unavailable to the public for thirty-one years. Patrick's death foreshadowed her husband's, she told him. Their new closeness made Jack's death two months later even more heartbreaking for her. She opened up to this virtual stranger in part for personal release, but with another purpose as well. She wanted to set down her version of her husband's presidency before the historians had a chance. "Only bitter old men write history," she told White. "Jack's life had more to do with myth, magic, legend, saga and story than with political theory or political science."

She was ready with the epitaph to the Kennedy years: Camelot. The lines her husband loved from the Lerner and Loewe Broadway musical *Camelot* were the ones that best expressed the way she wanted him to be remembered: "Don't let it be forgot, that once there was a spot, for one brief shining moment that was known as Camelot." There will be other great presidents, she told the reporter, but there will never be another Camelot. It was the beginning of the Kennedy myth, and the famed reporter was her willing tool in its creation. "She put it so passionately that, seen in a certain light, it almost made sense," White said later.

The conceit was too romantic to have suited John Kennedy's dry realism, and based on too much fantasy to endure. But Jackie was ruthless in her battle to control the history of the Kennedy White House. She broke with old friends who did not entirely share her misty vision of Camelot. She did not approve of Ben Bradlee's affectionate but familiar account of his times with Jack, *Conversations with Kennedy,* and never spoke to him after its publication in 1975. The man she herself enlisted to write a definitive account of the assassination, the historian William Manchester, would receive even harsher treatment years later. She had poured her heart out to Manchester, who based his *Death of a President* in part on her account. Later, she found the book far too personal and embarrassing and demanded that Harper & Row, Manchester's publisher, and *Look* magazine, which was to run an exerpt from the book, make hundreds of changes. She also tried to block any of the profits from reaching the author. She failed, but Manchester was hospitalized with a nervous breakdown from the ordeal.

◇

IRONICALLY, IT WAS JACKIE HERSELF who dealt her carefully crafted image of Camelot its body blow. When she married Aristotle Onassis in 1968 she slipped off the pedestal she had worked so hard to erect—perhaps, at a subconscious level, intentionally. Money, power and the security they purchase seemed her prime motives in choosing this hard, coarse man.

Most Americans no longer think of the Kennedy presidency as a thousand days of magic. The illusion has been shattered by revelations of unheroic conduct, and by public cynicism. Still, the Kennedy White House remains a metaphor for cool elegance and a combative self-assurance never again duplicated. Public fascination with Jack and Jackie goes on unabated. But now they are history. They were exquisitely of their moment, a time when Americans were unabashed and unquestioning of their preeminent position in the world. A respectful media and a still largely innocent public enabled them to project their chosen view of themselves on the world. It was a time before the lines between public and private conduct were blurred, many years before those lines were erased. In our memories the Kennedys are always young and beautiful, and so are we.

CHAPTER 5

LADY BIRD AND LYNDON JOHNSON

THE SINGULAR OBJECT OF THEIR AFFECTION

I am afraid it's politics . . . I would hate for you to go into politics.
— LADY BIRD JOHNSON TO LYNDON JOHNSON, *October 1934*

What I want is great solace—and a little love. That is all I want.
— LYNDON BAINES JOHNSON

He couldn't have been Lyndon Johnson without Lady Bird.
— KATHARINE GRAHAM

LIKE JACQUELINE BOUVIER KENNEDY, LADY BIRD JOHNSON PAID A HIGH PRICE
for forging one of the nation's legendary political partnerships. But while
many people considered Lady Bird to be both long-suffering and blindly
loyal, she never lost her own compass, nor was she consumed by her
husband. Beneath her endlessly accommodating manner, she retained a
core that was beyond even his reach. That fundamental independence
enabled her not only to survive him but to retain his respect. While Lyndon Johnson's legacy is still debated, Lady Bird's is assured. Since his
insecurities were as gargantuan as his ambitions, during six turbulent

years in the White House, Lady Bird's steady presence enabled him to perform to his fullest capacity.

Perhaps nothing so clearly demonstrates both Lady Bird's power and its cost than a conversation between the Johnsons on October 14, 1964, almost a year into the Johnson presidency. On that day, the first lady learned that Walter Jenkins, one of LBJ's closest and most hard-working aides for twenty-five years, had been arrested on a homosexual morals charge in a YMCA men's room a few blocks from the White House. With the presidential election just weeks away, LBJ wanted Jenkins fired immediately. Lady Bird decided that even on the eve of the election, consideration for Jenkins was essential. She called the president in New York. A remarkable tape recording of their conversation surfaced a few years ago in the LBJ Library. "I think a gesture of support on our part is necessary," she told her husband, shrewdly adding, "to hold our own forces together." She proposed offering Jenkins a job at the Johnson-owned television station. But Johnson wanted only to distance himself from trouble. "Talk to Abe [Fortas] and Clark [Clifford]," her husband instructed her, trying to end the conversation quickly.

But Lady Bird held her ground. As was often the case, she wanted to save Lyndon from himself. She knew her man, knew how to play him. "My poor darling," she cooed over the long-distance line, "my heart breaks for you, too." But at the same time she tried to lock in a small concession. "I'm going to say [to the media] that I cannot believe this picture put before me of this man I've known all these years."

But Johnson tried to forbid Lady Bird from calling on Jenkins's wife. The first lady, he warned, should not be making such a call. But she ignored him. "My love, my love, I pray for you along with Walter," she soothed, deflecting his rising temper. "You're a brave, good guy." She was determined. "If you read what I've said in Walter's support they'll [sic] be along the lines I've just said to you." Finally, she began to get through to him. "You think I ought to call her?" he asked. "I do. I think we ought to offer support in any way we can," she responded. Anxious to end the conversation, LBJ agreed to call Mrs. Jenkins, but still opposed giving her husband a job. "You won't have your [broadcast] license for five minutes," he warned his wife. "I'd almost rather offer it to them and let the license go down the drain," Lady Bird coolly replied. "Offer them something else," he suggested, "like running the [Johnsons'] ranch." All right, she agreed, quickly pocketing her small victory. "Good-bye, my beloved," she signed off. Lyndon never again saw or spoke in public of Jenkins, but Lady Bird issued a brave statement of personal support. "My heart is aching today for someone who had reached the end point of exhaustion in dedicated service to his country. I know our family and all of his friends—and I hope all others—pray for recovery."

Neither Lady Bird's public show of compassion for Jenkins nor the event itself cost Johnson electoral support. In November 1964 Johnson swept Barry Goldwater in a historic landslide, elected by the largest majority in modern history. Finally, the man who thought of himself as an accidental president had the overwhelming electoral mandate he hungered for. Not for the first time, the public surprised the politicians in its display of good sense. As Clark Clifford later noted, "The voters understood that [the Jenkins case] was a personal tragedy, not a public matter." Lady Bird had understood this when her husband had not.

The exchange shows how well Lady Bird understood LBJ's insecurities and his narcissism. It also demonstrates her ability to maneuver within the boundaries imposed by her overbearing husband. It illuminates her ability, limited but real, to manipulate her husband while simultaneously feeding his ego and soothing his rage. The contrast between her generous humanity and his single-minded focus on his political survival is clear. Both qualities were essential for the rise of the Johnsons.

With the exception of Andrew Johnson, no president ever started out under a darker shadow than Lyndon Johnson did on November 22, 1963. Lady Bird's sharpest memory of the nightmare flight from Dallas to Washington the day John Kennedy was assassinated was of "that immaculate woman, [Jackie] exquisitely dressed and caked in blood." At the same moment that Lady Bird became first lady, her predecessor, already the most famous woman in the world, became an iconographic figure. Lady Bird's husband wanted desperately to be president, but not this way. "I always felt sorry for Harry Truman and the way he got the presidency," Johnson told an aide, "but at least his man wasn't murdered."

JOHNSON, LIKE HIS HERO Franklin Roosevelt and his rival John Kennedy, followed more than his heart when he proposed marriage to Claudia Alta Taylor on their first date in the late summer of 1934. He was twenty-six years old and knew what he wanted. Politics were Lyndon's life—eighteen hours a day is all, he told the woman who would become known as Lady Bird. Given his boundless need for affirmation, his manic energy and his boredom with anything other than politics, his political ambition seemed preordained. Johnson instinctively grasped that Lady Bird would help get him there. Proposing to this intelligent and resilient woman revealed LBJ's early self-awareness.

As in many other presidential unions, she possessed what he lacked. Physical beauty was not his primary concern in his life partner. He needed her discipline and composure to moderate his excesses. He could also see she was capable of the total devotion he required. He did not want a wife who would draw attention from himself. He was looking for strength of character and loyalty. Lady Bird had both in extraordinary measure. To his credit, Johnson respected his wife and more often than not paid attention to her counsel. Given the confines of her role, Lady Bird's accomplishments are remarkable. Though married to one of history's most reviled presidents (despite notable achievements), she became one of the nation's best-loved first ladies and has remained so more than thirty years after the Johnsons left the White House.

Lady Bird did more than indulge this driven, egocentric man. She came as close to taming him as was humanly possible. She provided a loving, stable base and enabled him to channel his energies. "The best day's work you ever did," Johnson's law school classmate Russell Morton Brown told him in the late fifties, "was the day you persuaded her to marry you." Johnson knew it.

His six feet three inches overpowered her five feet two inches with what was later called the Johnson Treatment. With his rapid-fire salesmanship, he enveloped her with his long arms, big hands, his face not an inch from hers. "He was thin, but very good-looking," she later remembered, "with lots of black wavy hair, and the most straightforward, determined manner I had ever encountered." The force of his pursuit left her little time to breathe. "This morning I'm ambitious, proud, energetic and very madly in love with you," he wrote her on October 24, 1934.

"Lyndon, please tell me as soon as you can what the deal is. . . . I am afraid it's politics," she wrote him back, trying to restrain the onrushing train. "I would hate for you to go into politics." It was politics, all right, but she signed on anyway. Lady Bird, a shy girl whose mother died when she was five, and who had spent much of her life in rural solitude, was drawn to the voluble man. She had a taste for adventure. She had chosen to go to journalism school because journalists "lead less humdrum lives." Johnson promised an escape from sheltered Karnack, Texas. The gamble paid off for both of them.

It is hard to imagine that many women would have put up with Johnson's volatile, demanding and sometimes demeaning personality. Like Franklin Roosevelt and Bill Clinton, Johnson was a mama's boy who had been coddled, spoiled and adored. In the eyes of his mother, Rebekah Johnson, he could do no wrong. But Rebekah placed an extra burden on her son: to redeem his family's thwarted ambitions. Her life, her father's and her husband's had not turned out the way she had hoped. Rebekah's letters to Lyndon and Lady Bird are reminiscent of Sara Delano Roosevelt's to her son and daughter-in-law. "My darling boy," she wrote him on November 30, 1934, "I rejoice in the happiness you so richly deserve, the fruition of the hopes of early manhood, the foundation of a completely rounded life. I have always desired the best in life for you. Now that you have the love and companionship of the one and only girl, I am sure you will go far." Congratulating Lyndon on his election to Congress in April 1937, his mother transferred two generations of failed hopes onto her son's shoulders. "To me your election . . . compensates for the heartache and disappointment I experienced as a child when my dear father lost the race you have just won. . . . You have always justified my expectations, my hopes, my dreams."

Lyndon took Lady Bird from Austin to Washington in 1934. While she worked as secretary to Texas congressman Richard M. Kleberg, Johnson began to groom Lady Bird for political life. Early on he asked her to memorize the names of the county seats Kleberg represented and three or four of the men who could get things done in each. Early in her political education, Lady Bird discovered that her husband considered sex a prerogative of power. She showed remarkable intelligence and almost superhuman self-control in dealing with her husband's philandering. She was rarely confrontational. It helped that she was also used to strong, domineering, womanizing men. Her father, like Jackie Kennedy's, was also "that sort of man." Thomas Jefferson Taylor, known as "Mr. Boss," was a big man in Karnack, where he owned the biggest store and lived in the biggest house. Decades later, a longtime Johnson aide, Horace Busby, saw Lady Bird's father as the key to understanding her. "He was her role model. That's why she put up with Johnson's womanizing. She grew up with a father who had a wife and girlfriends. That was just the way men were in her mind."

Busby, who served as a sort of house intellectual, speechwriter and confidant, remembered Johnson, early in his marriage, courting a plain-looking secretary who had a reputation for running the best office in Congress. "Johnson bought her flowers, was real sweet with this woman. Nobody had ever done something like that before in her life. And he got with her one night and made love to her. And as soon as he finished, he turned over and said, 'Now about your files. . . .' That was on his mind the whole time. Lady Bird just didn't attach much importance to it."

She was a thirties wife, unembarrassed to assert her husband was "my lover, my friend, my identity." Later, she told her daughter Lynda Johnson Robb, "The need for women to have their individual identity belongs to your generation, not mine." She saw her role as "balm, sustainer and sometime critic" for her husband. Lady Bird learned to avert her gaze, in part to preserve her dignity. His long affair with Alice Glass, a tall Texas beauty who was at the same time the mistress of newspaper publisher Charles E. Marsh, was serious and painful for both Johnsons. During the many weekends they spent with Glass and Marsh at their Virginia estate, Longleat, Lady Bird hung back and listened to the political sophisticates, the bright and beautiful people of Alice's salon, and learned. Get the most from it, she later counseled her daughters, learn from your father's position and respect it. She did not apparently articulate the corollary to the admonishment: Don't expect much emotional support. Lady Bird was as fit for the grueling climb to the political mountaintop as Lyndon himself.

Lady Bird, familiar with loneliness from early childhood, had the capacity to take "psychic leave," to tune out things she did not wish to acknowledge, and it served her well. She was also a very shrewd woman. When she could, she befriended the women Lyndon was "courting." Busby recalled a long, warm letter of welcome Lady Bird left on the kitchen table for another woman frequently linked to her husband, Congresswoman Helen Gahagan Douglas. She even credited her husband's "ladies" with improving *her*. "I learned how to dress better from this one, to always wear lipstick from another, about art or music from another." She reacted to the "other women" by making herself even more indispensable to her husband. She was confident that in time the infatuations would pass, while she endured. When told that former Texas governor John Connally's memoirs included a passage about Lyndon's affair with Alice Glass, she coolly commented, "I would've thought Alice was too plump for Lyndon." Her comment regarding Eleanor Roosevelt's lifelong emotional estrangement from her husband as a result of his affair with Lucy Mercer sums up the philosophy that sustained Lady Bird. "What a shame," she said of the Roosevelts, when Lucy was only a "fly on the wedding cake."

Temperament is destiny not only for politicians but for their spouses as well. Lady Bird in some ways possessed the ideal temperament for her role. A natural optimist with a well-centered ego, she was also tough. "If I had wanted him to do without the stimulation, knowledge or assistance other women offered him," she recalled years later, "it would have after a period diminished me." She did not let them impede her life, she said.

As saintly as this stoicism may seem, there is another reason Lady Bird may have at times actually welcomed Johnson's temporary diversions. Lyndon was the world's most exhausting man, and he could not stand to be alone. "Bird!" he would boom upon entering the house. "Where are you, Bird?" And from then on she was his, serving his insatiable needs. Ultimately she was confident of his deep love and need of her, and understood what she called the "help and support" of other women. In 1998, she expressed profound discomfort with the media's scrutiny of President Clinton's private life. "We are narrowing the field of those who will run for office," she noted, "when we allow them so little privacy. We elect a man president for his devotion to every one of us. Not because of his private life."

In her eighties, she still recalled a rare moment when her iron self-control slipped because it so shocked both husband and wife. After seven years of marriage and ten different moves, the Johnsons, trekking back and forth between Austin and Washington, did not have a real home of their own. One day, Congressman Johnson was talking politics with John Connally in the living room of the Johnsons' tiny rented apartment in Washington. "I had been wanting a home after a few years of marriage," Lady Bird recalled. "My idea of being rich was to have enough sheets not to have to carry them back and forth from Washington to Texas. So that day, I burst out that I never had anything to look forward to but one more damned election! And Lyndon was just so absolutely startled that he went back the next day to the house we'd looked at and told the owner we had to have it right way. I was embarrassed for having said all that and gave myself very poor marks for it. But then I heard lots of times Lyndon talking to a new congressional member, telling him, 'Sure be a good idea if you bought a house, make your wife happier.' I held my laughter to myself."

In December 1941 things began to shift in the dynamic between Lyndon and Lady Bird when he became the first member of Congress to go on active duty in World War II. He asked her to run his congressional office while he was away. Lady Bird was not the only congressman's wife who ran her husband's office during the war. However, most people agree that she was the only one who considered it a full-time job. She did not get paid for her work, but her personal compensation was substantial. "It gave me a . . . sort of reassurance about myself," she later said. "I finally emerged thinking that—well, I could make a living for myself." It was more than a question of self-esteem. Lyndon was startled by the originality and intelligence of her correspondence with key members of his constituency. "Your letters are splendid . . ." he wrote her. "I don't think I have ever sent any better letters out of my office."

Seeing how effective she was, he wanted her to do more. If she reached more people, he wrote her, "we would be invincible. Think of the effect it would have if 2,000 of our best friends in the District had personal notes from you written at the rate of 25 a day for 60 days. I don't know how you are going to find time to do all this and still take the people to lunch that I want you to take, and see the people in the evening that you must see, but I guess with your methodical planning you can work it out." This was the Johnson formula: the more she gave, the more he expected. But she was up to it. "He could load you up with more jobs," Lady Bird remembered with a laugh. "He thought you could do more than you could do and he kept teasing or ridiculing you until you did. 'You mean to say you got two degrees from the University of Texas and you don't know how to do such and such?' "

Johnson returned from naval service in late 1942 and reclaimed his office. He was still a needy narcissist who patronized and occasionally humiliated her in public. But now he saw that she could play a bigger role in his political ascent. Henceforth she would be his political partner. She had demonstrated subtlety, intelligence and humanity that could advance his larger ambition.

Together they became a Washington institution, she beloved, he feared. In the fifties Lyndon became the most powerful Senate majority leader in history—and Lady Bird was always beside him, his balance. Not everyone in the Washington political establishment approved of her stoicism. Her fellow Senate wife Jacqueline Kennedy observed with characteristic bite, "Lady Bird would crawl down Pennsylvania Avenue over splintered glass for Lyndon." In fact, Lady Bird and Jackie had more in common than was obvious, including the fact that both were married to husbands who assumed sex as a prerogative of power—and both wives pretended not to notice.

❧

IN JULY 1955, just shy of his forty-seventh birthday, Johnson suffered a massive heart attack. It should hardly have been a surprise. A three-pack-a-day smoker and a legendary boozer, Senator Johnson had virtually no life outside the ornate chambers and smoky back rooms of Congress. He had no hobbies, no sports, no real friends outside Congress. Lady Bird moved into a room next to his at the Bethesda Naval Hospital. When he was discharged in August he told reporter (later Lady Bird's White House press officer) Liz Carpenter, "Everybody's disappointed me except Lady Bird. My close friends have disappointed me. But Lady Bird never has. I never turned over in bed that I didn't hear her feet on the floor."

Johnson quit smoking but returned to the only life he considered worth living, at the only pace he could keep: overdrive. When Jack Kennedy chose him as his running mate in 1960, the Johnsons embarked on their political life's least joyful chapter up to that point. Johnson's persona was simply too big for him to be vice president. He needed to be at the center of attention. To serve under a senator as undistinguished as Kennedy rankled. Nobody ever made Johnson more self-conscious of his rough beginnings than the Kennedys. They brought out the worst in him. "He would often say he wished that just once one of those 'Harvards' would run for sheriff," Lady Bird recalled.

Johnson turned to drink for solace. As always, his wife stayed steady. She could see that others might judge them by the sound of their vowels or the cut of their clothes, but she did not want to be anybody except who she was. Nor did the worldly and stylish new first lady shake Lady Bird's sense of herself. "It would've been out of the question for any jealousy there," she noted, "because Jackie was close to twenty years younger."

In truth, Jackie admired Lady Bird. "I remember . . . she and my sister and I were sitting in one part of the room [at the Kennedys' summer house in Hyannis Port]," Jackie recalled many years later, "and Jack and Vice President-elect Johnson and some men were in the other part of the room. Mrs. Johnson had a little spiral pad and when she'd hear a name mentioned, she'd jot it down. Sometimes if Mr. Johnson wanted her, he'd say, 'Bird, do you know so-and-so's number?' And she'd always have it down. Yet she would sit talking with us, looking so calm. I was very impressed by that."

The Johnsons never seemed more Texan than after Kennedy died. Lyndon had a big voice, a big physique, big hands, big appetites. Gold jewelry flashed from his wrists and fingers. His initials were emblazoned on almost everything he owned, pets included. His critics winced every time he reached for a microphone, for it brought back memories of the murdered man's dry wit. At first, Lady Bird suffered as well. She was petite, but no match for the world's most famous widow. Her twang was unmistakable and her style nondescript. Austin and the Texas hill country suddenly supplanted Boston, Newport and Hyannis as the presidency's cultural axis. To make matters worse, the bullet that ripped through Camelot had been fired in Texas. The country was in shock. The nation's loss was personal, familial.

But the thirty-sixth president of the United States had something the thirty-fifth did not. Lyndon Johnson had a partner whose mission in life was to serve her husband's ambition, who was as committed to the Johnson presidency as he himself. For Lady Bird, the presidency was always a matter of "we." "We were knocked flat by the assassination," she recalled, "but we performed." Better than anyone, she understood her husband's need for every light to shine on him. Not for a minute did she have her own agenda. It was always about Lyndon, how best to serve Lyndon. He could not have tolerated a free-spirited, independent-minded spouse. "I did not have Eleanor Roosevelt's courage," Lady Bird admitted. "Her energy, her determination. . . . Mrs. Roosevelt just didn't pay any attention to all the snide things that were said about her. I respect that. But I could not be like that." For her devotion, she was rewarded in a way Eleanor was not. She knew that without her steady presence Johnson was quite rudderless.

As with almost all presidential couples, the White House worked its subtle alterations on the Johnsons' relationship and their roles. Her marriage remained the center of Lady Bird's universe, but her power inside the marriage was considerably enhanced. Lyndon may have moderated his overt philandering once in the White House, but monogamy was not in his nature. Texas reporter Hal Wingo remembered a conversation with the new president one month after he assumed office. "About five of us reporters who covered Johnson were sitting around the bar of the old Driskill Hotel in Austin on New Year's Eve, 1963. Suddenly the President appeared and pulled up a chair. Johnson leaned in toward us and in his folksiest style said, 'Now, boys, let me tell you something. Sometimes you may see me coming out of a room in the White House with a woman. You just remember,' he said, wagging a long index finger at "the boys," 'that is none of your business.' So he was pretty up front about it. He wanted the same rules for himself that Kennedy had. We just said, 'Yes, sir,' and stuck to it pretty much. That's just the way things were then."

Though as president Johnson could no longer afford to maintain the "nooky room" he kept for his affairs in Congress, he still wanted to be surrounded by beautiful women. He ordered director of White House personnel John Macy to find "the five smartest, best educated, fastest, prettiest secretaries in Washington. And don't send me any broken-down old maids. I want them twenty-five to forty."

It wasn't just LBJ who loved women, women loved him, too. "One thing you've got to remember about LBJ," his consumer affairs adviser Betty Furness recalled, "is that he looked like a president. He had enormous presence. In the first place he was an enormous man. I think he was larger physically than most people think. It took my breath away to walk through the door of the office to meet this man."

In the White House, Lady Bird exercised firm but loving control over her husband's appetites. She could assert herself more because he needed her more. She could even remove some of his "women friends." Sometime in early 1964, Lady Bird told her husband that now that they were in the national spotlight, he must do something about his "friendship" with Eloise Thornberry, the wife of Texas congressman Homer Thornberry. Thornberry held the seat vacated by Johnson and was a long-standing political ally of the president. His tall, blond wife was known to be something more. Johnson appointed Congressman Thornberry to a federal judgeship in Texas.

Barbara Howar, an attractive blond writer and fellow southerner, was in and out of the White House during the Johnson years. Lady Bird always kept an eye out for her. "She was very vigilant. But I always felt there was a kindness to it," said Howar. Lady Bird stepped in just when the young Howar most needed her. "She knew how to interfere in his flirtations. When the president and I were too long in another room, she would call, 'Lyndon, don't be a hog, we all want to talk to you and Barbara.'" Even on the dance floor, Lady Bird knew how to minimize a potentially embarrassing situation. After her husband danced for fifteen minutes with Howar, for instance, Lady Bird took him firmly by the arm. "Now Lyndon," she told him, "I know a young girl who is very tired and a president who has a mighty big day tomorrow."

Lady Bird would even enlist the help of presidential aides to keep her husband in line. Television reporter Nancy Dickerson recalled staying in a Chicago airport motel along with the presidential party. A pajama-clad President Johnson knocked on her door. "It wasn't very romantic," Dickerson remembered. "He kept pacing back and forth in his bare feet, waving his arms, and I had curlers in my hair." Within minutes, Bill Moyers, the president's press secretary, arrived at her door, dispatched by Lady Bird. Moyers suggested that everyone get some sleep—alone. "LBJ was astonished to see Bill but not really angry. He just muttered something like 'What the hell is he doing here?' "

Lady Bird knew that she was among the few people in the world from whom Lyndon would—grudgingly—accept criticism. "You want to listen for about one minute to my critique?" she asked the president following his March 7, 1964, news conference. "Or would you rather wait until tonight?" "Yes, ma'am," the president replied without enthusiasm, "I'm willing now." As always, Lady Bird packaged her review in a thick coat of praise. "You looked strong, firm and like a reliable guy. Your looks were splendid," she told her husband. "During the [opening] statement you were a little breathless and there was too much looking down and I think it was a little too fast. Not enough change of pace. Dropping [your] voice at the end of sentence[s]. There was a considerable pickup in drama and interest when the questioning began. Your voice was noticeably better and your facial expressions noticeably better. . . . I really didn't like the answer on de Gaulle. . . . I believe you actually have said out loud that you don't believe you ought to go out of the country this year. So I don't think you can very well say that you will meet him any time that is convenient for both people."

There was no one else in the White House who would have given the president this bold an appraisal. Yet even with her he was defensive. "I didn't say where I'd go. I didn't say I'd go out of the country at all, did I?" Lady Bird pressed on undeterred. "When you're going to have a prepared text, you need to have the opportunity to study it a little bit more and to read it with a little more conviction and interest and change of pace," she told him. "The trouble is," he interjected, "they criticize you for taking so much time. They want to use it all for questions. Then their questions don't produce any news. And if you don't give them news, you catch hell." His wife was not so easily put off. "In general, I'd say it was a good B plus."

Johnson attacked the presidency like a starving man attacks a square meal. All his manic energy, banked during three frustrating years as vice president, rushed out now in an unstoppable torrent. "I would stand back and watch Lyndon Johnson," his defense secretary, Clark Clifford, recalled. "He reminded me of those great massive steam locomotives that at one time was the major source of transportation power in this country and you'd see this great locomotive coming. It would be big and noisy and would go by with a tremendous rush that was truly awe-inspiring and, to a great extent, that would describe Lyndon Johnson. He was accustomed to getting his way, and as a result of that, people would give him his way."

Above all, he needed to prove he was the man in charge. "He derived a certain enjoyment from being in a superior position to the person with whom he was talking," Clifford noted. "He was superior to his staff people, he was superior to his Cabinet people, he was superior to practically everybody, unless he wanted something from the Hill." The Kennedys haunted him, tied him in a bizarre love-hate knot. "There was some defensiveness on his part with eastern intellectuals. He felt at a disadvantage with them—they had had the benefit of educations at Harvard or Columbia . . . and had connections and opportunities that he had never had," Clifford said. He simply could not reconcile himself to anybody not loving him, and Bobby Kennedy could not love him. "I recognized it," Lady Bird remembered, "knew it was something we had to be aware of and have sense enough to understand, that to Bobby his brother was a knight in shining armor and Lyndon was a ruffian intruder."

Johnson relied on his wife to smooth his way in delicate human relationships. Unlike her husband, Lady Bird's sense of self was not tied to the approval of others. She also had almost bottomless patience for human frailties. "I grieved for Bobby," she said, her voice trailing off for a moment. "But I did not feel inferior to the Kennedys." Johnson, though not a reflective man, innately understood her ability to calm not only his storms but those of others. He summoned her to say the soothing words he could not. In the middle of a conversation with Secretary of Defense, and Kennedy ally, Robert McNamara, Johnson put Lady Bird on the line. "Anybody like you who would take time to say a word to me, not to Lyndon . . . ," she cooed in her molasses-thick southern drawl. "You-all are the big staff we lean on."

Lyndon and Lady Bird approached human relationships from opposite poles. Johnson sought to exploit the weaknesses of others. He bullied people and observed how they withstood the bullying. Lady Bird tried to disarm them with charm. She worked her magic on the influential *New York Times* columnist James Reston with an invitation. "Sometime, I would like to show you, quietly and serenely, if possible," she purred in her most honeyed voice, "the wonderful country which has made our life, and which has made Lyndon whatever he is because it is the Lord's blessedest piece of real estate. . . ."

In his first two months, the new president received almost seven hundred people in the Oval Office. Johnson was desperate to have Congress pass the Civil Rights Bill. In theory it was to honor his predecessor, but in fact the bill was about Johnson. He worked friends and enemies as only he could: cajoling, harassing, terrorizing and charming until they cried uncle. "He knew the men on the Hill quite well," Clifford said, "and he knew how he could get them to support him in reaching whatever goal that he had. He was devious. He was complex. He could be duplicitous. He used all of his natural assets and almost every artifice to persuade persons on the Hill to agree with him."

Johnson drew no boundaries between his public and personal lives. Unlike during the Kennedy stewardship, the White House under the Johnsons did not have an "Upstairs/Downstairs" divide. The president's staff was part of his family. Johnson liked to bring aides upstairs for dinner, unannounced. Chief Usher Rex Scouten recalled that arguing with the Johnson family cook, Zephyr Wright, was one of the president's great joys. "Zephyr was not a bit intimidated, gave as good as she got." At first the staff were astounded at the president's crudeness, but they soon got used to it. "He was one of those people that you just accepted as, This is Texas. This is the way he does business. Our biggest concern was Mrs. Johnson," Scouten noted, "how he affected her." But after a while Scouten said he realized that "He loved her. In his way he loved her. She was his. Lynda and Luci were his. He was not your average kind of guy." Scouten, a former Secret Service agent, said, "At Secret Service conventions, even now, agents tell one hundred stories about Lyndon Johnson for one story of every other president."

"He was the same with everybody," Scouten asserted. "You knew sooner or later your turn would come. Even if you were just standing there, you'd get bawled out or fired. Just standing around could get you in trouble. The clearest sign of how different he was from other presidents was that normally a half a dozen staffers and hangers-on would walk the president from the Oval Office to the residence. With President Johnson, only the Secret Service agents walked home with him."

On most mornings, the couple would be woken by a soft rap on their door, and aides Jack Valenti and Bill Moyers would be beckoned to enter. "And there was Mrs. Johnson," Valenti recalled, "in bed with her husband. She would perform the most extraordinary act of grace. She would remove herself from bed and instead of saying, 'Oh, my hair!,' she would say, 'Jack, Bill, how are you?' and then to her husband, 'Now Lyndon, don't work these young men too hard.' And then, in her nightgown, with marvelous dignity, she moved into the other bedroom." No matter how exhausting life with her human dynamo was, she always thought of him first. "Bone tired . . . ," she wrote in her diary on January 8, 1964, after her husband delivered his first State of the Union address. "If it is that way with me, what must it have been like with Lyndon?"

Valenti recalled many times when Lady Bird would step in to temper her husband's outbursts. "One time he was beating up on me and she said, 'Lyndon, no one serves you with more devotion than Jack. Do you think he deserves that?' Johnson would not say 'I am sorry'—he never said that—but he would move on. Only she could do that. Because when he crossed that line, she knew it, and she would put up a barrier there and he would stop." Scouten recalled Lady Bird scurrying in her husband's wake, dispensing soothing words. "He didn't mean that," she'd say to abused staff. "He has so much on his mind." She tried to atone for his misdeeds, Scouten said, noting that Johnson knew just how far he could push people. "He knew people's limits. He never abused Bill Moyers because he knew Moyers would walk out. With Valenti he'd call him every name in the book." Nor did he abuse the aristocratic Clifford. "He had nothing that I wanted . . . I never asked him for anything—I had never suggested even obliquely that I was interested in coming into his administration, so that placed me in an unusual posture with him," Clifford explained.

So hungry was Johnson for affection and affirmation that at times he resented his wife for getting more of it than he himself got. Philanthropist Mary Lasker told the president she was thinking of giving Lady Bird a letter autographed by Thomas Jefferson, since members of Mrs. Johnson's family had the middle name Jefferson. "I told [Lady Bird] about the letter," Lasker remembered, "and she sounded delighted. And then I told the President when he got on the phone and he said, 'Why are you giving anything to her? Do you like her better than you like me?' and I said, 'Well, it's her family name. Besides the letter is from Jefferson explaining that since he's out of office he no longer has any influence with the federal government.' The President said, 'Come to think of it, neither do I.' "

One evening in the upstairs residence, Clifford complimented Lady Bird, adding in a teasing manner, "I think we ought to arrange a ceremony and canonize Lady Bird. . . . Wouldn't it be great if we had a St. Lady Bird?' And I looked over at the president expecting to find the same kind of amusement on his part, and his face was just as glum as it could be. I got a little signal from that. I had seen on other occasions that when you were with Lyndon Johnson the main subject that you should devote yourself to was Lyndon Johnson."

NO GOAL seemed beyond Johnson's powers of persuasion his first year as president. He cajoled big business, and he got the so-called Rockefeller Republicans and hard-right Democrats who hated him to respond to his pleas of "I need your help." In the White House, he was everywhere, his voice echoing through the downstairs marble foyer, reverberating through every corner of the mansion. "Here, comb your hair," he would order startled UPI White House correspondent Helen Thomas, offering a comb from his pocket. "Put on some lipstick," he commanded his wife. No detail of the running of the ship of state or of his household was too trivial to merit his attention. He persuaded a pricey New York hairdresser to come and "do" all his "womenfolk": his wife, daughters, secretaries—not for money, for the millionaire president pleaded poverty, but for the privilege. "If you don't want me running around the White House naked," he told Joe Haggar, the president of a clothing company, "you better get me some clothes." The president then proceeded to instruct Haggar on how to cut his pants. "Make the pockets at least an inch longer. My money and my knife and everything fall out. . . . The crotch, down where your nuts hang, is always a little too tight. . . . Give me an inch that I can let out there because they cut me. They're just like riding a wire fence."

Years later Lady Bird would admit grudgingly that she "did feel Lyndon should tone down his behavior at times. I did not manage to convey that to him very successfully, however. Generally, my advice was couched in very tempered terms." Texas congressman Ralph Yarborough described Johnson as a "bank walker." In his best east Texas twang, Yarborough would explain, "When I was a boy we'd all get in the swimming hole, go skinny dipping. There was always one boy who liked to walk the bank, cause he was pretty well hung. That was Johnson."

When his wife was away, Johnson was often off balance. He would sometimes ask Homer Busby to sit in his bedroom and talk to him until he fell asleep. "Don't just lope off," he pleaded with Moyers. "I want to know where I can reach you on a minute's notice." At times he tried to fill the emptiness with alcohol. Lady Bird chided him about this recurring weakness for drink in lonely, stressful or idle moments. Johnson let fly that Jack Kennedy had been "shacked up" twice a day in the White House. His wife replied that if the Russians "press the button," a president can always jump out of bed. It is harder to get out of a bottle. Johnson switched from scotch to Fresca.

Unlike most of his predecessors, Johnson would allow himself no relief from the annihilating pressures of the job. April 6, 1964 was a red-letter day, prompting Lady Bird to write in her diary, "Something happened that I have been wanting to happen for about nine years or more. Lyndon played golf! Maybe he'll do it once a week and it would make a lot of difference for him . . . in health, in joy in life." But it turned out to be a nearly unique event.

In the spring of 1964, LBJ announced his plans for a Great Society: "to move not only toward the rich society and the powerful society but upward to the Great Society." Fearing failure as much as he yearned for glory, he wavered about running for election in the fall. He felt he was "from the wrong part of the country," too different from his predecessor.

The mounting uncertainty of the war in Southeast Asia added to his anxiety. In August, American destroyers were attacked in the Gulf of Tonkin by North Vietnamese PT boats, or so he and McNamara claimed; it was a much disputed event. But with his genius for persuading Congress to do his bidding, Johnson rammed through the Tonkin Bay resolution, clearing the way for full-scale war in Vietnam.

Still, unlike JFK, foreign affairs had been neither his passion nor his strength. Lady Bird noted with foreboding, "That's not Lyndon's kind of presidency." She wrote him a nine-page letter, outlining why she thought he should run: there was too much he still wanted to achieve, he had too much energy to retire. "And I dread seeing you semi-idle, frustrated, looking back at what you left. I dread seeing you look at Mr. X running the country and thinking you could have done it better. You may look around for a scapegoat. I do not want to be it. You may drink too much—for lack of a higher calling. . . . Stay in. . . ."

How many other presidents faced with equally hard choices might have been saved by letters this blunt, this knowing and this loving? Could anyone but a spouse write with such authority? It is not enough, however, to have a wife willing to confront her husband's weaknesses head-on—as Lady Bird was. Her partner must also be open to her counsel. "Through our years together I have come to value Lady Bird's opinion of me, my virtues and flaws," Johnson wrote in his memoirs. But so tortured was Johnson that he could not come to a decision for months. All of his self-doubt, his bruised feelings from media depictions of him as the buffoon in Camelot, surfaced. "I was not thinking just of the derisive articles about my style, my clothes, my manner, my accent, and my family—although I admit I received enough of that kind of treatment in my first few months to last a lifetime. I was also thinking of a more deep-seated and far-reaching attitude—a disdain for the South that seems to be woven into the fabric of Northern experience."

As usual, there was only one person with whom he could share his torment. "At 3:30 or 4 A.M. Lyndon woke up," Lady Bird wrote in her diary on July 15, "and I don't think either of us went back to sleep the rest of the night. He described to me in detail the problems, the pros and cons, the good points and the bad, of every decision that faces him with regard to this campaign—every sensitive job to be filled, every spot on the battlefield that needs to be manned. So it was a wakeful night, with about two hours' sleep."

In late August, the day after the opening of the Democratic convention, the president finally made up his mind. "Our country faces grave dangers," Johnson wrote in his prepared statement to the nation. "These dangers must be faced and met by a united people under a leader they do not doubt. After thirty-three years in political life most men acquire enemies, as ships accumulate barnacles. The times require leadership about which there is no doubt and a voice that men of all parties, sections and color can follow. I have learned after trying very hard that I am not that voice or that leader."

The self-pity and the plea for love masked Johnson's desire to be begged to run. In a moment of remarkable candor, he told Walter Jenkins, "People . . . think I want great power. And what I want is great solace—and a little love. That is all I want." For Johnson, votes meant love. Before delivering his statement, he asked the person who best understood him what she thought. "Beloved," she wrote him, "you are as brave a man as Harry Truman—or FDR—or Lincoln. . . . You have been strong, patient, determined beyond any words of mine to express. I honor you for it. So does most of the country. To step out now would be wrong for your country, and I can see nothing but a lonely wasteland for your future. Your friends would be frozen in embarrassed silence and your enemies jeering. I am not afraid of *Time* or lies or losing money or defeat. In the final analysis I can't carry any of the burdens you talked of—so I know it's only your choice. But I know you are as brave as any of the thirty-five. I love you always, Bird."

She understood better than anyone else that he needed reassurance more than reasoning. Whether or not he seriously considered withdrawing, Johnson credits his wife's letter with his final decision to run. "In a few words," Johnson wrote,

> she hit me on two most sensitive and compelling points, telling me that what I planned to do would be wrong for my country and that it would show a lack of courage on my part. The message I read most clearly in her note to me was that my announcement to the 1964 con-

vention that I would not run would be taking the easy way out. I decided finally that afternoon, after reversing my position of the morning and with a reluctance known to very few people, that I would accept my party's nomination.

The president's speechwriter, Harry McPherson, was astonished at the intimacy between the Johnsons.

They had a relationship that was everything that one would hope to have in a marriage. He trusted her advice and judgment. But more than that, we'd be in a meeting—it might include the Chairman of the Joint Chiefs and the Secretary of State and a couple of staff people from the White House and Lady Bird would walk through. And the President would stop and say, "Come here," and he'd look at her dress and say, "I don't like the yoke on the neck of it. Let me see the back." He really related to her and loved her.... He sure depended on her. Among public men that is a rare thing.

Richard Nixon was startled when he encountered the Johnsons' closeness. "As I got off the elevator on the second floor of the White House," Nixon recalled in his memoirs, "a butler greeted me and escorted me to Johnson's room. He was sitting in bed in his pajamas. 'Hello, Dick,' he said. His voice was extremely hoarse and he looked tired, almost to the point of exhaustion.... I had not been in the room long when the door opened and Mrs. Johnson walked in, wearing a dressing gown. She greeted me warmly, got into bed beside her husband and joined us for the remainder of our conversation."

The dark side of Johnson's dependence on his wife was his occasional cruelty toward her. Clark Clifford never forgot one particular family dinner. "From the moment she appeared he began attacking [her] dress, mockingly asking why she was wearing that 'dreadful yellow thing.' Finally almost in tears, Lady Bird left the room before we sat down to eat, returning a few minutes later in another dress. The rest of the evening went on as though nothing had happened. As Marny [Mrs. Clifford] and I drove home that night, we could not contain our anger at his treatment of Lady Bird."

Katharine Graham of the *Washington Post* did not contain her anger during another instance of Johnson's brutal behavior. Following the 1964 Democratic convention, during a stay at the Johnson ranch, the president obsessively berated his wife for accepting some social obligation without checking with him. He continued to berate Lady Bird until Graham could stand no more. "Yes, she did get you into this thing tonight," she told the president, "but she also got you where you are today." Johnson then shifted his attack to Graham until she blurted out, "Oh, shut up!" (Later she wondered if she should have added "Mr. President.")

He rewarded Lady Bird's love and loyalty with a growing dependence. The great and dangerous love affair with Alice Glass was long over. In February 1964 Johnson asked an aide to reply to a letter from Alice. "You read this," he instructed the aide, "and write a nice letter. She's an old friend. She's Charlie Marsh's ex-wife. She's alone—and an alcoholic."

During the 1964 campaign, his wife proved she could be much more than the provider of the stable base for Lyndon's pyrotechnics. She took off on a whistle-stop tour through the South, a region seething after passage of Johnson's Civil Rights Act. "It was the first time I focused on her as something other than the lady attached to my boss," McPherson recalled. "She took a dozen women with her—all dressed alike in red, white and blue—in a brilliant stroke to reassure the region it had a presidential nominee who would be attentive to the South." The train rolled out of Virginia and ended up in New Orleans, picking up politicians and their wives as it wound its leisurely way. In her soft drawl, which seemed to get deeper with each mile away from Washington, Lady Bird told crowds, "I wanted to make this trip because I am proud of the South and I am proud that I am part of the South. I'm fond of the old customs—of keeping up with your kinfolk, of long Sunday dinner after church, of a special brand of gentility and courtesy." But her message was not all honey and molasses. "We are a nation of laws," she affirmed, "not men, and our greatness is our ability to adjust to the national consensus. The law to assure equal rights passed by Congress last July with three-fourths of the Republicans joining two-thirds of the Democrats. . . . This convinces me of something I have always believed—that there is in this Southland more love than hate."

In Columbia, South Carolina, however, Lady Bird encountered more hate than love. Before she could begin her speech, there were angry shouts of "We want Barry [Goldwater]! We want Barry!" "My friends," Lady Bird said, with one hand raised, "in this country we are entitled to many viewpoints. You are entitled to yours. But right now I am entitled to mine." The crowd grew quiet and that night all three networks featured stories of the first lady's courage. But LBJ's reaction to her triumph was ambivalent. "The president was both very pleased with her success," his friend William S. White commented, "and, I thought, in a slight way somewhat jealous of it. I think he didn't particularly like it when people suggested that she'd made a major contribution to the campaign."

IN EARLY 1965, Johnson decided to commence the bombing of North Vietnam—Operation Rolling Thunder. What the Pentagon did not tell the commander in chief was that once the heavy bombing was under way, American ground troops would have to follow. Johnson and his closest advisers, especially McNamara, did not push the Pentagon hard enough for full disclosure of the operation's consequences. McNamara and Dean Rusk, along with Johnson's national security assistant, McGeorge Bundy, argued for a tough response to Hanoi's mounting aggression against South Vietnam. Eighty-three percent of the American people supported the bombing. When General William Westmoreland, the new American commander in Vietnam, requested the first American ground troops—ostensibly to protect American air bases—there was little public debate. It was sold to the nation as a defensive measure, when in reality the military was already planning offensive operations. Johnson's "credibility gap" had begun.

"Domino theory" entered the national lexicon: American withdrawal from South Vietnam would lead to the overthrow of weak democracies in Thailand, Korea, Laos and Cambodia by Soviet-supported Communist regimes. Pressure on the president to escalate was intense. But there was also an opportunity to declare, as Kennedy had done after the Bay of Pigs, that a mistake had been made, that this was not our war, before another 100,000 American ground troops were dispatched. Historically, the American people have been more likely to accept an open admission of error on the part of their leaders than to accept deception. But Johnson was constitutionally incapable of admitting error. He would not be the first president to lose a war, whatever the cost.

As always, Lady Bird shared her husband's burdens. By 1965, much of her natural ebullience had evaporated. "For some time I have been swimming upstream against a feeling of depression and relative inertia. I flinch from activity and involvement, and yet I rust without them. Lyndon lives in a cloud of troubles, with few rays of light." Not only the mounting death toll in Vietnam but the homegrown rage of the South dragged down the presidency. Lady Bird could offer little solace now, as the presidency veered away from Johnson's dreams. "Sometimes it makes me almost angry because he's spending himself so," Lady Bird wrote in her diary on June 10, 1965, "but then I don't know a better thing in the world to spend yourself for. Today has been one of those days, made up of long sessions with Maxwell Taylor, Rusk, McNamara . . . it's really strange the idea the press has of Lyndon's lack of interest in or grasp of foreign affairs. He spends so many more hours of his day working on foreign affairs than on anything else."

Johnson's aides remember a depressed president in 1965. "He would just go within himself," Moyers said, "just disappear—morose, self-pitying, angry. . . . He was a tormented man." His wife worried about his health. "He is much too heavy," she wrote in her diary. "I do not know whether to lash out in anger or sarcasm, or just remind him for the nine hundred and ninety-ninth time." He had few illusions about the domestic consequences of the escalating war. But his natural compulsion to win blocked him from doing anything else. "Losing the Great Society was a terrible thought," he said, "but not so terrible as the thought of being responsible for America's losing a war to the Communists. Nothing could possibly be worse than that."

By late summer of 1965, there were two hundred thousand American troops in Vietnam, and still the president had defined neither the mission nor his strategy clearly. The anti-war movement picked up steam. The White House itself was under siege. For Johnson, the blow was personal. He was crushed that he was losing America's youth, who chanted, "Hey, hey, LBJ, how many kids did you kill today?" "I guess the saddest thing was to think about all those years when Lyndon was the youngest," Lady Bird recalled. "He thought of himself as the champion of the young . . . felt he was one of the young. And then to have them turn against him, that was particularly poignant."

He continued to get important legislation passed, however, including the Voting Rights Act of 1965. "And we shall overcome," the president told Congress, dramatically embracing black Americans' slogan as his own. But there was no relief from the war's agony. The president and therefore also his wife were not sleeping well. "This day began in the early hours of the morning with a long talk," Lady Bird wrote in her diary on January 11, 1966. "Lyndon woke up as he often does these nights, and we talked about the prospects for the years ahead. They are so fraught with danger and with decisions whose outcome we cannot see. . . . And my advice to Lyndon is so mundane and uninspiring: stay healthy, laugh a little, remember you are as tough as other presidents who have lived through the same or worse." It was impossible for her husband to follow this advice. Late at night a pajama-clad Johnson wandered downstairs to the Situation Room to ask startled duty officers about the latest casualty figures.

"I had coffee with Lyndon about 8:30 this morning," Lady Bird wrote on March 10, "but these days I feel as if I'm part of a staff meeting. . . . [His aides] come to his room when he first wakes up and while he drinks cup after cup of tea give him reports, ask decisions, analyze the business of his day, discuss yesterday's triumphs and troubles and go over the appointments. It is a pattern of intense mental strain, totally unrelated to the luxurious idea of breakfast in bed. And I wait my turn to get a word in edgewise."

The toughest part was that he was not even sure he was doing the right thing. "It was a thorn stuck in his throat," his wife recalled. "It wouldn't come up or go down." Meanwhile, Lady Bird found release in another cause that suited her—flowers and trees and unspoiled scenery. She persuaded the president to support legislation to clean up the nation's blighted highways, and the word "beautification" became permanently associated with her. But she achieved far more than what that word normally implies. In those days, billboards hawking everything from cigarettes to motels lined the highways. Flowers were a rare sight in inner-city neighborhoods. She linked the sixties' crisis of the spirit with the ugliness of the urban environment. Lady Bird traveled to forty-eight states to promote conservation. She left a permanent mark on Washington, D.C., where each spring a profusion of wildflowers along the Potomac and in parks scattered throughout the city recall her tenure, and a park now carries her name.

Laurence Rockefeller, a fellow environmentalist and member of the great New York philanthropic and banking family, often traveled with Lady Bird. Like so many others, Rockefeller sensed that behind her soft-spoken facade was an iron will. "There's no question that Mrs. Johnson was a real professional person," Rockefeller recalled. "She worked hard to achieve great results. . . . I'm always awed by the way she focuses her attention and her conversation and her effort on things that she considered top priority." Lady Bird, like Eleanor Roosevelt, had a sharp sense of the media's role in getting her message out. She made good use of the White House as bully pulpit. The reporters who covered her liked her. Lady Bird called them by their first names and, unlike Jacqueline Kennedy, treated them like colleagues, not annoyances.

Away from her looming husband, a different woman emerged. Three decades of public life had altered the insecure girl. In the forests, parks and rivers whose reclamation she made her cause, she was herself. "To see Mrs. Johnson," wrote a reporter who accompanied her to Redwood National Park, "in the depths of that great, primeval, dripping forest is to understand immediately why she is called Lady Bird. Tiny, always a smaller woman than one had quite remembered, she is slimmer now than ever. She twitters. She is cheery, modest, persistent and alert and her avian qualities are intensified by those looming, green black and ultimately incomprehensible trees. Among them, dedicating the Redwood National Park, Lady Bird in her scarlet coat looked like a jaunty red cardinal."

Stewart Udall, Johnson's secretary of the interior, accompanied Lady Bird on trips that mixed politics and conservation through Wyoming, Montana and Utah. "She came back with quite a glow and really determined . . . that she wanted to carve out a career and a place of her own and do something in her own right," he reported. But Lyndon's needs did not leave enough time for her to achieve the great goals she set for herself. As always, she blamed only herself. "One thing I am sorry about was that I was not more businesslike, cool, determined and self-confident about trying to get what I thought the White House should have . . . ," she said later, typically underrating herself. "I did not use the leverage—and it is leverage—of publicity."

The sixties were an edgy time of transition, change and confusion. In 1963 Betty Friedan published her book *The Feminine Mystique,* in which she claimed that "the problem that has no name burst like a boil through the image of the happy American housewife." The same year, an American woman, the physicist Maria Goepper-Mayer, won a Nobel Prize for the first time. The civil rights and anti-war movements politicized and radicalized a growing number of women bombarded with contradictory expectations and images about work and family. While Lesley Gore's hit song "You Don't Own Me" climbed the charts, *Leave It to Beaver* and *Father Knows Best* dominated television. One in five women with children under six and nearly one-fourth of women whose children were over sixteen held paid jobs in the sixties. Their pay, however, was 60 percent of the male rate. Though equal pay legislation passed in 1963, that did not solve the problem of low pay in jobs that were classed as female.

During this muddled decade, the qualities that made Lady Bird essential to her husband also endeared her to the country. Modest, loyal and smart, she stood by her man, but just a little behind him too. "I'm terribly average," she said, "something like litmus paper." She saw her role essentially as the president's mainstay. "The best thing I can do for him is to try to create a pleasant little island where he can work—where you like the food and where you are not constantly bothered with questions about household and family and where you know you're coming back to somebody [*sic*] who, even if they don't always agree with what you are doing, are not going to [criticize you]." She provided reassurance not only for her husband but for the country in the throes of social upheaval.

SHE CALLED IT "THE MIASMA," the black mood that hung over the White House from 1966 until the end of the Johnson presidency. The man who took hold of the careening state in 1963, who had pulverized opposition to his domestic programs, was lost in a war he didn't even believe in. "I knew we were going to get into this sort of mess when we went in there," he told Georgia senator Richard Russell on May 27, 1964. "And I don't see how we're ever going to get out of it without fighting a major war with the Chinese and all of them down there in those rice paddies and jungles. . . . I just don't know what to do. . . ."

Kennedy's ghost hovered over the Cabinet Room. The Harvards still advised Johnson. The president had been dazzled by Defense Secretary Robert McNamara's precision and McGeorge Bundy's intellect, and they counseled against letting this "damn little pissant country" humiliate the United States of America. "When five of the most patriotic and wise experts come to you and say this is the path . . . ," Lady Bird noted, "well, ultimately you have to choose. But it was hard to know what was right." Vietnam brought out the worst in Johnson. He could not detach from it emotionally the way Kennedy had from the disaster of the Bay of Pigs. He wanted to be loved, but instead he was accused of killing kids. The sight of body bags coming home sank him deeper and deeper into depression and paranoia. His aide Eric Goldman remembered Johnson, the domestic reformer turned war chief, as "bitter, truculent, peevish— and suspicious of the fundamental good sense and integrity of anyone who did not endorse the Vietnam War. This Lyndon Johnson was not only depressing; at times he could be downright frightening."

More and more the president needed his wife beside him, even during news conferences. "At three o'clock I went down with Lyndon to the East Room for his press conference. My role was to sit in the front row and look pleasant and yet these conferences always affect me as though I were going into battle." Increasingly, the reporters' questions shifted from Great Society legislation to the war. "And then it was over and [Lyndon] took my arm. I threw him a congratulatory look with my eyes, which I meant to be all balm and velvet." By the final year of his presidency, many of his closest aides—Jenkins, Moyers, McNamara—had left

May 17, 1966. President Johnson kissing Lady Bird
on the forehead after a Rose Garden ceremony.

or were leaving. Lady Bird's legendary self-control was stretched thin, as she fought to maintain a calm veneer and keep her own anxiety from her husband. "I turned off the TV and went over to the bowling lanes, where I used up my energy in three games, hurling a heavier ball than usual and running up scores in the 150s—all by myself. Not much fun, but exercise, and while I'm doing it I don't think much about anything else," she wrote.

But in times of national crisis, there is no escape in the White House. The television vans by the West Wing, the army of commentators, microphone in hand, on the front lawn, the endless line of black limousines disgorging congressmen and national security staff in the driveway—all transmit the same message. The distant war had seeped into all aspects of life in the White House. On January 18, Lady Bird assembled a group of "Women Doers" in the upstairs family dining room to talk about crime in the streets. Suddenly, one of the invited guests, the singer Eartha Kitt, rose to her feet. Looking straight at Mrs. Johnson, she said, "Boys I know across the nation feel it doesn't pay to be a good guy. They figure with a record they don't have to go off to Vietnam. We send the best of the country off to be shot and maimed. . . . They don't want to go to school because they are going to be snatched from their mothers to be shot in Vietnam. . . . You are a mother too," she said, pointing a finger at Lady Bird. "I am a mother and I know the feeling of having a baby come out of my guts. I have a baby and then you send him off to war. No wonder the kids rebel and take pot. And, Mrs. Johnson, in case you don't under-stand the lingo, that's marijuana!"

An ashen Lady Bird fought for composure, feeling "first a wave of mounting disbelief. Can this be true? Is this a nightmare? Then a sort of surge of adrenaline into the blood, knowing that you are going to answer, that you've got to answer, that you want to answer. . . . Somewhere along the way—I think between the words 'gut' and 'pot'—I had a sense that maybe she was undoing her point. Miss Kitt stopped for breath to a stunned silence in the room and for a second I waited to see whether it was a comma or a period."

Her voice trembling slightly, Lady Bird replied, "Because there is a war on, that doesn't give us a free ticket not to try to work for better things—against crime in the streets, and for better education and better health for our people. I cannot identify as much as I should. I have not lived the background that you have, nor can I speak as passionately or as well, but we must keep our eyes and our hearts and our energies fixed on constructive areas and try to do something that will make this a happier, better educated land." With great presence of mind, Lady Bird turned a moment of supreme tension into a personal triumph. Her openness, her modesty and her fearlessness impressed everyone in the room. Only Lady Bird and her beleaguered husband knew the full price the daily stress exacted from them both.

Woodrow Wilson's portrait in the Red Room became a daily re-minder of the presidency's toll. "I . . . never looked at it that I didn't think that it might happen to me," Johnson said, "that I would end another term in bed with a stroke and that the decisions of government would be taken care of by other people and that was wrong. I didn't want that to happen." During a fall 1967 stay at the ranch, Lady Bird finally vented her feelings about her husband's political future. "I simply did not want to face another campaign, to ask anybody for anything.

Mainly the fear that haunts me is that if Lyndon were back in office for a four-year stretch—beginning when he was sixty years old—bad health might overtake him, an attack, though something not completely incapacitating, and he might find himself straining to be the sort of a president he wanted to be—to put in eighteen hours a day—and unable to draw enough vitality from the once bottomless well of his energy."

∞

BY 1967, HALF A MILLION AMERICAN TROOPS were fighting in Vietnam. Sixteen thousand of them were killed in action the same year. Americans were watching their first "living room war," and resistance was growing. The president talked of the need for peace talks, and of a "light at the end of the tunnel." But he shared his personal trauma, and his growing doubts about his own political future, with only one person. "Last night," Lady Bird wrote in her diary,

> was one of those bleak nights when the shadows take over. We both woke up about 3:30 A.M. and talked and talked and talked about when and how to make the statement that Lyndon is not going to be a candidate again. . . . In these discussions I feel that Lyndon reaches out to me more than ever, and yet I do not have the wisdom or the foresight for the answer. The only gift I have to give is the assurance that I will be content and happy saying good-bye to all this, much as I have loved it—deeply immersed as I have been in it every day, even the painful days.

In January 1968, during the Tet holiday period, the Vietcong launched a major offensive, mocking the "experts" who had predicted the end was near. No amount of number juggling or upbeat slogans about corners being turned could alter the basic fact: America's South Vietnamese allies were tired, corrupt and indifferent about their own government. American troops could not win the war for them. When the generals asked for two hundred thousand more troops, Johnson understood his Vietnam policy had failed. His job ratings at this point were the lowest they had ever been.

Lady Bird could no longer keep her fears about her husband's mental and physical state to herself. She poured her heart out to her husband's confidant, Abe Fortas. Did he agree with her that her husband could be "a happy man retired"? Couldn't he occupy himself as a rancher and maybe teach at the University of Texas? Fortas agreed the time had come.

Walking away from his life's greatest love was not easy for Lyndon Johnson. He kept postponing his decision, waiting for some deus ex machina to extricate him. Johnson's spirits rallied and he briefly reconsidered staying in the race after the Tet offensive. But it was a temporary lift. Sixty-three percent of his countrymen disapproved of his Vietnam policy. Bobby Kennedy announced he would run for president. Johnson's nightmare, that the Kennedy who seemed most hostile to him would reclaim his brother's throne, seemed to be coming true.

On March 31, 1968, the man who dreamed of greatness all his life faced the bright glare of television cameras in the Oval Office. "Remember," Lady Bird whispered in his ear, "pacing and drama." The president announced a partial bombing halt and called for Hanoi to join in peace talks to end the war. And then, looking momentarily off-camera at Lady Bird, said, "I shall not seek, and I will not accept, the nomination of my party for another term as your president."

The country and even many of his closest friends were stunned. Lady Bird, though, felt "immeasurably lighter." Relief was also her husband's immediate reaction. "The weight of the days and the weeks and the months had lifted. I had done what I knew ought to be done." But the awful year was not yet over. Within a few days, the president was back in front of the television cameras. The assassination of Dr. Martin Luther King, Jr., touched off a wave of arson, looting and terror in cities across the country. "I ask every citizen to reject the blind violence that has struck down Dr. King," the president pleaded, while smoke rose a few blocks from the White House.

Mindless violence struck again just two months later. Robert Kennedy was thanking his campaign workers in a narrow Los Angeles hotel corridor when Sirhan Sirhan emptied all eight bullets of his revolver into him. The Johnsons were ending their presidency as they had begun it.

Reeling from double grief, the country seemed to have lost its bearings. Through the year's convulsions, Lady Bird remained composed, even as her husband's legacy seemed in peril. The Democratic convention in Chicago revealed a party at war with itself. Lady Bird's gaze was fixed firmly on her beloved Texas hill country. She had no fears for her own future. That fall, another of her burdens was lifted when Jacqueline Kennedy married Onassis. "One of the oddest things is that as the result of the wedding which will happen tomorrow on a Greek island," she wrote in her diary, "I feel strangely free. No shadow walks beside me down the halls of the White House. . . . I wonder what it would have been like if we had entered this life unaccompanied by that shadow?"

Lyndon Johnson lived only four years after he left the White House. The great volcanic source of energy stopped flowing once he left politics. Rejected by the people and the country he had worked to change, he started eating and drinking more than he should. Lady Bird thought she was saving his life by getting him out of the White House. Perhaps she did. But she underestimated his need to stay "in the arena," as she put it. His old heart trouble flared up. In June 1972, he suffered a heart attack. His last speech, on December 11, 1972, was about civil rights, his proudest legacy. A humbler man than the one who left the White House, he claimed he was "sort of ashamed of myself, that I had six years and couldn't do more than I did. . . . To be a black in a white society isn't to stand on level and equal ground. While the races may stand side by side, whites stand on history's mountain and blacks stand in history's hollow. Until we overcome unequal history we cannot overcome unequal opportunity." His last speech was a reminder of LBJ at his best.

On January 22, 1973, Johnson suffered a fatal heart attack while he was taking an afternoon nap. A Secret Service agent who arrived within minutes with a small oxygen tank found Johnson unconscious on the floor. For once, the woman who had been by his side from the beginning was not there. Too late, Lady Bird rushed back from Austin. This man who hated being alone, died alone at his ranch. Afterward, Lady Bird said she was glad of one thing: her husband did not live to witness his successor's attempt to subvert the Constitution a few months later. Watergate would have broken Lyndon's heart, she said.

As for herself, she said she had no regrets about her life with him. He had delivered the adventure he had promised her on their first date in 1934. "Lyndon stretched me. He made us all perform," she said, laughing at some private memory. While Johnson's legacy is still wrapped in controversy, hers is beyond dispute. She made the Johnson presidency possible.

CHAPTER 6

PAT AND RICHARD NIXON

MISALLIANCE

For a long time I thought Daddy would be happier out of it all. Now I can see that he wouldn't. This is Daddy's whole life.

—JULIE NIXON EISENHOWER

They were locked in this dance of unhappiness. He felt indebted to her, and felt that he had won her and then imprisoned her. And she both admired him and hated the life. And there they were.

—DIANE SAWYER, *former Nixon aide*

THE TRANSITION FROM LYNDON JOHNSON TO RICHARD NIXON FOLLOWING so much national turbulence—was miraculously smooth. The contrast between the couple heading home to Texas and the new arrivals from California, however, was nothing short of stunning. The new tone was set the first night Pat and Dick Nixon moved into the White House. The president and first lady did not share the usual celebratory first evening meal. Pat asked for cottage cheese to be sent up to her bedroom, while her husband ordered steaks he shared with their two daughters and their husbands. It was the beginning of a presidency where the chief executive and his first lady lived virtually separate lives, carefully avoiding each other's company. The most betrayed first lady in American history was married to a president who never strayed from his marriage vows. He did not know how to flirt; he rarely even noticed other women. He betrayed his wife with his only real passion, politics.

Richard Nixon cut off the most valuable source of honest counsel a politician can have, that of the partner in the enterprise. He turned the lively redhead with the high cheekbones who had first caught his eye into a nearly silent partner. Nixon could never bring himself to ask his wife or his fellow citizens for understanding or forgiveness. He came close to embodying the Horatio Alger–type story of the self-made man, but in the end, his personal weaknesses doomed both his marriage and his presidency.

<hr />

THERE HAD BEEN WARNING SIGNS, assassination threats. In Caracas, Venezuela, the final stop on Pat and Dick Nixon's twelve-thousand-mile Latin American goodwill journey in 1958, they had been warned that there was going to be trouble. The local Communist party was expected to make maximum use of Vice President Nixon's arrival. The military junta was new, its enforcers were inexperienced. But Nixon was never one to retreat from combat; he felt most fully alive engaged in a good fight. As the Nixons emerged from *Air Force One* they could sense that the crowd below was not friendly. Skip the welcome speeches, Nixon instructed his military aide. Pat instinctively bent down to hug the little girl holding a bouquet for her. A grim Nixon pressed his wife toward the terminal. Just then, the Venezuelan army band struck up the country's national anthem. The Nixons froze where they stood. As if on cue, a shower of spit rained down on Pat and Dick from above. Saliva, brown from chewing tobacco, oozed down Pat's face and tracked her new red suit. Nixon stood rigid. He did not reach out to his wife with an arm or a handkerchief. Nixon preferred spit, or any other indignity, to betraying human emotion. It was not the first time his wife was reminded that no personal cost was too high for her husband's political ambition. In their marriage, the personal was always subordinated to the political.

By the time they reached the presidency, the Nixons were locked in a lifeless union, sustained by habit, a sense of duty and, on his part, political necessity. Could any woman have mitigated the blend of suspicion, anger and insecurity that propelled Nixon to the White House—and then destroyed him? Pat had long since stopped trying.

And yet it started as a love match. The Nixons' story began as a conventional pre–World War II romance. Twenty-four-year-old Dick knew the minute he saw Patricia Ryan that she was for him. He was proposing from the minute he met her, he said later. Like Lyndon Johnson, Nixon asked for his wife's hand on their first date. Pat was appalled and firmly declined. She was far from smitten. Nor did she understand Nixon's titanic willpower. But Dick knew that a small-town law practice would be the launching pad of his enormous ambitions. No matter how solitary a man he was, he would need a wife in that enterprise. Nixon was as determined in love as he would be in politics. For Nixon, life was combat.

Why a man with no natural charm, comfortable only in solitude and profoundly suspicious of everyone, would choose politics will forever remain a mystery. Pat surely sensed some hidden darkness and for a long time did not reciprocate his feelings. She had other beaus and a full life of her own as a Whittier, California, high school teacher. Her evasions only enhanced her appeal and his ardor. There was nothing he wouldn't do for the girl he called his "wild Irish Gypsy." Nixon even drove Pat on dates with other men. Nothing discouraged him. "Despite your refusal to let me be much more than an acquaintance," he wrote her with typical bathos, "by all that I hold sacred, Patricia, I say that you are a great lady—and now I think you know what I mean by that." His dogged pursuit—a carved pumpkin left on her doorstep at Halloween, a fully decorated tree at Christmas—finally wore her down. Together they would go places, he promised. Like Lady Bird, Pat longed for adventure and escape from small-town life. Like LBJ, Nixon delivered the adventure, but at an even higher price.

Pat and Dick were alike in some ways, dangerously different in others. Both were shaped by austere childhoods, marked by loss. Pat's mother died when she was twelve, her father five years later. Two of Richard's brothers died of tuberculosis. Neither Pat nor Dick had experienced much in the way of nurturing love. His dour, Quaker mother refrained from any show of physical affection and abandoned Dick for years while she nursed his sick brother. Pat and Dick were both secretive and self-disciplined to the point of near total repression. Dick did not find out until years later about Pat's mother's painful death from cancer. Pat did not even tell him that she had worked briefly as a movie extra and spent a few years in New York City. She kept hidden her mother's German birth and the fact that her father had died of the same disease that killed Dick's brother. She did not even tell him her real name, Thelma, until they went for their marriage license. They never broke through each other's defensive walls. This motherless daughter and this son of a hot-tempered Irishman survived by banking their emotions. Neither liked displays of feeling and would do almost anything to avoid confrontation. Dick was incapable of real sharing, of real love, perhaps because he had never really experienced it. He once revealed that his mother "never said 'I love you' because she considered that to be very private and very sacred. And I feel the same way. . . . I don't say . . . 'I love you' and the rest . . . that's just the way I was raised. . . . In my family we considered affection and love to be very private . . . we didn't think we had to prove it by saying publicly all the time 'I love you.' "

California at that time was a magnet for people prepared to give of their last measure to achieve their dreams. The citrus groves, the solitary pumping stations, the makeshift houses that dotted the dusty roads where both Nixons grew up marked a place of opportunity for only the most determined. The Nixons and the Ryans, of Irish and German stock, were of that unsentimental, dogged breed, prepared to keep moving until things worked out. Both families were religious, but theirs was a faith based on the belief that success comes to the tenacious, the uncomplaining men or women who put in the longest hours. Built in to that faith was a suspicion of the privileged—the wealthy, the smooth, the charming—to whom success comes too easily.

That bred-in-the-bone resentment fueled the Nixons' rise—as well as his eventual fall. "If your anger is deep enough," Nixon once told a friend, "and strong enough, you learn that you can change those attitudes by excellence, personal gut performance, while those who have everything are sitting on their fat butts." This bitter summation reveals a man whose success did not diminish his anger or his suspicion. "I can't let my hair down with anyone," he once confessed to the journalist Stewart Alsop, "not even with my family." Maintaining the facade was exhausting work, so Nixon's favorite companion was himself.

Pat was exceptionally independent for a woman of her generation. She colored her hair and wore bright red nail polish. But like her mother-in-law, Hannah Nixon, she was accustomed to hard work and keeping her own counsel. She had been the family's mainstay, keeping house and looking after her two brothers. "I am never tired," she once declared. Her father, like Nixon's, was a temperamental Irishman, so Pat learned to placate and look the other way.

Dick's courtship of Pat was as misleading about who he was as were his future political campaigns. "Dearest Heart," he wrote her, "I want to work with you toward the destiny you are bound to fulfill. As I have told you many times, living together will make us both grow—and by reason of it we shall realize our dreams." But even in courtship, he revealed his view that life was about struggle and called for a defiant attitude. Happiness was not a quality Nixon valued. When, much later, television journalist Diane Sawyer asked him if he was happy, Nixon cut her off, dismissing the question as both "stupid and trivial." "It is our job to go forth together and accomplish great ends and we shall do it too," he wrote Pat. And then, in a seemingly preemptive apology for all he would put her through, he added, "Whatever happens I shall always be with you—loving you more every hour and attempting to let you feel that love in your heart and life." Whatever passion, spontaneity and imagination he was capable of, Pat had stirred in him. For a brief period, she was the focus of all his drive and ambition. Never again did Nixon display affection so freely, except perhaps toward his daughters. His obsession with political success soon shut out anything else in his life.

Nixon married an ambitious woman who saw him as "going places." He promised horizons rare for Pat's generation. What he did not make clear was how he was going to get there. "There was no talk of politics or anything of that type," Pat said later, "I didn't even think in terms of that. He was doing well as a lawyer. He was well liked by everybody. He was always president of some group . . . so I knew that he would be successful in whatever he undertook." She aspired to the good life as the wife of an upwardly mobile California lawyer. A product of her time and place, Pat felt that a wife's duty was to help fulfill her husband's ambitions. But at the outset it was a marriage of equals, with the emotional advantage tilted in her favor. Nixon had been the cloying supplicant. With both of them fearful of emotions, communication between them stayed on the surface. Subjects more complex than those of everyday life were left unspoken. Thus began a lifetime of indirection and dismal miscommunication. Pat read in his intensity a zeal to make the world better. For, after all, Dick worshipped his remote mother, who retreated to her closet to pray and who dreamed her son would achieve great things. (Pat did not much like her crude, contentious father-in-law and discounted the father's influence on the son.)

In 1942, Pat had a premonition of what she had given up for this insistent young man. Like Lyndon Johnson, Dick joined the navy, leaving his wife on her own. "These many months you have been away," she wrote him, "have been full of interest and had I not missed you so much and had I been footloose, could have been extremely happy." And then, with a gentle warning that was really a plea, she wrote him, "So, Sweet, you'll always have to love me lots and never let me change my feelings for you." The intensity and the novelty of their early love—his particularly—compensated for their natural reserve. "I may not say much when I'm with you," he wrote her, "but all of me loves all of you all the time." She knew he was a loner, but felt she had penetrated his solitude. "I'm anti-social I guess," he wrote her, "but except for you, I'd rather be by myself as a steady diet rather than with most of any of the people I know. I like to do what I want, when I want. Only where you are concerned do I feel otherwise, Dear One."

His image enhanced by his snappy naval uniform, Nixon returned to launch the most unlikely career imaginable for such a man. In politics, he soon displayed the drive and tenacity of an Olympic champion. His first campaign in 1946, for a congressional seat, was against a five-term Democratic liberal, Jerry Voorhis. Nixon quickly developed a style of gloves-off campaigning that disoriented his opponent with insinuations impossible to prove but equally difficult to disprove. His skillful use of the nascent Red scare to tar his rivals with the dreaded label "Commie" won him two elections and the notice of Republican Party kingmakers. The paranoia of the time and the man meshed.

Pat and Dick adjusted to the California campaign trail. Within hours of their daughter Tricia's birth, Pat was researching congressional districts for her husband. She toned down her red nail polish, gave up smoking in public and, bit by bit, learned to drain her comments of any irreverence, personality or, God forbid, controversy. She had observed, first in the Voorhis campaign, then when her husband ran for the Senate against Helen Gahagan Douglas, what strong emotions Dick aroused in people. She came to realize that he was going to be a lightning rod for the rest of their lives. If she did anything that remotely fueled controversy, his career, the core of their existence, would be threatened. It was easier to assume the role her husband chose for her—a wife beyond reproach. A look of surreal serenity, the frozen smile that would soon earn her the Plastic Pat label, became her permanent expression. She had made her choice; she would believe in him. It was not in her nature to calculate the emotional cost of her sublimation.

Eight years into their marriage, her role as equal partner was over. "Once I make a decision, she supports it," he pronounced. The more self-effacing she became, the more he took her for granted. Whatever limited need he had for human interaction, Nixon transferred to a series of political operatives and subordinates. Murray Chotiner, a young Republican lawyer from Los Angeles, was the first aggressive, slash-and-burn campaign manager who preempted Pat's relationship with her husband. When Pat walked into a broadcast studio just before he was about to go on the air, Dick barked at her, "You know I never want to be interrupted when I am working!" He no longer welcomed her serious contribution to what was becoming his business alone. He could not take criticism from her or anyone else, so her role was reduced to bolstering his self-esteem. Always reticent, Pat became even more so.

It may not have been the marriage Pat once dreamed of, but the young California couple arrived in Washington in the winter of 1946 with bright prospects. The times were ripe with possibilities for Congressman Dick Nixon. Domestic terror marched in step with the deepening Cold War. J. Edgar Hoover told the House Un-American Activities Committee that communism was "a condition akin to a disease that spreads like an epidemic." Fighting it presented a fine opportunity for Nixon, who threw himself into his job. Dinners at home were reduced to once a week. He had no hobbies, no pastimes. "He can keep right on thinking about working at politics from the time he wakes up until he goes to sleep," Pat ruefully noted. Pat and Dick as a political couple were a thing of the past. She still believed her husband capable of great things, still clung to the belief that he was controversial only because he was so independent. There was not much left of her own sense of "destiny." She was his meticulous wife and the mother of his two children. Her role in his career was never to embarrass him and to look at him when he spoke, no matter how many times she had heard the same speech.

Nixon's reward came only six years after he arrived in the capital. His anti-communism and his willingness to take the low road in campaigning had catapulted him to national prominence. General Dwight D. Eisenhower picked him to be his running mate in 1952. The general saw Nixon's tough campaign tactics as complementing his own more conciliatory style, and also felt Nixon could help him in the West. Pat was less than thrilled by the honor. After six years of public life, she was tired and bruised. Her husband was the most vilified man in American politics. She was sick of campaigning, though her husband admitted she was better at it than he. She knew what a presidential campaign would require of the party's attack dog and his wife. She had borne up, done her duty and now wanted to head back to California, to the life she believed she had been promised. Nor did she want to leave her four- and six-year-old daughters. All this she told her husband.

He did not argue with her. They claimed they never argued about anything. Direct confrontation was not their way. He retreated and let Chotiner speak to Pat. Chotiner was powerfully persuasive. "I guess I can make it though another campaign," she sighed. Her husband then threw her a small bone as a reward. Before plunging into the presidential campaign that would take her away from her children for weeks at a time, Pat and Dick spent a few days in Hawaii. "It was the last carefree vacation I ever had," she later recalled.

AS WAS SO OFTEN the case in Richard Nixon's life, his moment of glory was shadowed by controversy. In the midst of the 1952 presidential cam-

July 12, 1952. A sight rarely seen later in their careers: Richard
Nixon, then thirty-nine years old, and Pat, as he was chosen
to be Eisenhower's running mate.

paign, press reports revealed that a group of seventy-six southern California businessmen had contributed to an illegal, secret fund that paid Nixon $900 a month to campaign continuously for Republican candidates. Suddenly, it was payback time for Senator Nixon the ruthless campaigner, his first taste of his own brand of personal attack. Nixon retreated into solitary gloom, unreachable to all, including his wife. "Dick was sitting in a huge leather chair," a House colleague recalled. "his arms stretched out, his hands dangling in that characteristic way of his. . . . I knew I was in the presence of total despair." Nixon knew Eisenhower was under pressure to dump him from the ticket. He had one chance to save himself—in a nationally televised speech. But two minutes before he was to go on, he was gripped by anxiety and threatened to bolt. Pat calmly took charge. "You must fight back," she urged him. Nixon rallied and delivered the legendary "Checkers" speech.

Nixon avoided political death, but in the process he devastated his wife. Again, he demonstrated how insignificant she was to him. Long before personal revelations became a staple of political life, he violated this most private woman's dignity. While his wife sat smiling her tight smile nearby, he laid out the family's finances and volunteered that, unlike corrupt Democrats, Pat did not even own a fur coat. "A Republican cloth coat" was good enough for his wife, he assured Americans. In his attempt to win sympathy, he went further.

> A man down in Texas heard Pat on the radio mention . . . that our two youngsters would like to have a dog. And believe it or not, the day before we left on this campaign trip we got a message from Union Station in Baltimore that they had a package for us. . . . You know what it was? It was a little black cocker spaniel . . . black and white spotted. And our little girl Tricia, the six-year-old, named it Checkers. And you know the kids love that dog and I just want to say this right now, that regardless of what they say about it, we're going to keep it.

The sentimental appeal worked. Eisenhower realized he had to keep Nixon on the ticket. "You're my boy!" he told him. But Pat felt humiliated. "Aren't we entitled to have at least a little privacy?" she meekly asked, knowing her objections counted for less and less. She and her husband continued to value above all else harmony in their marriage—at almost any price. So Pat kept quiet and Dick did what he had promised her he would not do. He thought only of himself. Pat's needs, her sensitivities, were plowed under her husband's single goal of vindication. Each perceived injury, and the Checkers incident was but one in a growing list, only fueled that need. For years after the Checkers speech, Nixon celebrated the anniversary as the day of his political resurrection. As for his wife, "She lost all heart for politics after that speech," he admitted. He wasn't oblivious to her pain, he just chose to ignore it. "She was the one person of whom my father never asked, 'Do you remember?'" his daughter Julie recalled.

Fame and success did not seem to affect Nixon's self-absorption or his insecurity. He did not think Eisenhower had shown him sufficient support in his ordeal. He had heard that, when asked about Nixon's contributions to the administration, Ike replied, "Give me a week and I'll think of one." Success only made him more determined and even more remote. Being vice president was an ego-crushing experience for a man as famished for power and affirmation as Nixon. He needed to be president.

The Nixons had virtually ceased direct communication with each other by 1958, when he was preparing his run for the presidency. Dick found a companion less demanding than even his wife. His name was Bebe Rebozo, a quiet, divorced real estate man who never disagreed with him, never challenged him, interacted with him only at Nixon's initiative. Rebozo was the closest Nixon could come to being alone while in the company of someone else. He often retreated to Rebozo's Key Biscayne, Florida, sanctuary when he wanted to escape from both Washington and his wife. Bebe is like a sponge, Pat said, he just listens to Dick and never disagrees with him. Dick loves that.

When Pat's old friend and fellow Whittier Union High School teacher Helene Drown spent a week with the Nixons, she was struck by the breakdown in communications between them. She sent Dick a memo, urging him to talk to his wife. "Have a talk about the future— what are the roads [available]," continued public life or returning to the practice of law. Drown's note is unexceptional. What is noteworthy is that it took a visitor to point out to the couple that they needed to talk to each other.

All the while, Pat had also become famous and much admired. She seemed the fulfillment of the ideal wife of the fifties, as depicted in situation comedies and advertisements. Perfectly groomed, smiling, loyal, she seemed uncomplicated and satisfied that her kitchen floor was shiny and her husband's pants pressed. Occasionally, the mask slipped. "We don't have as many good times as we used to," she admitted to one reporter. On a 1959 trip to Moscow, Pat turned to the wife of Ambassador Lewellyn Thompson, asked for a cigarette and said, "You don't know what it's like to be a politician's wife. I'd only voted once in my life—and that was for Roosevelt."

To protect herself and her daughters, Pat canceled their subscription to the *Washington Post*. She did not want their daughters to see Herblock's famous front-page cartoons depicting her husband with his perpetual five o'clock shadow as a sleazy Red-baiter. In public she was the tireless campaigner and goodwill ambassador who never put a foot wrong. "You probably have never seen a more exhausted woman than Pat Nixon," Washington columnist Betty Beale wrote. "When she and the Vice President showed up at the Women's National Press

Club . . . the evening they returned from South America . . . Pat stood on a platform beside her husband as he spoke, with her arms hanging limp beside her, her face so numb with fatigue it couldn't smile. . . . She seemed to move like an automaton. . . ." Did her husband even notice?

Pat almost never complained. Secret Service agent Rex Scouten was astonished at her self-discipline during an eighteen-country Asian tour in the 1950s. "The weather, the food—Mrs. Nixon was such a picky eater—but she bore up under everything without ever complaining. . . . I remember an endless ballet in Cambodia, even I couldn't stay awake. But she did. She was made of steel."

Her husband knew she hated his chosen profession. As to why he stayed in it despite continued promises to get out, Nixon blamed *destiny.* "Once you get into this great stream of history you can't get out. You can drown. Or you can be pulled ashore by the tide. But it is awfully hard to get out when you are in the middle of the stream—if it is intended that you stay there." Of course, he had no intention of leaving the stream. But Pat's sad, drawn face was a daily reminder of his betrayal. He wasn't home much, but when he was, he closed the door behind him and played the sound track of *Victory at Sea.* The music's martial sound drowned out all else.

In the 1960 presidential race, Pat campaigned as hard as he did. Her husband insisted she be there for public appearances, silent and perfect. She rarely expressed an opinion. Her standard line, "I don't give my husband advice because he doesn't need it," made reporters wince and fueled her reputation as being "unreal." Few people ever saw her and her husband touch. Mostly he seemed oblivious to her presence. On her own, she was different. Photographs reveal a woman spontaneously affectionate with her daughters, with children in hospitals, even with reporters and officials. The contrast between Pat's natural warmth and Dick's awkwardness was stark. Once, searching desperately for small talk with reporters in a restaurant, Nixon commented on the pretty flowers on the table. "But, Dick," his wife said, "they're plastic." Those present said Nixon's face darkened and he made no further attempt at small talk. No wonder Pat retreated behind the silent smile.

She hated reminders of the past and pleaded with others not to look back. Those who saw her after many years' absence were struck by the change. CBS White House correspondent Robert Pierpoint had been a student at Whittier Union High School when Pat was a teacher. He remembered the lively Miss Ryan. "She had changed drastically. She was extremely uptight, difficult to talk to, very nervous and not at all the happy, outgoing personality I remembered from high school days." Pierpoint was astonished at Pat's reluctance to talk about their shared past, "She became stiff and wooden and acted as though she didn't want to talk to me or hear of the other students and teachers."

Losing the presidency to John Kennedy was devastating to the Nixons. The Kennedys were everything Nixon most resented: rich, charming, Harvard-educated, socially connected, at ease in the world. Nixon was convinced they mocked him behind his back. Jack, the "light-weight playboy," beat Nixon in the only game Nixon cared about. For Pat, the defeat sealed her determination to get out of politics. "Nineteen fifty-nine disillusioned her beyond redemption," her younger daughter wrote. Nixon believed that voting irregularities in Cook County cost him Illinois. Though Nixon did not contest the results, Kennedy's popular vote total was only 118,574 more than his. In the electoral college, the results were 303–219. "[Pat] saw a stolen election and could not understand why so many were indifferent." The Nixons headed back to California, Pat determined to build a new life, Dick full of rage.

For a brief period now, she was happy. She led the life she had always yearned for, tending her garden and looking after her daughters. Her husband, meanwhile, plotted his return from exile. When the polls indicated that incumbent governor Pat Brown was vulnerable, he saw his chance for a comeback. This time Pat did not mince words. "If you run . . . I'm not going to be out campaigning with you as I have in the past." Her husband left the family council, gloomily mumbling, "Well, that's life. . . ." Pained at the sight of her deflated father, Tricia turned to her mother and said, "If it means so much to Daddy, maybe we should change our votes, Mother." Pat sighed. "You run upstairs and tell your father." In his *Memoirs,* Nixon describes his conversation with his wife that night. "I thought about it some more," Pat told him, "and I am more convinced then ever that if you run it will be a terrible mistake." But he knew she would come around. All he had to do was wait it out. "If you weigh everything and still decide to run," she finally said, "I will support

your decision. I'll be there campaigning with you just as I always have."
The next day he plunged back into the only life that mattered for him.

"You won't have Nixon to kick around anymore," the bitter Nixon declared to the media following his loss to Brown, "because, gentlemen, this is my last press conference." Julie Nixon never forgot the humiliation. "We were waiting tearfully for my father in the hallway at the front door when he arrived. Mother spoke first. She said brokenly, 'Oh, Dick.' He was so overcome with emotion that he brushed past and went outside to the backyard. That afternoon was the first and the only time my parents gave way to their emotions simultaneously and it bewildered Tricia and me. Mother lay on her bed, the room darkened by closed shutters, and cried in front of us for the first time we could remember. Tricia and I sat on the floor by the bed and cried also."

Ordinary mortals, even ordinary politicians, would have taken that searing defeat on the heels of the bruising presidential loss as a sign that it was time for a career change. The sight of his broken wife, his weeping children, would have been enough to convince even the most driven politician that the sacrifice was too high. But Nixon's demons would not rest, no matter what the human cost. Transplanting his family to New York, he saw them briefly thrive again. Pat was content to be the wife of a corporate lawyer. But by 1967 the restless Nixon was set to reenter political life, determined to make another run at the presidency. His wife and nearly grown daughters would just have to go along with his decision, as they always had.

Not only did he expect them to support him, Nixon required that they campaign full-time. The times may have changed—the Age of Aquarius supplanting the Age of Conformity—but Pat Nixon had not. Her proud assertion, "I may be dying but I would never say anything about it," sounded off-key in the new climate. For much of the country, Father no longer knew best. Dick Nixon was equally out of touch with the mood shift. His own opinion of himself was so low, he was so hungry for the public's admiration, that he could not cede any of the limelight, not even to his wife. It wasn't as if he was oblivious to her attributes. "Whatever you think of me," he often told audiences, "I'm sure you'll agree that Pat would make a fine first lady. . . ." Feminist writer Gloria

Steinem touched a nerve with Mrs. Nixon. When Steinem tried to draw out Pat to say just who she really was, she replied in a torrent, "I never had time to think about . . . who I admired, or to have ideas. I never had time to dream about being anyone else. I had to work. My parents died when I was a teenager . . . I never had it easy." This was not the happy, fulfilled woman of a thousand campaign appearances. This was a neglected wife who was at the end of her rope.

∼

VIOLENCE AND DISSENT DESTROYED the chances of LBJ's vice president, Hubert Horatio Humphrey, in the 1968 presidential race. Nixon won by almost as narrow a margin as the one by which he lost to JFK in 1960. Still, the presidency conferred its blessings and its privileges on the Nixons. However circumscribed a role Nixon wished for his wife, the country has expectations of any first lady. For a while, Pat allowed herself to savor her hard-won reward. But though she was now the wife of the president, he was still Dick Nixon, still the most polarizing politician of his day. As first lady she would be her cautious self. "She knew," her husband asserted, "you could not have two voices coming out of the White House."

The White House brings most couples closer. It had the opposite effect on the Nixons. For Richard Nixon, the White House was a place where he could finally indulge his love of solitude. Nixon gloried in his self-imposed isolation. Sheltered by a retinue of aides and the trappings of the office, it was easier than ever to ignore Pat. Finding the Oval Office too exposed, he often retreated to a secret hideaway next door in the Executive Office Building. After dinner he would escape to the Lincoln Sitting Room, a small room with a fireplace and huge windows, and play his martial music—alone. "A major public figure is a lonely man," Nixon told Stewart Alsop. "You can't enjoy the luxury of intimate personal friendships. . . . You can't confide absolutely in anyone. You can't talk too much about your personal plans, your personal feelings."

Henry Kissinger said he never heard Nixon directly address a word to his wife. Nor did they ever go alone to Camp David. His real "wife" was a tall former advertising man with a buzz cut, H. R. Haldeman. He was the one Nixon relied on to keep the world at bay, including his wife. Haldeman, like Rebozo, made no emotional claims on Nixon, required no intimacy. He, unlike Pat, did not remind Nixon of three decades of broken promises. Haldeman did not criticize. Haldeman called him Mr. President, which, no doubt to her husband's regret, Pat could not.

The staff served dinner quickly when the First Couple was dining alone. The silence hung like a curtain between them. The Nixons shared few activities, or even the same space much of the time. "I'll have to have a room of my own," Pat told Chief Usher J. B. West. "Nobody could sleep with Dick. He wakes up during the night, switches on the light, speaks into his tape recorder or takes notes—it's impossible."

The tone of the Executive Mansion is set by the relationship between the president and the first lady. A Cold War soon raged between the East and West Wings of the Nixon White House. Much as Nixon would show contempt for the constitutional limits on the office of the chief executive, he tried to subvert the traditional role of first lady. Power would flow from only one source: Richard Nixon. The president's men did not need explicit instructions on reining in the first lady's role. Nixon communicated with the first lady largely through memoranda exchanged between his aides. Nixon's chief of staff tried to run the East Wing as well as his own, and treated the first lady's domain with undisguised contempt. The communications to the first lady's office were remarkable for their condescending tone, and sometimes for their astonishing rudeness. When Pat's office recommended inviting the celebrated Russian-born pianist Artur Rubinstein for a White House gala, Haldeman answered with a single-word memo: "No!"

In an effort to control the first lady's role, Haldeman put the wife of Charles Stuart, one of his lieutenants, in charge of the East Wing. The move backfired. Constance Stuart was appalled by the demeaning treatment of the first lady. "She was one of the most experienced individuals to come into the White House," she said of the first lady she was meant to "keep under control." "[Mrs. Nixon] had long ago learned how to have a good public, political face. She could keep a stiff upper lip and a stiff lower chin in the face of the most difficult circumstances . . . a very warm, outgoing, funny, delightful woman."

"Funny and delightful" was not the image Nixon, whose ideal was Charles de Gaulle, sought for his presidency. "I would like to know who was responsible for selecting the entertainment, who checked the backgrounds of the entertainers, how this incident happened," began a typically accusatory November 5, 1971, Haldeman memo, one of a blizzard that crossed the White House's east-west divide, "and what are we doing to make sure that similar incidents don't occur in the future?" The "incident" was the presence of a longhaired guitarist as part of the entertainment at the state dinner honoring Indian prime minister Indira Gandhi. Haldeman was enraged by a mildly humorous description of the evening by *Washington Post* reporter Sally Quinn. Mrs. Stuart fired back.

> As you know, Mrs. Nixon selects the entertainers for White House functions . . . [their] background is checked out by the Secret Service, the FBI, [White House Counsel] Len Garment's shop. . . . May I say I found Sally's story about the hairy guitarist quite funny and no reflection on the White House whatsoever. I'm sure you are not indicating we shouldn't have long hairs in the White House just because they don't shave. And if you ever find a way to [ensure] that Beverly Sills's zipper won't pop, Anna Moffo's neckline won't plunge, Johnny Cash doesn't lose his baby in the Lincoln bedroom and accompanists don't turn out to be more difficult to deal with than the artists, we would appreciate your counsel. We do the very best we can, but the unknown looms menacingly when dealing with the entertainment profession. It's kind of like dealing with politicians.

Though Nixon tried to impose an image of frozen perfection on his wife, others penetrated her shield. Diane Sawyer, then an aide in the president's press office, recalled,

> She did this beautiful thing that melted me when I first met her. I had written something for her and took it over and as I was going to leave, Mrs. Nixon said, "Do you remember when you were a little girl, and just made a new friend, and didn't want them to leave and you said, I'll walk you 'halvers,' halfway home." She took my hand and walked me halfway back. And then hugged me—just like a little

girl. She was full of affection and gaiety. . . . She loved having fun. She loved it when [press aide] Frank Gannon played the piano and we would all sing and carry on. That was the Irish in her. You could even tell her a dirty joke. Well, not terribly dirty. But she was no prude. She was a real person. She got a kick out of people.

Though the Nixons' marriage had become a charade, the country still expected the president and the first lady to behave like a warm, loving couple. Increasingly the Nixons failed to convey that image. In the media age, the public has developed keen antennae for judging a presidential marriage. That perception has much to do with how the media covers the first lady. Nixon, obsessed by the attention the Kennedy women received in the media, could not understand why the press did not consider his dutiful wife a "good story." "Here's the point that I wish you would make in terms of building up Mrs. Nixon's activities," Nixon instructed Haldeman. "She's done a helluva job. . . . But did you ever have any biographies on Mrs. Nixon, who goes to Peru and all those goddamn things around the country?" Nixon seemed oblivious to the fact that his treatment of his wife might impact on the country's perception of her. Ironically, he assigned Haldeman to improve Pat's image. "There's a strong feeling," Haldeman wrote Connie Stuart, "that we have dropped the ball in getting across the story on the First Family in a warm and effective way. For example, there's an awfully good story in the fact that Mrs. Nixon is the most underestimated first lady. She thought of the lighting of the White House, the Thanksgiving Dinner [for the elderly] idea, the use of the boats for underprivileged children. . . . There is so much of this in the material that we now have that hasn't gotten over."

The women reporters who covered Pat Nixon admired her doggedness but felt sorry for her. "Nixon seemed to forget about her in big moments," Donnie Radcliffe of the *Washington Post* recalled. "He didn't want her to upstage or embarrass him. She was so controlled there wasn't the excitement associated with covering the first lady. Perhaps she had been burned in the past. . . . At any rate, she didn't have the flare or maybe the showmanship." But Pat once had both. When she traveled on her own, to Africa or to Russia, reporters glimpsed the warmth and the playful side of Plastic Pat. "She looked happier than I'd ever seen her," Barrie Dunsmore, the ABC correspondent who covered Mrs. Nixon's solo Africa tour, noted. "She didn't have her usual gaunt look. She seemed comfortable dancing and putting on the tribal headdress. The limelight was on her and she was treated with tremendous dignity everywhere she went."

Pat did not share her husband's visceral suspicion of all reporters. When away from him, she treated them as colleagues and even friends. On a Moscow trip, Associated Press reporter Saul Pett was about to be hauled off by Soviet security when she came to his rescue. She claimed Pett as a member of her party, even offered the reporter a lick of her ice-cream cone in front of the agent. Pett later wrote her, "I just wanted to express my gratitude to you for being so nice to me during phase I and phase II of the biggest, noisiest floating crap game in town. You've been a heckuva good sport and the ice cream was especially good."

Beneath the prim June Cleaver facade was a sharp eye. "She knew Brezhnev was having girlfriends in," Sawyer recalled. "She knew how unsteady he was." Her husband, for whom all social interaction was exhausting, was puzzled why she returned from her travels more rested than when she left. "The amazing thing," Nixon wrote in his diary after her 1972 Africa tour, "is that Pat came back looking just as fresh as a daisy despite an enormously difficult, taxing schedule. She had press conferences in each country, had conversations with Presidents, and carried it all off with unbelievable skill." Yet when the first lady accompanied her husband, he reduced her to an ornament. Planning his historic 1972 trip to China, the president assigned a very clear role to his wife. "If she goes," Haldeman wrote in his diary, "then the P[resident] doesn't have to go out into the people. If not, he will have to. If she goes, she goes solely as a prop."

She was Nixon's most underused asset. "I used to see her in the White House," her aide Patricia Mattson recalled, "with three, four hundred people coming through and she would stand there in the Green or Blue or Red Room and greet every single one: shake their hands, look into their eyes and they would come away feeling they had met the first lady of the United States." She spent hours each day answering her mail, refusing to let her staff use an auto pen on her behalf. "This is a woman who didn't expect anybody to do anything for her," Mattson noted. "She worked every single night. You always got the file back the next morning. Often it was a very used envelope, not to waste the government's money. She saw it as a job and a responsibility. . . . But we also saw a different Pat Nixon than the rest of the world did. She had the most wonderful sense of humor. She always had fun with the Secret Service agents, always teasing them about one thing or another. Their girlfriends, their ties. . . ."

Pat entertained more people, gave more White House tours and did more and better interior decorating than most of her predecessors or successors. "She told me exactly how she wanted to change every room, and all of it was in her head," White House curator Clement Conger said. "She didn't carry a notebook. And every change that she suggested was the right one. She had a marvelous eye for line, color and design." Room by room, Pat restored all the major public rooms to their nineteenth-century elegance, raising money for the project herself. While she was first lady, the White House acquired 65 valuable paintings, 156 pieces of period furniture, 19 chandeliers and 22 rugs. But her husband did not wish her to take credit for even this most traditional of the first lady's many roles. As usual, Haldeman was the messenger. "A recommendation has been made," he wrote Pat, "that Clement Conger appear on 'The Dinah Shore Show,' a daily television show on NBC aimed primarily at women. He would discuss his work here, with basic emphasis on the guidance and encouragement he has received from you. . . . The interview would be conducted at the program's normal studio in Hollywood and he would take along photographs which demonstrate some of the changes made." The contrast between Jackie Kennedy's highly personal and enormously successful tour of her White House restoration and Nixon's scenario for a studio conversation with the curator spoke volumes about two presidential styles.

This time, Pat fired back. "Mrs. Nixon and I have discussed your memo," Connie Stuart replied to Haldeman, "that Clem Conger appear on 'The Dinah Shore Show' to discuss the redecorating work Mrs. Nixon has done in the White House. . . . Once it [the entire White House] has been opened we hope to interest one of the networks in doing a television special on the completed White House with Mrs. Nixon as the focal point."

Only when one of his aides reminded Nixon that his wife could enhance his image did he temporarily react. "I think it is important for the President to show a little more concern for Mrs. Nixon as he moves through the crowd," Roger Ailes wrote. "At one point he walked off in a different direction. Mrs. Nixon wasn't looking and had to run to catch up. From time to time he should talk to her and smile at her. Women voters are particularly sensitive to how a man treats his wife in public. The more attention she gets the happier they are."

The stories of Nixon ignoring his wife in public are legion. The one told most frequently involves the Nixons' flight to San Antonio in separate planes. Pat, waiting on the tarmac, approached her husband with open arms. Senator John Tower reached her first and gave her a kiss. Her husband offered a stiff handshake. Did Pat remember the letter her husband had written her from the navy, "Whether it's the lobby of Grand Central or the Saint Francis bar, I'm going to walk right up to you and kiss you—but good! Will you mind such a public demonstration?"

Pat and Dick were together mostly when protocol required it. They stood side by side bidding their guests good night after state dinners, and then went their separate ways, he to his study, she to her bedroom. Their daughter Julie was startled to find her mother in the upstairs residence after one such dinner, ". . . still dressed in her evening gown. She was swaying to the faint sound of music coming from the Grand Foyer where some of the guests were still enjoying the dancing. On tiptoes she moved gracefully across the gleaming parquet floor. . . ." Whatever thoughts, regrets, lost dreams floated with Pat Nixon across that polished floor, she kept to herself.

Everything was left unspoken between them. "When you've been married as long as we have," Nixon told Frank Gannon, "you don't have to put things into words." It is unlikely Nixon ever told his wife something he wrote in his memoirs: "I knew that the road had been hardest of all for Pat. For almost twenty years of public life she had been wife, mother and fulltime campaigner. . . . She had done it all, not because she loved the attention or reveled in the publicity—she didn't. She had done it because she believed in me. And she had done it magnificently. Now she was loved by millions and no woman ever deserved it more. My deepest hope was that she felt that it had all been worth it." Most revealing in this passage is Nixon's uncertainty as to the answer.

THE EMOTIONAL COST of giving her husband advice was too high, so Pat stopped giving it. "Her way of dealing with conflict," Julie Nixon Eisenhower noted, "was to ignore it." On those rare occasions when she spoke up, as when she suggested he appoint a woman to the Supreme Court, he paid her no heed. She hated emotional confrontation and prided herself on never forcing an issue with her husband. Her greatest contribution to his life, she said, was "I never nag him." She let him make all the political decisions because that's the way he wanted it. She believed in him. She believed he was a great man who would never get a fair shake from the media. Her role was to protect him. She was temperamentally ill-suited for the more difficult and more important role of the fully engaged partner. Nor was he capable of engaging in such a relationship.

Diane Sawyer blames the turbulent times of the Nixon presidency for the Nixons' estrangement. "They got to the White House in the middle of the Vietnam War. Nixon was making Silent Majority speeches and bombing Cambodia and people were taking to the streets. He was getting up in the middle of the night to go out to talk to the protesters. Can you imagine being married to a man who is basically walking in and out of nuclear explosions, one after the other?"

Nineteen seventy-two should have been a triumphant year for the Nixons. He had just won the presidency by a greater margin than any Republican in history, nearly twenty million more votes than his opponent, George McGovern. It was his final election. At last he could appease his Quaker conscience by forging disarmament and peace treaties with Moscow and Beijing. Triumph was not Nixon's preferred state, however; combat was. He could not savor with his wife the second-largest landslide in American history. The morning after his victory he slumped into a strange melancholy. As always, he chose the most secluded corner of the White House as his retreat, the Lincoln Sitting Room. "I was not as upbeat as I should have been. . . . I think the very fact that the victory was so overwhelming made up for any failure on my part to react more enthusiastically than I did."

During his first post-election Cabinet meeting, instead of thanking his team for their support, he asked for their resignations. A stunned Cabinet staggered out of a session they expected to be a celebration. "I did not take into account the chilling effect this action would have on the morale of people who had worked so hard during the election and who were naturally expecting a chance to savor the tremendous victory, instead of suddenly having to worry about keeping their jobs," he wrote. An act this callous was surely a sign of a man who had lost his political survival skills, along with his humanity.

A single, overwhelming emotion washed over the first lady the morning after her husband's final election: relief. "I'm going to relax in these last four years," she told her staff. "I want to enjoy my family, spend more time with Tricia and Julie. I want to enjoy my grandchildren as they come along. I'm going to spend time with my friends, go out to lunch. . . . I'm going to shop." Her plan, simply, was to reclaim her life. She was not even going to replace her departing chief of staff. Pat was going to peel off the plastic shell of public life and finally live the way she had always wanted.

On June 17, 1972, a "third-rate burglary" shattered those dreams. Watergate would be the signal event of the Nixon presidency and permanently alter the American political landscape. As always in times of crisis, Nixon became less communicative than ever with Pat, relying more and more on Haldeman and Rebozo for companionship. Increasingly, the Nixons used their daughters as the bridge between them, and were lost without them. Tricia and Julie loved both of their parents but saw their awkward, beleaguered father as the more vulnerable. Julie took on the role of trying to explain her father to the world, while Tricia, who suffered from migraine headaches, retreated from public view. When their daughters decided to spend Christmas in Europe with their own partners, Pat and Dick were bereft. "It is inevitable," Nixon wrote in his diary, "that not only the President but the First Lady become more and more lonely individuals . . . who have to depend on fewer and fewer people who can give them a lift when they need it." The Nixons could not even bring themselves to open their presents on Christmas morning in Key Biscayne. "Later," Dick said, when his wife suggested they comply with the ritual. But later never came, and they took their presents back to the White House unopened.

When Pat heard her husband had been taping his conversations with his aides, her immediate reaction was "Destroy those tapes." They are like love letters, she said, private. It was advice that might have saved his presidency. But her husband did not consult her, and she had stopped offering him advice. For the country obsessed with Watergate, Pat knew that nothing she did would have much meaning. She dutifully answered her mail, for the volume was up to five hundred letters a night. In April, Nixon was forced to fire his two closest aides, Haldeman and John D. Ehrlichman. Typically, he could not bear to face them, and asked his old friend Secretary of State William Rogers to do it. Rogers refused, so Nixon had to fire them himself. Following a television address informing the nation of the latest development in the unfolding scandal, the president's family gathered to show support. Lifeless, his arms limp by his sides, Nixon mumbled, "I hope I don't wake up in the morning." His daughters hoped their mother had not heard.

The country was transfixed by the sordid details of CREEP (the Committee to Re-elect the President), of hush money, plumbers and bagmen with tentacles into the CIA, the FBI, the Justice Department and, finally, into the Oval Office itself. By March 1974, Attorney General John Mitchell and seven White House aides, including Haldeman, Ehrlichman and counsel John Dean, had been indicted on charges of conspiracy and obstruction of justice. The president was named an unindicted co-conspirator.

Pat and Dick did not discuss the scandal that was gradually engulfing them. "We never sat down as a family to talk about Watergate," Julie recalled. Knowing only the bare outlines of the scandal, Pat urged Dick to fight on. That had always been her role.

Nixon's spokesman, Ron Ziegler, advised that he go before Congress and admit everything he knew about Watergate. "Just tell it and tell us why it happened," Ziegler urged, knowing that the American people are forgiving of their leaders' mistakes, as long as they face them honestly. Nixon shook his head. "It won't work," he replied. "What has been done has been done. . . . People's basic character just doesn't change. Some try to change—some try very hard—but generally it ends up either good or bad. It all depends on one's strength of soul." The president's fatalism, his essential pessimism, his low self-esteem, as well as his grandiosity, are all contained in this brief, sad exchange.

Almost to the end, Pat carried on with her duties. Her final trip as first lady was to South America for the inauguration of the presidents of Brazil and Venezuela in March 1974. She received standing ovations in both countries for her courage in returning to the scene of violent anti-Nixon protests. On March 16, Pat's sixty-second birthday, she flew to Nashville to join her husband for the opening of the Grand Old Opry. Seated at an upright piano onstage, the president surprised his wife by playing "Happy Birthday" for her with the audience joining in. Flushed with pleasure, Pat sprang from her seat at the back of the stage and, with arms outstretched, rushed toward her husband. Nixon turned away from her and signaled the master of ceremonies to proceed with the program. Those present never forgot the shocked expression on her face.

∽

SPRING BROUGHT ITS USUAL STUNNING flamboyance to Washington that year. It went unnoticed by those inside the White House. The president still had not discussed the approaching disaster with his wife. He had not solicited her opinion on what they should do to salvage the public life they had jointly crafted. As always, he admired her "dignity"—but from afar. Pat's meals were brought to her upstairs in her bedroom, the trays returned barely touched. Her husband was aware of what he was putting her through. "God knows how she could have gone through what she does," he wrote in his diary, "I simply don't know." But he did not reach out to her. He asked Rebozo to prepare the Nixon family for his resignation, while he shut himself in his favorite sanctuary. "That night I began the painful task of telling my family about the June 23 tape and preparing them for the impact it would have on my attempts to remain in office," wrote Nixon. The three women were shattered by what the tapes revealed. The conversation of June 23, 1972, in which the president discussed the plan to use the CIA to head off the FBI's investigation of the Watergate break-in, left no doubt about the presidential cover-up.

Tricia wrote in her diary, "Julie and I talked some more and I learned that Mama had not been told of Daddy's tentative decision [to resign]. Mama was in her sitting room at her desk. It is strange how you try to spare those you love from worry. Strange because worry is contagious and is difficult to conceal other than with words. So in the end it is kinder to reveal what the person you are trying to spare already feels." Pat was not spared.

Even as their lives were crumbling, the three women thought only about propping up the tortured man. Tricia wrote during the final week in the White House, "Now we must all be as stoical as is humanly possible and show him [our love] more than ever. We must not collapse in the face of this ordeal. We must not let him down." There is no reproach from his wife or his daughters, no hint that it was he who had let them down.

On the eve of his resignation Nixon summoned the White House photographer to the upstairs solarium for a final family portrait. "Ollie," an astonished Pat greeted the photographer, "we're always glad to see you. But I don't think we need pictures now." The president signaled the photographer to proceed. "I tried to hide partially behind Mother," Julie remembered, "because tears were in my eyes and I didn't want them to be recorded in the photograph . . . it is very difficult to tell that I am crying. But my mother hates that picture and when it was being considered for inclusion in my father's memoirs she told me why, 'Our hearts were breaking and there we are smiling.' "

On August 8, 1974, Richard Milhous Nixon walked into the Oval Office for the final time. His family had wanted to be there when he made his announcement, but he told them he preferred to be alone. The man who had fought harder, and against greater odds, than almost any other to reach this office, announced, "I shall resign the presidency effective at noon tomorrow."

His wife's ordeal was not yet over. A final indignity awaited her in the East Room where the Cabinet, members of the administration and the White House staff had gathered for a last good-bye. "Who authorized television?" Pat asked, for the room was ablaze with lights. "I did," the president said. With his family standing behind him, Nixon stepped up to the podium and thanked his staff for "the sacrifice all of you have made to serve in government. . . ." Then, in a voice thick with emotion, he spoke of his father and his mother, Hannah. "She will have no book written about her," he said, his voice breaking, "but she was a saint." Nixon closed by reading Theodore Roosevelt's tribute to his first wife, Alice, at the time of her death. He said not a word about his wife, who stood just behind him fighting back the tears. It was as painful a spectacle as any he had ever staged.

Pat and Dick walked out of the East Room, across the red carpet flanked by the color guard at attention. Before boarding the *Marine One* helicopter, they smiled their terrible smiles at the wreckage below. One last time Nixon executed his jaunty over-the-head wave. Pat murmured, "It's so sad, so sad." And the Nixon presidency was over.

Pat was never rewarded for her loyalty, by her husband or by her country. Even her official White House portrait looks sad, a woman on the brink of tears. In San Clemente, California, she retreated from public view and stopped performing even for her husband. She declined to be her husband's official hostess and spent her days cultivating her small garden. "I think she had lost heart," Julie said. "It didn't matter to her anymore what happened. I don't think she felt things could ever be what they were."

In 1976, Pat suffered a stroke from which she never fully recovered. Her friends say it was stress-related. Her bubble of denial about her husband's treatment of her was burst by one of her own friends. Helen Smith had worked for her in the White House and was appalled at the depiction of Pat as a broken-down alcoholic in Bob Woodward and Carl Bernstein's book *The Final Days.* To counter that image, Smith wrote her own account, an entirely sympathetic portrait of a woman loved and respected by her staff but cruelly ignored by her husband. The article had a powerful effect on Pat. Given the source, she could not easily dismiss it. This public lifting of the veil on her marriage shattered her fragile emotional balance. She had lived a lifetime evading hard truths about her own choices; now there was no further escape. The article's publication coincided with the decision of the New York State Bar Association to disbar her husband.

At Pat's 1993 funeral, her husband wept openly and publicly for the first time. Was it guilt or a realization at last of what he had lost that shattered his lifelong emotional control? Following the burial, in Nixon's private eulogy to a small group, he talked about a boy who seventy-six years before, in a small house in Whittier, used to listen to the train whistle in the night and dream of places he would go. "I have always been fascinated by trains," Nixon said. "My favorite campaign was 1952, the last whistle-stop campaign." During that campaign, he recalled, he would often hear a line from a song, " 'I like the sunshine of your smile.' . . . And that's how Pat would want you to remember her," he told his friends. One final time, Richard Nixon passed up an opportunity to talk about his partner of over half a century, and chose instead to reminisce about his one true love.

CHAPTER 7

BETTY AND GERALD FORD

ORDINARY PEOPLE

What Betty Ford said was, We're real people in this house.

—MORLEY SAFER, *60 Minutes*

I do not believe that being first lady should prevent me from expressing my views.

—BETTY FORD

THE HELICOPTER THAT CARRIED RICHARD NIXON TO POLITICAL EXILE STILL hovered over the South Lawn when Gerald Ford grabbed his wife, Betty's, hand and said, "We can do it. We're ready." The country was also ready. The sigh of relief at the departure of the tortured president and his emotionally battered wife was palpable and nationwide.

At a moment in the nation's life when everything seemed up for grabs, when the punches of Watergate and Vietnam left the country reeling, the Fords allowed us to see who they were and thus reassured us about who we were. Their names speak reams about them: Betty and Jerry. They were midwesterners, plain and simple. Their presidency had less to do with statesmanship than character. The Fords were an accidental presidential couple. They had not sought the office. Ford was the only man who reached the presidency without ever facing a national election.

The Fords' blend of integrity and openness was the perfect antidote to Richard Nixon's stilted, dishonest attempt to make the presidency imperial. While her husband restored honesty to the White House, Betty Ford transformed the blameless role of the presidential wife that Pat Nixon had played into an engine for change. She responded instinctively to the country's hunger for honesty and openness. Her greatest contribution to her husband's presidency was bridging the gap between the White House and the rest of the country. She demonstrated the power of authenticity. In the process, Betty found her role: an Everywoman suddenly lifted to an extraordinary position. That it was a drug-dependent, stay-at-home political wife who grasped the moment and played this pivotal role is nothing short of astonishing.

❦

WHEN, IN AUGUST 1973, President Nixon called Congressman Gerald R. Ford to offer him the vice presidency, Ford asked him to please call back. Nixon had used the Fords' private number, which had no extension in their Alexandria, Virginia, home. Betty could not hear the president firsthand. Nixon and Ford both wanted her to. The Ford marriage was a real partnership: he made no major decisions without first talking to his wife. "I didn't know whether to say thank you or not," Betty wrote later. "If I had known what was coming," she added, "I think I probably would have sat right down and cried." Less than a year after this phone call, the Fords lived in the White House.

They were people with seemingly nothing to hide, and no aspirations to be anything but who they were. They were the most compatible couple to reside in the White House since that other pair of midwesterners, Bess and Harry Truman. They seemed unafraid of the social turbulence triggered by the Nixon presidency and the Vietnam War. They dealt with the unruly times in the open, matter-of-fact way Americans like.

Right from the start, Ford told the country what sort of man he was and what his wife meant to him. "Our long national nightmare is over," Ford announced in his most famous address to the nation. "Our Constitution works. Our great republic is a government of laws and not of men. . . . I assume the presidency under extraordinary circumstances never before experienced by Americans. . . . I feel it is my first duty to make an unprecedented compact with my countrymen. Not an inaugural address, not a fireside chat, not a campaign speech, just a little straight talk among friends. . . . I am indebted to no man and only one woman, my dear wife, Betty, as I begin this very difficult job."

Ford's fearless expression of his partner's importance was like a balm for a nation pained by Richard Nixon's treatment of his wife. Ford's style worked because it was not an act. The night the Fords learned that their old friend Dick Nixon had lied to them as well as to the country and that Ford was about to inherit the presidency, Betty and Jerry talked through the night. "As we lay there in the darkness, our hands reached out and touched simultaneously without either of us having said a word," Jerry Ford later wrote. "Then we began to pray."

The Fords had no driving sense of Gerald Ford's destiny. Politics was his profession, not his salvation. Ford was a popular congressman whose highest aspiration was to be Speaker of the House. He was a collegial man, used to the give-and-take of congressional horse-trading. He was a man of comfortable ego who knew his own worth. Ford did not need the presidency to fill a yawning personal void. He had always been loved and was comfortable loving. He had a sure sense of place: he was a man from Grand Rapids, Michigan. There are few places more emblematically American than that. A decent, smart and uncomplicated man, he was raised by his adoptive father and religious mother to, above all, do the right thing.

One month into the office, he did what he saw as the right thing and doomed his presidency. Without much warning, Ford announced Nixon's unconditional pardon. Betty agreed with him that the country had to move beyond Watergate. She thought that Nixon had suffered enough and felt great sympathy for Pat and the girls. It was a gross miscalculation born of the Fords' own temperament. Vengeance was not part of their makeup; forgiveness was. They thought the country needed to let go of its anger, but it was too soon for that. People were furious and suspected that Ford had made a secret deal with Nixon. Overnight, Ford's popularity took a nosedive, from a 71 percent approval rating to 49 percent. With his usual equanimity, Ford accepted the furor and understood the decision might cost him the next election. "But damn it," he wrote, "I don't need polls to tell me I'm right or wrong"—extraordinary words to come out of the White House. And it was only the beginning of an administration whose candor and decency reflected those of the First Couple. When Ford told his wife, "We're ready," he meant it. As a couple, they had already been tested, and would be again.

In April 1954, Mrs. Gerald R. Ford, wearing the square-shouldered, cinch-waisted suit and obligatory hat and white gloves, declared that wives of congressmen look better on a speaking platform when they're saying nothing. Politics should be left to your husband, Betty advised a gathering of political spouses. A bright woman with green eyes and a model's figure, she herself had abandoned her early passion for modern dance and was raising two boys in suburban Washington. She saw herself mirrored a thousand times at her women's club, at congressional wives' luncheons, at her sons' Sunday school and pushing the shopping cart around the Safeway near her Fairfax, Virginia, garden apartment. Raising a family, having a place of your own, greeting your hardworking husband in the evening with a smile and, above all, supporting his career—that was the code of conduct for a middle-class wife in the fifties and sixties. Mamie and Ike were in the White House, and women like Betty were supposed to feel fulfilled. For a time she did. Her husband's career was progressing nicely. Jerry loved the House, where he held a safe seat. Two more children arrived in rapid succession. The Fords were the picture of the healthy, well-adjusted, postwar American family.

But by the mid-sixties, life felt flat for Betty. Her husband was away up to 285 days a year. She was stranded in the suburbs with four children, virtually a single parent. There were no available outlets for her growing unease and resentment. What Betty did not realize was that she was not alone. "Women's Lib" was in its embryonic stages. "Nobody," *Time* magazine reported on November 22, 1963, "is more noisily dissatisfied these days than that symbol of stability—the fortyish housewife with teenage children and a reasonably successful husband." But for women like Betty, the style was still set by Jacqueline Kennedy's quiet, feminine elegance. Male supremacy was an article of faith for mainstream America. Betty concluded that the "fault" must be hers.

She had married Jerry with her eyes wide open. When he was courting her, he rarely turned up at her apartment before 10 P.M. and often much later. "I'd like to come by and see you tonight," he often told her, "but I've got to go to a meeting first." Ford did not tell Betty he loved her—that would have breached his generation's unwritten code for male behavior—only that he wanted to marry her. He also told her they couldn't marry before the following fall. There was something he had to do, which he could not share with her—he was planning to run for Congress that year. At his wedding he turned up late, wearing muddy shoes; he had been campaigning on a farm and forgot to change his shoes.

In 1965 Betty suffered a nervous breakdown. "I'll never forget it," her youngest child and only daughter, Susan, recalled, "I was eight years old. And Daddy was on the *Sequoia* with President Johnson, and Mother was in her room crying and very upset about something and I ran and called [the housekeeper] Clara, and Clara came and settled Mother down and got hold of Daddy and he came home and while he was in seeing her and the doctor, Clara pulled Steve [one of her brothers] and me outside. She said that Mother was very sick and she had to go to a psychiatrist." Later, Betty said her collapse had been building for a very long time. "I'd felt as though I were doing everything for everyone else, and I was not getting any attention at all. I was so hurt that I'd think, I'm going to get in the car and I'm going to drive to the beach and nobody's going to know where I am. I wanted them to worry about me . . . I wanted them to say, Well, my gosh, Mother is gone, what are we going to do?"

She expressed the sublimated rage, as well as the confusion, of so many women of her generation. "Who do they think is making it possible for [Jerry] to travel all over the United States giving all those speeches? He gets all the headlines and applause, but what about *me*?" she wondered. "On the one hand, I loved being 'the wife of,' on the other hand, I was convinced that the more important Jerry became, the less important I became. And the more I allowed myself to be a doormat—I knew I was a doormat to the kids—the more self-pity overwhelmed me. Hadn't I once been somebody in this world?"

Jerry did not deny the problem or abandon his wife because she was proving "difficult." He accepted some blame. "I wasn't aware. . . . I thought she had been a wonderful mother. I felt we had had a fine marriage. I felt our lives were developing very constructively." Never again did Jerry take his wife for granted as he had in the period leading up to her breakdown. In a move considered bold in the sixties, Betty sought psychiatric help. Their marriage was dangerously close to being destroyed, as was their family life and Jerry's dream of becoming Speaker of the House. "I think we were all so really tied up in his career," Betty said later, "that we weren't looking at each other the way we should look at each other."

After more than a decade and a half together, Betty and Jerry now recast their marriage into something more textured and very much in keeping with their times. Unlike most political couples, the Fords did not merely endure, they assimilated changing currents and evolved. Jerry responded to his wife's needs. Ford's balanced personality, his lack of self-absorption, may not have ultimately helped his political career, but it certainly made him a better husband than most presidents.

A decade later the Fords faced a greater personal challenge when, within an eight-month period in 1974, they went from Congress to the vice presidency to the White House. Now Jerry was caught in a sudden blaze of attention and Betty had to define her own role and identity. She found the answer in the most unexpected place. During the first month of the Ford presidency, a routine checkup revealed a lump in one of her breasts. Surgeons eventually performed a radical mastectomy. Breast cancer was a subject only whispered about in the seventies. Lying in the hospital recovery room, Betty was seized with the idea that from her platform she could save lives. If the most prominent woman in the country talked openly about her cancer, others could. She could encourage women to put their health ahead of their vanity, as she had, and to go for checkups.

In a widely read February 1975 *McCall's* magazine article, she openly expressed her fears regarding her appearance and her husband's reaction. "Jerry and I had a chance to talk alone that afternoon in the hospital," she wrote of the day of her surgery. "I think Jerry's real concern was to make me as comfortable as possible—and to express his love. Perhaps even more so because he realized I might feel disfigured or mutilated. He wanted to reassure me that it made no difference to him; that after all we still loved each other and were just as happy after twenty-six years of marriage."

Jerry described the night before his wife's surgery as "the loneliest of my life. . . . The thought that the woman I loved might be taken away from me was almost too much to endure. Before I went to bed, I asked the florist to send three dozen red roses—Betty's favorite—to the hospital." The president described his emotions upon hearing that doctors found a cancerous lump. "I put down the phone and tried ineffectually to focus on the speech [on the economy] again. But too many emotions were churning inside me. Excusing myself, I stepped into a small bathroom adjacent to the office and attempted to wrestle those emotions under control. After a minute or so I returned to my desk. [Speechwriter Bob] Hartmann looked at the expression on my face and understood immediately. 'Go ahead and cry,' he said. 'Do cry.' All my tensions and fears poured out in a brief flood of tears."

There was a new atmosphere of informality and unpretentiousness in the White House. Staff, under orders to be silent in the Nixons' presence, were amazed by the new occupants' friendliness. Betty's director of correspondence, Gwen King, recalled Betty, working in her slip, getting a call from a presidential aide. The first lady was late for the swearing-in of the new attorney general. "You just tell Jerry to hold his horses!" the first lady breezily instructed.

Betty, who did not expect to like being first lady, took to the role with relish. "Truthfully," she recalled, "I flowered. Jerry was no longer away so much. And I was somebody. The First Lady. When I spoke, people listened." Some mysterious alchemy between the time, the place and the woman made her tenure memorable. The seventies were, of course, famously charged. The *Roe v. Wade* decision had made abortion legal, giving women an unprecedented feeling of control over their bodies. While still only 14 percent of working women were in the professions— most worked because they had to—more and more were moving into the workforce; women's salaries were still far less than those of their male counterparts. But role models were suddenly everywhere: on television, in politics, in films and in sports. In 1971, Billie Jean King had been named *Sports Illustrated*'s first-ever Sportswoman of the Year. There were more choices for women than ever before. By 1975, there was one divorce for every two marriages.

Intuitively more than intellectually, Betty grasped the enormity of

these changes on American life. Rather than turn her back on them as
Pat Nixon had, she decided to encourage them. For unlike Pat, Betty
knew her husband stood behind her, pleased rather than anxious at her
sudden high profile. The fact that her husband had never been a controversial public figure also freed his wife to be herself. Seemingly bemused
by his wife's candor, he was not looking for a political Stepford Wife. As
with most healthy couples, his happiness was very much tied to hers. He
had learned the hard way how much he had to gain by having a fulfilled
woman at his side. Ford, former Yale quarterback and Grand Rapids'
most eligible bachelor, was fearless about sharing the limelight with his
wife.

Their daily life in the White House resembled the Trumans'. They
relished living and working under the same roof. On most evenings they
sat side by side talking and working together. "They were a playful couple," David Kennerly, their official White House photographer, recalled.
"They joked around with each other. They enjoyed each other. His idea
at the end of the day was to sit around with her, have dinner with her, just
be with her." Betty had converted Richard Nixon's bedroom into a little
study. Like the Trumans, the Fords shared a bedroom and a bed. With
typical candor, Betty told a reporter she liked to "sleep with my husband
as often as possible." Given their open relationship and their twenty-six-
year history, there was little they did not discuss. Getting more women
appointed to high office was one of her regular topics. "I kept pushing,
trying to influence him," she remembered. "I used everything, including
pillow talk at the end of the day, when I figured he was most tired and
vulnerable." Betty is credited with the appointment of Carla Hills as secretary of housing and urban development and Anne Armstrong as
ambassador to London.

Because she was in many ways a traditional homemaker, as well as a
mother of four children, she had credibility in advocating passage of the
Equal Rights Amendment. Betty worked the phones with congressional
legislators, an unprecedented role for a first lady. "Feminist" was still a
dangerous label for a politician, and her campaign was not without political risk for her husband. "Betty Ford," one anti-ERA public information advertisement ran, "will be remembered as the unelected First Lady
who pressured second-rate manhood on American women." After see-

ing that ad on television, "I went to bed laughing," she claimed. "Jerry did too." Though her mail was running three to one against her outspoken feminism, she knew she had her husband's support. She regretted only that the wife of a rising California politician named Ronald Reagan opposed making the ERA the law of the land. "I couldn't understand," she wrote, "how a woman who had had a professional life could show so little interest in working women."

Betty's mantra, "It is time for abortion to come out of the backwoods and into our hospitals," was her own idea and was widely quoted. She called the still controversial *Roe v. Wade* decision "great." "Jerry has never stepped on my toes," she wrote. "He's never turned around and complained, 'Well, *that* was a dumb thing to say.' " The president may not have "stepped on her toes," but his advisers were concerned about the first lady's activism. Presidential aide Ken Cole drafted a memo advocating a sharp line between the president's and the first lady's views on the subject of abortion. "As you are well aware," Cole wrote on September 6, 1974, "the controversy . . . is one of the most emotional and volatile issues this year and could become even more so as the elections approach." Cole signaled the danger of having Betty take a stand similar to Ford's liberal vice president, Nelson Rockefeller.

Why didn't Ford, a pragmatic centrist, rein in his wife, as other presidents have? He certainly liked being president. He hoped to be reelected. But he was not as consumed as those who have spent their lives fighting for it. He was unwilling to sacrifice his relationship with his wife for the office. And he knew how important it was for Betty to have a sense of her own autonomy. They had paid a high price for his earlier neglect. He needed her, and he needed her to be happy. He was—and this, too, seems refreshingly unpresidential—a little bit afraid of his wife. "If she got unhappy," Kennerly noted, "or frustrated, she would certainly tell him about it. Like most men, he liked to avoid those situations."

BETTY, A BORN PERFORMER, loved the role. Like Jacqueline Kennedy, though from another world, she understood the symbolic power of her undefined position. She grasped what Pat Nixon did not: that it wasn't the number of hands she shook or the letters she personally answered but the image she projected to the country that mattered. So, like Jackie, Betty established who she was in just a handful of appearances and through the canny use of her platform.

She loved to entertain and she loved to party. She quickly transformed the White House into a lively place. Jackie's small, round tables returned, replacing the Nixons' long ones. The First Couple were often the last to leave the dance floor after state dinners. Betty did the bump with Tony Orlando and the dignity of the republic was not shattered. The presidential couple stomped to "Bad, Bad Leroy Brown" at a state dinner for King Hussein of Jordan, and the country relaxed a bit. The poison of Watergate was oozing out of the nation's bloodstream.

While President Ford was meeting with the heads of thirty-five nations on the question of security and cooperation in Europe and hammering out the historic Helsinki Accord on Human Rights, Betty's profile soared to a new level. In August 1975, she sat down with *60 Minutes* correspondent Morley Safer and overnight became the most talked-about woman in America. "I expected a much earthier first lady than any previous ones," Safer recalled, "but not as earthy as I got. I found an attractive woman who was the first politician I have ever met who absolutely let her guard down. It was a conscious thing with her. This was going to be Betty's moment. She declared who she was." Safer did not think Betty had "cleared" her answers with her husband. "The interview liberated all those Republican women who nodded appreciatively at every Neanderthal statement made by the party," said Safer. "She was not out for self-aggrandizement or self-promotion. Betty Ford said, We're real people in this house."

Safer asked all the "hot button" questions first ladies generally evade with puffery. Betty took each one head-on. Infidelity: "He doesn't have time for outside entertainment. I keep him busy." Her breakdown: "I was giving too much of myself and not taking any time out for Betty. . . . I was a little beaten down and he [the psychiatrist] built up my ego." The secret of their successful marriage: "You go into it, both of you, as a seventy-thirty proposition. In other words, here I'm giving seventy, he can give thirty, he's giving seventy, I give thirty. When you're going overboard trying to please each other, you can't help but be happy." Abortion: "I feel strongly that it was the best thing in the world when the Supreme Court voted to legalize abortion. . . . I thought it was a great, great decision." The possibility that her seventeen-year-old daughter was having an affair: "I wouldn't be surprised." Marijuana: "I'm sure they [her children] have all tried it. . . . I probably would have been interested to see the effect. . . . It's the type of thing young people have to experience, like your first beer or your first cigarette. . . ."

Reaction to the interview was as unprecedented as the interview itself. The American people saw an open, honest woman talking about issues they were dealing with every day. Suddenly, the distance between the White House and their houses melted away. The White House was barraged with thousands of letters, with those opposing her at first running two to one. But that soon changed. *Newsweek* named Betty Ford "Woman of the Year" and claimed, "Not since Eleanor Roosevelt championed civil rights and organized labor in the 1930s has a First Lady spoken out more freely—or aroused more controversy. . . . In a year when women are continuing their climb into public visibility, Betty Ford seems the symbolic Woman of the Year. But her soft, hesitant voice seems to speak as much from her heart as her politics." A Harris poll found her post–*60 Minutes* approval rating soaring twenty-five points from 50 percent to 75 percent.

She appeared immune to controversy because of who she was: a seemingly ordinary American housewife and mother. She had come to be seen as the woman every child wanted as a mother, every man as a wife. She was smart, warm, funny, whimsical and she could even do the bump. When Rabbi Maurice Sage suffered a heart attack on the podium in the middle of a June 1976 benefit for the Jewish National Fund, Betty took charge. Pandemonium erupted in the New York hotel ballroom as hundreds of guests stood up to see the commotion. The Secret Service tried to lead Mrs. Ford off the dais. She refused to leave and stepped up to the microphone and asked people to bow their heads. The noisy room fell suddenly quiet as she led the guests in a spontaneous prayer. Rabbi Sage did not survive his massive heart attack. And no one present ever forgot the first lady's spontaneous humanity and presence of mind.

The still unanswered question was whether support for Betty translated into support for the president. Or was it a zero-sum game? Did greater support for *her* mean less for *him*? Many of President Ford's aides, notably his press spokesman Ron Nessen, were concerned that his wife's extraordinary candor would damage his reelection chances. Ford took it all with his customary good humor. "You've just lost me ten million votes!" Ford said, watching the *60 Minutes* interview. "No," he said, correcting himself, "twenty million," and threw a pillow at his wife. Later he wrote, "I was under no illusions as to what the reaction to her remarks would be. . . . Conservatives grumbled, their grumbles swelled to a roar." But it was not Ford's way to silence his wife. "I had admired her candor from the moment we met and had always encouraged her to speak her mind," he wrote. "We had few disagreements, but when we differed, we respected the other's opinion." This level of tolerance was something new in presidential history. Was the country ready for it? The extremely conservative New Hampshire daily, the *Manchester Union Leader,* said no. "President Ford showed his own lack of guts by saying he had long ago given up commenting on Mrs. Ford's interviews. What kind of business is that?"

But Betty's struggle to carve out her own identity alongside a high-profile spouse had wide appeal. "Why should my husband's job or yours prevent *us* from being ourselves?" she asked the hundreds of women gathered in Cleveland to celebrate International Women's Year. "Being ladylike does not require silence. The best way to celebrate International Women's Year is to examine the very real problems women face today, not the progress of *yesterday.*" Men and women alike are inhibited by out-of-date ideas of what they each can do, she said. "But the limits on women have been formalized into law and structured into social custom. . . . My own support of the Equal Rights Amendment has shown what happens when a definition of proper behavior collides with the right of an individual to personal opinions." Americans sensed this was no mere politician's wife, reading someone else's script. "Change by its very nature is threatening, but it is also often productive. And the fight of women to become productive, accepted human beings is important to all people of either sex and whatever nationality." In 1976, the American people pronounced Betty one of her husband's strongest assets, with 71 percent of those polled expressing a favorable opinion of her.

The country did not know how hard she had struggled against her demons for the confidence to pronounce such brave words. Though she had made great strides since her breakdown a decade before, the woman the president loved still walked near the edge. As much as she took to the role of first lady, she often felt isolated in the White House. "She was very lonely," Chief Usher Scouten remembered. "She had been very close to her kids, and now they were gone. She always wanted to talk. She'd say, 'Let's go over the schedule while I'm having lunch.' And she'd go on and on. I used to think, I have so many things I ought to be doing. But then I thought, if that is what makes her happy. . . . We'd talk about her kids, events around town, people in politics, Grand Rapids. . . ."

There were clues along the way that this suburbanite with the immaculate bouffant hairdo and winning smile was not exactly what she seemed. She was taking painkillers for a pinched nerve and arthritis, and Valium to take the edge off her high-velocity life—all washed down with alcohol. Barbara Walters noticed that Betty's speech was "heavy and slow" when Walters arrived at the White House before an interview. Betty's press secretary, Sheila Weidenfeld, at the time refused to accept her boss's condition—despite overwhelming evidence. "She was out of it a great deal of the time. I was stupid about it. I didn't know what was wrong. I used to see her with a drink, but everybody had a drink. But I did not know she popped a lot of pills. I knew she had osteoarthritis, that she was under the weather a lot. A nurse was constantly with her, traveled with her."

Betty did not acknowledge her own condition. "My makeup wasn't smeared, I wasn't disheveled, I behaved politely, and I never finished off a bottle. So how could I be alcoholic?" After all, cocktails were as American as a Saturday game of golf. "At home my parents always served cocktails, come five o'clock," Betty wrote. "It was a habit, like brushing your teeth in the morning. . . . I can see alcohol did not agree with me, but in those days, we didn't even know alcoholism was a disease, or that it might be inherited. . . . My father was an alcoholic, though I never knew it until after he died, and so was my brother Bob."

And so, it turned out, was Betty. Despite the overwhelming fact that for close to thirty years she had been mixing a variety of painkillers with alcohol, her husband and children had been avoiding the painful truth. President Ford's longtime political aide Stuart Spencer was not blind to her addiction.

> Her problem with alcohol was very apparent to me. When we'd go out to dinner I used to say to her, "Hey, Betty, you are floating." She would get bombed. And it was tough on her husband. Really, really tough. He was a gentleman. He would take her home. He struggled with being a father of teenagers and a husband in this high-profile place. He stuck in there. But he didn't really know what to do. We weren't as sophisticated then about alcoholism. The medical profession was very derelict in those days in their understanding. Jerry Ford carried a load only a few people were aware of.

It was not until 1987, eleven years after she left the White House, that Betty acknowledged to herself, her family and the country her true condition. Once again, she spoke for many. "I had a great deal of pain and back pain, so the medications that I was taking for my back and my neck became considerably multiplied . . . [and] I had always used alcohol." Again she turned private adversity into public good by destigmatizing a common disease. She started a clinic for drug and alcohol abusers that has made her name better known than her husband's. Just as he did not try to silence her outspoken activism when he was in the White House, he encouraged her to be open about her addiction to drugs and alcohol.

BETTY AND JERRY FORD DID NOT consciously set out to make the presidency less imperial. It happened because of who they were. The presidency did not change them. Betty did not deliberately blur the lines between the public and the private sides of the presidency. By speaking out on issues never before touched upon by a first lady, she opened that door. She was not interested in making policy. But by boldly speaking out, she made controversial social issues an acceptable part of the national conversation.

"Elect Betty's Husband" became a favorite campaign slogan in Jerry's bid for the presidency in 1976. But the public seemed to prefer

Betty to her husband. Ford had too many obstacles in his way. Unlike his wife, he was no performer. His plain words and slow speaking style did not fire up a hall. He came across as somewhat dim, rather than the solid, methodical thinker he was. Ford had a habit of bumping into things in full view of the cameras. Once he became the focus of a *Saturday Night Live* skit, there was no shaking his image as a clumsy, oafish kind of guy. Most damningly, he had pardoned the man whose betrayal most Americans had not yet forgiven. And the Republican Party's right wing, left cold by the Fords, had already begun its love affair with Ronald Reagan. By a slim margin, Ford lost to an unknown southern governor who promised a fresh start. Considering that the Republican Party had been shattered only two and a half years earlier by Nixon's resignation, there was nothing shameful in Ford's narrow loss.

The Fords ended their brief tenure the way they had begun: the picture of a solid, united couple. The morning after his defeat, Jerry woke up with a bad case of laryngitis, unable to deliver his concession speech.

Betty and Jerry Ford dance at the National Symphony Ball, December 4, 1976. Jimmy Carter has already won, and the Fords are lame ducks.

He asked Betty to give his final speech as president. Her composed, heartfelt message from her husband to the nation stood in contrast to the bitter memory of Richard Nixon's final moments, his final public humiliation of his wife. The Fords walked away holding hands.

It is hard not to conclude from the Fords' fulfilled partnership and failed presidential bid that devoted husbands rarely make successful presidents. But the same qualities that made Gerald Ford a good husband—compassion, the ability to engage in the real give-and-take, the controlled ego—are not necessarily the qualities of a great leader. History is driven by needy, dominating, narcissistic personalities who let nothing and no one stand in their way. "Everything trends towards catastrophe and collapse," Winston Churchill wrote his wife on the eve of World War I. "I am interested, geared up and happy. Is it not horrible to be built like that?" Ford was not built like that. Lacking Churchill's drive and ruthlessness, he did not achieve a Churchillian career. Together the Fords did, however, play their part for history. At a confusing time for the nation, their sheer straightforwardness reminded Americans of who they were: imperfect, honest and hardworking.

CHAPTER 8

ROSALYNN AND JIMMY CARTER

VIRTUE UNREWARDED

I have found that the more that she and I can share responsibilities, with her being in an unofficial position and me in an official position, then that tends to strengthen the personal kind of relationship between husband and wife.

—JIMMY CARTER *to the* New York Times

He makes up his mind and I follow along. That is how it is. —ROSALYNN CARTER

Mama, we'll go down in the history books!

—MENACHEM BEGIN TO HIS WIFE, ALIZA, *upon the signing of the Camp David accords*

NOT SINCE EDITH AND WOODROW WILSON HAD THERE BEEN A COUPLE THIS close in the White House. As with the Wilsons, the remarkable rapport between Rosalynn and Jimmy Carter did not necessarily enhance his presidency. The very qualities that made Jimmy a devoted husband mitigated against his political success. He did not need a bracing dip into a crowd to confirm who he was. Carter did not even like large crowds. He was not possessed of that giant hole of neediness that drove men like Johnson or

Clinton, time after time, to "press the flesh." He did not really enjoy people, other than Rosalynn. Beyond his wife, and to a lesser extent his children, Carter felt an abstract connection to others. He loved her and really needed only her approval. Their airtight bond, the fact that they were self-sufficient and self-contained, sometimes shielded them from reality.

They were an exemplary pair: close, loving, supportive and open. From the beginning they were everything to each other: friend, lover, confidant, business, and later, political partners. Eminently suited, they were raised in the same corner of rural Georgia and had known of each other all their lives. From the day he first kissed the shy seventeen-year-old, Jimmy was determined to make Rosalynn "an extension of myself." It was more than the sweetness that radiated from Rosalynn's perfect apple-shaped face and upturned wide eyes that drew him to her. She shared his seriousness and fierce determination to improve herself, a trait neither of them has ever lost. Three decades of marriage had not cooled Jimmy and Rosalynn's need, or their ardor, for each other. They shared the same goals for their marriage: unlimited mutual support and a closeness that made them function like an autonomous republic. Neither liked being without the other even for a day. But it was not a relationship of equals, and never would be.

One presence was more dominant than Rosalynn's in Jimmy's life: God. A born-again Christian, Jimmy felt that God's hand had chosen him, that he was accountable only to Him. By living an exemplary life, Carter believed he could reconcile his deep commitment to God with a career in politics. His belief that he was a messenger of God had fueled the political novice's extravagant dream: to run for president. Armed with a moral certainty that bordered on the messianic, Carter was a singular presence on the American political landscape.

He had run a brilliant race in 1976 and had then become the anti-politician, beyond the reach of advisers, including even his wife. His vice president, Walter Mondale, remarked that Carter had the coldest nose of any politician he'd ever encountered. Carter seemed proud of that fact. Once he made up his mind, there was no one, not even Rosalynn, who could change it. For ultimately Rosalynn was the beloved instrument of his will. It had always been so between them. It was so in the White House.

The Roosevelts, the Kennedys and the Reagans were master manipulators of the trappings of the presidency. Jimmy and Rosalynn were not. The most remarkable thing about Jimmy Carter is that he was ever elected president in the first place. But the American people like their leaders to radiate confidence and strength, to reassure them that they are in charge. As president, Carter often seemed smaller than life.

Rosalynn had no agenda other than her husband. Her marriage came ahead of everything else in her life, though she had other interests. "If you ask me which were his ideas or hers," Mondale concluded, "I couldn't tell you. They worked together." The Carters, however, are an object lesson of the truism that no matter how good the partnership, how successful the first lady, it is still the president's performance that determines their legacy.

∽

BY NOVEMBER 1979, the third year of her husband's presidency, Rosalynn Carter had grasped the power of her office. A journey to Thailand demonstrated her strength as first lady. She was not prepared for what she now saw: thousands of wasted humans—babies, small children and the very old—lying very still on the ground or on dirty mats as the sun beat down and flies buzzed around them. The smell of human waste and disease hung over the Sakeo refugee camp at the Thai/Cambodian border, as did a chilling silence. Among the human wrecks suffering from cholera and malaria walked healthy young men wearing red-checkered bandannas, members of the Khmer Rouge, the organization responsible for the killing fields that brought the refugees to this camp. Their leader, Pol Pot, had already exterminated more than one million Cambodians in an effort to create a "new society." The first lady had come to call attention to the growing refugee crisis, but there had been no advance work done for this visit. Instinctively, she touched the elderly and whispered hello to people who could no longer hear her, as she moved with solemn dignity through the camp. She cradled a dying infant in her arms. Although tears sometimes filled her eyes, she retained her composure through the visit.

This was Rosalynn at her best, fulfilling her country's expectations of a first lady without overstepping the invisible boundaries that tripped her up earlier (when, for example, she attended Cabinet meetings). On the flight home from Bangkok to Washington, she pulled the State Department veterans traveling aboard her military aircraft to her side and talked about the urgent need to organize a large-scale, coordinated relief program for the refugees. The diplomats were moved by the intensity in her soft, modulated voice. She said she would summon to the White House all the various refugee organizations for a meeting. They needed to appoint a strong, high-profile leader for the effort. There should be no duplication, none of the usual bureaucratic paralysis. She would make maximum use of her platform.

Physically and emotionally exhausted when the plane touched down at Andrews Air Force Base late at night, Rosalynn was surprised when her husband bounded up the ramp. With a characteristic cool greeting to her entourage, he swept her up in a warm embrace. It was obvious to those present that the president had badly missed his wife. Rosalynn switched seamlessly from her official role back to the one she had filled for nearly her whole life, Jimmy Carter's essential partner.

One of those who helped choreograph Carter's stunning victory, Pat Caddell, learned fast about this couple. During the 1976 Michigan primary, two of Carter's closest aides, Hamilton Jordan and Gerald Rafshoon—famous pranksters—egged on the young Caddell to call the candidate with new poll numbers. Call him in Plains at midday, they urged him, he'll just be getting home from a week on the stump, he'll want to know right away. Rafshoon and Jordan knew what Caddell did not, that calling candidate Carter before he had his "Rosalynn fix" was dangerous. But Caddell, the new kid on the team, foiled the practical joke by not calling until later in the afternoon, much to Rafshoon and Jordan's disappointment.

Luck, politicians will say, is more important than skill in politics. They also say that politicians make their own luck. By the time Rosalynn returned from her transforming trip to the Thai refugee camp, President Carter's legacy was sealed. That same week, on November 2, 1979, several thousand Iranian youths seized the American embassy in Teheran and took fifty-two members of the staff hostage. It was the beginning of the end of a singularly unlucky presidency.

⌇

LIKE MOST COUPLES, the Carters established the rules governing their marriage early on. She adored him and felt privileged to have been chosen by Plains' most desirable, most glamorous son. In their tiny universe, he was at the top of the social pecking order, she much further down. Neither one had ever loved, or would ever love, anyone else. Rosalynn lost her father, an auto mechanic, when she was thirteen, so Jimmy was literally the only man in her life. Though only twenty-one himself, Jimmy was self-assured enough when they met to play the role of both father and suitor, and soon husband.

To stroll down Plains, a "town" of a single row of stores whose chief businesses are peanuts and worms, is to realize the enormity of Jimmy's ambition and achievement. Carter was different from all the other youths Rosalynn Smith had ever met. Most of them finished twelfth grade and either went off to the service or returned to their farms. But Jimmy, a restless youth with big dreams, was not going to stay under his authoritarian father's thumb for long.

Jimmy began planning his future before adolescence. He wrote letters to people who might recommend him as a candidate for the U.S. Naval Academy in Annapolis, Maryland, the school his father wanted him to attend. As the scion of the tiny community's best-known tribe, Jimmy already had an air of infallibility. His parents had ambitions for their brilliant son. Rosalynn was not part of their scheme.

Rosalynn's pleasure, like Jimmy's, came from hard work and self-improvement. Shortly before her father died, Rosalynn had promised him she would go to college, and so she did, the only one in her high school class to do so. Responsibility had been thrust on her early. As a teenager, she became a parent to her three younger siblings while her mother worked. Rosalynn fell in love with the twenty-year-old naval academy cadet when she was seventeen and still living at home. "I thought [Jimmy] was the most handsome young man I had ever seen."

Carter used the Bible as his manual for living. He imparted to Rosalynn a biblical sense that a wife's role was to serve the husband. Even then there was an air of piety, a gravity, about Jimmy. At Annapolis, his

classmates would not tell off-color stories in his presence. On his days off
in the navy, while others went carousing, Jimmy conducted Bible classes.
Rosalynn learned to fulfill his expectations. She strived for the qualities
Carter prized: tenacity, self-sufficiency and spirituality.

He whisked her from dusty southern Georgia to San Diego; New
London, Connecticut; and Hawaii, glittering ports of call for a girl from
Plains. As far as Jimmy was concerned, there was nothing she could not
do. She rarely disappointed him. In his early years in the navy he was
gone much of the time. Three babies were born in rapid succession. "I
felt I became independent that way," said Rosalynn. "When you're away
from home and your husband's gone, you just have to take care of everything. And it was a good feeling for me. I liked it."

But Jimmy cut short her independence. After seven years of the free-
wheeling navy life, he decided it was time for the Carters to return to
Plains. His father had passed away, and Jimmy wanted to take over
the family peanut business. "I argued, I cried. I screamed at him. I loved
our life in the navy," Rosalynn wrote, but tears, she added, "instead of
being persuasive or eliciting sympathy, had quite the opposite effect on
Jimmy."

They were setting the pattern for their life. When they disagreed,
even though they were intensely connected, he prevailed. "I'm not going
to argue about this, Rosie," he would say, and that was that. "He had,
and still has, no patience with tears, thinking instead that one makes the
best of whatever situation—and with a smile," Rosalynn said. Sullen, she
was driven back to the small town she thought she had left behind. Rosalynn thought the best part of her life was over. "I became more and
more dejected the closer we got. I didn't want to live in Plains. I had
left there, moved on, and changed. But Jimmy was determined—and
happy. . . ." Approaching the dusty street of her childhood, seemingly
oblivious to her despair, Jimmy turned to her with the brilliant smile that
would one day be familiar to the whole country, and said, "We're home."

There was something almost ruthless in Carter's disregard of his
wife's feelings, and a chilling aspect to his dead certainty that he was
doing the right thing for both of them. She was his wife and he expected
her to be just as competent, just as stoic, just as determined as he was.
Happiness for him came from a job well done, not from a "good time."

Jimmy once said that if he could come back in another life, it would be as a Mennonite, a member of the austere religion that holds the Bible as its sole rule of faith.

When she rebelled against his demands, he ignored her. It was easier for Rosalynn to submit to his plan. Anyway, she adored him and considered herself the most fortunate woman to have landed her gifted, confident Jimmy. "I remember he called me one day and asked if I would answer the telephone [at the peanut warehouse] while he went out and did something," she recalled. "And I took the kids with me and cleaned and swept down there. And then I started going down answering the phone, and started writing tickets for supplies." Rosalynn gradually assumed more and more of the running of the peanut warehouse. She took business and accounting courses. She was good at it, grew more confident and stopped sulking. "I loved it. To make all those books balance? It was better than anything I'd ever done."

Jimmy's plan was working, just as he predicted. Rosalynn made her peace with Plains. He had a full partner. A husband and wife working together was not a radical idea in the rural South; it was often a simple matter of survival. "In Plains when I was a child," Rosalynn recalled, "if you walked down the street and you went into the grocery store there was the man and his wife working behind the counter. If you went out on the farm, the wife was working beside her husband in the field. This was what we did." But Jimmy was not content to be the most successful peanut farmer in Plains. He had a great appetite for self-improvement. While his wife mastered accounting, he learned speed-reading. They built their dream house. Within a decade, Jimmy and Rosalynn were the leading citizens of their small community. But a new ambition now animated his restless spirit.

"He got up one morning and put on some dress slacks instead of his khaki pants and I said why are you dressing up on a weekday? And he said, 'I'm going to Americus to sign up to run for the [state] Senate.'" Thus did Rosalynn learn that her husband intended to run for office in 1962. "He makes up his mind and I follow along," Rosalynn said. "That is how it is." He was thirty-eight and she was thirty-five and he had never shown the remotest interest in politics.

The Carters approached campaigning with the same dogged determination they brought to farming. They both had a powerful competitive streak. "If we were going to live in Plains," Rosalynn decided, "we might as well be really successful." Rosalynn called every registered voter in their native Sumner County. Her ears hurt, her mouth was cracked and her voice hoarse. It was a rough battle for the young, well-educated businessman from Plains, running against corruption and the southwest Georgia good-old-boy network. But Jimmy was elected against tremendous odds, and the Carters of Plains were definitively launched on *their* third career.

Rosalynn now ran the warehouse while Jimmy applied himself to becoming the best state senator in Georgia. He wasn't much of a politician, in the traditional sense. He bridled at the bonhomie and horse-trading. But he was smart, focused and impeccably honest. In 1966 he ran for Congress and had his first taste of defeat. Jimmy and Rosalynn learned that they did not like to lose. "I don't take defeat easily," she said later, "and for the first time since my father died I hadn't wanted to wake up in the morning." Profoundly shaken, exhausted and in debt, Jimmy turned to his Baptist roots for solace. He renewed his Christian faith with a convert's zeal and never strayed from it.

By the time Jimmy ran for governor in 1970, his Baptist faith was at the core of his politics. The Carters had also honed their campaigning skills. Together they worked out a system for remembering something about each person they met on the trail. They competed with each other to see who could remember more names. Campaigning was more of a trial for Jimmy than for Rosalynn, whose self-confidence was growing. She had another powerful motivation in wanting Jimmy to succeed: she still wanted to get out of the little town that was both their sanctuary and their confinement. The overwhelming presence of her forceful mother-in-law, Miss Lillian, a sort of Georgian Sara Delano Roosevelt, was yet another reason Rosalynn yearned for escape.

Only seven years after Jimmy startled his wife by putting on his dress pants in the middle of the week, the reformist Carter was elected governor of a deeply conservative southern state. A famous *Time* cover hailed him as the symbol of the "New South." Rosalynn saw a breakthrough opportunity for her husband during the summer of 1972. On the heels of news reports of his past psychiatric treatment, presidential nominee George McGovern's running mate, Tom Eagleton, was suddenly removed from the ticket. Rosalynn quietly put out feelers to party operatives to consider Jimmy as Eagleton's replacement. Her overtures came to nothing, but henceforth Georgia's reformist governor was on the Democratic Party's radar screen. In his typical methodical way, Carter began the process of letting his countrymen take his measure: traveling, speaking and writing a short autobiography with the extraordinarily bold title, *Why Not the Best?*

As always, his staunchest ally in this seemingly quixotic quest was his wife. To Rosalynn, it was obvious that Jimmy was ready. "He knew a lot more about a lot of things than did these men who were running for president." After the national trauma of Watergate, it was clear that the next presidential race would not be about politics as usual. Carter, quoting theologian Reinhold Niebuhr, who said that the duty of politics is to bring justice to a sinful world, was running as an outsider. Such was the depth of the country's disaffection that Carter's inexperience was deemed a political asset. It was a remarkable meshing of a man and a moment; given his personality, it is unlikely that he would have succeeded except in the unique circumstances of 1976.

Few believe he could have been elected without Rosalynn. Gerald Rafshoon, the Atlanta advertising executive who helped shape Jimmy's image, was among the first to realize that Rosalynn was a more natural politician than her husband. "She was good door-to-door. He couldn't do that. He wasn't much good at retail politics. He was a solitary man with a fantastic ego. Nobody dreams of becoming president—certainly not from Plains, Georgia—without that. Carter is a very tough guy. Very controlled. I've never heard him raise his voice. To have those pale blue eyes bore into you, saying, You have failed, is much worse than shouting." Her husband could inspire a large audience with his earnest intensity. He spoke the language of religion and morality. He was the first presidential candidate to use the word "love," as a Christian concept, in almost all his campaign speeches. He inspired audiences much as a priest might, in a lofty and impersonal way. But Rosalynn was down-to-earth, feminine and strong, every inch the self-made woman. Like many others in that confused time, she seemed to be pushing herself to be more than the wife and mother society asked her to be. She was also free of her husband's often overbearing piety. In the eyes of the world, she humanized him. Unlike him, she enjoyed the game of politics. "I loved the politics and Jimmy never did," she said. "I had my own rules for the road:"

- Stop at courthouses, the center of political activity and gossip.
- Insist on the front page of the newspaper.
- Head for the large radio and television antennas, usually the most visible landmark in town.
- Stay in people's homes. You save money, learn about people's real concerns, establish close ties and loyalty, and end up with access to a network of their friends and relatives.
- Be intrusive—on meetings, events, carnivals, anyplace people gather.

The sheltered, shy girl Carter married had been transformed into an independent political operative, no longer waiting for her instructions. "I'm Mrs. Jimmy Carter and I thought you might want to interview me," she would say, marching unannounced into broadcast studios. She even had a prepared list of questions they "might like to ask" her. Rosalynn wanted the White House as much as Jimmy did. In fact, she had left Plains farther behind than her husband had. No matter where Jimmy campaigned, even if it meant catching the red-eye from Los Angeles, he felt a powerful urge to return to Plains. "I preferred taking a day off in Malibu," Rosalynn remembered. But Jimmy would insist and get his way. Then he would change into blue jeans, walk into Plains and talk to people who still called him "Jimmy," and feel restored.

Sometimes the days were so long Rosalynn felt numb with fatigue, unable to form words, reduced to nodding and smiling. But she pressed on. Unlike Lyndon Johnson, Jimmy Carter was a secure enough man not to feel threatened by his wife's growing prominence. "I have never seen a political performance as good as hers on *Meet the Press* in my life," Jimmy enthused. "She even has a better awareness of people and issues than I do. I'm too encapsulated by staff and the Secret Service, local officials, and so forth. She's there, is more intimate with the average voting citizens than am I during this part of the campaign. Her advice on debate points and techniques is almost infallible."

In Roslynn, Virginia, in the fall of 1976, Jimmy heard his wife's stump speech for the first time. "I've known him all my life," she began, in her soft, lilting southern accent. As she went on, Carter's aides were astonished to see tears trickling down their usually controlled boss's cheeks. When she finished, he kissed her so hard he lifted her off the ground. "That's beautiful," he whispered. Stepping up to the mike with his arm around her, he asked, "How many of you would like to have Rosalynn as first lady?" When the crowd roared its approval, he said, "So would I!"

But for all his respect and admiration, he never saw her as anything but his "Rosie," "a perfect extension" of himself. "I have just met two Jimmy Carters" was how one politician summed up his meeting with Mr. and Mrs. Carter.

Jimmy stood for moral leadership at a time the country was receptive to it. This slight man from the Deep South was offering a way to heal the twin wounds of racism and Washington's excesses through his ministry of love. Carter's promise to the American people, "I will never lie to you," was so powerful it drowned out concerns about his inexperience. With Hamilton Jordan's help, the Carter team made maximum use of the primary system to catapult Jimmy to the party's top spot. Occasionally during the campaign Carter revealed flashes of a quality well known to his wife, which would ultimately define and doom his presidency: a stubborn disregard of others' views.

Even Jimmy's odd 1976 *Playboy* confession that he had "lust in his heart" seemed proof of their openness. Everybody who knew the Carters knew there was no other woman for Jimmy. "Jimmy talks too much" was Rosalynn's blithe put-down of his clumsy admission in *Playboy*. When a reporter asked her if she had ever committed adultery, she shot back, "If I had I wouldn't tell you!" They projected closeness and an unabashed enjoyment of each other. Walking hand in hand from the Capitol to the White House on that frosty inaugural day in January 1977, they electrified the country. "Be kind to us," Barbara Walters famously said at the end of an ABC interview, and she seemed to speak for the nation.

YET FIRST IN SMALL WAYS, then in large, the new president began to mis-read the country. Carter underrated America's attachment to the tradi-tional presidency, with its pomp and circumstance. His Baptist faith, and not his political instincts—which suddenly seemed nonexistent—ruled his presidency. He did not feel that the people's chosen leader should live like a millionaire. He wanted to be seen as a modest, frugal, ordinary man. So he stripped the office of many of its trappings, the fanfare and flourishes that had inflated and embellished the presidency. Carter seemed to think that if he simply did the opposite of what Nixon had done, he would succeed. But the country did not like seeing their presi-dent carrying his own garment bag. The people missed hearing "Hail to the Chief" when he appeared. A physically small man, Carter made both himself and the office seem smaller.

Noting awkward lapses of protocol in the Carter White House, Ambassador Angier Biddle Duke, scion of an eastern establishment fam-ily and President Kennedy's protocol chief, offered his services. Protocol is more than empty ceremony, Duke assured the president; it is a formula for dealing with other states. "For example," he asked Carter, "do you know who the world's first chief of state is?" The president shook his head. "It's Haile Selassie, sir, because he has served the longest. And they expect us to know these things." But the president was implacable, telling Duke he wasn't interested in such things. "But Mr. President," Duke pressed on, "every president keeps the seat warm for his succes-sor." That conversation, Duke's widow, Robin, noted, "was the end of my husband."

In another show of disdain for the trappings of the office, Carter sold the presidential yacht *Sequoia,* thus losing an important political asset. He reduced the number of presidential limousines and cut the pay of White House staff. Rather than earn him respect, these small, cost-cutting measures fueled resentment.

Carter thought he was elected to usher in a new political age. But his margin of victory was much too small for such high-handed behavior. He alienated Congress by not dispensing presidential favors the way his pre-decessors had, to grease the legislative wheels. Because he did not wish to be beholden to anyone, Carter refused to show any personal gratitude toward the groups who helped elect him: labor, women, Hispanics; in fact, he eventually managed to alienate all of them. But he most alienated party elders like House Speaker Tip O'Neill, whom he deliberately snubbed in an assertion of his independence.

Even Carter's attempts to have fun were often marred by his sanctimony. When, during the fall of 1976, a group of high-powered businessmen and academics traveled to Plains to "get the measure of the man," Carter admonished them, "Now, we're not going to talk world affairs. We're here to clog dance!" He then proceeded to instruct the astonished luminaries in that fine southern art. "We'd come a long way to hear his ideas on issues," Robin Duke recalled. "Carter wanted to show us how uninterested he was in talking to a group of heavy hitters. It was another missed opportunity."

Not even Rosalynn was spared his steely blend of arrogance and piety. She wanted to make mental health her primary focus, like she had as the governor's wife. But when the president was presented with a $1 million budget for a mental health commission that she would chair, he balked, even though the sum was well below prior budgets for presidential commissions. Under great duress, he approved $100,000 in emergency funding for mental health. Nor would he allow her to have as large a staff as her predecessor, Betty Ford. Her pleas fell on deaf ears. "Everybody always wants more staff," he told her, "and that's why the federal government gets so overloaded." "But I'm not *anybody,*" she pleaded, "I'm your wife!" She loved him and forgave him. Others in Washington would not.

As honorary chair of the President's Mental Health Commission, Rosalynn testified before Congress and helped to draft legislation for a $47 million increase in funds for research in mental health. "But she did not understand how Washington works," Richard Beattie, general counsel to the Department of Health, Education and Welfare, recalled. When her mental health bill seemed to languish in Congress, she blamed Joe Califano, the secretary of HEW. "She wanted to know why this wasn't happening. If the first lady proposes legislation, she thought the secretary of HEW should damn well get it passed. She got more and more incensed. I was in the room a number of times when she expressed bewilderment and frustration that it wasn't happening. It was easy for her to believe Califano was the problem. She had a notion that he was part of the Kennedy team. She had seen him hanging out with Teddy Kennedy; she didn't think his first loyalty was to Carter. Joe was too much of an insider." When Carter fired Califano in 1979, many people, including Beattie, knew of the first lady's displeasure with him. "I saw private notes between Carter and Califano, so I knew what was going on, and it didn't seem to me that the president was that unhappy with Joe. Rosalynn was an important factor in Califano's firing by the president. No doubt about it." There were, to be sure, other reasons for Califano's forced departure, most notably his opposition to Carter's plan to create a separate Department of Education.

Nor did the Carters understand the Washington media's enormous influence in translating the presidency to the nation. "Image," Rosalynn wrote, "became a nuisance that wouldn't go away. I thought that if I were working productively and accomplishing something worthwhile, the image would take care of itself." When Rosalynn held her first news conference in the East Room to announce her Mental Health Commission, "I found not one word about the commission or the press conference [in the *Washington Post*]. There wasn't anything and I was crushed," she recalled.

"She wanted to be covered the way any member of her husband's administration would be covered," *Washington Post* reporter Donnie Radcliffe noted. "She didn't want to be in the women's pages. She didn't want to be identified with tea parties and fashion stories." Robin Duke attributes the Carters' problems to their combination of naïveté and insecurity. "They were both so guarded, so suspicious of people they called the 'socially prominent.' I think Rosalynn was frightened of us. The presidency is not a loner's game. You have to reach out. It's the only way you find out what people are thinking, how you're coming across. The magic of a good president is openness. The Carters were not open."

Nor did they attempt to win over the entrenched Washington culture, the lobbyists, the pundits, the wise men and socialites who are the capital's permanent ruling class. The Carters did not like to socialize. "We are from Plains, Georgia," Rosalynn said years later, "and we don't like that sort of thing. We work all day, so we didn't want to have to go out at night." But Washington expects newcomers, even those who reside in the White House, to play according to *its* rules. The president and the first lady may be at the top of the social and political hierarchy, but they are nevertheless expected to acknowledge and socialize with others who matter politically. The Carters stubbornly declined to play that game. They were happiest when there were just the two of them. "The Carters don't have friends," Stuart Eizenstadt, the president's chief adviser on domestic policy, noted, "they have each other."

Without expending time or energy in the requisite seduction of the town's elite, Rosalynn expected Washington to take her as seriously as her husband did. After all, they had been partners in all his previous ventures. When she talked fertilizer prices with southeast Georgia farmers, they knew she understood their business. But she did not penetrate the arcane rules governing Washington's social and political culture. "She made no attempt to ingratiate herself with Washington—'the cave dwellers' or the Georgetown set," Donnie Radcliffe recalled. "These people had been preaching to presidents and first ladies for two centuries on how to be successful. They still do. Rosalynn's lack of a light touch as much as anything may have been one of her weaknesses. She didn't have much humor. If she could have loosened up a bit, and shown us her playful side . . ."

Would a playful couple from Plains, Georgia, have made the passage from peanut farming to the White House in a decade? Of course they were earnest, single-minded and driven; those were the very qualities that got them there. They were not about to change now, even if they could have. Rosalynn's White House aide, Paul Costello, recalled the moment he finally "got" Rosalynn. "We were en route to San Francisco aboard a DC-9 military aircraft. It was the end of a very long day. It was about 1 A.M. Mrs. Carter and I were in the front cabin. Everybody was asleep—her chief of staff, the stewards, the press in the back. I suddenly woke up and there was Mrs. Carter with her glasses on, under a penlight, studying Spanish. That relentless striving epitomized her character. There she was, just disciplined to the core."

Those who recognized Rosalynn's role in Jimmy's life, like National Security Adviser Zbigniew Brzezinski, were better able to push their agendas and ideas. Those who mistook her low-key style and absence of a personal agenda as lack of influence, paid the price. "If Rosalynn didn't like you," historian Douglas Brinkley noted, "you started with a near fatal handicap. She was less tolerant than Jimmy. And very protective of him. She would often say to the president, 'Oh, he's not really a friend of yours, he just wants something from you.' " She frequently sat in on policy sessions, quietly taking notes. "Carter often relied on Rosalynn's notes as the record of events," Brinkley recalled. Rosalynn frequently interrupted the president at White House dinners, to clarify a point he was making.

In June 1978, Rosalynn set off on a seven-nation tour of Latin America and the Caribbean. It would be an exaggeration to regard this foreign policy as marriage therapy, but it certainly had an element of that. Jimmy knew that Rosalynn was happiest playing a part in their shared enterprise. "I have found," he told the *New York Times,* "that the more that she and I can share responsibilities, with her being in an unofficial position and me in an official position, then that tends to strengthen the personal kind of relationship between husband and wife."

Rosalynn prepared for her first plunge into serious diplomacy with all of her customary application, poring over enormous volumes of briefing books. "I was *determined* to be taken seriously," Rosalynn said, noting, "There was more than a little discomfort at the State Department, and on the Hill. I remember Congressman Dante Fascell coming in to a meeting and saying, 'Well, Latins are macho, they hate gringos and they hate gringos' wives. What else do you want to know?' That was their attitude."

Fortified by her husband's iron faith in her, Rosalynn set off. In Brazil, Jamaica, Costa Rica, Ecuador and Peru, she bypassed the traditional first lady's circuit of orphanages and ladies' lunches and held substantial, one-on-one talks with heads of state. "I am closer to the President of the United States than any person in the world," Rosalynn chided reporters who questioned her role as presidential envoy.

Her diplomatic mission was her husband's gesture of love, respect and trust, but it provoked a backlash against activist first ladies that lasted many years. Her two immediate successors would be more cautious about asserting their influence, and when Hillary Clinton trod even more visible terrain, the debate erupted again, even more violently. Rosalynn had assumed a role for which many felt she lacked credentials, a role not in keeping with her previous image as the supportive, traditional helpmate to the president. Campaigning for her husband, she had defined herself as his wife. Now she raised the age-old issue of the proper role of the unelected—and thus unaccountable—family member of elected officials.

"The question raised by [Mrs. Carter's] Latin American trip," Meg Greenfield wrote in *Newsweek,* "is not whether Rosalynn Carter is capable of serving as an agent of her husband's government, but rather whether she should." The *New York Times* was even more blunt. "The unspoken question behind many appraisals of Rosalynn Carter's journey to seven Latin and Caribbean nations has been 'Who elected her?' . . . We think Mrs. Carter's boast in Latin America that she was 'closer than anyone' to the President was unseemly and unnecessarily defensive. For her . . . the question should be not just who she is, but how well-equipped to handle a Presidential errand."

Rosalynn brushed off the critics. "What irritates me is that people in our country expect women to work now, but when the first lady tries to do something, she is criticized for it. It's ridiculous, but it's a way to get at the president." She knew she had the full backing of the only person whose judgment really mattered to her. Their staffs were in awe of the closeness between the Carters, and their perfect pitch in communicating with each other, almost as if they were one person inhabiting two bodies.

But in the eyes of the media and the public, Rosalynn did not have independent credentials for the role she was now claiming. She was seen as the president's wife, the first lady. To Jimmy, she was his most influential and forceful adviser, and she deserved a more public role. No previous president's schedule had lunch with his wife as a weekly ritual. The president would ask, "Well, Rosie, what's on your agenda this week?" Rosalynn would consult her manila folder. And for approximately one hour their worlds merged, and again it was just Rosie and Jimmy working in common enterprise. Only now, instead of discussing the price of a pound of peanuts, the Carters talked about political appointments, normalizing relations with China, the Middle East and dealing with the Panama Canal problem. Nor did many other presidents retreat to Camp David accompanied only by their wives.

AS ALWAYS, despite the Carters' closeness, there was a limit to how much Jimmy heeded Rosalynn's counsel. One bone of contention between the Carters was Jimmy's unwillingness to do the *political,* as opposed to the *right,* thing. Perhaps as proof of his moral purity, Carter seemed almost deliberately to embrace unpopular decisions. A speechwriter of his, Hedrick Hertzberg, recalled, "We used to joke that it was no accident that the man's initials were J.C." Such was his disdain for political showmanship that Carter succeeded in undermining his own achievements. One day he was scheduled to announce he was eliminating several thousand pages of federal regulations, Hertzberg remembered.

> We got a big stack of paper for him and the idea was that he would sweep it off the table or dump it in the wastepaper basket to illustrate how many regulations he was getting rid of. We thought this would be very dramatic—excellent footage for the evening news. The only problem was, the President didn't follow the script. "This is a prop prepared by my staff. It's supposed to represent the thousands of pages of regulations. Actually it's just a pile of blank sheets of paper," he said. He then ignored it for the remainder of his statement. The evening news found something else to lead with that night.

It was a losing battle for his politically more astute wife. "His standard answer when I talked about political expediency was . . . 'I'll never do anything to hurt my country.' "

During his second week in office, wearing a cardigan sweater, Carter announced on national television the need for the country to conserve energy. A severe winter had overtaxed supplies of natural gas and oil, creating an energy crisis. He admonished Americans to turn their thermostats down to sixty-five degrees during the day and fifty-five at night. In the White House, he went even further. "I couldn't believe it," Rosalynn recalled. "I had been freezing ever since we moved in. My offices were so cold I couldn't concentrate, and my staff was typing with gloves on. Even upstairs we were only comfortable if we were all wrapped up. . . . I pleaded with Jimmy to set the thermostat at sixty-eight degrees, but it didn't do any good."

Each of Carter's aides had only partial knowledge of his plans. Only to Rosalynn did he reveal the full picture. "When I come home very discouraged," he told the *New York Times,* "she listens to only just a few words of it and she looks at me and says that I've got a problem with this or that. She knows enough about the background of that problem that I don't have to sit for two hours and explain it to her." When Carter told longtime Democratic operative Robert Strauss he wanted him to be his Middle East policy coordinator, he silenced Strauss's protest by saying, "Rosalynn, Cy [Secretary of State Cyrus Vance], Zbig [NSC chief Brzezinski] and Ham [Jordan]" all confirmed his judgment. "In that order," Strauss recalled years later.

When Rosalynn began attending Cabinet meetings, she ran into another buzz saw. It did not matter that she sat quietly taking notes in the back of the Cabinet Room. No first lady, not even Eleanor Roosevelt, had ever attended a Cabinet session. Her chief reason for being there was so Jimmy wouldn't have to explain to her what he did at the "office" all day. "There's no way I could discuss things with Jimmy in an intelligent way," Rosalynn said, "if I didn't attend Cabinet meetings," a poor justification, since Cabinet meetings are famously not where sensitive issues are discussed. She just wanted to be the full partner she had always been. On the margins of position papers and memoranda, the president would often scribble, "Ros. what think?"

Ironically, it was women reporters who protested loudest when the first lady expanded her traditional role. She was once again breaking the first lady's unwritten code of conduct. Jimmy told her to do what he did: ignore the tongue wagging. "I never considered not attending [Cabinet meetings] because of the criticism," she said. "I had learned from more than a decade of political life that I was going to be criticized no matter what I did, so I might as well be criticized for something I wanted to do. If I had spent all day 'pouring tea,' " Rosalynn said, foreshadowing a certain future first lady's line about baking cookies, "I would have been criticized for that too."

Still, unlike Eleanor Roosevelt or Hillary Clinton, Rosalynn always put marriage first. "When Jimmy wasn't working he didn't want me working." Her ambition was to serve him, as well as to temper his excesses. "Rosalynn was the one to point out to him the tawdry practicalities of the situation," Carter's press spokesman, Jody Powell, noted. "I've had tremendous respect for the first lady since I observed Rosalynn Carter. It's an almost impossible role. She played a fine combination of Melanie and Scarlett."

The Carters' most historic days were spent in Camp David. It seemed entirely appropriate for a president at home with the Old Testament to summon Israeli president Menachem Begin and Egypt's president Anwar Sadat to the mountaintop for a Middle East summit in September 1978. To make Rosalynn's presence at the peace talks less conspicuous, the Carters invited the wives of the two old adversaries to join them. "The Begins," Jimmy wrote later, "always seemed very close, and I was sure Aliza [Begin's wife] would be as helpful to him during the coming days as Rosalynn would be to me. . . ." Carter assumed his interlocutors depended on their wives as much as he did on his and was disappointed when Jehan Sadat [Anwar's wife] failed to show up. "I had particularly wanted the three wives to be with us so they could ease some of the tension and create a more congenial atmosphere."

Carter's memoirs of the Camp David conference reveal what his wife's presence by his side meant to him.

Waiting for Sadat to arrive, I discussed the prospects with Rosalynn. . . . I got up at my usual early hour . . . then Rosalynn and I played tennis for about an hour, ate breakfast and discussed my talk with Prime Minister Begin and my plans for the day. . . . Rosalynn was a partner in my thinking throughout the Camp David negotiations, and I presumed that Begin discussed all the issues freely with his wife. Although [the two wives] took time out to have coffee a time or two and went shopping together at a nearby mountain folk festival, the two wives were, in effect, an integral part of their own national delegation. . . .

Rosalynn sat in on many of the Camp David negotiations and took more than two hundred pages of notes for her husband. When she was unable to sit in on the negotiations, she followed the drama from the next room, her mood rising and falling according to the tone of the muffled voices, which sometimes turned to angry shouts.

When Rosalynn was forced to return to Washington to attend to White House business, she couldn't wait to return to Camp David. "I wanted to be near Jimmy, to help him as much as I could. And I had become so caught up in the drama of the peace negotiations that as much as I wanted to get away from the tension, when I did I couldn't wait to get back." Upon returning, she knew that a deadlock had been broken. "When I looked into the room to see what [Jimmy's] mood was, he pushed back his chair and said, 'Come here.' I went in and sat on his lap. He was obviously pleased and hopeful and for a change I was happy for him. 'I think it's all coming together now,' he said."

The Camp David accords of September 1978 were the high point of the Carter presidency. On March 26, 1979, under a huge tent on the White House lawn, Menachem Begin and Anwar Sadat, flanked by a beaming Carter, formally ended thirty years of war. Israel would begin withdrawing troops from Sinai. Egypt would revoke the 1956 ban on Israel's using the Suez Canal. The accords were meant to signal the first step toward self-government for Palestine. Carter's determination, his prodigious patience and his profound understanding of the ancient roots of the Middle East succeeded in breaking the Gordian knot. Sadat and Begin shared the Nobel Peace Prize, but, in Rosalynn's words, "it was Jimmy who made it happen." Jimmy saw it as a joint achievement, his and Rosalynn's, and remained bitter for years that he had not been recognized by the Nobel committee.

∞

FACED WITH INFLATION, high unemployment and long lines at the gas station, Jimmy Carter was not skillful in deflecting bad luck. In fact, he seemed to embrace misfortune with martyrlike zeal. When national discouragement hung like a thick cloud over the White House, a frustrated Rosalynn urged Jimmy to do something dramatic—and politic. "The worst thing you could say to Carter," Mondale noted years later, "was that something was politically the best thing to do." The essential lubricant of Washington political life, its "let's make a deal" ethos, was an alien concept to Carter. He felt no great need to either explain himself or engage in political horse-trading. Just being Jimmy Carter had always been good enough. He never got over his mistrust of the powerful and never stopped letting them know it. (At a December 1994 gathering of some of Washington's media luminaries, Carter preempted the reporters by starting the news conference with a revealing question of his own. "Raise your hand if you have a poor friend," he asked of the reporters. When the startled media failed to respond, Carter, his voice cold and flat, declared, "Well, I see what we've got here.")

With inflation and unemployment soaring, Rosalynn pleaded with her husband to postpone harsh measures until his second term. But his mind was made up. Even more than is usual, the presidency isolated this already solitary man. By 1979, Nixon's corruption of the presidency was no longer at the forefront of public consciousness. Nor had Carter's pieties won him wide support. He had run as an outsider, but after three years in Washington, he could no longer claim that privilege. The Carter presidency was foundering. By June his approval rating hovered around 30 percent. Gasoline lines on the nightly news came to symbolize the administration's failure. There were news clips showing a pregnant woman getting punched in a gas line.

Rosalynn grasped the depth of the problem more than her husband. Mondale thought Carter should speak to labor unions. His chief adviser, Hamilton Jordan, recommended a staff restructuring. Rosalynn asked Jimmy to "change the context" of his presidency; return to the formula that got us elected, she urged.

A brooding, charismatic and heavyset young man of volcanic temper, Patrick Caddell had helped mastermind the Carter presidential campaign. "Pat Caddell was brilliant and crazy," a Carter insider recalled. "Out of a hundred of Caddell's ideas, ninety-eight would get you thrown in jail. Two would be absolutely brilliant. During the campaign, Carter was on the road; the rest of us would be around to vet Pat's ideas. But it is easier to get to the president than to a candidate. Caddell lobbied Rosalynn. He was relentless. Around 9:30 at night when the rest of us would be going home to our wives or girlfriends, we'd see Caddell coming in to the White House to see Rosalynn." Caddell came bearing books: John Maynard Keynes's essays, James McGregor Burns's *Leadership,* Christopher Lasch's *The Culture of Narcissism.* He persuaded Rosalynn that the problem lay not so much with her husband but with a loss of confidence in the future, a general feeling of impotence after fifteen disastrous years of war, Watergate, assassinations, riots, double-digit inflation and the energy crisis.

Caddell showed Rosalynn a memorandum for the president detailing how to revive the country's flagging spirit. The problem, according to Caddell, was not political but spiritual and cultural. It was no longer enough for Carter to be the soothing, humble anti-Nixon. Instead of standing for one or two or three big things, his presidency had turned into a hodgepodge. The country had tuned him out. The president should stop talking issues and touch on the intangible problems of society, minister rather than manage. Talk to the country about the need for rebirth, not gas prices or thermostats, Caddell advised. Jimmy must be more of a "transforming" leader and less of a "transactional" one. Deal from a higher place, he urged, reconnect with your roots.

Caddell's advice resonated with both Rosalynn and her husband. Returning exhausted after a June 1979 economic summit in Japan, the president suddenly decided against a long-planned Hawaii vacation. Instead, the Carters landed at Andrews Air Force Base and helicoptered to Camp David. Caddell joined them there. Vice President Mondale hated Cadell's message, saw it as ruinous for the administration. "I had majored in social psychology," Mondale recalled. "I figured it [Caddell's plan] was a dry hole. We had been elected on a platform of 'a government as good as the people.' This new message would come across as a search for 'people as good as their government.'" Mondale did not think there was anything "so wrong with the Carter presidency that couldn't be fixed by going out and talking to the people and asserting presidential leadership."

But Rosalynn and Cadell persisted. Carter summoned a group of "wise men" and fixers, seasoned politicos and civil rights leaders, to commune with him at Camp David. "I feel I have lost control of the government and the leadership of the people," Carter told his astonished guests. The exercise began to look like part group therapy, part religious atonement. Sitting on the floor in blue jeans and a polo shirt, a yellow legal pad perched on his knee, the president listened and took copious notes, filling page after page as if he were a graduate student and not the leader of the free world. "It's not easy for me to accept criticism and reassess my ways of doing things," Carter wrote in his diary on July 9,

1979. One of those in attendance wondered how Carter would distill rational policy from the "mishmash of people, prejudice and points of view." The country was equally mystified by the president's eight-day absence from the White House. Even for this unorthodox president, it was a gamble, both brave and dangerous.

On July 15, Carter faced the country. He delivered a strong, inspirational speech, while at the same time reminding the country that its resources were limited. Carter's approval ratings zoomed up eleven points. In a presidency branded by bad luck, the lift was temporary. The speech, called the Crisis of Confidence Speech by the president, was soon damned by a word that he never used in the speech—it came to be known as the "Malaise Speech." (He had, however, used the phrase at Camp David, and Clark Clifford, one of the wise men, had mentioned it to the *Washington Post*.)

Caddell's hoped-for transformation splintered into bureaucratic warfare. "We'd created an opening to the public," Caddell asserted, "but then institutional inertia took over. Carter had some serious organizational problems, but I thought we should start with the conceptual part first. People inside the White House were threatened by where we were going. I wanted to set up a creative workshop inside the White House to give the president new ideas, to drive this plan."

One of the many ideas tossed out during the Camp David retreat was one for which media adviser Gerald Rafshoon takes the blame. Rafshoon had a solution to Carter's problems with three of his Cabinet secretaries, Joseph Califano, Treasury Secretary Michael Blumenthal and Transportation Secretary Brock Adams. None of the three was deemed to be loyal or to be operating from the administration's script. "We knew Jimmy Carter did not have it in him to fire them outright," Rafshoon recalled, "so I suggested he ask the whole Cabinet, plus senior staff, to offer their resignations. Carter could then choose which ones to accept." Rafshoon says the idea—a way around Carter's aversion to personal confrontation—was never seriously discussed. When Jordan called Rafshoon and said his "plan" had been put in play, Rafshoon was astonished. But the mass firing meant to assert presidential leadership and a clean break with the past provoked the opposite effect, telegraphing the twin messages of chaos and disarray at the top. It recalled Nixon's Cabinet purge after his 1972 reelection. Carter's popularity now sank to record lows. Though he may have accurately analyzed the country's problem, his prescription—blame it on the people, shake up the government—aggravated, rather than eased, the situation. He had chosen a course that seemed a compromise between national psychotherapy and bureaucratic bloodletting, and no one was satisfied.

Just months after the Mideast Camp David triumph, the Carter presidency had lost its way. He had lost the support of the media and academic elites who had helped elect him and did not have the political skills to reach the people without them. The pall of failure hung over the White House. "I saw real despair there," Mondale remembered. "Jimmy Carter was an eighteen-hours-a-day man, but nothing he did seemed to be working." A relative stranger to defeat, Carter was also new to Washington's appetite for consuming the vulnerable. Rosalynn remembered 1979 and 1980 as a period of never-ending crises. "Big ones and small ones, potential disasters and mere annoyances." The downward spiral seemed irreversible and emboldened Carter's two most dangerous political enemies, Edward Kennedy and Ronald Reagan. The Malaise Speech became the Carter presidency's epitaph. It provided his many enemies and detractors, inside and outside his party, with the sword they were looking to finish him with. Carter had never played by their rules and did not take sufficient care of their sensibilities. The man who thought he could change Washington's culture was crushed by it.

The photograph that became the metaphor for the waning days of the Carter presidency perfectly illustrated this. His face drained, arms limp, the president is shown running a marathon near Camp David, straining for breath but still pushing mightily to cross some imaginary finish line. His aides had begged him not to run. "But there he was, running harder and longer than he should have," Mondale said, "and it was just typical of Jimmy Carter and the administration." So much effort, so much exertion, to so little effect.

And so it came down to the crisis that sealed the fate of his presidency: the Iran hostage crisis. The face of the Carter presidency morphed from gasoline lines to the far more alarming blindfolded Amer-

icans. Carter's humanitarian gesture, in granting the Shah of Iran temporary asylum in the United States for medical care, had boomeranged.
When Iranian terrorists seized the American embassy in Teheran and
held fifty-two American diplomats captive, it seemed a personal strike
against the hapless president. "America Held Hostage" became a media
slogan. (The name, in fact, of the ABC late-night news program that
became *Nightline*). Carter could do nothing to free the hostages or to
change his now fixed image as an inept, if morally pure, chief of state.

As Carter spent sleepless nights negotiating for the hostages' release
over the next year, Rosalynn campaigned for his nomination and reelection. Senator Edward M. Kennedy's challenge for the Democratic nomination was a fatal blow. The simple verities that worked for the Carters
four years earlier, authenticity and humility, no longer appealed to a
country yearning to feel good again. Kennedy hurt Carter, and Ronald
Reagan exuded rugged, unshakable confidence. Suddenly the Carters
looked small and dangerously naive. Jimmy's voice now seemed reed
thin, his personality, when compared to Reagan's manly assertiveness
and sunny certainties, too tentative.

While Jimmy followed a "Rose Garden Strategy" of barely leaving
the White House during the bitter primary fight with Kennedy, Rosalynn
was his designated voice. She still believed she could break through to
the people in a way the president could not. Where he was surrounded
by his jet stream of advisers, she traveled light. She could have real conversations with people and be a conduit to Jimmy. She was also completely exposed to the media's scrutiny of her every expression, every
furrowed brow of distress. "I bring greetings from Jimmy," she began
each stop on her relentless tour—Chicago; Pine Bluff, Arkansas; Fort
Worth; and Fresno. "I want you to know he's healthy and we're having a
wonderful time at the White House." She meant to reassure people after
the damaging image of the marathon. But it had the opposite effect.

Reporters dubbed her the nurse, him the patient. Now her strength
exposed his weakness. Her fear of public speaking long conquered, her
self-assurance on the stump was used against him. "She gets coy about
her role as adviser. . . . And the public continues to believe that she is a
major influence on her husband," the *Washington Post* reported, "maybe

too major." With the scent of failure lingering over Jimmy Carter's presidency, the sharks circled.

Returning to the White House, she urged her husband to "do something." Like what, he wearily asked her. Mine the harbors of Iran, she entreated. Jimmy patiently explained why that would be rash and probably lead to the death of the hostages. When her frustration boiled over, her husband told her she should quit campaigning. But after nearly a lifetime of following his lead, Rosalynn was in the game as much as he was.

So Rosalynn set off on another round of stumping, shaking every hand. Very rarely did her iron composure slip. Her aide Paul Costello recalled one night during the long summer campaign, aboard Rosalynn's DC-9 military aircraft. "We had started taxiing out and the Secret Service came to get her. 'Mrs. Carter, the president wants to speak to you.' So we taxied back to the gate and she went to a land line and took the call from the president. After she came back and while we were having dinner, she said, 'Jimmy wanted to know how things were going. So I told him, 'It's really rough. Everybody's beating up on you.' And he just cut me off. 'Rosalynn, I don't want to hear any of this.' So I told him, 'You can just go to hell.' And I hung up."

~

ELECTION DAY 1980 coincided with the first anniversary of the hostage crisis. "All the understandable disillusionment of the American people," Rosalynn later wrote, "fell on us. . . . Damn, damn Khomeini!" Determined and defiant until the very last day, Rosalynn vowed, "We'll just show them like we have so many times before."

But it was too late. Reagan swept to victory by a humiliating margin: 51 percent of the popular vote to Carter's 41 percent. Not only did the Republicans take possession of the White House but, for the first time in twenty-eight years, they gained control of the Senate as well.

On a weekend shortly before Reagan's inauguration, Rosalynn invited her staff to Camp David. It was a day to unwind, to swim, skeet-shoot and bike-ride around the breathtaking Catoctin Mountain trails. Rosalynn struggled desperately to put a bright face on her misery. "But it

The Carters ride a bicycle built for two in Plains, Georgia,
on Christmas Eve, 1980. Defeated by Reagan, they
have less than a month left in office.

felt as if we were on a plank," a member of her staff recalled, "waiting to
be pushed. She was just flabbergasted that this incredible man—her husband—had been rejected by the country." Rosalynn blamed the times,
the opposition, her own side's inability to get their message out. But she
found no fault with Jimmy. Jimmy was still the brightest star she had ever
come across, the handsome young man in his navy whites who had rescued the young girl from Plains.

The Carters stayed as close, as exemplary and as singular in their
behavior in private life as they had in the White House. Jimmy continued
his biblical quest to end wars and eradicate disease with barely a nod to
political or practical considerations. His office walls at the Carter Presidential Library feature such suspected war criminals as the Bosnian war
lord Radovan Karadzic, whom Carter sees not as a mass murderer but as
a soul to save. When President George Bush prepared to mount Operation Desert Storm, Carter wrote every member of the United Nations
Security Council urging them not to support Washington.

The Carters were a transitional first couple, a bridge between the
traditional and the postfeminist eras. Rosalynn tried to carve out new territory as first lady but came under tremendous criticism, in part because,

unlike Eleanor Roosevelt, she had neither the credentials nor a strong enough political base. Her public identity was as a mate and not as a political partner. Two decades later, when Hillary Rodham Clinton was still pondering whether to run for the United States Senate, someone asked Rosalynn why she had never run for the Senate. "What would I have done in Washington," she asked, "with Jimmy in Georgia?"

CHAPTER 9

NANCY AND RONALD REAGAN

VIRTUALLY PERFECT

Without Nancy, Ronnie would still be driving his red Lincoln up and down California's beaches and talking to Republican women's clubs.

—MICHAEL DEAVER

[Nancy] was the ignition and the battery of [Reagan's] whole political career, and I persist in thinking this essential relationship is the clue to Reagan.

—MEG GREENFIELD

THE CHANGE COULD NOT HAVE BEEN MORE DRAMATIC. THE PRESIDENCY NOW passed from a man who zealously controlled its most minute components to a man whose motto was "Show me an executive who works long overtime hours, and I'll show you a bad executive." But those who thought Ronald Reagan would be a pleasant figurehead and his wife a lady who merely lunched were equally far off the mark. Nancy Reagan was the most powerful first lady in terms of influence on the president since Edith Wilson; she was not the most creative nor the most compassionate first lady, but probably the most indispensable to her husband.

Politics, the great wedge between many political couples, drew the Reagans closer. They shared every step of his rise. By the end of their remarkable partnership—always presented to the public as a Hollywood-style love story—Ronnie and Nancy had effectively fused into a single persona, completing each other almost seamlessly.

Reagan radiated optimism and a return to simple American values. This, of course, is a truism. What is less well understood is that his wife acted as a sentry guarding him, guarding the gate to power, enabling him to present his sunny face. Nancy was far more transparent in her ambitions and motives than Ronnie, whose determination was camouflaged by a self-deprecating smile, a one-liner or a witty anecdote. His wife was the lightning rod, he the magician. As the Reagans made their way from Hollywood to Sacramento to Washington, this arrangement worked with astonishing success.

As president, he saw his job essentially as being Ronald Reagan, acting like a president (FDR, of course, being his role model). An intuitive politician, he was dependent on his wife's analytical sense. Policy was what his staff did. He summarized his management philosophy as "Surround yourself with the best people you can find, delegate authority and don't interfere." Reagan usually treated the office simply as a ceremonial one, trusting his lieutenants to carry out his intentions. "He listened, acquiesced, played his role," in the words of one of his chiefs of staff, Don Regan, "and waited for the next act to be written."

Historically, great and powerful leaders have been entitled to both their courtesans and their consiglieri. In Nancy Davis Reagan, Ronnie had both. He could not have been elected president without her drive and will. Without Nancy as his sterner half, he could not have conveyed the image of well-being that was key to both his election and his presidency. Nor would he have achieved the easing of Cold War tensions, perhaps his most enduring legacy, without his wife's encouragement and intrigues.

Nancy, like several of her predecessors, served her husband, not the country. He was her career. She was the ultimate "insider" first lady. Unlike Eleanor Roosevelt and Hillary Clinton, she had no separate policy agenda. Unlike Rosalynn Carter, she sought little recognition for herself as an independent policy maker or presidential emissary. His policy was the only one that mattered; his legacy would be inseparable from hers. The famous and much mocked gaze that she fixed on him when he spoke seemed to make this detached man perform at maximum capacity. During the greatest crisis of his presidency, this insecure, superstitious but politically shrewd woman helped bring him back from the brink.

There is perhaps no more important presidential power than choosing the right people to fill key positions. FDR, Truman and Kennedy made brilliant and consequential choices. In this critical presidential territory, Reagan ceded extraordinary ground to his wife. She made no apologies for her involvement in White House personnel decisions. "Most of my suggestions were about personnel," she admitted. "I don't know much about economics or military affairs, but I have strong instincts about people, and I'm a good judge of character. As much as I love Ronnie, I'll admit he does have at least one fault: he can be naive about the people around him." But Nancy *was* generally a shrewd judge of people. Those she backed—George Shultz, Mike Deaver, Jim Baker, Howard Baker and Bob Strauss—were the right ones for her husband's legacy.

ON THE SURFACE, she and Reagan could hardly have been more different. She was small and brittle. He was a big man, tall and muscular, with a strong sense of his own power—the power of his physical presence and that of his voice. No detail was too microscopic for her attention. He was indifferent to details. Worry etched Nancy's face and pitched her voice high, sometimes causing her to stammer. His voice—self-assured, yet humble, hopeful and intimate—connected with people. Her self-consciousness made those around her edgy. Ironically, his voice as well as the rest of his persona were really a way to keep people at bay.

And yet this easy man and this nervous woman became opposite sides of one coin. "In some ways," he wrote, "Nancy and I are like one human being." Both had been permanently scarred by traumatic childhoods. She could trust no one except the one person who was as dependent on her as she was on him. The wholesale intimacy her husband exuded that made him irresistible to so many masked an almost complete emotional detachment.

The son of a failed salesman who was an alcoholic, Ronnie learned to retreat from reality into his own world, to see and hear only what he wanted to. He was nine when his family finally settled down in Dixon, Illinois. The remote little boy did not learn to form real attachments, and he never would. Always the new boy in class, he had learned to please everybody. The trauma of finding his father passed out in the snow, or the routine chaos of life with an alcoholic, instilled in Reagan a fear of anything "unpleasant." For the rest of his life, he avoided confrontation and emotional entanglement. His sanctuary was an idealized America of solid, uncomplicated midwestern values. In this fable, he cast himself as a straight and simple hero, a man of action, not words. As an actor in films extolling American virtues and, finally, as president, Reagan, remarkably, realized his original vision of himself.

He called Nancy his "everything," and claimed she had "saved his soul," but even with her he kept a veil over his emotions and could be remote. Throughout their married life Reagan spent hours in solitary physical labor, chopping wood and building fences at his ranch. "There's a wall around him," she wrote. "He lets me come closer than anyone else, but there are times when even I feel that barrier."

WHEN RONNIE AND NANCY MET IN 1949, he was still bruised from his recent divorce from actress Jane Wyman. The breakup had stunned him, stripped him of his equilibrium. He was despondent in a way his friends had never seen. As always with bad news, for a long time he simply refused to believe it. "Janie is a pretty sick girl in mind," Reagan wrote the head of his fan club, Lorraine Wagner, in January 1948, "but I'm still hoping that things will be different when she gets over this nervousness, so don't listen to things you hear, please. I know she loves me, even though she thinks she doesn't. . . ."

Reagan, for whom marriage and family were articles of faith, was not supposed to be divorced. That he did not see the breakup coming was in keeping with his willed blindness toward anything smacking of "unpleasantness." But others remarked on Wyman's weariness with Reagan's new obsession. It wasn't their shared craft that stirred Ronnie's passion but politics, particularly the threat of Communist infiltration into the Screen Actors Guild. Like many politicians, he was mesmerized by his own voice and a set of repetitive ideas. He failed to see their effect on his wife. "Don't ask Ronnie for the time," Jane once dryly cautioned a friend, "because he'll tell you how the watch is made." Though she has rarely expressed herself on her marriage to Reagan, his inability to form an intimate emotional connection no doubt weakened their bond. The Reagans' two children, Maureen and Michael, could not compensate for the loneliness Jane felt alongside her husband. Not even with his children was Reagan able to drop his diffidence. His older brother, Neil, recalled that though Ronnie was a strong swimmer, "I taught Maureen to swim. . . . He didn't bother with her. . . . Dutch thought children should be on their own. . . ."

Reagan was on Nancy Davis's list of eligible Hollywood bachelors. With the help of director Mervyn LeRoy, she engineered a dinner invitation. Nancy was immediately, almost too easily, smitten. Indeed, she was looking for just such a partner: manly and commanding. By shoring up his ego and making herself indispensable, Nancy gradually wore down his resistance to a new emotional entanglement. "How come you moved in on me like this?" Ronnie asked Nancy once they were married. He would soon discover that what the thirty-year-old struggling actress lacked in beauty or talent, she compensated for in determination and focus.

No doubt it helped that she was almost as wary of intimacy as he was, after the incurable wound of having been abandoned by her own actress mother for six years, and left in the care of relatives. Later, Nancy rationalized her mother's neglect. "It nearly killed her to do it, but she had to make a living, since she wouldn't accept alimony. As long as Mother had to work, this was the best possible arrangement." But Nancy had to admit that she "missed her—terribly. No matter how kindly you are treated—and I was treated with great love—your mother is your mother, and nobody else can fill that role in your life." When Nancy was sick, she recalled years later, "I was angry that Mother was a thousand miles away in a touring company. I remember crying and saying, 'If I had a little girl, I'd certainly be there if she was ever sick.' "

Nancy saw her mother's precarious life as an actress suddenly transformed by a strong, wealthy, socially prominent man. Almost overnight, nine-year-old Nancy went from a poor relation, the ward of her mother's sister, to a world of privilege. Her stepfather, whom she revered, was Dr. Loyal Davis, the noted Chicago neurosurgeon. He became Nancy's role model for a husband. In Dr. Davis's universe, men were the leaders, and women their devoted helpmates. Nancy brutally severed all ties with her own father so Davis could adopt her.

Later, Nancy understood that Jane Wyman had been too interested in her own career and insufficiently interested in politics. Nancy was not about to make the same mistake. She knew how to listen. She knew how to make Ronnie feel like an American hero. Nancy must have recognized certain vulnerabilities behind his winning cowboy grin. He seemed to need the love of the faceless, distant crowd, but not too much intimacy. She, in turn, needed a single person who would be all hers, who would provide the comfort and security withheld from her as a child and would allow her to adore him, protect him, even *create* him. Thanks to her stepfather's devotion to conservative causes, Nancy was already genuinely interested in politics. She married Ronnie on March 4, 1952.

Thus began the transformation of a forty-one-year-old movie actor with declining career prospects into one of the dominant political figures of the latter part of the twentieth century. Nancy discovered that she had never really wanted a career after all, and had pursued acting "only because I hadn't found the man I wanted to marry."

Ronnie and Nancy, and before long two children, soon became the very image of the wholesome American family, circa 1964. Looking for a positive corporate face, General Electric found Reagan appealing and admired his ease before the camera no matter what he was selling. He had an uncanny ability to connect with the audience not as an actor in character but as Ronald Reagan. From the small screen, Ronnie, Nancy, Patti and Ron beamed out the message that all was well in the land.

If something seemed unreal about the appearance of perfection in the Reagans' marriage, it was because they wanted it that way. Each had sampled reality and found it wanting. The artificial could be controlled more easily. The Reagans were not who they appeared to be. Nancy was never really a housewife; she did not intend simply to play the role of Harriet to his Ozzie. Ronnie's evangelical zeal was more rhetorical than real. With few exceptions—he genuinely hated communism and big government and loved missile defenses—he, with Nancy's help, chose his politics opportunistically. They were sure only of Ronnie's magic. It was clear he had a personal magnetism that went beyond the actor's craft. People warmed to the optimism he exuded. "They look at me and they see themselves," he liked to say.

To be sure, others, like Lyndon Johnson and JFK, had also been masters of invention and hyperbole. Politicians tend to exaggerate as a professional way of life. But Reagan's great strength was that he seemed to *believe* his own fantasies. Facts were less important than his larger message. Even before he became an actor, Reagan had perfected the ability to make the unreal sound real. As a sportscaster in Davenport, Iowa, he never left his studio, yet conveyed the thrill of the game by embroidering on the spare information coming over a Teletype. He never left the United States during World War II, but decades later he seemed convinced he had. "When I came back from the war," he used to begin stories, even though he spent those years making army training movies at a military base in Los Angeles. His stories about the liberation of the concentration camps and all those brave G.I.'s were so personal, so gripping, his style so engaging, it almost didn't matter that he had not been an eyewitness. (Israeli prime minister Yitzhak Shamir, leaving a private meeting with Reagan, told his staff he had just learned that Reagan had witnessed the liberation of Dachau. Of course he had not.)

This was Reagan's magic: the ability to convince people that something had happened when it hadn't. With his masterful storytelling ability, he pulled people into his narrative. He learned this from his father, Jack. His mother, Nelle, much like FDR's and LBJ's mothers, imbued Ronnie with a sense of his own destiny. The son was to redeem the father's failure. For though Reagan's politics evolved over the years from Roosevelt Democrat to Goldwater Republican, then from Cold War zealot to peacemaker, Reagan was essentially always selling himself.

The Reagans' love and need of each other, however, was authentic.

"It's time to move on to the next town," Ronnie wrote Nancy in March 1955, when he was traveling for General Electric, "and every move is a step toward home and you. I love you so very much I don't even mind that life made me wait so long to find you. The waiting only made the finding sweeter."

For a long time, Reagan hovered on the fringes of the country's consciousness as a pleasant, second-tier actor and corporate spokesman whose ex-wife was more successful than he was. Nancy, conservative by nature and upbringing, no doubt influenced the rightward shift in her husband, as did the network of newly wealthy businessmen and industrialists they spent time with in California.

The years with GE were invaluable. He traveled the country, honing and polishing his speaking style, and learning what was on people's minds. In 1964, in a nationwide sermon urging Barry Goldwater's election, he shattered his soft-lens image. Angry and absolutist, he declared his new Republican credo. "You and I have a rendezvous with destiny . . . ," he said, appropriating his old hero FDR's words for a different cause. "We can preserve for our children this last best hope of man on earth or we can sentence them to take the first step into a thousand years of darkness." The overheated rhetoric did not save Goldwater's candidacy, but it put Reagan on the nation's radar. The *Washington Post* called it "the most successful political debut since William Jennings Bryan electrified the 1896 Democratic convention with his 'Cross of Gold' speech."

Two years later, campaigning for governor of California, Reagan transformed a speech about Depression-bound Dixon, Illinois, into a gripping parable of small-town America. Reagan, no longer simply the angry man of the 1964 Republican convention, electrified audiences. He had the actor's skill at persuasion, but now he had a part he could play better than anyone: himself. His wife was always beside him, her hands clasped, her unblinking gaze fixed on him, transmitting a current of love, support and security. And Reagan, a man who believed deeply in luck, now got his first big dose of it. Californians' fear of chaos, fueled by the recent Berkeley riots, helped Reagan defeat the incumbent governor, Edmund G. ("Pat") Brown, in a landslide in 1966.

In those early days, Nancy had not yet learned to camouflage her insecurity. Governor Reagan's secretary Nancy Reynolds recalled finding her looking forlorn at Sacramento Airport, one week after her husband's election as governor. "She said, 'I don't know what to do. He just left me here. I need to get to Los Angeles.' She seemed completely lost. I asked her if somebody was going to meet her at the other end in L.A., and she said yes, we have a car and driver. So I said, 'I'm going to get two tickets and fly down with you.' She was very relieved. But my memory is of a lost soul, unsophisticated and completely vulnerable."

Mike Wallace, the CBS journalist and an old friend of both Nancy Reagan and her mother, recalls a moment that crystallized for him the relationship between Ronnie and Nancy. On board the U.S.S. *Independence* en route to a governors' conference in the Virgin Islands,

> There was Michigan Governor George Romney and his wife, and Governor Nelson Rockefeller and Happy, and Governor and Mrs. John Connally of Texas, all interacting with each other and the press—a lot of banter, very informal. And as we were all getting off the ship, I wanted to go say good-bye to Ronnie and Nancy, whom I had known since before they were married. And there they were, just the two of them, sort of huddled in a stateroom, all alone. They were not mixing, or glad-handing like everybody else. They were really into their own world. I don't know why this had such an impact on me. It was as if for a split second I caught them as they really were—alone, together.

Nancy had to surround Reagan with aides almost as dedicated to him as she herself. Ever alert to the slightest hint of disloyalty or less than total commitment to Ronnie, she developed antennae for staffers with their own agenda. With the laissez-faire Reagan, staff support took on a whole new meaning. His staff, with Nancy as invisible producer/director and Mike Deaver as her executor, enabled a stellar performance artist to function as an effective politician.

Nancy's role as her husband's unofficial chief of personnel dates from his time as governor. Stu Spencer, who worked with Reagan during this period, remembered that "She made judgments about the people around him. She knew what type worked best with Ron. She tried to determine who would be loyal to him. She inserted herself into that role and he appreciated it. He respected her judgment and opinion."

Trained as an actor, Reagan liked direction, a sense that everybody had a role to play in the production. "Once in 1966 when he was running for governor," Spencer remembered, "at the end of the day we were in some cow town like Fresno, talking about scheduling for the next day, sitting in his room, and Reagan turns to me and says, 'I think I figured this thing out.' What do you mean? I asked him. 'Politics,' he said, 'I figured it out. It's just like show business. You have a hell of an opening. You coast. And then you have a hell of a closing.' That was his view of the process, and there's a lot of truth in that."

Reagan had a handful of core beliefs. Once he made them known, he expected others to turn them into policy. The power to charm, persuade and, like his friend Jimmy Stewart, make Americans feel good about being American—-those were his gifts. He could convey a stronger message with his crinkly grin and his jaunty step than Jimmy Carter could with a briefing book of facts at his command.

Reagan was incapable of dismissing people, no matter how incompetent. This trait dated from his days as head of the Screen Actors Guild. Reagan's longtime Hollywood agent Taft Schreiber worried about how this would play out once the actor became a serious politician. "We better have lunch, kid," Schreiber told Stu Spencer. "Something you are going to have to learn. You are going to have to fire a lot of people." Startled, Spencer asked what he meant. "I was Ronnie's agent for twenty years and he never fired anybody," said Schreiber.

Nancy Reynolds, who observed the couple over many decades, concluded that "Nancy was Ronald Reagan's first line of defense, politically and personally." She recalled an incident during a flight with Mrs. Reagan when her husband was governor. "Behind us was somebody lacing into Ronald Reagan and his budget cuts. I could see the blood rising in Nancy's face. Suddenly she flips back the seat, turns around and says, 'That's my husband you're talking about and that budget is what this state needs.' Nancy didn't shout, but she was very firm."

Even though Nancy is a tough-minded, practical woman, she sought help in the occult. She believed in the alignment of planets and stars as predictors of events. An astrologer had chosen the precise moment of Reagan's swearing-in as governor of California. Nancy started relying on astrology. Spencer claims that Reagan did not believe in it but humored his wife. Whatever made Nancy happy was all right with Ronnie.

In 1968, Joan Didion interviewed Nancy for a *Saturday Evening Post* profile that would forever seal Nancy's distrust of the media. Didion had spent a day with her subject at the governor's residence in Sacramento. Nancy, who thought the interview had gone well, was shattered by the article when it appeared. Entitled "Pretty Nancy," it was etched in acid—and missed Nancy's essential insecurity. "Nancy Reagan has an interested smile," Didion wrote, "the smile of a good wife, a good mother, a good hostess, the smile of someone who grew up in comfort and went to Smith College and has a father who is a distinguished neurosurgeon . . . and a husband who is the definition of Nice Guy, not to mention governor of California, the smile of a woman who seems to be playing out some middle-class American woman's daydream, circa 1948."

After this article, a newly wary Nancy set out to befriend key members of the media. She never again granted an interview without a careful vetting by her friends. Former CIA director Richard Helms became one of her favorite "controllers." Arrangements for an interview with her were (and remain) akin to obtaining clearance for a sensitive national security position. Unlike her husband, who used wit and charm to disarm the press, Nancy used fear and intimidation. Almost two decades later, *Washington Post* reporter Sally Quinn still remembered a confrontation with Nancy: "She gripped both my shoulders while she chewed me out about a comment I'd made on TV a few weeks before. I could feel that grip for a long time."

∞

IN 1976, Reagan took a bold and dangerous step: he challenged a sitting president from his own party for the presidential nomination. A politically wounded Gerald Ford ultimately carried the day and blamed Reagan for dividing the party. "How can you challenge an incumbent,"

Ford asked in his autobiography, "and not be divisive?" Reagan, who preached the mantra of never attacking fellow Republicans, deflected blame for the party's humiliation that fall through charm, persuasion and a quality later dubbed "Teflon." Ronnie and Nancy had electrified the convention. They had a close-up view of the summit and they savored the excitement.

As Ronnie's national prominence grew, so, too, did the Reagans' interdependence. "When one of us has a problem, it automatically becomes a problem for the other; an attack on one of us is an attack on both of us. When one suffers, so does the other," he wrote. The insecure woman abandoned by her own mother now felt secure with a man who didn't seem to need anyone else. "Everything began with you," Nancy wrote Ronnie in 1967, "my whole life—so you'd better be careful and take care of yourself because there'd be nothing and I'd be no one without you."

His impressive physical presence was an important part of their bond and continued to be until very late in their married life. "I remember being upstairs in her office in the White House," White House social secretary Gahl Burt recalled, "and he would walk in wearing his gym shorts and I was just stunned with his physique. Stunned. He had this broad chest, long, strong legs and arms. And there wasn't an ounce of flab."

Decades into their marriage, he still left her love notes ending, "I.T.W.W.W."—"in the whole wide world"—as in "I love you more than anything." Not surprisingly, their children felt left out, sidelined by their parents' passionate need only of each other. When Ronnie wrote, "I love the whole gang of you," he meant all of Nancy. "Mommie, first lady, the sentimental you, the funny you and the peewee power house you. . . . I couldn't and don't sleep well if [you aren't] there—so please always be there." For Reagan, his children were a responsibility to be fulfilled. "But what is really important," he wrote Nancy in May 1963, "is that having fulfilled our responsibilities to our offspring, we haven't been careless with the treasure that is ours—namely what we are to each other." Late in his father's life, his son Ron admitted, "I never had a real conversation with my father."

Ronnie called her Mommy and liked to sort out her vitamin pills before she left for a trip. Nancy Reynolds traveled with him during the 1980 presidential campaign and often fielded Nancy's nightly calls.

> We were at a hotel in New Hampshire during the primaries. I had ordered his breakfast for him and said good night. No sooner do I get to my room and start undressing than the phone rings. It's Nancy and she said, "Is Ronnie asleep?" I said, Gee, I don't know. She said, "You go and tell him to turn out the light. I bet he's reading. He needs his sleep. You go right out of your room, knock on his door and you see if he's undressed and in bed!" So I went past the Secret Service and knocked on his door in my robe and whispered, "Governor, it's me. Nancy wants to know if you have your pajamas on and have the lights out." "Between the two Nancies in my life," he grumbled, "I'm never going to have a peaceful moment!" But, in fact, he loved it.

In 1980, Reagan had the perfect foil in Jimmy Carter. In politics, optimists always trump pessimists. Like FDR, Reagan had a winning temperament. He seemed to enjoy life, and found no issue too complex for a solution. Reagan, who could capture an audience with a single one-liner, famously did so that year with the line "There you go again!," disorienting the earnest Carter. Reagan did not sound like a politician, which of course is the highest goal of all politicians. "He knows so little," his national security adviser Bud McFarlane once marveled, "and he accomplished so much." Carter lost not solely on issues but on how he came across to the country: a small man who filled Americans with self-doubt. The big, tall, radiant man of the West who talked to the country like a Depression-era man of the people said, "I can fix this!" He seemed glad to be alive. The country wanted to be sprinkled with some of his magic dust.

When his advisers made the mistake of treating Reagan like just another politician, cramming him with facts for a televised debate, he fizzled. When it happened, memorably, in his first debate with Walter Mondale in 1984, Nancy stepped in to refocus him. She knew how to extract his best performance. It was Nancy who made sure the house lights were on when he addressed a large group because he needed to see faces and make eye contact. By telling his aides to back off and let Ronnie be Ronnie, Nancy enabled him to make that connection in the second debate, and he recovered from the disaster of his first encounter with Mondale.

∽

THE PRESIDENCY TIGHTENED the Reagans' bond. Living and working in the same house enabled Nancy to exercise unprecedented control over Ronnie's staff and schedule. Her vehemence was a counterweight to his nonchalance. While with others Nancy could be brutally direct, with Ronnie she had to be indirect, subtle. "Ronnie can't be pushed," she said. "He can be coaxed." She ordered others to do her bidding, even prepping her guests before dinner to raise certain delicate issues that she knew her husband was not eager to confront. She would feed guests their lines, and at a given moment during what seemed to be a casual gathering, she would cue them. "Ronnie, so and so has something he wants to raise with you. . . ." When the news was bad, she absorbed it and acted on it, while he deflected it. "Nancy will be livid," Ronnie would say when presented with a negative article.

At various times she identified deputy secretary of state/then national security adviser William Clark, Attorney General Ed Meese, CIA director William Casey, Secretary of State Al Haig and—most famously—chief of staff Don Regan as not serving Ronnie's interest, being guilty of too much ideology or demonstrating insufficient loyalty. Nancy succeeded in getting rid of them all, one way or another. But she would never say to her husband, Fire that man. Instead, she would plant the seed and nourish it to life. Once she made up her mind, she was relentless, while the president barely seemed to notice the carnage. To Reagan, a new chief of staff or a new national security adviser seemed of no greater moment than a new producer. It was the leading man who filled the theater.

Whatever tension there was in the Reagan White House came not from the genial host of the nation but from his wife. "She can smell fear on you," Spencer once said to political consultant Ed Rollins. Presidential speechwriter Peggy Noonan ducked behind a pillar when she heard the tap-tap of the first lady's high heels around the corner. Nancy never attended Cabinet meetings and rarely showed up in the West Wing. Her weapon of choice in asserting her influence and in staying on top of all aspects of life in the White House was the telephone. "If I did not hear from her for twenty-four hours," deputy chief of staff Mike Deaver noted, "I would call her and ask, 'Nancy, do we have a problem?' " Gahl Burt recalled, "Mrs. Reagan liked to joke that she will be buried with a telephone. And I knew when there was a problem to call her and tell her first because I knew she would find out anyway, one way or the other. It was fatal if you didn't keep Nancy in the loop. Because she wanted to know *everything*." Burt recalled the frustration of dealing with violinist Isaac Stern, who was to perform at a state dinner. "Suddenly Stern wanted to invite twenty-two people of his choosing. And he wanted another friend to give a lecture on Mozart. You would not think that the first lady would want to get involved with that level of detail. But I knew Nancy would find out about it, so I kept her informed of all his demands."

Even the normally composed Jim Baker, when chief of staff, broke out in a sweat at the thought of the first lady's ire. Baker had come into the Reagan administration as a Bush loyalist, not an original Reaganite. But the canny Texan soon discerned that the way to become an insider was to connect with the first lady. Reporter Lesley Stahl described sitting in Baker's office late one afternoon. Suddenly the president's helicopter hovered into view over the South Lawn. "Oh, my God," Baker exclaimed, looking at his watch and springing to his feet. "I think I may have missed the helicopter. The president is leaving for Camp David any minute. Maybe I can still make it." With that, Baker sprinted toward the helipad. Returning minutes later, breathless, he announced, "I made it!" When the reporter asked what was so urgent, Baker replied, "I didn't have anything special to tell *them*. I just wanted them to see me standing there as they left for the weekend." Later, hearing the story, a White House official wryly noted, "It wasn't Reagan Jim was afraid of. It was Nancy. Reagan wouldn't have noticed whether Jim was there or not."

The White House was a perfect theater to display Ronald Reagan's talents. It was a highly controlled environment for a man who thrived in controlled situations. A disciplined man of remarkably low intellectual curiosity, he seldom strayed from the schedule his staff prepared for him. His aides knew how to get his attention first thing in the morning. Vice President Bush kept a file of jokes, replenished by his sons, to start the president's day. "Bush and I would get into the White House at 6:15 every morning," Deaver remembered, "and we'd call each other and trade two or three stories that we'd heard the day before and decide which one was the best one to tell Reagan at quarter to nine when we'd see him. Then it would start. We'd tell the president a story and then the president would tell a couple. He loved stories. That was Hollywood. He and his old friends Pat O'Brien or Fredric March would sit around telling Irish or Jewish stories on and on."

In coordination with Nancy, Deaver, Baker and Meese formed the troika that ran the Reagan White House during the first term. "Nancy and I were a team," Deaver recalled, "united by our shared belief that her husband needed to be protected." Deaver's day began with a call to Nancy. What's his mood? he would ask. The Reagans' always close partnership was tightened by the president's slipping memory, impaired hearing and the total invasive scrutiny of the post-Watergate White House media. With the Reagans' accurate sense for what played in the heartland, they even turned his dependency on his wife into an asset, a great American love story played out on the world's biggest stage. No other presidential couple was ever seen kissing, holding hands, dancing and romancing with as much ardor as this pair of septuagenarians.

The country was the better for the Reagans' closeness, according to Nancy. "It would be far better and more realistic," Nancy argued in her memoir, *My Turn,* "if the president's men included the first lady as part of their team. After all, nobody knows the president better than his wife. The president has a host of advisers to give him counsel on foreign affairs, the economy, politics and everything else. But not one of these people is there to look after him as an individual with human needs, a man of flesh and blood who must deal with the pressures of holding the most powerful position on earth."

Of course Nancy did much more than take care of her husband's "human needs." Those closest to Reagan were grateful for Nancy's vigilant involvement. "Ronald Reagan was the most trusting human being I've ever known," Deaver asserted. "If you were walking down the street and a guy came up and started talking to him, Reagan would believe him. Now, he wouldn't believe a Russian commissar or maybe a Democratic chairman of a congressional committee. But everybody else he trusted. Nancy was much more cynical and also had better antennae. Particularly about the moment. Reagan always thought in terms of years, whereas Nancy would think about polls that were published in the *Washington Post* today."

Two months into his presidency, on March 30, 1981, America witnessed Reagan's familiar, lopsided smile turn to bewilderment, and then twist into pain, as he was shot. John Hinckley, Jr.'s, bullet missed Reagan's heart by one inch and permanently shattered his wife's always fragile emotional balance. Reagan now revealed his bravest, most appealing side. His now famous quips, "Honey, I forgot to duck," and "On the whole I'd rather be in Philadelphia," were old Hollywood chestnuts whose very corniness in the face of crisis calmed the country. He said God had spared him for a special purpose; he would make the most of his time. During his first hospital meeting with his national security team, still in his pajamas and robe, he pulled out a yellow pad and said, "You know, I wrote this four-page, handwritten letter to Brezhnev. 'Do you remember, I met you at Nixon's house in California and we talked about peace? Well, I have just been shot and I'm thinking about our grandchildren. . . .' "

The assassination attempt exposed something elemental in Nancy, too. All of her insecurities found a rational focus now. After the gunshots, no one could dismiss her paranoia as excessive. Her seventy-year-old husband had suffered a near fatal attack, leaving physical and mental scars. "Nancy called me ten days after the president was shot," Deaver remembered, "and she said, 'Joan [Quigley, the astrologer] told me that she had wished that I had called so she could have told me that was going to be a bad day.' What do you mean? I asked. She said, 'Well, she knows bad days and good days and days not to be in public and that sort of thing. Not to be around crowds. I want you to send me Ronnie's block schedule for three months. I want Joan to take a look at it. To give us the bad days.' It made sense to me, if that's what she wanted to do. If it would help her get through, it was easy. I'd send Nancy his schedule, and she'd call me and say, 'April 9 we ought not to do anything in public.' My personal reaction was that I would do anything to help her peace of mind. I gotta tell you something, there were four of us who walked out of the [Hilton] door, and I was the only one who didn't get shot. That has an effect on you. I was indelibly altered from having Mr. Hinckley put his .22 on my shoulder and shoot those people."

Reports of Reagan's memory lapses and verbal slips started early in his presidency. Princeton historian Arthur Link related having dinner at the White House in 1983 when conversation turned to the TV miniseries *Winds of War.* "What would the world be like," the president mused out loud, "if the Second World War had actually taken place?" There was a notable deterioration in both Reagan's memory and his hearing. "How are you, Mr. Mayor," the president greeted his own housing secretary at a reception for big-city mayors. Three months later, Reagan met for the first time with the leaders of the industrial nations in Ottawa. Afterward, Reagan "could not remember the substance of any subject that had been discussed, apart from Mitterand's anticommunism," according to writer Lou Cannon. Television correspondent Barrie Dunsmore attended a small Christmas party in the upstairs residence later that year. "The contrast between the first lady and the president was so stark," said Dunsmore. "Nancy was conscious of everything that was going on. The president was charming, but he seemed out of touch, in his own little world. He didn't seem to know who Sam Donaldson was. Nancy was clearly in charge and the president was pretty much out of it."

Nancy moved closer, doubled her vigilance. She had to protect him not only from any further violence but from close public scrutiny. She had to control his movements, set his schedule, watch him as she had never done before. She had always played a big part in picking the right people to serve him, but now she assumed a behind-the-scenes role in pushing the policies that would assure his legacy.

At the same time, Nancy was fighting her own battles. Part of the Washington media's unwritten code is not to attack both presidential partners with equal force simultaneously. In the first few years of the Reagan presidency, Nancy took most of the hits. It seemed as if everything she did aroused the media's ire. Taking a page out of Jacqueline

Kennedy's book, she tried to restore Camelot's glitter to the White House. But the eighties, a time of unemployment and recession, were not the sixties, and Nancy was not Jackie. When Nancy raised $700,000 in private donations to restore the private quarters and another $200,000 for new china, the public was offended, not beguiled. Her expensive designer frocks and perfect lacquered hairdos were mocked, not imitated. Her husband was shocked by the vehemence of the criticism. "Why wasn't the same thing said about another first lady some years ago," a bewildered Reagan asked a reporter, "who set out to contribute to the beauty of the White House and there was nothing but praise?"

At a time when 70 percent of twenty-five- to forty-four-year-old women were in the workforce, Nancy seemed out of step, an embarrassment to women struggling to reach still uncharted male territory. Her assertively traditional marriage and her adoring gaze made many women squirm. The business suit, not the couture gown, was the preferred image for women of the eighties. The beaming face of astronaut Sally Ride was tacked to thousands of dormitory doors. Nancy, and not her

The Reagans during a barbecue for members of Congress on the South Lawn of the White House, September 30, 1982.

husband, became the symbol of compassion-free conservatism. She was deemed too brittle, too artificial, too cold and much too much the material woman of the new gilded age. Polls showed that 68 percent of the people felt the first lady was too concerned with style and fashion, at the expense of other concerns. Her husband did his best to defend her as a warm and caring soul, without whom his life was unimaginable. "How do you describe someone that makes your life like coming into a warm room?" he asked. The contrast between her Marie Antoinette hauteur and his down-to-earth innocence seemed to burnish his image while damaging hers.

By the second year of the Reagan presidency, Deaver, the public relations genius of the administration, decided it was time for a Nancy makeover. Almost overnight, a new Nancy—funny, self-deprecating and, best of all, shabby—sprang to life. The venue for the metamorphosis was carefully chosen: that sacred spring ritual of the Washington media and political establishment, the Gridiron Dinner. Nancy astonished and disarmed the luminaries with a surprise appearance as a bag lady and her deliberately off-key rendition of "Secondhand Rose." "I wore white pantaloons, with blue butterflies, yellow rubber rain boots, a blue blouse with white dots, and over that a really ugly sleeveless red cotton print house dress," she wrote later with obvious relish. "Over that I wore a blue print skirt pinned up on the side with a sequined butterfly, a long strand of fake pearls, a mangy boa, and a red straw hat with feathers and flowers. I was gorgeous!" Never mind that Nancy would rather be incarcerated than ever appear in such a costume in real life; she had surprised and entertained the media. She was game. Suddenly, they loved her.

ABOVE ALL, it was Nancy's instinct for her husband's legacy that led her to nudge Ronnie away from his evil-empire posture toward a role as a man of peace. But in part it was also the lure of the new culture she aspired to join. "Nancy had a tropism toward high society," Peggy Noonan noted. "She liked to rock at the best parties." And Washington was different from Orange County. No longer surrounded by self-made millionaires who spent poolside lunches talking about "welfare queens," the insecure little girl still aspired to be at the peak of the society she happened to

inhabit. A keen observer, she was always learning. Before she was introduced to Beverly Hills decorator Ted Graber, a velveteen-framed photograph of John Wayne graced the Reagans' mantelpiece in a decor friends
characterized as early Holiday Inn. Jacqueline Kennedy Onassis, Nancy's
great icon, who had little to learn from decorators, archly commented to
a friend, "Can you imagine, Nancy Reagan's first call when she got to the
White House was to her *decorator*?"

The social and political arbiters of Washington society are the handful of socialites who run the salons of Georgetown and the select ambas-
sadors, senators, editors, anchors and columnists who grace their tables.
As she set out to carve a place for herself among the capital's aristocracy,
Nancy was exposed to a worldview different from the confines of both
Hollywood and southern California Republicans. Less an ideologue than
an opportunist, she bristled when her husband was described as one of
those "jump-off-the-cliff-wrapped-in-the-flag" Republicans. With skill
and intelligence, she cultivated the friendship of Katharine Graham,
who, as publisher of the *Washington Post* and *Newsweek,* was both a
social and media doyenne. "I liked Nancy," Graham said, "and I thought
she was getting a raw deal from the press" (meaning, among others,
her own publications, with whose coverage Graham did not interfere).
Nancy was soon a member ex officio of the capital's most rarefied social
circle. Being *inside* suited her need for social acceptance and served her
husband's needs. It was a lesson Rosalynn Carter and Hillary Clinton
never fully grasped.

In fact, other than her marriage, her social position was the one thing
Nancy was zealous about. There was room for only one hostess in the
Reagan administration. Nancy was determined to keep Barbara Bush, a
popular figure in the capital, in her place. Drawing up the guest list for a
state dinner honoring Prince Charles and Princess Diana, Nancy deliberately left off Vice President and Mrs. Bush. When an aide cautioned
against such a blatant breach of protocol, Nancy tartly replied, "Just
watch me."

Her husband's evolution was proceeding, too. Nancy's urgings and
his recent brush with death worked their transforming power on him.
The handwritten letter to Brezhnev was only the first step. For some
time, given Brezhnev's failing health and the short tenures of his two

immediate successors, Yuri Andropov and Konstantin Chernenko, there was nobody to negotiate with in the Kremlin. But in 1985, a vigorous new Soviet leader presented himself as a negotiating partner. "There was something likable about [Mikhail] Gorbachev," Reagan noted. "There was warmth in his face and his style, not the coldness bordering on hatred I'd seen in most senior Soviet officials I'd met until then."

It was not personal chemistry alone that turned the crusading ideologue into the peacemaker. One of Reagan's core beliefs was an almost mystical faith in America, its indomitable strength, its essential civilizing role in the world. "The bureaucrats were telling him, We have to figure out ways to coexist with the Soviets," Deaver noted. "Reagan said, No, we don't." He thought he could bring the Soviets to their knees by outspending them. He would build up to build down. "He felt that if an American president faced down the Soviets, they would fold like a cheap suit," Peggy Noonan recalled. So before he "faced down" the Soviets, Reagan pushed through the largest peacetime military spending budget. He initiated Star Wars, as the Strategic Defense Initiative was soon dubbed. For a man who saw his role as a sort of national lifeguard, SDI was more than a bargaining chip. Like lower taxes and less government, the shield against nuclear missiles was something Reagan could *visualize,* something that struck him as quite real.

While her husband had an almost mystical belief in the power of SDI, for the pragmatic Nancy it was a means to get the Soviets to the table. "Nancy believed this was her husband's destiny: a man of his age who had lived through two World Wars would be the one to break the deadlock of the Cold War," Deaver said. "It was the only thing she really got into as an issue. She worked with me and [Secretary of State] George Shultz and George Bush. 'Don't let the bureaucrats get in the way,' she would say. She was afraid they would block the back channels she and the president were working." She had already cleared out one man she saw as a roadblock. In October 1983 she prevailed on her husband to replace the hard-line National Security Council adviser William Clark with the former Kissinger staffer Bud McFarlane. The new man at the NSC shared Nancy's view that Reagan had to evolve from cold warrior to peacemaker.

Once she got Clark out of the way, Nancy used back-channel diplomacy to reposition her husband. When she heard that Soviet foreign minister Andrei Gromyko was scheduled for a working White House lunch on September 28, 1984, she called Shultz and asked if she could join the secretary of state and the president. "I had a lot of talk with Nancy about the Gromyko visit [to Washington]," Shultz remembered, "and we arranged a role for her. I said that we were coming to her home for lunch, and I thought it would be most appropriate if she greeted Gromyko on his arrival and stayed until the reception was over." The signal sent by the unexpected appearance of the first lady was not lost on the veteran Soviet leader. Gromyko seized the opportunity. "Does your husband believe in peace?" he asked Nancy. Yes, of course, she replied. "Then whisper 'peace' in your husband's ear every night," Gromyko urged. "I will," she agreed, "and I'll also whisper it in your ear." Then, leaning in, she softly whispered, "Peace." In such small and seemingly insignificant ways did the ice between two superpowers begin to melt.

"Ronnie's got to have his chance to do his stuff," Nancy instructed chief of staff Jim Baker. "Work this out so Ronnie gets a chance to sit down with Gorbachev," she urged, knowing better than anyone the power of Ronnie's "stuff." "George Shultz couldn't believe he had Nancy in his corner," Deaver noted.

On a bitter cold Geneva morning in November 1985, the hatless, coatless, smiling seventy-four-year-old American president grabbed the hand of the fifty-four-year-old Soviet in heavy overcoat, muffler and fedora, and led him inside. Without having uttered a single word, Nancy and Ronnie had the image they wanted beamed around the globe and into the history books. Nancy had chosen the perfect location for the historic Soviet-American facedown—a cozy lakeside cottage with a roaring fire was the ideal setting for Reagan's style of homespun diplomacy.

He did not try to dazzle the Soviet with his grasp of missile-to-missile ratios, as Richard Nixon or Jimmy Carter surely would have. He made Gorbachev feel as if the two of them had been friends for years. Reagan bonded instantly with the Communist leader. He compared the story of his humble origins to Gorbachev's and, with his uncanny ability to connect intimately with strangers, told him, "We [are] possibly the only two men in the world who might be able to bring peace to the world." Their meeting, scheduled for twenty minutes, lasted more than an hour and a quarter. Thanks in some measure to Nancy, the chemistry between the two men was so good that they agreed then and there to meet again in Moscow and in Washington.

Nancy also played a big part in staging the Reagans' triumphant 1988 Moscow summit. Fierce competitiveness was part of what drove her. Gorbachev had been mobbed when he strolled down Connecticut Avenue during his Washington visit in December 1987. Nancy wanted the same image of her man when he was in Moscow. "Nancy and I talked extensively about how her husband could be pictured interacting with the Russian people," Reagan aide Kenneth Duberstein remembered. "She liked the idea of a stroll down the famous pedestrian street in Moscow, the Arbat. But the Secret Service said no, it wasn't safe. But she was firm that this was the way for Ronnie to connect with the Russian people. They should touch and feel him. He was better with people than anything and he needed to be inspired by that sort of contact."

The Secret Service continued to veto the idea. They had an agreement with the KGB that they would give an hour's warning before the presidential party made a move. But Nancy was equally determined to provide Ronnie his essential plunge into the Russian crowd. So when the presidential limousine arrived at the Arbat, the Reagans unexpectedly stepped out. Startled Moscow strollers closed in on the big, cheery American and his chic wife. The KGB closed in just as fast, trying to scatter the crowd. That night, CNN and the networks carried the shot Nancy had choreographed for her husband: the leader of the Free World ignoring the KGB and reaching out to touch the Soviet people.

BY 1985, however, the man who always attached himself to causes, not people, seemed nearly oblivious to the fact that his friends had left the White House. Chief of staff Baker had bizarrely switched jobs with Treasury Secretary Donald Regan, and Ed Meese had become attorney general. The Reagans' most intimate ally, Mike Deaver, left to set up his own public relations firm in Washington. "If by some miracle," Nancy later noted, "I could take back one decision in Ronnie's presidency, it would be his agreement in January 1985 that Jim Baker and Donald Regan should switch jobs. . . . Of the four people who had been closest to Ronnie during his first term . . . I was the only one left."

One month after the October 1986 Reykjavik summit with Gorbachev, the Reagans were reminded that this was no longer the same White House that they had run like a family franchise. Suddenly, Reagan's cavalier management style, his near total dependence on his staff, his almost chemical inability to make hard choices, all exploded. Iran-Contra, the most serious crisis of the Reagan presidency, was borne of the sort of man Reagan was: trusting, vague and dangerously passive. Reagan's detachment enabled members of his staff to abuse their power and withhold information from him.

For fifteen months, the White House had been the nerve center of a conspiracy spanning several countries and three continents. It appeared that the commander in chief, or those using his name, was making deals with Iran, the country Reagan had recently described as "Murder Inc." The first lady was caught completely by surprise. McFarlane and an NSC staffer named Oliver North had been secretly trading arms to Iran in exchange for the release of American hostages held by Shiite Muslim terrorists in Lebanon. North, a gung-ho marine with a limited attachment to the truth, was a fantasist who thought he was doing his president's bidding in other ways as well. Reagan had compared the Nicaraguan Contras to the Founding Fathers. That seemed enough for North to hatch his conspiracy to funnel profits from the Iranian arms deal to the guerrillas. "Ronald Reagan was a big-picture guy," Deaver noted, "so he would leave a lot of this stuff to others. I was always careful that Oliver North did not ever get left alone with Reagan in the Oval Office when I was there. North was bad news: bright-eyed and bushy-tailed, power-hungry and ambitious."

Iran-Contra again revealed the indispensable role Nancy played in the Reagan political partnership. For the first time, Reagan could not rely on his wife to protect his flank. Nancy had been out of the loop, sidelined by a new and insensitive chief of staff who saw her as a meddlesome wife, instead of a powerful, potential ally. "I don't think Don Regan understood the dynamics of the marriage," Deaver explained. "If you didn't understand that, you didn't have any business being there."

Rather than win her trust, Regan set out to bar her from the West Wing. It turned out to be the grossest miscalculation of the presidency and ultimately of Regan himself.

Now, as questions about her husband's competence and integrity dominated the headlines, Nancy reasserted herself. She once again became a constant but invisible presence in the West Wing. Regan was helpless to stop her. "By now," Regan wrote later, "in the middle of January [1986] the First Lady's telephoning was so frequent that I was spending two or three times as much time talking to her as to the President." Nor was Regan as tolerant of the first lady's dependence on the occult as Deaver. "Apparently Deaver had ceased to think that there was anything remarkable about this long-established floating seance," Regan wrote. "But the president's schedule is the single most potent tool in the White House, because it determines what the most powerful man in the world is going to do and when he is going to do it. By humoring Mrs. Reagan we gave her this tool--or more accurately gave it to an unknown woman in San Francisco who believed that the zodiac controls events and human behavior and that she could read the secrets of the future in the movements of the planets." Though the president's job approval ratings were steadily dropping, Nancy, acting on her astrologer's advice, still prevented Regan from scheduling a presidential news conference to explain the president's role in the Iran-Contra scandal.

Just as Reagan denied other unappealing truths, he now denied his administration's sale of arms for hostages. We were merely making overtures to Iranian moderates, he explained, when Nancy finally permitted him to face the country on March 19, 1987. "We weren't dealing with the kidnappers, and it was not ransom." Shultz felt the president truly believed he had not traded arms for hostages. "I had to keep trying to make him realize that indeed we had. The president had completely buffaloed himself about this matter." For a long time, Reagan refused to believe the mounting evidence against the marine who nearly brought down his presidency. "I kind of hope," Reagan said to friends, "that maybe North isn't as bad as some of the media people have suggested. Maybe he really is an American hero."

He needed desperately to hold on to his positive view of the world. He now made himself believe that he hadn't gone behind Congress's back, hadn't broken the law of the land. "Sometimes," Shultz noted dryly, "President Reagan simply did not seem to care that much about facts and details."

For the first time, the country did not believe him. How could any president be so detached from his own administration that he would be oblivious to the movement of arms and men around the globe, all done in his name? When his reviews were consistently bad, Reagan fell into a despondent state. He was, after all, first and foremost a performer. His oxygen was public approval. Without it he seemed lost and bewildered. "It was the first time I'd seen him with the wind completely out of his sails," his son Ron recalled. At some level surely he realized Iran-Contra was a direct result of his inattention to the office he had sworn to uphold. The instincts that had carried him so far in life had betrayed him.

Slowly and, as always, with Nancy's help, he shook off his depression and inertia. Only she could prevail upon him to go before the country and admit he had made a mistake. It was a bitter pill for a man so unaccustomed to dealing with hard facts. He still could not face the truth head-on. "It was a mistake," he finally told the nation, which more or less forgave him. With that semi-admission and the gradual regaining of public approval that followed, Reagan partly restored his emotional balance. But, at seventy-eight, he was not the same vigorous man who first bounded into the White House. The assassination attempt, cancer, prostate surgery, diminished hearing and memory—probably early signs of Alzheimer's disease—compounded the emotional shock of Iran-Contra. He was even more the ceremonial president, less and less attentive to details, ticking off items on staff-prepared memoranda without comment. But he still had the old trouper's ability to perform for the lights and cameras.

⟨∾⟩

REGAN HAD THOUGHT he and Reagan had a genuine bond: two men of similar working-class Irish backgrounds who loved to swap bawdy stories. But Reagan could not find a moment or a word for a man who had worked for him for six years, and whose career was now ending. It was not from the boss but from CNN that Regan learned that the president was replacing him with Howard Baker. The two never saw each other again.

Deaver went much further back with Reagan, far enough so that on rare occasions he slipped and called him Ron. Yet during one Christmas dinner following Deaver's departure from the White House, when he suggested possible candidates for the Medal of Freedom, the president cut him off. "Mike, I've got competent people at the White House who make those decisions." Deaver, the president thus made clear, was no longer serving him. His opinions were no longer of great consequence.

In fact, Reagan had no real friends except Nancy. He preferred strangers or fans. For fifty-two years Reagan corresponded with Lorraine Wagner, from his fan club days. She saved 276 of his letters, some of them five or six handwritten pages long, on subjects that ranged from his first wife to Iran-Contra. None of Reagan's four children can claim such communication. "We missed him while he was here," his son Ron said when Reagan was diagnosed with Alzheimer's. "We're not missing something that we ever had."

Nancy never cared passionately about anything besides Ronnie and their marriage. When she left the White House, she pretty much said no to the war on drugs that had been her cause as first lady. She had a chance to stay involved, to have a drug rehabilitation center named after her in Los Angeles. "I think she felt for the kids," Phoenix House chairman Dr. Mitchell Rosenthal recalled. "Her tears were not artificial, her heart went out to people who are vulnerable. But those of us who were trying to get her to go to the next level, becoming a vigorous, informed public spokesperson, were disappointed in the end. Phoenix House lost $3–$5 million when Mrs. Reagan abandoned the L.A. project. But that's small potatoes compared to the legacy she would have left had she sustained this work. But that did not seem to be a strong enough motivation for her."

Her lifework was Ronnie. His legacy was the one she cared about. The depth of her commitment to him and to his presidency was made clear when she was diagnosed with breast cancer in October 1987. Forgoing the vastly less deforming option of a lumpectomy, Nancy opted for a radical mastectomy because, in her husband's words, "She realized she wouldn't be able to perform her duties as first lady if she had to undergo the radiation that would be required after a lumpectomy. . . ."

Presidential couples are masters at presenting a certain image of themselves. Sometimes it is only later, when they are no longer so relentlessly scrutinized or so wary, that they reveal flashes of the real dynamic between them. On November 17, 1989, the Reagans were interviewed by Barbara Walters. "You are remote," Walters said to the former president. "And even [Nancy] finds it hard to get through." His wife answered for him: "I think . . . the way we were brought up . . . what our background was . . . that is what makes us the way we [are]. Ronnie's father was an alcoholic. They moved from town to town to town to town. He never had a chance to put down any roots anywhere and establish friends. . . ."

"So do you get a shell?" Walters tried again, but again Nancy answered for her husband. "He doesn't know that. But he is so gregarious and so loves people and they love him. But there's a certain point . . . when it comes down on me." Walters asked Reagan if he was aware of that. "Well, no, I'm not. I feel very much for people . . ." Walters interrupted. "I mean *individual* people . . . I'm talking about *one* and he doesn't understand . . ." she said, turning to Nancy. "No," Nancy agreed, "he doesn't. He doesn't understand because he doesn't feel it and it's something buried way, way, back. . . ." Then, as though addressing a child, she said soothingly to her husband, "We'll have a long conversation, honey, tonight."

Walters then broached another sensitive topic: how Nancy's views on abortion differed from her husband's. "There's nobody," Nancy answered, "that you're going to agree with 100 percent all the time." Again her husband tried vainly to interject. "Can I add one thing here to this whole thing that maybe you don't know and a lot of people don't know?" Nancy cut him off again. "No," she said, "I think you should just let it go." But this time he would not "let it go." "I want to add one thing," Reagan insisted. "One thing about this, that we're not dealing with a fetus, we're dealing with a living human being." In a few, painful moments, the Reagans had revealed their interaction.

No president since Wilson had a more fiercely devoted partner. This most powerful modern first lady was in some ways also the most traditional. She had no substantive agenda of her own, she craved no lime-light or credit. Her only ambition was for him, and she fulfilled that beyond imagining. A Reagan presidency without Nancy's constant presence—her all-seeing gaze, her whispered cues, above all her unfailing radar registering every current for or against her husband—would not have been possible. Presidents don't benefit just from good marriages, but also from partners who understand the demands of political life and are willing to assist in meeting those demands. In Nancy, Ronald Reagan had both. Nancy not only helped elect her husband president but helped to keep him on course in the White House. In the end, the Reagan presidency is as much her legacy as his.

CHAPTER 10

BARBARA AND GEORGE BUSH

MOTHER KNOWS BEST

She's got this great, ramrod steel backbone. She is such a gutsy gal. She can stick that jaw out. Nothing is too much for her.

— LUD ASHLEY, *a Bush intimate*

Why does [Mrs. Bush] "take the Fifth" on the issues she has every right to talk about? The disappointing result is she leaves the president alone with his West Wing advisers who have a long history of ignoring women's issues.

— LIZ CARPENTER, *press spokeswoman for Lady Bird Johnson*

The difference between Barbara and Nancy was that people knew Nancy would go to Mike Deaver or Jim Baker if she were upset about something. If Mrs. Bush felt strongly, we knew she would go directly to her husband. We would hear from the president, "Bar is really unhappy about . . ." or "Bar says we ought to . . ."

— A WHITE HOUSE STAFFER

AT FIRST, IT WAS ENOUGH THAT SHE WAS NOT NANCY. "I WANT YOU ALL TO take a look at me," Barbara Bush said three times during the inaugural festivities. "Please notice—hairdo, makeup, designer dress. Look at me good this week, because it's the only week." It was a brilliant, if not too subtle, put-down, a demonstration that she grasped the country's need for a new beginning after eight Reagan years. It was also a way of getting back, just a little, at Nancy. Like Ronald Reagan, and *un*like her husband, Barbara knew the power of a well-aimed one-liner. She had an innate sense of what works in politics. She would be the un-Nancy: plain-spoken, authentic and unthreatening. In private, as well, Barbara was not Nancy, nor Rosalynn; she made no effort to project herself on foreign missions, or to shape history by whispering in a foreign minister's ear. Unlike Nancy, she would not be continually involved in the politics and process of her husband's career. Policy was for men; her role was to keep *her* man on a steady, focused path.

But there was a deep irony behind Barbara's skillful one-liner about Nancy: it wasn't true. Barbara had been wearing designer clothes, "hairdo" and makeup for years and would continue to do so. In reality, Barbara's matronliness was as carefully packaged as Nancy's rail-thin look. Manipulative, judgmental and tough, Barbara was not quite what she seemed. So skilled was she at managing her image that she gave almost everybody something to like about her. The traditionalists saw a woman who reminded them of their mothers or grandmothers. Feminists saw a feisty woman speaking her mind. She managed to turn every potential negative into a positive: her age, her weight, her wrinkles, even her privileged lifestyle. It wasn't that the times had fundamentally changed; it was that Barbara was shrewder than Nancy in presenting herself.

After eight years of Nancy's thinly disguised palace intrigues, Barbara calculated that the country was ready for something else. She would play the country's good-natured grandmother who left the business of state to her husband, an unabashed throwback to a time when everybody knew his or her place and fathers knew best. The image was contrived, but the act worked.

Barbara thought that who she really was, or what her marriage was really like, was nobody's business but hers and her husband's. Coldly determined, she would prove more successful in her role as first lady than her husband as president. George never learned the political skills that Barbara seemed to grasp intuitively. It was she, in conversation with her husband, who inspired the "kinder and gentler" line he proclaimed in his 1988 convention acceptance speech. She let others, primarily Peggy Noonan, craft the words, but she had the idea. This Connecticut Yankee had been outraged by the nouveau riche California White House. She was offended that while Ronald Reagan declared ketchup a school lunch vegetable, champagne flowed in the White House.

But, unlike Reagan, George Bush did not owe his wife the presidency. Bush had the drive, the tribe, the energy and the charm to get elected. His talent for male bonding nearly compensated for his tin ear for politics, as well as his aversion to grand ideas. But Bush needed Barbara. She had iron will and an antenna for danger. She was the memory bank for slights. "Bar's the one who'd remember that kind of thing," her husband would say. Those inside the Bush camp treated her with immense respect. "Barbara was always taken into consideration," Roger Ailes, Bush's longtime media adviser, noted. "She was forceful in protecting the president. Barbara was always aware of what was going on." She was also the source of one of Bush's strongest assets: his image as the patriarch of a large and appealing brood.

Barbara compensated for George's shortcomings. Unlike her husband, whom the press routinely (and cruelly) referred to as a "wimp," she seemed like granite. George could indulge his enthusiasms—pork rinds, horseshoes, odd, tribal ways of talking—because Barbara was watching his back. Somewhat ruefully he called his wife "Miss Frank," knowing he could expect something approaching the unvarnished truth from her. In an office as cushioned with sycophants as the presidency is, that is no minor role. And, unlike many presidents, George seemed to relish his wife's sometimes brutal candor. "He's much nicer than she is," said an old friend. "She is fierce and snobbish. She can freeze him out if she thinks he is pandering too much. Once, when we were having lunch with them and he was saying nice things about Pat Robertson and Jerry Falwell, she cut him dead. 'Come on, George,' she said, 'you don't really believe any of that, do you?' "

As much as the Carters and the Clintons, and much more than those accidental presidential couples the Trumans and the Fords, the political ascent of the Bushes was a shared enterprise. Barbara understood that she had to be understated in order to be effective, not to overshadow her husband, who often suffered from an appearance of lightness. He was not a man whose presence filled a room. Nor did he have a natural constituency. Throughout his political life, Bush had to cobble together both his platform and his base. Unlike Roosevelt, Reagan or Clinton, Bush could not afford the appearance of an assertive, strong woman as his visible partner. Like Jacqueline Kennedy and Lady Bird Johnson, Barbara was a strong woman who presented herself publicly as a submissive and supportive wife.

As first lady, Barbara did not take chances. She did not try to carve out new territory as Rosalynn Carter had. Her agenda was her husband: electing him to office and then keeping him healthy and happy once there. Beyond her family, she was not passionate about a cause, though she was serious about literacy. Skirting sensitive issues, she did safe things. She was coy on the subject of abortion, which was opposed by her husband and ever so quietly favored by her. She identified herself as pro-choice only once she was out of the White House. But through subtle pauses, inflections and body language, she gave moderate Republicans a feeling that she was with them, that they had an ally in the Bush White House. Nobody ever successfully pinned her down. She was brilliant at sending a signal without leaving an imprint.

She had her views, but they were always subordinated to her husband's political needs. Unlike Eleanor Roosevelt or Hillary Clinton, she would not take on her husband in public. "We stopped discussing [gun control and abortion] about fifteen, twenty, thirty years ago," she admitted once. "What's the point?"

But her husband, while usually upbeat, was never able to convey what FDR, LBJ and even Jimmy Carter did: a feeling of authentic connection with his territory, geographic and political. He always seemed a shade off somehow: the cigarette boat whipping around the Maine coast, the velvet embroidered slippers and striped watchband in Texas. He seemed an outsider, not a man rooted to his terrain. His capacity for friendship and his good manners were not enough. The same index cards with "talking points" that transported Reagan to inspirational heights worked no magic for Bush. In the end, Barbara, the more natural performer, could do little to alter that fact.

❦

SHE WAS RAISED in a traditional, prefeminist era, and accepted that. Her generation of women was supposed to fulfill its destiny within the context of marriage. Her prewar credo held that a woman's first and last career choice was her marriage. "I'll tell you in one sentence how you train to be first lady," she said in 1987, in a typical bit of self-deprecation. "You marry well. That's all you need to know." When she was in her sixties, she said she might have become a corporate CEO had she been born later. But she seemed to have no regrets. Her sublimated message—I am who I am, I have made the best of my life, I'm comfortable with myself—had tremendous appeal, especially after Nancy Reagan. In the late-twentieth-century confusion caused by the shifting power balance between men and women, the Bushes exuded old-time clarity. He was the provider, she tended the home fires. She never expressed remorse for leaving Smith College after only one year to marry, or for staying home to have five babies in rapid succession and raising them mostly by herself. "All our children were planned," Barbara stated. "By me." Her matter-of-fact optimism was a balm after Nancy's striving angst.

The Bushes' marriage was based on shared expectations and values. Each upheld his or her end of the unspoken bargain. George and Barbara had a fixed goal: his ascent in his chosen field. Everything else, their relationship, family life, comfort and well-being, was sublimated to that. How else can one possibly justify twenty-nine family uprootings in forty-four years of marriage?

If, later in life, they seemed more like old chums than husband and wife, it is perhaps because George and Barbara virtually grew up together. When they met as Connecticut teenagers, from classically WASP families, their attraction to each other was immediate. She later said she had trouble breathing when he was in the room. He wrote his mother, "I have never felt towards another girl as I do towards her." Barbara Pierce would marry the first boy she ever kissed. George was more sentimental and prone to tears—but equally inexperienced. "I have never kissed another girl," he wrote his mother at age eighteen. They were raised in the same strict school of conduct. "I would hate to find that my wife had known some other man, and it seems to me only fair to her that she be able to expect the same standards from me," he wrote. George and Barbara chose their mirror images: two tall, athletic adolescents from large, affluent families who loved dogs, picnics, boats and the sea more than books and ideas. Their fathers took the same commuter train to New York each morning.

Duty, discipline, good manners and service were implanted in George's and Barbara's DNA. They shared their parents' view that men should tend to the outside world and women should rule the family and household. Emotions were suspect, something to control. Displaying affection in front of others was a sign of bad manners. So was expressing real feelings. "You shouldn't have to tell that," Bush insisted. "You see it. You know it." Barbara said George did not even have to propose marriage. It was just understood they would marry.

There were few mysteries between them. Neither was rebellious, probing or introspective. They both have frequently asserted how little they think of "psychoanalyzing." They neither challenged each other nor complicated each other's lives. George picked the perfect partner for public life: a woman who would not embarrass him or be an emotional drain, a woman raised to keep their private lives private and keep any problems *inside* the marriage.

But the Bushes were also different in important ways—and those differences were critical to George's success. "Barbara knows how to hate," Thomas "Lud" Ashley, George's Yale classmate and closest friend, noted. "George does not. Barbara is the memory bank. George will get ticked off at somebody and then forget about it. Barbara remembers." Ashley claimed there was a key disparity in George's and Barbara's upbringing. Barbara's father, Marvin Pierce, who worked his way up the ranks in the McCall Publishing Company, taught his children to be aggressive. "Her brothers were linemen," Ashley noted, "taught to hit hard, to play both sides off. That was also part of Barbara's personality." George, scion of a crustier WASP dynasty, was taught to be competitive

January 6, 1945. George and Barbara Bush on their
wedding day.

but not aggressive. His mother, who had the strongest influence on him,
trained George never to talk about himself, never to boast, never to
shove his way to the front. George was raised to trust people, to see the
good in them. Barbara, according to Ashley, "reads people differently
than George. She doesn't mind impugning motives. He's more ready to

take people at face value. It's just not in his nature to see beneath the surface. It is in hers."

Nobody knew George better than Barbara. "George Bush, and maybe this is a fault," she once said, "looks for the best in everybody. He does not question motives." She knew he hated conflict. Barbara had no such compunctions. "I can always find a tricky reason someone did something, because I could have done it myself. George can't." Anticipating people's motives and a fearlessness about hitting hard were qualities Barbara brought to her marriage. "He learned to rely on her judgments of people," Ashley noted. "It is hard to imagine George going as far as he did without Barbara."

During a family gathering shortly after their wedding, Barbara was asked if she would like George to be president. "I'd like it," she answered without hesitation. "Because you know, I'm going to be the first lady sometime." This was not grandiosity speaking but rather her conviction that there was *nothing* her husband could not achieve. Was he not among the most admired and beloved boys at Andover, voted the Best All-Around Fellow, president of his senior class, captain of the baseball team, secretary of the student council? And he loved her and only her. Bar was the luckiest girl in the world and ready to do almost anything for George.

The length of the road to the White House, rutted with defeats and setbacks, explained both Barbara's occasional flashes of bitterness and her triumphant smile. Reaching the White House justified her choices and sacrifices: the dislocations, the lonely years raising her children virtually alone, the loss of privacy.

Early in life, Barbara honed the sharp retorts and subtle put-downs that became her signature as first lady. As the large-boned daughter of a coolly critical mother and the younger sibling of a thin and graceful older sister, she survived by irreverence, a cutting wit and the ability to see what she wanted to see. Feistiness and humor, rather than feminine charm, were the core of her self-image. "Good night my beautiful," George wrote his fiancée from the navy. "Every time I say beautiful you about kill me but you'll have to accept it." But she did not want the burden of beauty. She lacked the narcissism required for its maintenance, and perhaps sensed her claim on it would be too fleeting anyway. There were other qualities her ambitious suitor valued in her. "She's got this great, ramrod steel backbone," Lud Ashley said. "She is such a gutsy gal. She can stick that jaw out. Nothing is too much for her."

Barbara and George yearned to get out from under authoritarian, controlling parents. The parents' metronomic, privileged lifestyle, with each season accompanied by its ritual passages, did not appeal to the young couple. George was too exuberant to be incarcerated in Wall Street like his father. He had demonstrated courage and an affinity for risk-taking by signing up for the navy at age nineteen. "He was a stand-out at Yale," Ashley remembered. "It would not have surprised any of us that he would be elected president. There were about thirty people at Yale who had also been shot down in the war, who'd been taken prisoner. But here was George, already married to an extraordinarily pretty girl, with a newborn son, who did two varsity sports, soccer and baseball, and knocked out grades that got the Phi Beta Kappa key." George was going places.

FLAT AND BROWN, Odessa, Texas, was a planet away from the soft, green lawns and ancient oaks of Greenwich. "I've always wanted to live in Odessa, Texas," said Barbara dryly when George informed her they would move. In her view, happiness was a matter of will. It was only the first of many moves: from Odessa to Huntington Park, California, to Bakersfield and back to Midland, Texas, as George, eased along the way by family and friends, made his name and fortune in the oil business.

Barbara bore the greatest burden. While George was testing himself in adventuresome ways, she had babies, packed and unpacked and let her mind go "dormant . . . just dormant." She later said that in a marriage "where one is so willing to take on responsibility and the other so willing to keep the bathrooms clean . . . that's the way you get treated." It was not a relationship of equals. But she never blamed George.

"She is something, Mum," George wrote his mother,

> the way she never ever complains or even suggests that she would prefer to be elsewhere. She is happy, I know, but anyone would like to be around her own friends, be able to take at least a passing interest

in clothes, parties, etc. She gets absolutely none of this. It is different for me, I have my job all day long with new things happening, but she is here in this small apartment with people whose interests cannot be at all similar to Bar's because they have never had any similar experiences. I continue to be amazed at her unselfishness, her ability to get along with absolutely anyone, and her wonderful way with Georgie. . . . I am so very lucky, Mum. I am grateful and I must always work to make Bar happy. She has made my life full and complete; she has given so much and never asked a return. How lucky I am!

It was almost inevitable that a man as well connected and as relentlessly extroverted as Bush would end up in politics. His father, Prescott, had moved easily from Wall Street to the Senate in 1952, where he was popular with both parties. The word "networking" had not yet been coined, but Barbara and George applied themselves to the task with as much zeal as Hillary and Bill Clinton would decades later, collecting endless friends as they crisscrossed the Sun Belt. Barbara's job was to keep index cards about each of their growing list of friends. By the mid-seventies she had somewhere between four thousand and five thousand index cards. By 1986 the Bushes sent out thirty thousand Christmas cards. Like Lady Bird Johnson, she did not protest George's last-minute invitations to six more for lunch or dinner. She had never known any other life, any other man. If George liked it that way, she would adjust to a life of constant motion, an endless stream of people filling her kitchen and dining room. Like LBJ, Bush had an insatiable need for company. When he was not entertaining, he was on the telephone. "How George loves the West Coast," Barbara wrote in her diary, "because he can call anybody he wants when he wakes up. I have to hold him at bay on the East Coast."

Like so many other men of his generation, Bush saw his wife as an extension of himself. Bush's legendary acts of kindness and generosity were directed not at his wife but at outsiders. It was snowing hard the day that the congressional freshman's moving van arrived in Washington in 1966. George could not bear to make the movers drive home in the storm. So he dispatched Barbara to Sears to buy extra sheets for the moving men. Later, he would insist on keeping the family home for the holidays, so he could send his Secret Service agents home. Unlike Reagan, Bush possessed the gift of genuine friendship. He remembered people's wives, mothers and children. "One of the reasons I fell in love with George," Barbara wrote later in life, "was that he was so kind and nice. He always thought of the other fellow. Sometimes that caused me some pain and jealousy, which I'm now ashamed to admit. I just didn't think there was enough time for us."

In 1953, their lives crashed. Their only daughter, four-year-old Robin, was diagnosed with leukemia. It was during the months she spent looking after her fatally ill child that Barbara, still in her twenties, started to turn gray. The Bushes' way of dealing with scorching pain is revealing. "The day after Robin died, George and I went to Rye to play golf with Daddy, at his suggestion," Barbara wrote. It was not a lack of feeling, rather that physical activity of almost any kind was George's preferred form of therapy. He, the great extrovert, would not allow Barbara to turn inward. It was the first time in his life that he was actually looking after someone else. "When I wanted to cut out," Barbara wrote in her memoirs, "George made me talk to him, and he shared with me. . . . He made me remember that the loss was not just mine. . . . Many times he held me in his arms and let me weep myself to sleep." The shared loss no doubt deepened their bond.

Their life of constant motion soon picked up again. After twenty years in the high-stakes oil business, George moved Barbara and their five children to Houston and plunged into Texas politics. In 1964, Bush showed just how determined he was to please his constituency, opposing the Civil Rights Act. "I still favor the problem being handled by *moral persuasion,* at the local level," he explained. The man who had once led Yale's United Negro College Fund was willing to pay almost any price to win. It was not the last time he would deep-freeze his conscience for politics. Bush denounced the United Nations, where he would later serve as ambassador. When he lost the Texas Senate race to Democrat Ralph Yarborough in 1964, Bush swore he'd never again pander so blatantly for right-wing support. From then on, Bush tried to avoid issues and ideology and showcase his personal qualities. Barbara and their photogenic family became a central part of the image he was marketing. This is who I *really* am, Bush seemed to be saying. The rest is just political accommodation. Barbara's reward was that her husband needed her more than ever.

"In a sense it was a matriarchal family," their son Jeb recalled. "Mom was always the one to hand out the goodies and the discipline." The bleeding ulcer George developed early in his business career was a reminder that he did not deal well with stress. He possessed neither the rhinoceros skin nor the reptilian cunning that politics demanded. "Ivy League connotes privilege and softness," he wrote his sons in the seventies when Richard Nixon appointed him ambassador to the United Nations, "in a tea sipping, martini drinking, tennis playing sense. There's an enormous hang up here [in Washington] that comes through an awful lot. I feel it personally. . . . But I must confess that I am convinced that deep in [Nixon's] heart he feels I'm soft, not tough enough, not willing to do the 'gut job' that his political instincts have taught him must be done."

Barbara's role was to keep tension at home to a minimum. She absorbed a great deal of it herself and provided both diversion and stability for her husband. Robin's death was a wound that never fully healed. There were other heartaches. Son Neil was diagnosed with dyslexia and Marvin was expelled from Andover for smoking marijuana. Barbara chain-smoked Kools and ground her teeth until they hurt. Their daughter Dorothy, born after Robin's death, remembered her mother saying how lonely she sometimes felt, spending endless hours alone with her small children. "She did it all. . . . She brought us up. Not to say that my dad wasn't there some, but definitely she did all the disciplining and she was at every game with my brothers and all of that."

Those were the gender roles George was used to. His beloved mother, Dorothy Walker Bush, and not his austere father, was the heart of the Bush family, the one who exerted the greater influence. Dorothy's relentlessly competitive spirit infused all that George did. Well into his seventies, George would still recall his mother's admonishments and her gift for cutting him down to size. "Mum used to tell me, Now, George, don't walk ahead [of your wife]." In October 1999, when Bush returned for a visit to his former home, the United Nations ambassador's residence in New York City's Waldorf Towers, he asked the housekeeper, "Show me to the room my mother used to stay in." His mother's hold on him did not loosen.

Bush never quite managed to define what he stood for. When he made another run for the Senate in 1970, he gave as his reason "upward mobility." It seemed as if politics, campaigning, was just another athletic event for him. There was a hustle-for-the-sake-of-hustle feeling about the man, an absence of thoughtfulness. The throwaway grace with which he led at Andover and Yale did not thrive in Texas. His mother had done too good a job scrubbing him clean of the magnetic force called self that a politician must summon to fill the room.

When George was defeated a second time, at forty-six, the wind seemed to have gone out of the Bushes' political sails. Their relationship was affected by their thwarted ambitions. During the summer of 1970, in an act that generally symbolizes resignation for a middle-aged woman, Barbara stopped dyeing her gray hair. "George Bush never noticed," she said. "So why had I gone through those years of agony?" At the same time, to rescue his flagging public service career, her husband was forced to lean on a man who stood for everything his mother and father despised: Richard Nixon.

Nixon came through with the UN ambassadorship. Hearing the news, Lud Ashley, by now an Ohio congressman, stopped George in the House Speaker's lobby. "What the hell do you know about foreign policy?" Ashley asked his friend. "Not much," Bush answered, "but ask me in ten days." The presidential favor was not cost-free. When Nixon became enmeshed in Watergate, he "offered" Bush the less prestigious job of chairman of the Republican National Committee, hoping Bush could protect him. Ashley was appalled. "I remember being at the Waldorf at a Yale football get-together and we got talking about the R.N.C. and I said, 'For Christ's sakes, George, you got it backwards. You go from that to this. Not the other way around.' Especially when it was clear that Nixon was going to be in deep trouble. Very few people would have accepted that job. But that was George."

This time Barbara could not keep her disappointment to herself. Bush wrote Nixon,

> Frankly your first choice for me [as head of the Republican National Committee] came as quite a surprise, particularly to Barbara. The rarefied atmosphere of international affairs plus the friendships in New York and the Cabinet seem threatened to her. She is convinced that all our friends in Congress, in public life, in God knows where, will say, "George screwed up at the UN and the President has loyally found a suitable spot." Candidly, there will be some of this. But— here is my answer: Your first choice was the Republican National Committee. I will do it!

In the space of two years, there had been two more uprootings, two more cities for Barbara to adjust to. He served the president, she served him. But while her husband trimmed and shaded his image to suit the times, she did not. She was unabashedly middle-aged and patrician in looks, speech and conduct. And not since Jackie Kennedy—of similar background—had an American political wife drawn such clear boundaries around her privacy. "You have two choices in life," she often said. "You can like what you do, or you can dislike it. I have chosen to like it." Disappointments and failures were kept inside the Bush family. The trouble was that George's important assignments seemed to add no heft to the man. Bush's reputation was for eagerly supporting almost anything the president and the party required. He was a team player, a utility infielder, not an innovator.

In 1974, George and Barbara suffered another public humiliation. President Gerald Ford chose Nelson Rockefeller as his vice president. "Yesterday was an enormous personal disappointment," Bush wrote his friend James Baker. "For valid reasons we made the finals . . . and so the defeat was more intense." But the Bush credo was to move on, look ahead, not dwell on disappointment. "That was yesterday," Bush declared. "Today and tomorrow will be different, for I see now clearly what it means to have really close friends . . . the sun is about to come out and life looks pretty darn good."

As always with the Bushes, hard on the heels of defeat came a consolation prize. President Ford dispatched them to head the American mission in Beijing. Just as she had once declared she always wanted to live in Odessa, Texas, Barbara now willed herself to love the gray and watchful capital of the People's Republic. "The Bushes have an ability to not acknowledge things that they don't want to acknowledge," observed Barbara's former chief of staff Susan Porter Rose. "They both have it. They don't see what they don't want to see." In politics, which is mined with setbacks and sustained by a public display of happiness, denial is an asset. When her husband was not appointed vice president, Barbara sent this description of her life to the *Smith Alumnae Quarterly:* "I play tennis, do vol. work and admire George Bush!" Her guiding philosophy was, If you put a bright face on it, it *will* be bright. (Two decades later, Hillary Clinton practiced her version of this credo of willed optimism—"fake it 'till you make it.")

Once again, Barbara packed and moved and sorted out the lives of her five children. "It's great," George wrote Baker from Beijing. "We are happy here, though Bar and I miss family, friends, news, even politics. It is funny how fast we get cut off. . . ." Bush was perhaps less isolated than his wife. Accompanying him to Beijing was Jennifer Fitzgerald, his new executive assistant. In her early forties, the divorced, English-born Fitzgerald was the only woman other than his wife ever publicly linked to him. Their relationship was, at a minimum, emotionally close. Barbara's many absences from China fueled the rumors of a liaison. Barbara's recollection of taking leave of George for a short trip home is poignant. "Although this was planned for months I was heartsick. I had never been so far away from George and could hardly stand saying goodbye to him."

In her absence, her husband was seen outside the office with Jennifer. They shopped and dined together and often traveled together. Jennifer controlled access to him. She imposed martial order on a man known for his lax management style. In both looks and style, Jennifer vaguely resembled Barbara. Though roughly ten years younger, her appearance was matronly and comfortable rather than stylish. The order and discipline Barbara provided at home, Jennifer imposed on the office.

Bush liked strong women. For two decades, Jennifer, like Barbara, freed him to be the easygoing, universally loved figure. "I'm not saying she's Miss Popularity," Bush said of Jennifer. "She's doing what I want done. When you have to say no, particularly to friends, there's bound to be some level of frustration."

She was one of those women found in the upper reaches of corporations as well as in politics who give their lives to the great man. They have no other real interests. Sometimes they fall a little bit in love with him. If they are ready to work the hours no one else will, it is a labor of love. They feel they understand him, know his needs better than anyone else—better even than his wife. Very rarely, the great man reciprocates. Rarer still is the man willing to reciprocate for the woman's sacrifice with a sacrifice of his own. For there are always others willing to serve him, ready to step in when, inevitably, the intensity between the boss and the office wife becomes a problem.

In 1976, all the good cheer and I'm-the-luckiest-woman-alive bravado trickled out of Barbara. Her husband was summoned home from Beijing to a job they both felt would end his political life: director of Central Intelligence. "I was given no options," Bush wrote his friend William Steiger. "I was asked to take on the CIA—I agreed . . . because of a fundamental *sense of duty*. . . . It's just that uncomplicated. . . . I honestly feel my political future is behind me. . . ." As always, Bush rationalized the new position, put a bright face on it and failed to consider his wife. "She's shed a few tears. . . . But now she sees that in spite of the ugliness around the CIA, there's a job to be done. . . . I'm fifty-one and this new one gives me a chance to really contribute."

With her five children grown or away at school, Barbara now had too much time on her hands. She was bitter that all those years of relentless uprooting and campaigning and self-sacrifice were invested in a political future that now seemed to vaporize. Worst of all, there was no room for her in George's new position. For the first time, her husband could not even talk about his job at night. He disappeared into the world of covert operations with Jennifer Fitzgerald in tow.

"I was very depressed, lonely and unhappy," Barbara wrote of this painful time. "It is still not easy to talk about it today, and I certainly didn't talk about it then." She attributed her depression to her age and to the women's movement. "Suddenly women's lib had made me feel my life had been wasted." But hers was a more urgent cry for attention than a general unhappiness with the women's movement. "Sometimes the pain was so great I felt the urge to drive into a tree or an oncoming car." Unlike Betty Ford, who suffered a similar depression, Barbara never accused her husband of neglect. Her personal code required that she never be a burden to him. That a woman as steely as she was cracked under the weight of the political life speaks for itself.

It must have been quite a shock for the man who had always relied on his rock-solid partner to discover that she was the one in need of him. "He would suggest that I get professional help," she recalled, "and that would send me into a deeper gloom. He was working such incredibly long hours at his job, and I swore to myself I would not burden him. Then he would come home and I would tell him all about it. Night after night, George held me weeping in his arms while I tried to explain my feelings. Sometimes I wonder why he didn't leave me." This is an astonishing confession from a woman of such bred-in-the-bone reserve. The words take on deeper meaning since she published them two years after she left the White House, when she could hardly have been motivated by a political need for a display of public "intimacy."

Her collapse surely got his attention. "I love you very much. Nothing—campaign separations, people, nothing will ever change that," he wrote his wife on her fifty-fourth birthday. "I can't ever really tell you how much I love you." It is doubtful that Bush ever again took his wife for granted as he had in the period leading to her breakdown.

"George Bush is an extraordinarily flirtatious man," says a woman reporter who covered his presidency. "He loves women. He came on to a lot of women, but he never got close to the line. It was a game for him, something he enjoyed engaging in. Yet it didn't seem to be going on with Barbara. I think that says more good things about them. But she would often do something that marked him as hers. She can make fun of him and make jokes which the rest of us could not. Nor did she defer to him, even in the White House." Diane Sawyer recalled that when CBS first assigned her to cover President Bush, "Barbara came out and asked, 'Are you going to be joining us?' I said yes. 'Are you going to travel with us?' I said yes. She took her elbow and gored me in the ribs. 'He's my boyfriend, sweetie,' she said, 'now don't forget it.' "

As with many political marriages, his need for her was as much personal as political. Once, in Barbara's words, "*we* became vice president," his presidential hopes revived again. Barbara was again indispensable as he campaigned. She wanted the presidency as much as he did. What other purpose had their nomadic life, the near total loss of privacy and the cultivation of armies of "friends" had? There was only one prize that would compensate for having her husband labeled a wimp. Only the presidency would provide satisfaction for the years this most opinionated woman refrained from speaking out. Only being upstairs at the White House would make up for the humiliations Nancy Reagan had inflicted on her.

For eight years Nancy had treated Barbara with a pointed disdain. Only twice in eight years did the Bushes dine with the Reagans upstairs. Nancy deliberately withheld the most prized invitations from the Bushes. "Once," recalled a member of Nancy's staff, "when Nancy bailed out of an East Room ceremony, she called me and said, 'Make sure Barbara isn't on the platform without me there.' Mrs. Bush understood the situation. 'Just tell me where she wants me to stand,' she said." Just as she never complained about what she suffered as a wife, so she never spoke out about the Reagans' treatment of the Bushes. She was biding her time.

In 1984, George, reeling from harsh media coverage, again considered abandoning his presidential dreams. Barbara, raised by her father to fight hard and win, helped to keep him in the game. "During this time Barbara was a kind of rudder helping him steer the large ship of his public life," Bush's chief of staff Craig Fuller recalled. "He would not have reached out to some of us without her encouragement. He would not have started thinking about building his team for the presidential campaign."

It was Barbara's career, too. Her competitive instincts were fully engaged. She, too, liked being in the center of things. She had paid her dues and was not about to quit now. She was tougher, scrappier and possessed of finer public relations antennae than her husband. "I'm not sure his political instincts are that great," Lud Ashley noted. "They're good enough, but you need more than that for a presidential campaign. She had that." Barbara may have had another motive. "George is so much more fun when he's engaged in something he cares about," in the words of an old friend of the couple.

Once George made up his mind to run for president, Barbara's role in his personal and political life was enhanced. He was selling who he was: a family man with solid values whose kids came home to visit. When asked what made him fit to be president, Bush answered—almost surreally—"I've got a big family and lots of friends." Barbara was at the core of that image. But after eight years as Reagan's number two, it was hard to tell what Bush stood for. He had shifted his views on civil rights, abortion, gun control, China, the United Nations. She learned it was best never to express hers. When she went off her usual winning script, as when she said Congresswoman Geraldine Ferraro was a "$4 million rhymes with rich," she could cause an uproar. But even her slipups seemed calculated. Though she apologized profusely to Ferraro, she had made her point. It was an old Nixon trick: putting negative remarks into circulation by apologizing or denying them.

Nobody inside the 1988 Bush campaign doubted her essential role. Her eldest son, George, even boasted about it. "There were times [when] people did something that I think upset my mother. . . . Leaks and staff siphoning credit for ideas originating with the candidate especially infuriated her." George W. Bush claims credit for mediating between staff and his mother in those instances. "I would then go and talk to that person [sic] and inform [sic] that they had made a mistake and that they needed to mend their ways and explain to them that if they were not careful the wrath of the Silver Fox would fall upon them." George W. knew that was not an experience anyone inside the campaign, the government or the media relished. "Fear of Barbara" was a potent political weapon. "My mother was viewed as a very smart, intelligent, savvy person. People needed to be aware of her presence. No one wanted to irritate her. . . ." Very few politicians' wives could be as cutting as the woman who liked to claim she left politics to her husband. Of Rosalynn Carter, Barbara Bush once said, "There's nothing wrong with being a strong, supportive wife—if you have a strong husband. I think she [Rosalynn] missed on that. . . ."

George's running for the highest office offered another consolation for Barbara. Jennifer Fitzgerald, still George's faithful gatekeeper, would finally have to go. "I always thought less of George Bush for having Jennifer around as much as he did," a former White House staffer noted. "It was so in-your-face for Barbara." Fitzgerald had alienated nearly everyone by her proprietary attitude toward her boss. "She even had control of the children's access to their father," one staffer remembered. "She would undo what others had scheduled. The kids had to book their tennis games with their father through her." Craig Fuller recalled being warned not to accept the job of Bush's chief of staff. "As long as Jennifer was there, I was told I'd never succeed. She was powerful and influential and sat right outside his office. She tangled with other people on the staff and clearly exerted a lot of control, sometimes more than the chief of staff. Jennifer was somebody who managed to transcend all of George Bush's different activities. A lot of people were jealous of that, and maybe that's why the rumors of something else going on between them were started. I never saw anything myself. I never had any trouble with her. I suggested that maybe with the changes in the office she could do something else. I told her we needed someone on Capitol Hill."

Fitzgerald was indeed moved to the Hill as congressional liaison, but she continued to travel with the vice president. Sometimes, if Barbara was along, a seemingly innocent remark could spark tension. As the vice president descended *Air Force Two* during a tour of NATO countries, Jennifer was overheard to say, "You should wear a pocket hankie, Mr. Vice President, like Ambassador ———." Barbara, within earshot of the dapper ambassador, shot back, "I think it makes him look like a fag." But the following day, reporters noticed that Bush sported a pocket hankie.

Whatever the real nature of the relationship, Jennifer Fitzgerald was now a political, not a personal, matter. Only Barbara had the power to resolve it. "I decided to raise it with the vice president after our weekly intelligence briefing at their residence," Fuller recalled. "We were sitting out on the porch, and as we finished the intelligence briefing, [campaign operatives] Lee Atwater and Bob Teeter joined us. It fell to me to deal with the difficult issue. So I said, 'One more thing, sir. You won't like it, but you will be asked about adultery.' Well, Bush was just livid.

At that moment, Mrs. Bush appeared around the corner, back from a walk. She looked at us and said, 'What are you talking about?' And the vice president said to her, 'Well, I'm going to be asked the adultery question at the next news conference.' Mrs. Bush cut him off. 'The answer is *no*. End of discussion.' And that was the answer. That is how we dealt with it."

The morning after the *New York Post* published the story of Bush's rumored affair on August 24, 1992, "We debated asking Mrs. Bush about Jennifer," *Newsweek* White House correspondent Ann McDaniel recalled. "Just then, Mrs. Bush walked into the press room and said, 'OK, which of the Big A's do you want to start with? Adultery or abortion?' She wasn't about to wait for us to beat around the bush. She was going to control the story." That was the end of Jennifer Fitzgerald. Moved to the State Department's Office of Protocol, she was never again publicly seen with Bush. Whatever the real nature of their relationship, once Fitzgerald became a political liability and was no longer allowed to serve him, she had the good grace to disappear completely.

With her usual blend of steel and defiance, Barbara triumphed. Like Jacqueline before her and Hillary after, she would not allow anyone to see her humiliation. But the hurt from the Fitzgerald years lingered. In a supreme act of media manipulation, she even expressed sympathy for the woman who had caused her pain. "She's a wonderful lady," Barbara said with a clenched smile to Barbara Walters. "And can you imagine how hurtful that was to her?" But when pressed as to whether the public has a right to know if a politician has been unfaithful, her anger flared. "When you are married, it's different, dearie."

If it is possible to be temperamentally suited for the role of first lady, Barbara Bush was. Her rigorous training in noblesse oblige and good manners in the most awkward situations without ever betraying real emotions served her well in the White House. "Barbara Bush was an ideal first lady," presidential adviser David Gergen said. "She had a quality of steel about her." Barbara's popularity in the polls and her stature made her a force to reckon with inside the White House. "The difference between Barbara and Nancy," a staffer who worked in both administrations noted, "was that people knew Nancy would go to Mike Deaver or Jim Baker if she were upset about something. If Mrs. Bush felt strongly, we knew she would go directly to her husband. We would hear from the president, 'Bar is really unhappy about . . .' or 'Bar says we ought to . . .' Mrs. Bush's influence on her husband was direct. Nancy's was indirect. People in the White House respected her [Barbara's] power and influence because of her popularity. You certainly did not want her mad at you." When asked about Nancy's use of aides to bring pressure on President Reagan, Barbara tartly replied, "We do things differently. I have always been able to go through George."

It would not have occurred to Barbara to move her office into the West Wing, as her successor would. The notion of a declared "two-for-the-price-of-one" presidency was an alien concept for the tradition-minded Bushes. But even those who claim never to have heard her views on policy could not mistake her influence. Together, George and Barbara planned the tone of the Bush inaugural and White House. "We wanted very much for it to be a people's inaugural," Barbara said. It would be a family house, less formal and less glitzy than the Reagans'—a place where muddy dogs and sticky children were welcome. The new, relaxed atmosphere was one more way for Barbara to let the world know what she thought of Nancy. In public she was careful about her comments, proclaiming, "I am [Nancy's] greatest fan. I think she's done a wonderful job. The White House has never been more beautiful, the flowers prettier, the food better. . . . But"—Barbara paused for emphasis—"she and I are not alike and you can't compare apples and oranges. . . ." Once in a while, she abandoned caution for the satisfaction of a good swipe. "I think Nancy Reagan has done a wonderful job for American designers, honestly, and as I say, if I were a size two, they'd give them [couture dresses] to me too." Then, pausing a beat, she inserted the needle. "But I pay for mine."

Barbara refused to comment on a much publicized, scorching biography of Nancy. She told reporters she had "no intention to read that garbage." Her press spokeswoman, Anna Perez, recalled a flight during which the first lady seemed engrossed in a best-seller by Rosamunde Pilcher. Occasionally, however, Barbara would shake her head and make a comment about Nancy. Puzzled, Perez got up and peered over Barbara's shoulder. "Behind a fake cover, she was reading the Nancy bio," said Perez.

Barbara's self-assurance grew with her stature. For the first time, her husband needed her more than she needed him. "I'm going to approach my job as Barbara approaches hers," he said shortly after becoming president. "Call 'em the way you see 'em, as the umpire said." She had become his role model. "I don't think he would have guessed that his wife would have touched the country as she did," Craig Fuller noted. "He was very proud of her as a result, and yes, I would say there was some amazement at her success." President Bush now larded his speeches with the phrase "Barbara and I."

Since George hated any display of emotion beyond sentimental tears, Barbara channeled her anger at others. "She had this way about her to put you in your place," *Washington Post* reporter Donnie Radcliffe noted, "then come back quickly and attempt to make up for it. It was part of her way. She was very adroit." Almost everyone who has ever worked for Barbara has felt the cold snap of her irritation at some point. Rex Scouten said she never raised her voice, but "She could cut you down in a hurry. She knew everything that went on in [the White House]. I used to wear vests. I had an old pocket watch and I put it on a chain. Mrs. Bush noticed it right away. 'What's that, Rex,' she asked, 'your Phi Beta Kappa key?' I knew from the way she said it that she didn't like me wearing it. She thought it was too showy."

Few people who received Barbara's wrath ever forgot it. Once, Barbara arrived ahead of George for a dinner at the Chinese embassy. Spotting Barbara's car, deputy chief of protocol Bunnie Murdoch informed the Chinese ambassador, who invited Barbara to come inside the residence, rather than await her husband's arrival outside. "And just who told him I was here?" she said later, flaring at Murdoch. "I mumbled something about, 'Well, I assumed . . .' and Mrs. Bush cut me off," said Murdoch. " 'Never assume.' She was so quiet I was completely undone. She saw that I turned beet red and said, 'Just don't do that again.' "

The consequences for paying too little attention to Barbara could be severe as well. "Vice President Bush had a young military aide named Sean Coffee," Bush press spokesman Marlin Fitzwater recalled. "We were all guests of the Chinese government at a banquet in Shanghai. We had been instructed about the *Mao tai,* how you drink one for courtesy, but never two. Our Chinese hosts started toasting. They got up and went from table to table. Sean, in his dress whites, was going from table to table also. I turned to him and said, Before you do this, look up at the dais, which he did. Mrs. Bush was staring right through him. It was unmistakably a look that said, Sit down and don't say another word for the rest of the evening. Well, Sean ignored her. At the end of the dinner he made the fatal mistake of riding down the elevator with the vice president and Mrs. Bush, as a personal aide often does. By the time they got to the ground floor, Sean was history. He was sent back to Washington on a commercial plane."

∽

BARBARA DID NOT THINK it was in the Bushes' interest for the public to know how influential she was. "I'm not too sure the American public likes the spouse to be too front and center," she would write later. "A spouse has a fine row to hoe. Dennis Thatcher played it just right, in my eyes. He was supportive of Margaret always, yet had a life of his own." According to their friend former Canadian prime minister Brian Mulrooney, the Bushes have a more "modern" marriage than the Reagans. "Nancy and Ronnie lived for each other. The Reagans were interested in their family only insofar as it enhanced their relationship. Bar and George lived for their family. They were much less emotionally dependent on each other. Each was self-sufficient, each lived his own life separately. Ron and Nancy lived one life."

Like the best political wives, Barbara professed to a near total lack of interest in politics. Apart from occasional "slipups," deliberate or not, "She would not express her opinions in public," Bush media adviser Roger Ailes noted, "but she was a strong and respected voice inside." Fitzwater said that in seven years as Bush's press spokesman, "I don't know that I ever heard her comment on policy." This was part of her careful calculation. She had an upstairs/downstairs attitude about voicing her views—not in front of the staff and certainly not in front of reporters.

The cardinal sin, in Barbara's opinion, was for a strong, smart wife to call attention to herself. "Shortly after Bush's 1989 inaugural," *Washing-*

ton Post reporter Radcliffe recalled, "they were going to Japan to the funeral of Emperor Hirohito, and on to China. I wrote that Barbara was going to be the co-star of the trip, or something like that. I got a call from one of her aides telling me in no uncertain terms that Mrs. Bush did *not* want to be compared to her husband in any way. That she did not wish to detract from his center-stage role on that trip. She was downplaying anything that was on her schedule." Her view of the wife's "proper" role was made clear by a comment she made during the Clinton presidency. "Hillary Rodham Clinton is certainly very much a part of her husband's decision-making process. She seems much the stronger of the two. Does it make him seem weaker?" In Barbara Bush's view, the answer was self-evident.

Mulrooney saw the private face of the marriage and Barbara's role in it.

> I'd always go and see George when he was vice president and I was prime minister. He was silent in meetings when Reagan was present. But I wanted to get to know him. Barbara weighed in on issues during all our meetings. "Now just a second, George," she'd say if she disagreed. Before George's trip to Russia in 1989 I briefed him since I'd just come back from Moscow. Barbara was definitely involved. "Now why do you say there are cracks in the Soviet empire? Do you seriously think the place could implode?" She was there because he trusts her. I remember in August 1990 Saddam Hussein had just invaded Kuwait and the U.S. had no response ready yet. Bush called me and invited me to dinner. This was not a social call, but a full crisis meeting. Over dinner in the family quarters with National Security Adviser Brent Scowcroft and Acting Secretary of State Larry Eagleburger, George presided with Barbara at his side. Again, I had a feeling of a wife fully engaged in her husband's business. She particularly weighs in about people if she doesn't think they're serving George's best interest.

Those who did not perform according to her standards often found their careers cut short or sidelined, and not just military aides. Fuller did not get the coveted chief of staff job in part because Barbara felt he was leaking to the *Washington Post*—and not returning Barbara's calls fast enough. Aboard *Air Force Two* following her husband's defeat in the Iowa straw polls, she summoned campaign operative Rich Bond. "So," she said with a hard smile, "when are you going back to Iowa to manage the vice president's campaign?" It was not a question but an order. Bond relocated to Iowa for the next five months.

Though she was content to leave policy to the "hired help," no one cared more about President Bush's image or his legacy than his wife. Sometimes the president is the last to know when a staffer serves his own interests with greater zeal than he does those of the president. This is particularly so in the case of the chief of staff, who controls access. "I've known very few chiefs of staff who didn't in the end feel that 'If I could just get rid of that dumb guy down the hall in the Oval Office . . . everything would be fine,' " Roger Ailes noted. Barbara concluded that John Sununu had fallen into what Ailes calls the "ego pit" of the chief of staff. Lud Ashley credits Barbara with Sununu's demise: "She picked up that he had his own agenda. She alerted George to the problem." After a series of embarrassing press reports charging Sununu with abusing the privileges of his office, Bush fired him in December 1991. But, unlike Nancy Reagan, Barbara stayed in the shadows. When asked about her role, Barbara answered with the same sweet attitude with which she brushed off the Jennifer Fitzgerald story. "I love John Sununu and I love his wife and they know it and I guess that's what counts." Barbara rarely lost her composure or let an injury go unanswered.

She had found her winning formula: praise her husband and bolster his policies however she could. In so doing, she even befriended Nancy Reagan's nemesis, Raisa Gorbachev. There was something gleeful in Barbara's great show of friendship for Raisa. "She is a lovely-looking creature," Barbara wrote of her, adding with characteristic irony, "I don't know how old, but I think the paper said fifty-three or fifty-five. That's funny, we don't know if Nancy Reagan is sixty-five or sixty-seven, and she won't tell. I guess Raisa won't tell, either." Barbara scored a double hit when she took Mrs. Gorbachev to Wellesley College to share commencement-speech honors with her. Campus protests had preceded Barbara's appearance, as a number of students felt the first lady—who came by her position through marriage, not personal achievement—was the wrong choice to address them. Barbara's combination of charm and guile disarmed her critics. "Somewhere in this audience," she told the Wellesley graduating class, "may even be someone who will one day follow in my footsteps, and preside over the White House as the president's spouse." Then she delivered her punch line: "I wish him well!" The women roared their approval of the most traditional first lady in recent memory.

Only rarely did her convictions trump her political caution. In the wake of a school shooting incident, a reporter asked Barbara if she thought assault weapons should be illegal. "Absolutely," she answered. Within a week, her husband declared, "Absolutely not." For her subsequent silence on the issue, Barbara was publicly chastised by Lady Bird Johnson's press spokeswoman, Liz Carpenter. "Americans have come to expect a first lady to care about her family and her country in visible ways that lead others to action," Carpenter wrote, "and to stiffen the spine of the president when he needs it." In a letter Barbara never sent but included in her memoirs, she answered the charge. "Long ago," she wrote Carpenter, "I decided in life that I had to have priorities. I put my children and my husband at the top of the list. That's a choice that I have never regretted. . . . I realized that a more literate America would benefit every single thing I worry about: crime, unemployment, pollution, teenage pregnancy, school dropouts, women who are trapped into welfare and therefore poverty, etc. You name it I worried about it. . . . Abortion, pro or con, is not a priority for me. ERA is not a priority for me, nor is gun control. I leave that for those courageous enough to run for public office."

Her answer to the charge of political cowardice was typically shrewd. Barbara was quite disingenuous in implying that she had to choose between literacy and gun control and literacy and a woman's right to choose. Barbara needed no handlers to contrive this winning formula. Though possessed of the same accommodating spirit as her husband, she was more successful because she *seemed* more believable.

To glean how she really felt, one must examine her statements before and after the Bush administration. In 1980 she declared, "George has always been against gun control. Well, I have always been for gun control. For thirty-five years I have been for gun control. . . ."

By 1992 George and Barbara seemed out of step with their own party. The GOP had turned too sharply right for the Bushes. Something else had also changed. The candidate was bone-tired. For the first time in his political career, Bush did not relish the race. "I haven't made up my mind," he told concerned friends and family. The effort to keep the Gulf War alliance together left him weak and low. "I have never felt like this a day in my life. I am very tired. I didn't sleep well and this troubles me because I go to the nation at nine o'clock. My lower gut hurts, nothing like when I had the bleeding ulcer. But I am aware of it and I take a couple of Mylantas."

Bush had discovered something known only to a handful of members of the world's most exclusive club: there is never any downtime for the president. "I come over to the house about twenty to four to lie down. Before I make my calls at five, the old shoulders tighten up. My mind is a thousand miles away. I simply can't sleep. I think of what other presidents went through." There was another reason he seemed sapped of his competitive juices. On May 5, he started off on a jog at Camp David. "I . . . got tired right away, or got out of breath, so I stopped and walked. Then I ran a little but couldn't run more than a hundred yards, so again I stopped. I did this for about thirty or forty minutes and I told Rich [Miller, a Secret Service agent] to get the doctor. . . ." The president was diagnosed with Graves' disease, the same thyroid deficiency his wife suffered in 1989, only in his case it affected the rhythm of his heart.

For a president to be sick while in office is a unique experience. Even more than normally, the eyes of the world, through the camera's unblinking lens, are on his every move. "I got up and went to the bathroom and ABC carried a picture of me standing there. . . ." Such was the high cost of the office that even with her husband's condition uncertain, Barbara's first consideration had to be the political consequences of his illness. How would this play in the country, and the world? Edith Wilson had had similar considerations. Knowing that her every gesture could set off speculation, Barbara decided against spending the night in the hospital with her husband. "I went home . . . partially to reassure the world and our own children that it was not serious." Her husband was not fooled. "She's a little more worried than she indicates and I'll probably be thinking tomorrow, Have I really told her how much I love her, and it's going to be okay?"

Medication restored Bush's heartbeat to normal. But the convergence of the Gulf War and his illness depleted the once hyperkinetic man. On June 10, 1991, he added this to his White House "funeral file": "I want the song 'Last Full Measure of Devotion' sung by a good male soloist. . . . Gravestone—the plain stones we see at Arlington. I would like my Navy number on the back of it. . . . Also on the stone in addition to what I already requested: 'He loved Barbara very much.' "

<hr>

FOR BARBARA AND GEORGE the worst year of their political life was the year that ended it: 1992. On January 9, a photograph showing the president throwing up on the lap of Japanese prime minister Kiichi Miyazawa was beamed across the globe. The image of the stricken president became as much a metaphor for Bush's final year in office as the one of Jimmy Carter collapsing while jogging. Nothing Bush would do that year could erase that devastating image. Barbara could do little to inject into her husband's final campaign the momentum it never had.

"The wheels came off in '92," Lud Ashley remembered. "Every day I shook my head at his disastrous campaign. The people running it were bickering among themselves. There was no theme. George wasn't telling the American people where the country was going. I was so upset I wrote him a memo telling him he wasn't coming across to the electorate. But George assumed ultimately the character issue would sink Bill Clinton. He just could not believe a man who had dodged the draft and all those other facets of his personality would be elected president." But Bush never articulated an alternate vision. Nor would he agree to get rid of his running mate, Dan Quayle. "George felt Quayle had served him as he wanted to be served," said Ashley. "He never admitted that choosing Quayle had been a boneheaded move."

Barbara did not hide her own view that Quayle was a liability. Ashley recalled a family gathering at Camp David before the 1992 Republican convention. Every time Quayle's name came up, "Barbara rolled her eyes. She did not say anything, she just rolled her eyes." You made your views on Quayle pretty clear, Ashley later teased her. "Yes," Barbara admitted, "but you'd have a hard time quoting me, wouldn't you?" which was in keeping with her style. But this time her husband did not heed her message. For him, the private virtue of loyalty trumped the political advantage of dumping his running mate.

Bush seemed out of touch with his country's gravest troubles: a sluggish economy, inflation and the downward-spiraling quality of life in the inner cities. His tin ear for politics was never more conspicuous than during the rioting set off by the announcement of the Rodney King verdict in Los Angeles. Fifty-three deaths, two thousand injuries and five thousand fires ripped the city, and from the safety of the White House all the president could find to say was that it was "wrong." When he finally flew to the ravaged city he missed another chance to heal and inspire. Standing at the bedside of a critically injured firefighter, he mumbled, "I'm sorry Barbara is not here. She's out repairing what's left of our house [in Kennebunkport]. Damned storm knocked down four or five walls. She says it's coming along. . . ." What, one wonders, was the man who lay flat on his back thinking, hearing the president's hard-luck tale? And what would Ronald Reagan or Bill Clinton have made of this moment? How differently Bush's own wife would have treated the injured fireman.

The 1992 Republican convention in Houston's Astrodome was a surreal nightmare for George and Barbara. Loudly and proudly, the party's triumphant right wing thumbed its nose at Bush's moderate roots. Former Nixon speechwriter Pat Buchanan, in a speech worthy of George Wallace, whipped up xenophobic fervor. "There is a religious war going on in the country," Buchanan roused the convention. "It is a cultural war as critical to the kind of nation we shall be as the Cold War itself. . . . Take back our country!" Buchanan urged a wildly cheering minority who had hijacked the convention, shredding Bush's right flank in the process.

"Mila [Mrs. Mulrooney] chided Barbara about the right wing," Brian Mulrooney recalled. " 'You've got to get this under control,' she told her. Barbara got quite upset and turned on Mila. 'We've had just about enough advice, thank you very much,' she said. 'I'm *trying* to get it under control.' "

But Buchanan wasn't George's biggest problem; George Bush was. The Cold War was over and he lacked the political instincts to seize the new moment. He wasn't interested in domestic problems. Tone deaf to the new beat, he allowed other voices in the GOP to define the times. Bush's lifelong struggle to placate and accommodate his party's right wing was fruitless. To many in the party, Bush's most memorable line of 1988, "Read my lips. No new taxes," was pivotal, because Bush never successfully explained why he had abandoned that pledge. Unlike in 1988, when he spoke movingly of hearing "the quiet America that others don't," this time Bush had no soaring rhetoric, no ringing promises. The party's platform—anti-gay, anti-abortion and distinctly pro–Christian right—did not reflect his views. He had failed to move his party to the center, where he was most comfortable.

"This is all extraordinarily tough on Barbara," her husband wrote in his diary. "She is still wildly popular and gets a wonderful response, but I can tell she is hurting for me. She refuses to watch the television; refuses to read the papers; and she tells me to turn [the television] off when I turn it on because it is always hammering away at me." During his second debate against Clinton, a dispirited Bush bemoaned that his wife was not running. She would surely win, the president said. "But it's too late."

As always in tough moments, he found solace in his family. "Everything is ugly and everything is nasty," he wrote in his diary. "But we are a family, and I have a certain inner quiet peace, which I'm not sure I've ever had in a situation like this." For a man who fled introspection, he had gained a measure of self-knowledge. "I agree on Clinton," he wrote speechwriter Noonan. "He's got more facts—he's better at facts-figures than I am. I'm better at life."

The pain of the actual defeat was beyond anything Bush had experienced. In the greatest competition of his life, he lost massively. Thirty-two states chose Clinton over Bush. "It is hard to describe the emotions of something like this," he wrote at fifteen minutes past midnight on November 4, 1992, "but it's hurt, hurt, hurt and I guess it's the pride too. . . . I was absolutely convinced we would prove them wrong but I was wrong and they were right and that hurts a lot." Bush's lament is as good a description as there is of a loss so abrupt, so deep, so personal and so public—only a handful of men and their wives have experienced it in the republic's 224 years.

When, on January 20, 1993, the presidential helicopter, *Marine One,* carrying Barbara and George Bush on the first leg of their homeward journey, made the traditional farewell circle around the White House, Barbara whispered, "It's so sad." Twenty years earlier, Pat Nixon had uttered the same three words.

CHAPTER 11

HILLARY AND BILL CLINTON
UNLIMITED PARTNERSHIP

Eleanor Roosevelt was strong, but she did not try to beat men at their own game. Hillary does.
— ARTHUR SCHLESINGER, JR.

Being first lady is a very different position than I've ever had before. . . . I've always had jobs and worked for a living. I'm here, as everyone else in the White House is here, because of one person, the president. It was bewildering to me and has taken a while to get used to.

— HILLARY RODHAM CLINTON, *April 1997*

TO AN EXTENT THAT WOULD HAVE SEEMED UNIMAGINABLE BEFORE 1992, TO A degree that dwarfed even the saga of Franklin and Eleanor, the story of the Clinton administration was the story of a marriage. Bill and Hillary Clinton said they sought a "zone of privacy" for themselves, but their own actions, both political and personal, made it inevitable that the press, the public and ultimately a relentless barrage of investigators and prosecutors would invade their private lives and make Hillary Rodham Clinton the most controversial first lady in history.

The Clintons understandably blamed their enemies for their difficulties—and, to be sure, an unusual number of people hated them. But even their admirers would ultimately have to admit that the Clintons brought on to themselves the attention and most of the crises.

First came the determination of both Clintons that Hillary would be a first lady unlike any of her predecessors. She would be the first to have an office in the West Wing, rather than the traditional East Wing space. The symbolism was clear: only policy makers had precious, if cramped, West Wing real estate. ("You can't put Hillary in the West Wing," Vernon Jordan whispered to his friend the president-elect in January 1993. "You don't understand," Bill Clinton replied. "That's a done deal.") She would attempt the reform of the nation's health care system—an awesome job, the handling of which damaged her immensely early on in her husband's presidency. And finally, eight years and countless crises later, she would become the first wife of a president in history to run for public office.

And then there was the unprecedented and relentless furor surrounding a sitting president's sex life.

Americans ended up knowing more about Bill and Hillary's marriage—and, in excruciating detail, his reckless behavior—than about those of their closest friends. The Clintons had almost nothing left to hide at the end of their tenure. Even after leaving the White House, when other ex-presidential couples normally fade into the background, the unique circumstances of the Clintons—she a sitting U.S. senator, he a beleaguered high-profile defender of controversial, last-minute presidential pardons—meant that the invasive attention would continue.

The memory of this accomplished and intelligent partnership would be that Hillary saved both their marriage and the Clinton presidency even as he exposed her to the most searing public humiliation of any spouse in American history. Ironically, the woman who measured herself against Eleanor Roosevelt and once publicly scorned Tammy Wynette's famous song, "Stand By Your Man," ended up resembling both Eleanor and Tammy.

FEBRUARY 6, 2000. "Ladies and gentlemen. Please welcome the next senator of the United States, Hillary Rodham Clinton!" Three hundred fifty-two Democratic party delegates and an audience of thousands roared their approval from the bleachers of the Albany State Capitol as the candidate strode briskly to the podium to accept the nomination of the New York State Democratic Party.

It was, quite simply, astonishing. An incumbent first lady was running for office in a state where she had never lived. Few doubted Monica Lewinsky's role in Hillary's Senate run. "After Monica, Clinton had to give Hillary whatever she wanted," a White House aide said. And, on that night in Albany, in a low-key manner, she neatly flipped the traditional note of spousal appreciation uttered by countless politicians. "I am delighted that the president is here this evening," she said. "And I am so grateful for his support." And, with a line that stunned some and amused others, she added, "I would not be standing here tonight were it not for Bill and were it not for all he has done for me. . . ." It was the perfect echo of a thousand conjugal grace notes from a thousand candidates. Only now, the gender roles were reversed.

Nine months later, New Yorkers elected Hillary Clinton as their first woman senator. Standing quietly behind his wife as she thanked hundreds of cheering supporters in a downtown Manhattan ballroom, the president wiped tears from his eyes. Once again, the Clintons had rewritten the rules.

LOVE AND AMBITION cohabited seamlessly with the Clintons. A quarter of a century and countless tales of infidelity after they had first met, they still loved to match wits, test their ideas on each other. Clinton chose Hillary rather than any of the blond beauty queens he usually dated or wanted to date. "It's Hillary or nobody," he told his mother, who dreamed of other women for her son. "This is a very bonded couple," said her longtime friend and former secretary of health and human services Donna Shalala. "As much as anything else, when he goes home at night he wants to talk policy and so does she. He was smart enough to marry a serious grown-up." Hillary never bored him intellectually, and he understood instinctively that she would help him achieve his ambition.

Clinton knew enough about himself to know he needed one steadying presence in his life. He knew, said a friend years later, that "Hillary would never quit on him." She loved him and she loved the idea of the life they could build together: he the natural politician, she the intellectual strategist. Bill needed and valued Hillary's discipline, decisiveness and fierce devotion. She was the serious academic who landed the charming rogue. "Clinton was the first man who made her feel beautiful, not just smart," observed George Stephanopoulos, who saw a lot of them as a couple.

Hillary endured—but barely—her husband's philandering because she knew that his attachment to her was based on feelings beyond guilt and indebtedness. He empowered her because she, and later their daughter, were the only people he really needed. In the blunt judgment of a friend who had known Clinton since college, his affairs were simply "recreational."

At Yale Law School, Hillary was smitten by Bill, but she also saw his political potential. "My boyfriend," she told her bemused friends, "is going to be president." Bill and Hillary discovered that they balanced each other's strengths and weaknesses: his magnetism and her organizational skills forged a single, smooth-running political machine. She was smart and efficient, he was comfortable with ambiguities. He was intuitive; she was deductive. Yet he was probably more emotionally detached than she when confronting adversity or adversaries. He could cajole strangers and seduce adversaries into a common position. She was a fighter. Like Nancy Reagan, she would learn to watch his back, remember slights and urge attacks before their adversaries mobilized. He would compromise and beguile. She would keep him focused and steady and pounce when danger knocked. If she couldn't tame his vanity, his compulsiveness and his capacity for denial, she could at least temper them.

HILLARY RODHAM WAS always remarkably self-contained. Even as a child she did not need much parenting. "She was already a perfectionist when she was eight," her mother, Dorothy, recalled years later. "She always set very high standards for herself. She was almost scary." In the sixties, when Hillary was in high school, not many girls thought about running for public office. Hillary, however, already thought of the political world, if at first only through marriage. Her stated ambition in high school was "To marry a senator and settle down in Georgetown." By the time she was at Wellesley, she had become a student leader receiving national attention and a *Life* magazine cover for a provocative valedictory challenging establishment values.

With her suburban Chicago background she also seemed to provide Bill some of the respectability he needed. "He thought she was the best thing he had ever encountered," said Brooke Shearer, whose husband, Strobe Talbott, was Clinton's Oxford classmate and later became deputy secretary of state. "He was amazed that she was interested in him." In 1974, when Clinton was running for Congress in Arkansas (he lost) and Hillary was on the Watergate investigative staff in the House of Representatives, she often called five or six times a day with suggestions for his staff. "Anything Hillary says," Bill instructed them, "do it. She's the smartest woman I ever met." He never swerved from that conviction. "Each thinks the other is the smartest person they know," according to Stephanopoulos. Their friends see a balance in their relationship. "She has achieved a level of prominence that she never could have gotten on her own," one of her closest political advisers remarked. "If she hadn't married him she would have gone back to Chicago or New York and become a first-class lawyer."

Hillary was the thread in his thirty-year political career, his Colonel House and Louis Howe and much more. While Eleanor Roosevelt was a separate political and moral center in her husband's presidency, Hillary was integrated into the Clinton White House. Had Eleanor disappeared, Franklin would have been fine (perhaps, some would say, a bit relieved). Bill Clinton needed Hillary to function and survive. "If something ever

happened to Hillary," said Ann Stock, White House social secretary during the first Clinton administration, "he would be lost. He depends on
her for political judgments. She can cut through stuff. When things happen to him, she just comes in and goes right to the core."

Clinton was the first president to support his wife's political aspirations. As early as 1990, Governor Clinton asked pollster Dick Morris to
gauge how Hillary would fare in a governor's race in Arkansas. When the
poll showed that she was viewed solely as the governor's wife and would
lose on her own, "Clinton told Morris to go back and rephrase the questions," recalled one of Morris's former pollsters. "It was the first time in
twenty years that Clinton questioned one of Morris's polls." The results,
however, were the same.

Most of their friends believe Clinton, even with all his political skills,
would not have been elected without Hillary. "She brought discipline
into the operation," Ruth Goldway, a friend of three decades and the former mayor of Santa Monica, California, noted. "He was allowed to play
the emotional part because she was taking this tough role." Their friends
always assumed that if they reached their goal, the Clintons would have a
co-presidency. "They were so used to handling things, just the two of
them," said Derek Shearer, Ruth Goldway's husband and a friend since
Yale. "She was in on all of his political decisions. She is not just a policy
person, she is a political person. They managed his campaigns together.
She met with the pollsters, she signed off on the media buys. And she
always had an area of policy responsibility; in Arkansas it was education."

In 1980, Clinton was defeated in a re-election bid in Arkansas.
Suddenly, he was the youngest ex-governor in the country's history.
Hillary called Morris, and together they repositioned a shaken and devastated Clinton. By 1990, he was back on top, preparing his run for the
White House. In May, as Clinton ran for his fifth term as governor, a
Democratic challenger named Tom McRae declared that five terms was
too many. Standing in the state capitol's rotunda, McRae called Clinton
a coward for refusing to debate him. Suddenly, a woman's voice interrupted him, "Give me a break!" Hillary, from the middle of the crowd,
shouted, "I think we ought to set the record straight. Many of
the reports you issued praised the governor on his environmental

and . . . economic record. . . ." Hillary had stolen McRae's spotlight and left him spluttering.

Bill's debt to his wife was growing. On January 26, 1992, with his presidential prospects slipping away after Gennifer Flowers claimed an extramarital relationship with him, Hillary famously saved her husband's career. Sitting beside him during a *60 Minutes* interview, looking squarely at the camera, she confronted the rumors of "problems" in their marriage. "We think that's between us. . . . We don't owe anyone else besides each other. . . . And you know, it is something that we are just not going to go any further into. . . . If that's not good enough, don't vote for him."

Hillary seemed to alternate between endangering and saving her husband's political life. She was most effective when helping him and least effective when pursuing her own agenda. Whenever she tried to carve out an independent policy role as first lady, the public resisted. It is hard to avoid the conclusion that this paradox, which she fully understood, contributed to her decision in 1999 to seek office on her own.

❦

IF AMERICANS DID NOT at first perceive the complicated and seemingly contradictory layers of the Clintons' relationship, many of their friends and closest associates did. "Her public image is so brusque and so efficient," Mandy Grunwald, a key campaign aide in 1992 and later one of Hillary's advisers, remarked. "The notion that she is crazy about him is hard [for people] to imagine. But there is no other rational explanation for a Wellesley and Yale graduate to move to Arkansas, and without even a proposal of marriage there."

Journalist Joe Klein accidentally witnessed their intimacy in January 1992. Bill had just delivered a rousing address to a Columbia, South Carolina, audience. Klein chanced upon Bill and Hillary kissing, in his word, "passionately" in the dark. This was not, he recalled later, a staged moment for the cameras.

But with the Clintons, other images intrude. On Hillary's West Wing office wall there was a large photograph of her speaking at a podium,

unexceptional except for the inscription, "You are so good, Love, Bill"—
the essential affirmation of her political mentor and partner.

⌖

IT MUST BE SAID: the Clintons left behind a substantial record of achievement in their eight years. The economy was the strongest in history,
the budget had gone from a huge deficit to big surpluses, welfare was
reformed, crime cut, the largest amount of land protected and preserved.
Despite errors of judgment, the Clintons had outmaneuvered their enemies. They had survived. By his final year, Bill Clinton was the master of
the office, with the highest eighth-year approval rating in the history of
polling, even higher than Eisenhower or Reagan. (These would drop
precipitously in his first month as an ex-president because of the pardons
scandal.) But the cost was high. The country was exhausted from their
eight-year psychodrama, and Hillary, by becoming a senator, helped
keep the past alive.

⌖

IN JANUARY 1993, there was the promise of change in the air. Bill Clinton,
the first president born after World War II, was richly talented. Hillary
Rodham Clinton was a New Woman: confident and polished, the first
wife of a president with a serious professional life. The Clintons had
turned traditional gender roles on their head. Hillary had been the
family's chief breadwinner, the one responsible for their finances. Even
their affect challenged tradition: she of the implacable composure, the
crisp, trenchant style; he, languid, the sentimental man of a hundred
hugs and easy tears. He was among the proudest and most publicly supportive husbands in the presidential chronicles. "In my whole life," he
told an Arkansas group in May 2000, "I have never known anybody who
had a better grasp of the issues, a better ability to organize, a better ability to get people who thought they would never get along to work
together and to get up every day and just keep going than Hillary.
Never."

Two for the price of one, they proudly proclaimed during their campaign. It had worked in Arkansas, they assumed it would work in the White House. But Washington was different, and they would learn the hard way. When David Gergen was hired to improve presidential public relations during the Clintons' first year in office, he was told he would have to deal with three separate chains of command: the president's, the vice president's and the first lady's. But such a system, if one can call it a system, could not work. It would take four years and many missteps to learn the lesson.

Though many things in American life had changed by the final decade of the twentieth century, what had not changed was the public's view that the presidency should not be shared by a husband and wife—not overtly, anyway. Was it sexism, or something else? "The same thing," asserted Stephanopoulos, "would happen to a man, if a woman were president. It's about the role of the spouse in the presidency. Everybody will forgive the influence if the spouse appears to respect that line. Why did Hillary need to have the world see her influence, since she had the last word at night and the first word in the morning?"

TO MANY AMERICANS, Hillary presented a bewildering image. Many people, especially women, were disturbed by her numerous makeovers through the years. Was this proof of her own inner confusion? Her friends remembered Hillary changing her glasses as often as every month, even in college. She herself admitted to some deliberate role playing, trying out different personalities and lifestyles, "now the social activist, now acting as outrageous as a moral Methodist can get." But was it Hillary or the times that were confused? "All the reporting on Bill Clinton revels in his complexities and contradictions," Grunwald noted. "He is smart. But he is a Bubba. He loves Elvis, but he reads philosophy and theology. Isn't he fascinating? Meanwhile, Hillary bears the burden of [society] not being used to women being complex."

Hillary's generation was the transitional one in the women's movement. She was among the fortunate few granted provisional membership in male bastions—if they worked twice as hard and were twice as determined. "Hillary does not believe she'll be taken seriously if she isn't strong," said Shalala.

"In some ways she was a victim of feminism," Stephanopoulos contends.

> She was fulfilling her generation's goal. There was this sense among her core support that We want a woman to break this barrier. Her institutional, formal success would be of political benefit to the community which was her base. Just like the gay community wanted gays in the military, a lot of Hillary's friends and colleagues wanted her to be co-president, since Hillary would have deserved a job in any Democratic administration. There was the feeling that if she did it the traditional first-lady way, it would be a surrender. She would be accepting that she was just serving her husband, that all her power was derivative. Whereas, if she had an office in the West Wing and her own policies, it was not derivative. She was being recognized in her own right.

IN AN AGE when personality trumps other qualities in the public's eyes, Hillary's desire to make policy, not stand for something ill defined, troubled many more traditional Americans. Like Eleanor Roosevelt and Rosalynn Carter, Hillary and her efforts to play a public policy role met with considerable public disapproval, but she persisted.

In some ways the country's expectations of the first lady are almost as specific as those of the president. Certain values had not changed as much as the Clintons thought, or hoped. Two hundred years of myths and memories are vivid in the collective consciousness—Dolley Madison saving George Washington's portrait from British fire, Eleanor as the moral beacon (not policy maker) of the Depression, Jackie and her son in front of the flag-draped coffin. Hillary sought a public role greater than that of Eleanor and a private influence greater than Nancy Reagan's. Eleanor, Jackie, Lady Bird and Barbara Bush instinctively understood, or quickly learned, the power of the nonelected office, and used it to help set the tone of their husbands' presidencies. These women were willing to reveal a humanity and at times a vulnerability; Hillary was not. By trying to present a perfect facade, she lost a chance to connect with people in the way these women did.

But always, there was the paradox: while she *seemed* cutting-edge, a strong advocate of women's and children's rights and health care reform, Hillary was also, in many ways, old-fashioned. She preached the sanctity of marriage and did not permit unmarried couples to stay overnight at the White House. Her Methodist faith became increasingly important to her. "Whenever I think I am like her," Grunwald noted, "religion is the part that I know is most different about Hillary. It really is a comfort for her and sustains her in a way that's hard for the rest of us to understand." Ann Stock recalled that Hillary carried a daily prayer card with her and was, for a time, part of a bipartisan weekly women's prayer group that included Jim Baker's wife, Susan. Shalala, a solid Lebanese Christian who had no trouble understanding this aspect of Hillary, observed, "She was a suburban church kid. It was reinforced when she moved to Arkansas because religion is important there. People who move to the city get over that. She never did."

"We don't talk about deeply personal things," Dorothy Rodham said. Her pastor, Ed Matthews, explained that Hillary "knows that she has been given many gifts and graces and has greater obligations than ordinary people." That sense of special mission often came across as self-righteous, a feeling, in the words of Gergen, that "You're lucky to be in my presence." Her speaking style, her body language, her unwilling-ness to talk about herself—all this made her seem inauthentic. Some of Hillary's harshest critics were angered by her professed spirituality and sought to unmask what they felt was her sanctimoniousness. But in fact her faith was real—and indispensable to her survival.

Not surprisingly, Hillary often seemed to wish she could inhabit a separate, hermetically sealed universe where people were oblivious to her husband's reckless behavior and his wife's constant need to forgive him. In August 1998, at the height of the Lewinsky scandal, Hillary refused to acknowledge, as even Britain's Queen Elizabeth had after her public pain, that it had been a "horrible year." Instead, Hillary's press secretary issued a statement. "Clearly this is not the best day in Mrs. Clinton's life. But"—in the language of the Bible—"her love for [her husband] is compassionate and steadfast." This was not what most of the country wanted to hear from the wronged wife. It seemed to many that power—not love—was the tie that bound this couple. But the Clintons were much more complicated than that. Many of those who have spent time in their company felt that there was an almost sexual charge to their intense interaction and arguments. "They get into arguments about substance. He's gregarious and all over the place," Shalala said, "but he's a political genius. She melts when she looks at him. She is both infuriated and totally in love with him."

The Clintons loved to watch each other perform. They both had an uncanny ability to recall names and obscure details about people they barely know. They could recall thousands of people, people they had known since kindergarten or collected along the way. Bill and Hillary vied with each other for who could recall more names, more personal details. This vast network of public policy–minded baby boomers is part of their shared territory. When Clinton was introduced to Zoe Baird, his first short-lived nominee for attorney general, he seemed surprised there was an overachieving baby boomer who was not his friend. "I don't know why we haven't met before," he told her.

In December 1998, aboard *Air Force One,* returning from a Middle East trip during which the cameras captured Hillary's ice-cold body language toward her husband, she astonished a fellow passenger, Congressman Sander Levin, when she said, "The president made history during this trip." As if in answer to Levin's unasked question, she said, "He's my president too, you know." She seemed always to accept, if sometimes reluctantly, her husband's need to walk near the edge, in both his personal and political life. With Hillary, as with the country, he had the knack for working his way back. "They didn't get me that time, did they?" he gloated to James Carville in 1992, after his near-death experience in the Gennifer Flowers affair.

What the public did not often see, except in regard to their daughter, Chelsea, was the conventional side of this unconventional union. "He acts like a baby around her sometimes," Stephanopoulos remembered. "The way he calls her name, Hirrree . . . dropping the l's. She loves it." While a world seemed to separate Nancy Reagan from Hillary, there were some surprising similarities between them. Like Nancy, Hillary was very protective of the president's schedule. " 'You are putting too much on it, these meetings are lasting too long,' she would tell us." Grunwald recalled:

She had a very clear sense of what he needed, intellectually and emotionally, to be himself, to work best, to be the best president. That sometimes he had to play golf. That if he didn't see Chelsea for a while he went crazy. Or that he needed to feed his brain. Many times, she said, I tell you he will blow this if you don't give him time to run, time to think, to prepare. Hillary's first role in the 1992 campaign was to teach everybody how he operated best. And to intercede if she thought it wasn't happening. Anybody who tried to close him off too much from people just found out he would hit the phones at midnight and start dialing around because he needed his mind fed. He doesn't want [advisers] telling him that his choices are A or B. In his mind he knew there was a C. He always knew what wasn't told him. I have seen Hillary most angry when she thought he was being put at risk in some way. You don't understand, she would say, he will blow this debate, or speech or whatever, if he doesn't do this or that. Let him go goof off with Vernon [Jordan].

"They developed an arrogance you don't get in a place like New York or Washington where you get knocked around and there are a lot of people who are just as smart as you are," a member of the Clinton Cabinet noted. "You make mistakes and you learn to pick yourself up again. The Clintons never went through that in Arkansas. It's like they didn't grow up in some ways." They behaved, in the words of one of their closest Washington friends, "as if they had LBJ's [overwhelming] 1964 mandate." But they didn't. Clinton won only 43.5 percent of the popular vote, a 5 percent margin over Bush, while Ross Perot got 19 percent as a third-party candidate.

At no point in the entire process was Hillary's role more important than in that murky, ill-documented but critical period between election day and the inauguration called the "transition." How much the president-elect owed Hillary was clear. Had she not handled the *60 Minutes* interview as she had, had she not focused him and rallied his troops, it is hard to believe he would have been elected, or even nominated. Now it was Hillary's turn. It is hard to reconstruct the precise details of the conversations that took place around the kitchen table in the governor's mansion in Little Rock, with Vice President Al Gore, Vernon Jordan, Mickey Kantor and Warren Christopher—the transition team leaders. But while the process was chaotic, the outcome was historic. By insisting that half of all senior political appointees be women, Hillary transformed the Washington political culture. It was her most enduring contribution. The women who ultimately headed the Justice Department, Health and Human Services, Energy and, in the second term, State and Labor, all owed Hillary a tremendous debt. (The selection process for attorney general was sloppy. After two women nominees had been found wanting, a third, Janet Reno, was picked, but she was diminished by the fact that her gender had been announced before anyone was chosen.)

Having achieved her constituency's initial expectations of her, Hillary stumbled. In the exhilaration and high hopes of the early months, the Clintons failed to heed the principle that in politics, the more radical the idea, the softer the approach should be. "Right away she announced she would go by Hillary Rodham Clinton," *Time* magazine White House correspondent Ann Blackman recalled, "when all during the campaign she was Hillary Clinton. She was making a statement: take me seriously. Then she took an office in the West Wing. Another statement. She was often on the Hill, and outspoken at meetings. She could have changed the way the first lady operates if she had better advice, or if she took advice on how to do things gradually. First ladies have been very traditional. They've all had their own personalities and have emerged gradually. She offended people by moving so fast."

Hillary, who had studied all her predecessors, nonetheless underestimated the nation's attachment to the traditional role of first lady. She was succeeding one of the most popular presidential wives in modern history, and one of the most traditional. But she believed she could change things rapidly.

"The president was worried," noted Betty King, ambassador to the United Nations Economic and Social Council, a friend from Little Rock since the early 1970s. "It was the first time Hillary was not going to be working. He really wanted her to do something big," Melanne Verveer,

Hillary's White House chief of staff, recalled. "Early on, Hillary said, 'I don't want to be a symbol.' She is a doer, a worker who gets things done." Donna Shalala saw the danger of a too powerful first lady. "They came in talking about a co-presidency. Her friends were talking about her running eight years later. There was an unreality about it. A total misreading of politics. I told her she should go and teach law at Georgetown."

But Hillary's passion was for policy making at the highest level. Originally, she wanted to be her husband's domestic policy chief, but after the president's pollster, Stan Greenberg, showed the Clintons data indicating that people weren't ready for such a dramatic move, the president pulled back. Instead, King recalled, "They appointed a woman to that office who was only there because Hillary trusted her, Carol Rasco, a very nice woman from Little Rock, [who] was not up to the job." They filled the White House with young and inexperienced people and old friends with proven loyalty to the Clintons. Two of Hillary's partners from her Little Rock law firm, Vincent Foster and William Kennedy, and another old friend, Bernard Nussbaum, took over the White House counsel's office. They did not want a strong chief of staff because it was understood that Hillary was essentially going to fill that role. Clinton's childhood friend Thomas "Mack" McLarty, a genial, conciliatory man lacking Washington experience, got the job. "Hillary would come to staff meetings," a ranking member of the Clinton White House recalled, "and take over. She got things done. But it was humiliating for Mack." When Erskine Bowles became chief of staff at the beginning of the second term in 1997, he told the President, "Sir, I love Hillary, but I cannot have more than one boss." Bowles won: he would report only to the president.

❧

HILLARY'S NEED FOR A DEFINED ROLE led to the Clinton administration's biggest political mistake. In 1993 health care accounted for 7 percent of the U.S. gross domestic product. Almost 37 million Americans had no health insurance. Others had inadequate packages costing thousands of dollars. One of President Clinton's goals was to guarantee all Americans a standard package of health care benefits. It was to be the new administration's single most ambitious enterprise. His choice to lead the effort to reform America's health care system was his wife. "We needed a talented navigator," he explained later, "someone with a rigorous mind, a steady compass, a caring heart. Luckily for me, and for our nation, I didn't have to look very far. . . ."

The president knew that giving his wife the largest domestic portfolio was risky. "We knew it would be easier to get at her than at somebody else," said White House Deputy Chief of Staff Steven Ricchetti. "But he had done this with her in Arkansas, with education reform." Clinton's Cabinet was less sure. Lloyd Bentsen, Robert Rubin, Alice Rivlin, Laura D'Andrea Tyson and Donna Shalala all expressed concern, although very cautiously. "There were difficult feelings within the administration," Melanne Verveer recalled. "Some people felt that it should be run from within Health and Human Services, instead of under Hillary. But the president felt she would make the process move forward. He knew she would bring to it a passion and an expertise that no one else could." Clinton himself said, "People would know I was serious about trying to do this. I thought if we were going to take this on against all the odds, we had to give it our best shot. We had to stretch to the last degree."

Interestingly, her qualifications were not the issue. "I was always wowed by the extent to which both Hillary and the president understood this stuff," Tyson, chief of the Council of Economic Advisers, recalled. "She was often the smartest policy analyst in the room." Clinton's political blindness to the consequences of his appointment was a blindness born of need and total trust. The president instructed the Cabinet and his staff that Hillary should be treated like anyone else— challenge her, question her. But it simply did not work. The Clintons seemed oblivious to something that was obvious to everyone else. "She absolutely thought that this was the right thing for her to be doing," said Robert Boorstin, one of Hillary's media advisers. "But who in the White House is going to say to the first lady, You can't do that. Nobody thought carefully about how this would look." One Cabinet member who had grave misgivings reflected later: "You can make your point only once to the president's wife, and if it is not accepted, you just don't press it."

Hillary claimed she was prepared to take public heat for her unprecedented power. "I understood, as many people never tired of telling me, that this could be a disaster, that I could get blamed. . . . That didn't bother me. Heat comes with anything. If I had done nothing, I would have gotten heat. So better to get heat trying to do something important for people." Health care reform would be an achievement to rival FDR's creation of Social Security. It would also demonstrate how effectively the presidential couple worked together. "H—" began a typical note President Clinton scrawled atop a memo intended for his wife. "Speechwriters should see this if they haven't—also I like the idea of having series of issue events—but I'll defer to you and your team on that. Love, B."

There were problems from the moment the president announced that his wife would head the task force on health care, just five days after the inauguration. The size of the task force that Hillary headed (at one time as many as six hundred people), the secrecy of their proceedings, divisions within the Democratic Party, increasingly partisan Republican attacks—all should have set off alarm bells in the White House. But the Clintons were totally committed to creating a national health insurance system. While Hillary and her task force worked behind closed doors, congressional Republicans under Newt Gingrich, working with the physicians' lobby, mobilized to defeat it.

Before Hillary met with fifty senators, her aides advised she not use the $100 billion figure as the estimated cost for health care. "I don't care how they do things here," Hillary retorted. "If they can't take the truth, at least they're going to get it from me." Her political judgment was clouded by her growing antipathy to the invasiveness of the Washington culture. She was angry and frustrated that other members of her husband's team, working on their economic reform package, were giving short shrift to her health care initiative. His economic advisers worried about its cost, its timing and its scope. The debate was intense. Unable or unwilling to take on the first lady directly, the opponents of her plan resorted to leaks. On May 23, 1993, a *New York Times* headline declared,

"White House Fight on Health Care: It Is Hillary Clinton Versus the President's Economic Advisers." The first lady was furious. "Are these people part of the administration or not?" she asked.

One of the few people in the process who expressed her reservations to Hillary was Tyson. "Maybe because I was a woman and her contemporary," said Tyson,

> it was much easier for me to accept her as another person in the room, a policy analyst, rather than the wife of the president. It wasn't an issue for me. She and the president had encouraged us during our first weekend retreat at Camp David to express dissent inside the administration, not go outside with it. I took them at their word. The more I got involved in these health care discussions, the more concerned I became. I wanted to fulfill my role to provide economic analysis to shape policy. The others couldn't find a way to express their reservations. Rubin and Bentsen were remarkably quiet and unengaged. They acted like, Well, it's out of our hands. But Hillary reached out to me about the situation. I had a couple of really good people on my staff who had raised all sorts of concerns about the plan . . . Hillary at one point talked to me about being a sort of bridge between the health care team and Rubin and Bentsen, and the other economists. But I made it clear to her that basically I had the same reservations that they did. Never did I ever feel vindictiveness on Hillary's part for our differences. But there was a real possibility for us to become allies during the first term and that may have been undermined by this.

The West Wing, a confined place of narrow corridors and intertwined, rabbit-warrenlike offices, was now seething. If there is tension in one part, it radiates through the walls and into the cubbyholes of staffers hardwired to respond to every twitch from the president or the first lady. "Hillary liked to criticize the president's staff in front of him," said Boorstin.

> It was her way of saying, You are incompetent. Look at how your staff treats you. Rather than insult him directly, she used the staff. I

remember the day we had the first health care event on *CBS Morning News* at 7 A.M. Hillary is a morning person. The president is not. Hillary had already been on her treadmill, the president was in terrible shape. The president had a statement to give at the beginning. But there was no podium in the Rose Garden. In front of staffers and within earshot of a lot of other people, Hillary exploded. "What the fuck goes on here! How come there's no podium for him? What is your staff doing?" Nobody said anything. People were scared of her because they knew she could chop off their testicles if she so chose. You did not cross Hillary.

On September 22, 1993, Hillary appeared on the Hill to launch her plan. Sitting alone at the witness table, without a single note in front of her, she gave a stunning performance. "I still have little shreds of paper," Melanne Verveer said, "that senators would pass me saying, 'I'll be doggone if this isn't the most amazing performance.' " But Steve Ricchetti was worried. "I told Hillary, 'You're too good. They're gonna try to knock you down.' "

The process revealed both Hillary's strengths and weaknesses. She showed remarkable ability to get out into the country and listen to peoples' health care concerns, and explain the administration's reform proposal. She knew how to use the spotlight almost as effectively as her husband did. Whether in the inner cities or on Indian reservations, her patience and her eloquence were unlimited. The clarity of her speaking reflected the orderliness of her thought process. But in the end, many asked themselves, had she really *listened?* She was at her weakest in the area where her husband was strongest: finding common ground, building consensus. "She was really smart on policy," Tyson noted, "but not the politics of Washington. That was not her strength at the time." Once she had made up her mind as to what was right, Hillary was unmovable—a striking contrast to her flexible, politically astute husband.

By the summer of 1993, the president's budget fight with Congress had pushed health care off the radar screen. When she and health care adviser Ira Magaziner presented Congress with a 1,342-page bill, it was doomed. The plan pledged universal coverage by 1998 and would have prevented insurers from denying benefits to patients with "preexisting conditions." It was also extremely difficult to follow and pleased almost no one. Conservatives cried "big government," while the left attacked it as "pro-industry." Partisan politics had much to do with the defeat. Later, both Clintons admitted they underestimated the political cost of the first lady's role. "The reaction was more negative than I thought," the president said. "I will admit, I underestimated this."

She was reluctant to deal with members of Congress who pushed for a less ambitious but more politically feasible plan. "Bill and I," she declared, "did not come to Washington to play the game as usual, and to fuzz the differences between universal coverage and access." She had not yet learned one of the hard lessons of Washington: that the stars in the capital line up on a big issue only once in a while. The Clintons did not understand that it would have been better to get an imperfect deal on health care and try to fix it later. "Hillary let the perfect become the enemy of the good," said Mandy Grunwald. Hillary's fondness for secrecy deprived the public of essential information. It also created suspicion and further alienated the media. "I saw that it wasn't going to work several months before it went down," Tyson recalled. "It was too big and would have dismantled things that were working fine for the sake of the 15 percent that wasn't. I could see supporters of the plan peeling off."

Putting such a huge issue under the first lady's leadership made her an irresistible political target. "She was not [solely] responsible for the failure," Tyson maintained. "The president had totally bought in to it. The policy was based on flawed and politically compromised thinking. But the cost of the failure was hers."

"There was a chance to get it done," Ricchetti recalled. "In the winter of 1993, Hillary was very popular in the country. She had demonstrated enormous substantive competence. The Republicans thought, Holy God. This is gonna happen! Several GOP strategists wrote, If the president succeeds at this, it's all over. They will win in '94. Then two days before Christmas, Troopergate erupted. Then came Whitewater, followed by the cattle futures deal. All of that combined to erode the

Clintons' political capital. With more capital to spend, they could have got something."

⌘

HILLARY HAD LOST more than a chance to shape national health policy. She had lost much of the shield that traditionally protects first ladies. Henceforth, she would be treated like the policy maker she wanted to be—and an unsuccessful one at that. She was fair game for political attacks in a different way from other first ladies. A deeper wound was a loss of standing with her husband. He had always relied on his wife not only to look out for his best interests but to do the politically smart thing. He had placed in her hands the most far-reaching social legislation since the Great Society, and she had misread Congress, the media and the acceptable parameters of her role as first lady. After health care, the magic was gone.

It was a terrible personal disappointment. But humility and retreat were not Hillary's way; at least not public humility. Even the double tragedy in 1993 of her father's death and the suicide of her closest colleague and friend from Little Rock, Vince Foster, who had become deputy White House counsel, did not reap much media support. Hillary's glacial self-control seemed to repel sympathy.

Rather than reaching out to the women who covered her—many of them fellow baby boomers—she alienated them. *Washington Post* reporter Martha Sherrill, for one, was at first excited about covering the first lady. Weeks went by, and though she had interviewed all members of Hillary's family, her childhood friends and her Methodist minister,

> I began to get this funny feeling that maybe I was never going to sit down with her. The first time I actually laid eyes on her was at a public event where she sort of toured around like Florence Nightingale. She would not give any interviews. She would not talk about the role of first lady. I was told by her press people that she was pondering the role. That she was letting it percolate and hadn't decided what her role was going to be. So we ended up writing about her clothes and her hair, because that's all we had. And I was getting frustrated. I

thought I was asked to cover her because she was supposed to be this new kind of first lady: a serious intellectual and a career woman. And she was turning out to be this sort of ornament, showing off American designers. I became good friends with her staff—Maggie Williams and Melanne Verveer and Neil Lattimore—and they kept telling me she was too busy.

Hillary eventually sat down with Sherrill.

I found her warm and folksy but at the same time sort of preachy. There was a lot of, Let me impart my wisdom on that subject. A mix of Bible and ancient wisdom. There was an attempt to manipulate the press, which backfired. She wasn't telling us who she was or what sort of first lady she wanted to be. So then all these stories came out about her being Lady Macbeth or Saint Hillary, because she didn't speak or give interviews for such a long time. With Mrs. Bush you would be told, She doesn't want to do this story because she doesn't think it's good for her. Period. You would never get a straight answer from Hillary's office. Their arrogance was something. They didn't know that you produce a schedule for the people covering the first lady the night before. They would say, Well, we're doing things differently. And then they realized after several months of total chaos that there were certain things they had to do that way for a reason. I think that came from Hillary not wanting to do anything the way it had been done before. Basically she didn't want to talk about what kind of first lady she was going to be. She was going to *show* us. If Eleanor had gone down in the mines, Hillary was going to do one better.

As far as Hillary was concerned, there were good reasons to avoid the media. "I think at different times she has tried to engage reporters and has come to believe it is a losing proposition," Grunwald recalled. "She wanted them to focus on substance and they wrote only psychobabble pieces about her."

Hillary did not think the public had to know who she was, only what her positions on issues were. This was a misreading of the times. In times as prosperous and peaceful as the 1990s, character and personality tend to be dominant. Hillary tried to defy the trend and return to a less personality-driven political climate. "She wants to be in public service," said a close friend, "but not in public life. She wants to practice politics the way it *was,* not the way it is."

Behind this aloof posture was more than a midwesterner's natural reserve. Hillary probably had more to hide than any other first lady in recent times. "It's all that scar tissue," a close friend asserted. "She cries. She doesn't have his hide. He is spooky, how lightly he takes things." Jackie Kennedy had floated above her husband's philandering, which, in any case, never became public until after his death. Lady Bird had rationalized it for her own peace of mind and lived in a different social and media climate. Whatever humiliation she suffered was private until years later. But the revelations and accusations about the Clintons occurred in real time, while they were in the White House—a situation unique in American history.

Hillary tried to rationalize this most intimate of problems by turning it into a political issue. Sex was another weapon that their enemies would use to try to bring them down. "She doesn't treat the stories about women any differently than any of the other scandals," Mandy Grunwald said. "So we wonder, how does she feel about Gennifer Flowers or Paula Jones or Monica Lewinsky. She believes it's part of the same story. *They* are out to get the Clintons. She has pretty good reason to think so, if you look at what she considers the invasion of their lives. She puts it all in a box called 'Politics.' "

Early in 1995, Hillary invited a group of women reporters who covered the traditional aspects of her office—style and entertaining—to lunch at the White House. She asked them for suggestions as to how she might present herself in a more favorable light. On January 10, 1995, the *New York Times* ran a front-page article entitled "Hillary Clinton Asks Help in Finding a Softer Image." She emerged as human, warm and fallible. Quoted by reporter Marian Burros as telling the women she was "shocked" by the harsh way she came across in news reports as "a woman she herself would not particularly want to know," the first lady said, "I am surprised at the way people seem to perceive me, and sometimes I read stories and hear things about me and I go 'Ugh.' I wouldn't like her, either. It's so unlike what I think I am or what my friends think I am." For the first time since October 1994, when her health care plan died on the floor of Congress, Hillary accepted blame for its failure and called herself "naive and dumb" about national politics. "There was a lack of politically savvy advice. No one figured out the dynamics," she said. "I take responsibility for that and I'm very sorry."

The article was, in the words of *Times* editor Andrew Rosenthal, "about as positive a piece as the White House could ever hope for." But Hillary demanded a correction and an apology. The first lady's office claimed Burros had violated the agreed-upon off-the-record rule for the lunch. "I was dumbfounded," Burros recalled. "There was nothing unflattering in that piece. On the contrary. I had taped the whole thing, including where she gave us permission to quote her. I used only what was on the record. But the battle went all the way up to the highest levels at both the White House and the *New York Times*. The whole thing became the subject of every late-night talk show."

Five years later, Rosenthal still shook his head in wonder. "What was that all about?" Hillary's need for control and perfection turned a favorable story into an embarrassment. "For somebody so smart," Burros (who remained an admirer of the first lady) noted, "she had amazingly poor judgment." A savvier politician would have seen the opportunity to win points, and hearts, simply by saying, "I made a mistake." But Hillary still wanted to appear infallible.

Christmas of 1993 was an unhappy one for the Clintons. Whitewater, Hillary's cattle futures trading and the firing of seven travel office workers—which the press dubbed Travelgate—targeted her, not the president. Clinton's long-rumored use of his Arkansas state troopers to procure women was in the news. According to the trooper's allegations, the same week in 1991 that Clinton had dazzled the Democratic National Committee in Cleveland, he had summoned Paula Jones to his room in the Excelsior Hotel in Little Rock. As always, Hillary defended her husband in public, absorbed the body blows in private. Their friends have speculated that the Clintons live by an unspoken principle of "Don't ask, don't tell—but don't embarrass us."

A less resilient person might have crumbled. But Hillary was preeminently a survivor. "Hillary does not waste time on regrets, does not waste time on ambivalence," one of her oldest friends from Wellesley College, Jan Piercy, said. "She is impatient with people who dwell on what might have been. When you give her advice you feel you can influence her about 10 percent. The other 90 percent, no. She is very sure."

As usual, her husband took his cues from her. "Saying [Hillary's] name," Stephanopoulos recalled, "flipped a switch in his head. Suddenly his eyes lit up, and two years worth of [her] venom spewed out of his mouth. You could usually tell when Clinton was making Hillary's argument: even if he was yelling his voice had a flat quality, as if he were a high school debater speeding through a series of memorized facts."

"I'm very confused by her," says her old friend Donna Shalala. "I've known her since the early seventies and it's almost as if she is tone-deaf to politics. She's funny and smart and fun to be with, but it's as if she wakes up every morning in a state of rage against what the press has done to her." Bob Boorstin recalled, "As the only former journalist in the room, I told Hillary to get every single document they could find relating to the land deal, everything about Arkansas, and give the press a three-foot-high stack of papers. That way at least you look like you are telling the truth. Very few reporters take the time to go through it and write the stuff. Her reaction was stunned. No reaction. Silence."

Looking back, another Clinton Cabinet member pointed to still another reason for Hillary's discomfort with the many investigations: "I don't believe they did anything wrong, other than try to make a quick buck because of Hillary's total financial insecurity, married to a man who was making $35,000 a year. What these deals were really suggesting was that she wasn't a good lawyer. Her identity was not just tied to her marriage to the governor but to her being a good lawyer. This investigation was threatening her identity."

By the spring of 1994 the White House was like a bunker, with an increasingly isolated president and first lady. Behind the scenes, the White House staff was often frustrated at the Clintons' failure to reach out to many of the people they needed most. In 1994, when the Whitewater allegations hung over the White House, her staff tried to get

Hillary to answer the media's questions. "Her view," Mandy Grunwald remembered, "was that it is nobody's business whether she invested in this stock or that stock." It was a view more appropriate to a court-room than the White House, and ignored the fact that reporters want most what they cannot get. It overlooked the biggest lesson of Water-gate: it is not the crime, but the perception of a cover-up that can destroy a president. "And here was a woman," said Boorstin, still amazed several years later, "who had been on the Watergate committee. I wanted to scream."

"She was adamant that she wasn't going to talk to reporters," Grun-wald noted. "It wasn't their damned business. It was a legal situation. She had done nothing wrong. We worked on her. We got our heads chopped off. 'Well, I'm just not going to do that.' But a week later she was in her pink suit doing the press conference. And she was great."

Grunwald's memory of that press conference on April 22, 1994, is not universally shared, although White House counsel Lloyd Cutler, who prepped her for the session, believed that "She did about as well as she could, considering how close to the edge she skated." Hillary sat for more than an hour, her face an expressionless slate, patiently answering every question asked of her in the same even, give-nothing-away tone, never losing her composure while reporters pressed her about Whitewa-ter, her cattle futures trade and allegations that the Clintons were trying to obstruct the investigation. But her eyes were hooded, and the press thought there was a robotic quality to her promise of greater openness. "I'm certainly going to be more sensitive about what you all need," she said stiffly.

"She basically lied to us," said correspondent Ann Blackman.

I asked her if she had authorized Maggie Williams to go into Vince Foster's office to take papers the night he was shot. And she said no one went into his office that night. Well, it was the next day that she authorized people to go into his office. Instead of saying that's not exactly how it was, she tried to be so lawyerly. It was the equiva-lent of "I didn't inhale" or "I didn't have sex with that woman." That's what they'd done in Arkansas and had gotten away with. But here all of a sudden they were dealing with reporters who were much more worldly and politically experienced. Hillary does not want to be challenged. I'm not sure she's guilty of anything, but she acts as if she is.

Unlike the Reagans or the Bushes, but somewhat like the Carters, the Clintons did not attempt to win over either reporters or the Washington elite. "The Nixons were better at getting their story out than the Clintons," Blackman asserted. "In the thirty years I've been in Washington, the six presidents I've covered, every one of them had at least one person that they called in regularly to talk to. Not shills, but good reporters whom the rest of us trusted. Johnson had Frank Cormier from the AP. Reagan had Lou Cannon. Bush had Ann Devroy. These people told the rest of us the president's mood, his thinking and what the first lady was up to."

Befriending the handful of people who are not only the city's social arbiters but also have access to the national soapbox would not have been difficult. As Bob Woodward, one of the city's leading journalists, noted, "No group is more susceptible to presidential flattery than the Washington establishment." But the Clintons did not really try.

THE COMBINED PUNCH of the defeat of health care and the sweep of the midterm elections by the Republicans in 1994 left the Clintons reeling. Hillary had been outmaneuvered on health care by the Republicans and the pharmaceutical and insurance companies, and with Whitewater and the cattle futures she seemed to have mismanaged the Clintons' personal finances. When Stephanopoulos tried to persuade Hillary that the Clintons had to accept a special prosecutor to investigate the multitude of rumors, Hillary actually wept. "I'm feeling very lonely right now. Nobody is fighting for me."

She had lost some of her certainty. Privately, she regretted not having agreed to a compromise health care bill. Polls in 1995 confirmed that her style was not admired by the public. Moreover, Dick Morris's research showed she made her husband look weak. Fifty-one percent of the public had an unfavorable view of her. She had become a political liability to the president.

As always with the Clintons, the arc of their public and personal lives ran a parallel course. Hillary had to resurrect her public life to revive her relationship with her husband. Typically, this remarkable woman found the strength to do both. She recast herself as a different first lady. She scaled back, and gained in approval. In 1995 she no longer ran staff meetings. Mack McLarty was succeeded as chief of staff by the more seasoned Leon Panetta, a former congressman who knew Washington. He gave the first lady private weekly briefings, and she largely stopped going to strategy or policy meetings. Instead, she busied herself in areas other first ladies might have identified themselves with: breast cancer, women's and children's issues. Her domain, called Hillaryland by White House staffers, peopled by loyal, admiring women (and a few men), formed a more effective protective shield around her. They kept the outside world at bay. It was the end of the public co-presidency.

Hillary had recast her image yet again. "I really believe you can change the way you feel and think if you discipline yourself," she told friends. She wrote a book, *It Takes a Village: And Other Lessons Children Teach Us,* a best-selling collection of anecdotes mixing serious parenting advice with lighthearted glimpses of the Clinton family. The center of Hillary's universe, as portrayed in *It Takes a Village,* was Chelsea and Bill. Her strongest words were reserved for divorce, which Hillary depicted as the absolute last resort for dysfunctional families. With a few revisions, it could have been a book Barbara Bush or Marilyn Quayle might have written—a traditional, upbeat look at families. Next, taking a leaf out of Eleanor Roosevelt's book, she started writing a syndicated newspaper column. But unlike Eleanor, Hillary adopted a tone resolutely uncontroversial and apolitical. Writing about her New Year's resolutions at the end of 1995, she promised, "I will try to keep the same hairdo for at least thirty days, I will try to show more enthusiasm for my husband's golf game . . . I will try to act nonchalant when my daughter's sixteenth birthday approaches and the issue of a driver's license becomes more important than breathing . . . I will try to show new appreciation for my friends in the press. . . ."

She especially found her platform, and renewed confidence, overseas, in Pakistan, India, Nepal, Turkey and Romania, reinventing herself as an emissary for women and children of the Third World. There, almost always treated with adoration, she held out her hand to the powerless and displayed emotions she could not show at home. "I saw her get off that plane with the United States of America markings," Joe Klein recalled. "It had a power that she had not expected. Just by being there she could draw attention to women who live in a society where most marriages are still arranged." Her press coverage was different abroad than at home, more substantive, more serious, more respectful. "If she does a micro-credit event in Bangladesh," Grunwald said, "it tends to get covered as a bank event, without the political filter." When, suddenly, a group of women in Ahmadabad, India, joined hands and began singing "We Shall Overcome," tears welled in Hillary's eyes, and even the most cynical Washington journalists were moved.

In poor neighborhoods in Chile and Nicaragua she talked to women about starting small businesses with a tiny bit of credit. "Where women prosper, countries prosper" became her global mantra. She thrived away from the White House. "I'm so totally engaged when I'm abroad," she admitted. "You know Washington is a tough place to be . . . I'm going from one thing to the next when I'm at home. But when I'm in Africa . . . it's twenty-four hours of just total immersion. And I think that in itself is very relaxing. Because you just feel like you know exactly what you're doing for the next week or two weeks and you can just give it a hundred percent."

The culmination of her role as global advocate for women came on September 5, 1995, at the UN Conference on Women, in Beijing. In a speech interrupted by thunderous applause from thousands of women delegates, she took on the conference's Chinese hosts and the Indian government. "It is a violation of human rights when babies are denied food, or drowned, or suffocated or their spines broken simply because they are girls," she said. "It is a violation of human rights when women are doused with gasoline, set on fire and burned to death because their marriage dowries are deemed too small. . . ."

People stood for hours along dusty roads waiting to catch a glimpse of the famous American first lady and bask momentarily in her smile.

From the Indian subcontinent to North Africa to South America, Hillary Clinton became a global icon. Not since Jacqueline Kennedy had an American woman stirred such excitement overseas. Many of her earlier critics now hailed Hillary as the administration's most forceful human rights advocate. And, for this moral Methodist, there was the satisfaction of becoming a voice for the voiceless.

After the debacle of the 1994 midterm elections, she summoned Dick Morris, the man who had saved Clinton in 1980 in Arkansas, to reposition her husband once more. For a long time the president did not even tell his chief of staff, Panetta, or Stephanopoulos about Morris's role. "I like subterfuge," the president admitted to Morris, as they worked in secret in the East Wing. It was Morris, code-named "Charlie," and not Hillary who helped recast Clinton as a moderate centrist, skillfully co-opting elements of Newt Gingrich's "Contract with America."

Typically, rather than opt for a quiet family New Year's as 1995 came to a close, Bill and Hillary joined a thousand other networking baby boomers. Tension and drift in their marriage seemed apparent to many of their friends during the annual Renaissance Weekend celebration held on Hilton Head Island, South Carolina. "It was clear from their body language they were in the middle of a big fight," said one observer. Just before midnight Hillary delivered what Klein called "a self-righteous, overlong policy speech" to a crowded ballroom and returned to her table. Moments later, she returned to the microphone. "They tell me I have to introduce the next speaker," she said coolly, before presenting her husband.

The following week, Hillary's executive assistant Carolyn Huber found her missing Arkansas law firm billing records and related papers in the book room on the third floor of the White House. "If you're about to begin a campaign, you've got to get all that stuff out," Klein speculated. But there were more unpleasant surprises ahead.

Despite her overseas triumphs, 1996 began on a bad note. The first lady, called a "congenital liar" by William Safire in the *New York Times,* received a subpoena from special prosecutor Kenneth Starr to appear before a federal grand jury on January 26. She would never forgive Starr for forcing her to walk the media gauntlet into the federal courthouse. Smiling and waving and flashing her least sincere "glad to see you" smile, she became the first wife of a president to testify under oath before a grand jury. The reporters cut her little slack. "Whenever I go out and fight I get vilified," she told Stephanopoulos, "so I have just learned to smile and take it. I go out there and say, Please, kick me again, insult me some more. You have to be much craftier behind the scenes, but just smile." Even her mother observed to friends that Hillary's smile and her eyes no longer matched.

Still more bad news came cascading down. A memo from the former head of White House management, David Watkins, discovered the same week, seemed to hold the first lady accountable for the firing of the travel office. "There would be hell to pay," the memo read, "if we failed to take swift and decisive action in conformity with the First Lady's wishes." Watkins later testified he was basing this on hearsay, not direct instructions. As President Bush's spokesman, Marlin Fitzwater, noted, "Mrs. Bush would have known that one call to the chief of staff about the travel office is the same as firing them." Hillary later tried to explain her misreading of the situation: "Part of the urgency that my husband felt about the agenda he brought with him to Washington made all of us rush in and try to do things before we really understood how Washington worked."

Hillary was still paying the price for having approached a symbolic, ill-defined situation—being the president's spouse—as if it were a specific job. Now she understood something she had refused to accept earlier. "It's not a defined responsibility. I'm absolutely aware of that now," she told this writer in 1997. "I've always had jobs and worked for a living. I'm here, as everyone else in the White House is here, because of one person, the president. It was bewildering to me and has taken a while to get used to."

⚮

BY THE SUMMER OF 1996, her surface transformation was complete. The combination of her lower political profile, her new global stature and her best-selling book had successfully recast her image. Democrats gathered in Chicago to renominate her husband greeted Hillary with sustained, rolling cheers and applause. But Hillary, looking soft and pretty in a sky-blue suit, seemed impatient with the display. With both hands held up, she urged the crowd to quiet down. Where Bill would have basked in the moment, Hillary was eager to get on with her message. Her melody seemed at war with her lyrics. Her crisp, flat, sometimes edgy tone seemed out of sync with her words, which were relative boilerplate. "For Bill and me," she told the delegates, "no experience has been more challenging than raising our child. . . ." Her speech was larded with references to Chelsea doing her homework, homilies about the Clinton's family life and repeated use of the phrase "my husband wants to. . . ." The speech may have seemed a retreat for the woman who had wanted to take charge of her husband's domestic agenda, but politically, it was the right move.

Donna Shalala said that during Clinton's second term, Hillary no longer called her with personnel suggestions. "I don't see her as [having been as] much of a player the second term. She didn't go to meetings . . . [but] we all briefed her, especially when we thought she could be helpful. . . . She [didn't] want anybody to be able to write [another] story that she [was] a major policy player." Hillary sent stand-ins such as Maggie Williams or, later, Melanne Verveer, Harold Ickes or the president's deputy chief of staff, Evelyn Lieberman, to meetings.

Although Hillary had lowered her public profile, she remained an important political player in the White House after the 1996 election— ironically a bit more like Nancy Reagan. "She was quietly present throughout," Ricchetti maintained. "The president respected her judgment so much that her impact was always huge. Her influence was felt especially on children's issues, education, drugs, social issues and politics. She processes people differently than he does. She's more demanding, harder on people, more suspicious, more definite than he is. Her commitment to ideology is more severe, his is very pragmatic. He likes to get things done and move the ball. But it's a very strong partnership."

Verveer said that, in her final years as first lady, Hillary became a better politician as well as a better first lady. "Hers is an instance of successful human development. She did not collapse, she changed. She came to grips with the fact that she had a platform she could use. She became a much more effective speaker, and I think she realized that at times it wasn't useful to come across that strongly, just because of the way our society perceives women, that you can say the same thing but be less threatening. She became much smarter about the process and how things work in Washington."

⁂

BUT THEN CAME another disaster, by far the most serious, and once again Hillary had to rescue her husband under the most painful and embarrassing circumstances imaginable. Monica Lewinsky changed everything, obsessing the entire nation for a year and almost destroying the Clinton presidency. Thanks to the Starr Report, anybody interested in the precise and sordid details of this sorry affair is already familiar with them, but some questions may never be answered. How, for example, could a president who was already the target of the world's most famous sexual harassment suit engage in this guilt-ridden, joyless, breathtakingly risky business? The fact that Clinton understood the risk he was taking makes it all the more outrageous. When his attorney, Robert Bennett, asked him if he had an affair with the intern, the president answered, "Bob, do you think I'm fucking crazy? . . . I know the press is watching me every minute. The right has been dying for this kind of thing from day one. No, it didn't happen."

Of course, Clinton was not the first politician with an overactive libido and a reckless sense of his own invulnerability. But this was not about sexual satisfaction. Clinton tried desperately to deprive himself of that, as if by holding back he was making it all right. Nor was it emotional or, even more laughable, intellectual. Perhaps Hillary drew a small measure of comfort from the thinness of the "relationship." Clinton knew Monica was not a woman who could keep anything to herself. When she flashed her thong underwear at him, why did he not push the buzzer and ask that she be immediately removed? What was he thinking? The answer could only be Clinton's dangerous combination of compulsive reckless behavior and his breezy presumption that he could extricate himself from any situation, no matter how tangled, as he always had.

Clinton's oldest friends from college, men like Tom Caplan and Tom Siebert, claimed ignorance of their friend's philandering and rejected outright the idea that he could have harassed women. Caplan says it's a ridiculous charge to make against a man who always had women lining up. Like John Kennedy, Clinton compartmentalized. "His best friend is Hillary," said Derek Shearer. "If you're cheating on your best friend, who are you going to talk to? Bill had developed a whole way of functioning, where he wasn't dealing with any of this—until presented with the evidence."

In the Clinton White House, there was an unofficial role that female staffers and certain Cabinet members played: "We all protected the president from flirtatious girls," said Shalala. "Any one of us would

The Democratic Convention, Los Angeles, August 14, 2000.
The transition from Bill to Hillary begins.

walk right up to him and interrupt the conversation before Hillary had to. But I have seen Hillary body-block the president when a woman was coming on to him." The president's deputy chief of staff, Evelyn Lieberman, was the first lady's designated eyes and ears in the West Wing.

Women aides had been aware of an intern named Monica Lewinsky—whom they had called "Elvira," after the dark-haired, big-bosomed television character—since well before the scandal broke. "We kind of felt sorry for her," one aide recalled, "she was always so overdressed, and so eager to please and kind of out of it. And always just hanging around." Then Evelyn Lieberman moved her out, getting her a job at the Pentagon (where she fell in with Linda Tripp). Stephanopoulos remembered a "flurry" about Monica in late 1995, "when Evelyn was buzzing about it. But then nobody thought about it any more until the day of Clinton's [January 17, 1998] deposition. I think he came home from that deposition and had to tell Hillary. They canceled their dinner with Erskine Bowles and his wife. You could tell he was in a panic that weekend because he called Betty Currie on Sunday in an anxiety-ridden state."

Months later, after Lieberman had become the head of the Voice of America, she was accosted by Monica's mother at a V.O.A. event. "You ruined my daughter's life," Marcia Lewis said to the startled Lieberman, "by moving her to the Pentagon. And I know why. It's because she is too beautiful."

"Monica was not just another political crisis," said a close friend of the Clintons. "It was not like health care. It was both a constitutional crisis and their own marital crisis." First, it took place in the White House, a place of nearly spiritual power for many Americans. Most serious, however, was that not only did Clinton lie to his wife, but he let his wife lie for him to the nation. On January 27, 1998, clearly not knowing the truth, Hillary appeared on *The Today Show* and told Matt Lauer that a "vast right-wing conspiracy" was behind the latest charges against her husband.

White House correspondent Helen Thomas recalled an astonished Melanne Verveer exclaiming, "Hillary really believes him!" Had Hillary known the truth, she would not have said those things, Verveer said.

"Her credibility was on the line. I have no doubt that she believed him." He lied to his wife because only she could save him. "What else can she do but believe him," Stephanopoulos noted, "or lose everything she's worked for. But that's too cynical. She has to believe him because she also loves him. At another level she was complicit. If she went along with it for eighteen years, how could she be the person who stabs him in the back now?"

Clinton had betrayed the unspoken promise he had made to his staff and supporters who had endured the nearly fatal Gennifer Flowers tapes in 1992. "We believed certain things were not going to happen," Stephanopoulos said. "Even when it looked like it was happening, we said to ourselves, It's not possible. He's just not that dumb." Until evidence of the most appalling and explicit nature—a stained dress—forced his hand, Clinton did not tell even his lawyers the truth.

Shortly after the Monica story broke, some of the president's oldest friends gathered at Camp David for President's Weekend in February 1998. Former ambassador (to Sweden) Tom Siebert was there with his wife, Debbie. As Georgetown freshmen, Siebert said, they "had all talked about changing the world, but [we felt] Bill was really going to do it." Hollywood producers and old Arkansas friends Harry Thomason and his wife, Linda Bloodworth Thomason, were there. While Hillary and the other wives sat at the opposite side of the room, the men formed a semicircle around the fireplace. "Bill started to attack Ken Starr in a very profane, very personal, very bitter way," one friend recalled. "Bill said no other president had ever had this kind of scrutiny. From his tone I could tell it was true about Monica. It was such a non-denial denial. I felt just terrible for him and for [Hillary] and for the country."

Shalala also got a non-denial denial from the president. "I said to him, 'Look, I'm not going out there and defend you unless you tell me straight out.' And he told me the same thing he told the press. 'I didn't have sex with her.' I said, There's something inappropriate going on. And he just shrugged his shoulders." Still Shalala and Secretary of State Albright publicly defended the president.

From the beginning of 1998, Hillary virtually disappeared from the West Wing. Like Pat Nixon during the final days of Watergate, she stopped reading the newspapers. "She blocks it out," said Grunwald during the most fevered days of the media's Monica obsession. "She knows it's just going to drive her nuts, so she blocks it out. I was over there two weeks ago. It was a pretty big day in the life of the scandal. No one in the first lady's office was talking about it. They would talk about how Betty Currie had been in a car accident because some reporter had chased her or something, and Betty had sat in her office crying that day because she had banged up her car. That was how they were relating to the story."

"I waited for Hillary to call," Shalala remembered. "I left messages for her, If you need anything just yell. But basically she didn't want to talk about it. She just wanted people to distract her. She's got to be furious and disappointed. And maybe that stiffness was just covering up. I think she understands his weakness and she may have believed him because she wanted to. And it's too outrageous. She couldn't believe he would risk everything they worked for all these years." "This was not something we talked about," Verveer said later. Even Diane Blair, Hillary's closest friend before Blair's death from cancer during the summer of 2000, said that she and the first lady had never discussed Monica Lewinsky or her husband's adultery.

Not since the state of siege that gripped Nixon's final days in 1974 had the White House been ground zero. The remote trucks and camera crews transformed the lush front lawn into mud, often covered by brown garbage bags. Late into the night, hot television lights bathed the gleaming facade.

Hillary inhabited a separate universe. But there was no more room for illusions after August 14, 1998, when an FBI lab test showed a match between the president's blood and a semen stain on a blue dress. For the president, it was the first time in a lifetime of evasions that he had to face the full consequences of his sexual behavior. "We were told there was no blue dress with DNA," said one of his inner circle. "We could not talk to the president, so we talked to his lawyers. They didn't know either."

How could Hillary, whose husband credited her with teaching him "The definition of insanity is doing the same thing over and over again and expecting a different result," not have known? Historian Arthur Schlesinger, Jr., had the same answer for the mysterious willed blindness he perceived in both Jackie Kennedy and Hillary Clinton: "Never under-estimate the power of protective denial." Until August 1998, Hillary said she thought the "problem" was behind them. "I thought he had con-quered it; I thought he had understood it."

First she had to save his presidency. She switched the personal rela-tionship off, turned the political one up full throttle. She summoned old friends and trusted aides like Mickey Kantor, Harry Thomason and Linda Bloodworth Thomason, Paul Begala and Steven Ricchetti to help with her husband's defense. "We have to fight. They are out to destroy his presidency," she told the people whose help she was asking. "The other thing is between Bill and me. We will work it out in our own terms." When Virginia Democratic congressman James P. Moran began to waver in his support of the president, Hillary confronted him. "I'm the field general of this operation," she told Moran. "I believe in my hus-band. I believe in what he has accomplished and what he'll be able to accomplish once this is all over. He is my best friend. And I still believe in him."

But, on a personal level, her body language was clear. Her husband was about to give the most important speech of his political career, explaining his long deception. She refused to help him. "Hillary was so angry," said one of his speechwriters, "that she did not want to have any-thing to do with the guy. She wanted him not to exist." All she said to him was "It's your speech."

It was indeed. In some ways Clinton's four-minute speech on August 17, 1998, was his most revealing. Full of anger and self-pity, it was hardly an apology. The dichotomy in the man's character had never been laid so bare: self-awareness intertwined with self-justification. "I answered their questions truthfully . . . questions no American citizen would ever want to answer. Still, I must take complete responsibility for my actions, both public and private. . . . I was motivated by . . . a desire to protect myself from the embarrassment of my own conduct . . . in a politically inspired lawsuit . . . This has gone on too long, cost too much, and hurt too many innocent people. . . . " Petulant and reproachful, his speech tried to shift the blame to Ken Starr. But a man who hated to apologize did admit, for the first time, that he had "misled" people, including his wife and daughter.

In a season of extraordinary humiliations for the first lady, surely one of her worst days was August 19. On that day the Starr Report was released. CNN asked that children leave the room because of the "inappropriate nature" of the report. Newspapers and talk shows argued over the precise definition of various types of sex. Hillary's tight, drawn features as she held her daughter's hand and crossed the White House lawn to a waiting helicopter mirrored the nation's emotional landscape. But once again the Clintons were stronger than their enemies. The image of the three Clintons was poignant and sad, but without the presence of his wife and daughter beside him, the shamed president would have cut a different figure. Blessed by enemies in Congress like Gingrich, Tom DeLay and Henry Hyde, Clinton still could not have survived without Hillary; with her great inner strength on public display, she led the country from denial through rage to grudging acceptance of her husband's evasions and lies. If she could stand it and maintain her dignity, the American people decided, so could they.

BILL AND HILLARY, who always related on two levels, would take longer to mend their personal relationship. "She had to forgive him," Melanne Verveer said, "so their lives could go on." Their religious beliefs helped. "I believe deeply in forgiveness and reconciliation," she told CNN's Christiane Amanpour. "I'm very gratified that my husband and I have a very strong relationship and a lot of understanding of one another and a great commitment to each other. . . . Part of it is our religious faith and part of it is just our experience of human nature and how one always has to be ready to forgive if one wants to go on and live without bitterness. . . ."

As a southern Baptist, Clinton believed in the redemption of the sinner through constant effort. For Clinton, character was not a fixed quality but an evolving one. Unlike Nixon or Johnson, Clinton was not a tormented soul. His remarkable capacity for self-renewal, the flip side of his reckless sense of invulnerability, served the nation and saved him. In many ways, he resembled that other president whose father had been an alcoholic, Ronald Reagan.

At the White House holiday parties at the end of 1998, the Clintons stood as rigid as two sentries in the receiving lines. At the Kennedy Center honors in early December, they sat side by side without touching, barely acknowledging each other. During the intermission, Hillary was surrounded by friends and well-wishers in the presidential box. Her husband stood apart, virtually alone. But the couple with the surreal survival skills were moving on. The Clintons were back among old friends for the year-end Renaissance Weekend at Hilton Head. In a forty-minute speech there, the president hailed the successes of 1998, never even alluding to his impeachment. Following his speech, *Newsweek* columnist Jonathan Alter wished him a better year in 1999. "I hope the Constitution has a better year," Clinton replied coolly.

In February 1999, a friend visiting them in the upstairs residence found the couple still estranged, their conversation strained and artificial. "Have you walked the dog?" Hillary asked her husband. "No, I thought you had," the president replied tersely. "All right, I'll do it," she snapped. "No, let me," he said. It was, the visitor recalled, "an atmosphere of complete unreality. This was not about Buddy the dog."

But a thaw was necessary and inevitable. In April 1999, the Clintons played host to Nobel laureate Elie Wiesel and more than a hundred scholars, philanthropists and human rights activists at a White House millennium evening. In the white-and-gold, classically elegant East Room, beneath a Gilbert Stuart portrait of George Washington, the Clintons were at their best. Husband and wife took turns speaking and answering questions, dazzling in their discussion of war, genocide, the nature of evil and human responsibility. The frost between them was melting. They interrupted each other with a relaxed ease. "You can tell we're obsessed with this," President Clinton said. "Yeah," Hillary said, laughing, "we talk about this a lot. . . . When Bill and I are either entertaining people from other countries here, or traveling abroad, we'll get together at the end of the day and trade notes and stories about what occurred." It was not by chance that Hillary publicly volunteered this small but positive detail about their shared life. The

Wiesels stayed the night and saw the Clintons reaching out to each other privately.

During this period, Hillary was nourished by an unaccustomed form of sustenance: massive public approval. Her conduct during the year's tawdry soap opera had won her unprecedented support. The public's attachment seemed to have transferred from Bill to Hillary—and she liked it. With magazines running features on her—in one she was called "the better half"—and a glamorous *Vogue* cover, her public approval ratings had never been higher. When *Time* magazine considered making her Person of the Year, however, Hillary expressed mixed feelings. She understood her support came from the very thing she did not want to be known for: standing by her man. But for a woman raw from public humiliation, sudden popularity was a balm. For the first time in their three decades together, she was the object of more adulation than her husband. It was no longer just in Bangladesh and Morocco that people lined up to touch her. Now they lined up in New York City, too. At the lowest point in her personal life, the public reinforcement was welcome.

Fellow Democrats began to see her as a potential candidate herself. If the Lewinsky affair had never taken place, Hillary might not have felt the same compulsion to run for the Senate; she might have been more patient and waited a few years. "I want independence," she said in September 1999. "I want to be judged on my own merits. Now for the first time I am making my own decisions. I can feel the difference. It's a great relief." A friend who advised her to run explained why: "Hillary understood that if she did not carve out her own political life she would forever be remembered for all the scandals. . . . She could not bear that."

By vigorously supporting her campaign, Bill Clinton played by the rules the couple had always lived by. On their twenty-fourth wedding anniversary he said as much. "I am very grateful that now my wife has a chance to do what I thought she ought to do twenty-six years ago when we finished law school," he told a group gathered in October 1999 to support her Senate race. "The only thing that really worried me about our getting married was that somehow she would be denied the opportunity to share her gifts in the most important way."

Bill and Hillary still rose and fell together. "Hillary does not listen—really listen—to anybody except her husband. This is his campaign," one friend said at the time. He did not just follow it, he worked on it, behind the scenes. At 3 A.M. on September 6, 2000, for example, after an exhausting day of meetings at the United Nations, President Clinton was still up in his suite at the Waldorf-Astoria, hunched over a yellow legal pad working on a campaign speech Hillary was to give on education. It was a typical moment in an unusual campaign: throughout her campaign, drafts of her speeches went back and forth between the White House and New York. "B, what do you think of this?" Hillary scribbled on top of texts. After extensive editing, the president signed, "I love you, B."

IN FEBRUARY 1992, a young woman had driven over icy New England roads from her Boston college to Manchester, New Hampshire, to volunteer for the Clinton campaign. After Clinton's victory, she had worked her way up the ranks to a notable position in the White House. Eight years later, in January 2000, as she watched the president deliver his final State of the Union address, working his magic one last time, dazzling his supporters and dumbfounding his enemies, she wept. "So much time and talent wasted," she said through tears. She spoke for many for whom the Clinton presidency, despite a surprisingly energetic and successful final year, represented as much a lost opportunity for true greatness as well as a series of achievements.

Did Bill Clinton understand how much time and talent he had squandered, how much more he could have achieved? "Don't let anyone fool you," his friend and former chief of staff Erskine Bowles said. "He knows. He knows and he feels terrible about the might-have-beens." When, years before, Clinton was asked if he believed in life after death, he had replied, only half in jest, "I have to. I need a second chance." His second chance was Hillary's Senate run. In late July 2000, when a poll showed Hillary running behind her Republican opponent, Rick Lazio, Clinton revealed to what extent he saw her race as his. "Everybody that always hated me all those years and were so mean to me," he said, "they've all transferred all their anger to her now. It's almost as if they've got one last chance to beat me."

Never closer than when campaigning, the Clintons ended the presidency as close as they had ever been. Never before had Hillary appreciated him more than while running herself. Hillary's friend and adviser Harold Ickes acknowledged that she has "a deeper appreciation . . . she understands now how good he is, and how difficult it is to do what he does."

In the planning and the organizing of a political campaign, and in once again outmaneuvering their enemies, the Clintons' personal and public lives were most harmoniously joined. And the answer to the question which for so long obsessed the nation—is theirs a *real* marriage or a political arrangement?—seemed clear. It was both. For though the Clintons's marriage had perhaps a larger area of mystery than most, a decades-long relationship of deep interdependence cannot finally be *unreal*.

It was not by chance that both candidates to succeed Bill Clinton presented perfect marriages to the electorate, stressing family values, morality and putative first ladies who, despite their advanced degrees and substantial personal attainments, conducted themselves in a far more traditional manner than Hillary Clinton. Perhaps the final irony of the Clintons' turbulent tenure was that their experiment in co-presidency pulled Americans back toward an older attachment to tradition.

THE FINAL WEEKS of the Clinton administration were unique in American history. For seventeen days, the first lady was also an elected official. At Hillary Clinton's swearing-in as New York's junior senator, the president played a proud but distinctly secondary role, assuming a position normally reserved for political wives: he held the Bible. His mood at the end of his tenure was nostalgic. He spoke of his legacy, his accomplishments. For Bill Clinton the future no longer had a precise focus.

For Hillary it was the opposite. She had a new bounce in her step.

The media focus was on her, and for the first time it had nothing to do with the state of their marriage. Entering into the routines and rituals of a United States senator, she quickly got three choice committee assignments that would allow her to become publicly involved in almost any issue in the world: health, environment and banking.

Now her every move was receiving more attention than his. The early signs were that she would be the same kind of senator as she was campaigner: serious, intense and tireless, much more issue-oriented than her husband. She told friends that she would never again repeat the mistakes of her health care initiative in the White House and she was glad she was given a second chance.

She had also told the voters of New York that she would not run for president in 2004. Not everyone was sure this pledge was ironclad. But no one, not even her closest friends—especially not her closest friends—doubted that she would eventually think of the presidency. The only question was when and how.

During the last weekend of the Clinton administration, Bill and Hillary hosted a series of remarkable overnight parties at Camp David. On Friday, January 12, the Cabinet was invited for a last get-together. In historic Laurel Lodge, where the Clintons on their first presidential weekend in 1993 had asked the incoming Cabinet to sit around the floor and, in a classic piece of New Age psychobabble, reveal something secret about themselves, each member of the outgoing Cabinet now rose in impromptu farewell tributes. The mood combined pride and wistfulness, nostalgia and hope. The president did not talk about his own accomplishments but rather about the rewards of public service, despite its many pitfalls. The toasts and tributes were mostly personal reminders of early times with Bill Clinton, and there were frequent references to the future Senator Clinton. A few people referred to the possibility that there was a "future president" in the room. No one doubted who the object of the reference was.

As for Hillary, she looked radiant. She seemed to combine effortlessly the roles of first lady and senator, switching easily from conversations about the past to questions about staffing her Senate office. While the president rambled across the entire range of his voracious intellectual curiosity, Hillary stayed focused. She had undergone another transformation: liberated from the past, she had finally become the senior partner.

But the Clintons' roller coaster ride never seemed to end, and the euphoria of January was gone within a few days (along with Clinton's high popularity ratings). In his last days in office—largely circumventing his own staff and the Justice Department—President Clinton made one of the greatest errors of his entire eight years, pardoning Marc Rich and several other controversial felons. Denounced by his friends and enemies alike for abuse of presidential power, Clinton watched his two-year post-Monica effort to erase the stain on his legacy evaporate almost overnight. Revelations regarding Hillary's own brother's role in two of the pardons dragged the new senator into her husband's post-presidential swamp. Once again, Bill Clinton's worst qualities, his reckless self-indulgence and sense of entitlement, damaged their personal and political lives. This time, however, Hillary had a signal advantage: time and a platform from which to recover. Within months of her election, through hard work, determination and focus, Senator Clinton had converted her staunchest foes in the Senate into admiring colleagues.

CHAPTER 12

LAURA AND GEORGE W. BUSH

TRANSFORMED BY HISTORY

I've always done what really traditional women do, and I've been very, very satisfied.

—LAURA BUSH

I have the best wife for the line of work that I'm in. She doesn't try to steal the limelight.

—GEORGE W. BUSH

TEN MINUTES BEFORE THE END OF HIS 2002 STATE OF THE UNION ADDRESS, George W. Bush paused. "I hope you will join me in expressing thanks to one American for the strength and calm and comfort she brings to our nation in crisis," he said, "our first lady, Laura Bush."

The audience had been vocal in its support of the President's rally cry for victory in the war on terror, but many seemed ambivalent when Bush spoke of an "axis of evil" that included the strange bedfellows Iran, Iraq and North Korea. When Bush spoke of his tax policy, half of the assembled legislators shook their heads and folded their arms. Now fifty-two million viewers watched as both sides of the aisle stood in unison and whooped like teenagers at a high school pep rally.

The President looked up and nodded at his wife from the podium. From the balcony, she stood briefly, primly straightened her dress and acknowledged the applause with her signature smile. She mouthed "thank you" bashfully, and waved briefly. The applause continued. Finally, she reached for her neighbor, Afghan Chairman Hamid Karzai, as if to stop his clapping, and, hopefully, to get the rest of the class to settle down and listen to the teacher—who for the time being was her husband.

Bush, in his first State of the Union address, was right to recognize that his unassuming wife had changed her image since becoming first lady. Indeed, after the terrorist attacks five months earlier, Laura had become Comforter-in-Chief of the nation. The tragedy of September 11, 2001, had transformed Laura's role as dramatically as it had her husband's.

It was not the presidency either of them had prepared for or expected.

❧

AS GEORGE AND LAURA BUSH moved into the White House in January 2001, one thing seemed certain. The days of endless speculation about the state of the presidential marriage and precedent-shattering and controversial activities by the first lady were over. From what the nation knew of them, George and Laura appeared to be the most "ordinary" couple to inhabit the White House in decades. She would be a more traditional first lady than any of her recent predecessors, including her formidable mother-in-law.

The White House is not a glittering palace of culture or style under the Bushes. It is not an exciting place intellectually or socially. The Bushes prefer their own and their extended family's company and like to go to bed early. Washington's social life holds little appeal for President Bush. "He didn't like it when he was here," White House aide Mary Matalin noted. "[To Bush] this is a very insular, phony place." Nor is life in the White House an overpowering experience for this couple. They know the place.

The presidency is something else again. George W. Bush, like Ronald Reagan, delegates many responsibilities of the office. But Reagan's performance skills were breathtaking. In the campaign and during the transition, Bush conveyed acute discomfort in public. Ill at ease before cameras, he kept his remarks as short and scripted as possible, reaching for his smiling wife's hand whenever he could. Even some of his oldest friends wondered, "How did this happen?" But, as events would soon prove, one should not underestimate this man, or the shy Texan he married twenty-three years before.

⁓

LAURA BUSH WAS BORN in Midland, Texas, on November 4, 1946. The mid-sized town, built by oil money in the middle of the west Texas emptiness, is a gleaming corporate city "whose eye-popping wealth . . . retained the quaint virtues of a small town." Later, Laura Bush and her husband would describe Midland in only the most glowing terms—and particularly portrayed it in opposition to the Gomorrah of "Washington Deecee." It was "a place where neighbors had to help each other because any other help was too far away," Laura would say during the 2000 GOP Convention, "a place of family and community, and it had a sense of possibility as big as the West Texas sky."

Laura's sense of duty came early. Before Laura was born, her bookkeeper mother, Jenna Welch, had lost several babies, a fact that weighed heavily on young Laura: "I felt very obligated to my parents," she once said. "I didn't want to upset them in any way." Laura Welch was by all accounts a serious, self-contained child, who had inherited her mother's love of books and aspired to be a teacher. Years later, millions would hear her recount how she honed her teaching skills in her bedroom, with her dolls as her well-behaved pupils.

Unlike many men and women of her generation, Laura never questioned the values that shaped American society. "She would never have done any protesting," said her longtime friend Jan O'Neill, "or all that other '70s stuff." While her contemporaries became civil rights activists, she became a debutante; while others shouted protests against the Vietnam War, she sang in church.

At age seventeen, Laura's placid existence was shattered when, on November 6, 1963, she drove her Chevrolet sedan through a stop sign and hit another car, killing its occupant, who happened to be a close friend of hers. "It was a terrible, terrible thing," Laura has said. The early trauma no doubt reinforced her innate caution.

ALTHOUGH GEORGE W. BUSH spent just twelve years of his youth in Midland, his official White House biography says only that he "grew up in Midland and Houston, Texas," making no mention of the fact that he was born in New Haven, Connecticut, in 1946. Once his political career started, he did his best to play up his—and co-opt Laura's—"Midlandness" and downplay his East Coast pedigree. "This place," he has said, "has shaped the values that will shape my service to our nation." Indeed, Bush has said he wants to be buried in Midland.

Unlike his wife, George had much to prove, both to himself and to his parents. "Young George," his cousin Elsie Walker commented, "sometimes was sort of sensitive to the fact that he was too coarse, or, you know, rough-edged for his father." Life, in the words of the elder President Bush, is about "passing on legacy, passing on tradition." The unspoken burden weighed heaviest on the eldest son. "A lot of people who have fathers like this," George's younger brother Jeb noted, "or moms who have lived such extraordinary lives, feel a sense that they have failed because they haven't reached the same level . . . and it creates all sorts of pathologies." Barbara Bush—"a very ferocious mother," in Laura's words—described her eldest's desire to live up to the standard set by his father in simpler terms: "nuts." For the boisterous son of a patrician overachiever, competition was bred in his bones. The trouble was, young George had no real idea what to compete *for*, other than his father's affection and attention. George, in his own words, did not have "normal access" to his busy father. "My father doesn't have a normal life," he told friends at Yale. "I don't have a normal father."

At first, George didn't show much interest in the family business. As a Yale undergraduate during the sixties, one of the most politically charged periods of the last century, "George was never involved in any of that . . . [he] expressed no interest [in politics] and had no involvement in it," his college roommate Clay Johnson recalled. "I don't remember him saying anything profound," his old friend Bill Semple said. "I never knew what his passion was, I never thought of him as a passionate person. And yet he got there."

It did not happen right away. Though George consciously retraced his father's footsteps, he did not match the elder man's distinguished record at either Andover or Yale, or in the military or the oil business. Mostly he stood out for being fun-loving and unambitious. But he struggled to emulate his father. He even got engaged at the end of his junior year at Yale, just as his father had, though in his case the engagement (to Cathryn Wolfman, a Rice University student) did not last. Until midlife nothing really *took*. Bush calls those his "nomadic years." For a long time—virtually until George W. was elected president—his elders deemed his younger brother Jeb the more serious, the smarter and the more electable. When, early in the 2000 campaign, I asked the elder President Bush what if things did not work out for George W., without skipping a beat, he answered, "Jeb would make a very fine candidate."

AFTER TWO YEARS OF TRYING in vain, Jan and Joe O'Neill finally convinced their friend Laura—a thirty-year-old librarian who was contentedly single—to return to Midland from her new home of Austin and meet George in late July 1977. She had put off the O'Neills' prior efforts to introduce her to the wisecracking, hyperkinetic young man with the famous name. "I was so uninterested in politics," she later explained. "I thought he was someone real political, and I wasn't interested."

When she showed up at the O'Neills' backyard barbecue wearing a blue sundress, George was definitely interested. "Smitten, I must confess," he later admitted. Though for a while they had attended the same junior high in Midland together, and lived in the same apartment complex in Houston in the 1970s, George and Laura had never met. Now he found her to be "one of the great listeners. And since I am one of the big talkers, it was a great fit." He later said getting married was one of his toughest decisions prior to the presidency—as well as one of the best.

George's big dreams and high ambitions did not impress Laura. "The thing that I liked about him was that he made me laugh," she later said. He was avid to reach some as yet unspecified goal; she was content with her life. Young George surely perceived what a solid counterweight Laura would be to his still hazy ambitions. She would help him mature. All Laura ever wanted to do was teach: "I've always done what really traditional women do, and I've been very, very satisfied,"

Laura was still unconvinced and, days later, when George left for the family compound in Kennebunkport, Maine, he had trouble getting her on the phone. To prove he was serious, he interrupted the Bushes' annual rite of summer water sports to return to Texas. In three whirlwind months, she became Laura Bush.

∞

"AND WHAT DO YOU DO?" Dorothy Walker Bush, the starchy matriarch of the Bush family, asked her grandson's new bride during her first visit to Kennebunkport in 1977. "I read, I smoke and I admire," Laura replied. Barbara Bush later recalled that the elder Mrs. Bush "darn near collapsed." But Laura's answer revealed remarkable comfort about herself, even in the alien world of the Yankee establishment.

The marriage had a rough start. Their honeymoon was spent on the campaign trail, as an attractive congressional seat had opened up. Kent Hance, a native Texan—who had stayed in Texas—was Bush's opponent. It didn't take long for the carpetbagger accusations to fly. "My daddy and granddad were farmers," Hance twanged in a debate shortly before the election. "They didn't have anything do with the mess we're in right now, and Bush's father has been in politics his whole life." George was stunned. For her part, Laura had made George promise not to ask her to give any speeches, but he soon broke that promise and made her stand in for him at a speech in Muleshoe, Texas. Petrified, she spoke too softly and ran out of words.

Laura was learning how to handle her husband as well as politics. One evening, the newlyweds were pulling into the driveway after a full day of campaigning. "How was my speech?" George asked Laura. "It wasn't that good," Laura replied. George slammed their Pontiac Bonneville into the garage wall, and Laura learned to tread lightly when criticizing her husband's political performances. She would soon find that a lilting "Bushieee," and a knowing glance would suffice to calm him.

Bush lost his 1978 congressional bid. Laura was quietly relieved. It meant no more speeches—at least for a while. He returned to the oil business, while she hoped to start a family. But Laura had such difficulty conceiving that the couple finally began the process to adopt children. When she finally became pregnant, they soon discovered that she would have twins.

Five weeks before her due date, Laura's and the twins' lives were threatened when she developed toxemia. George could not conceal his alarm; Laura remained, as ever, a rock. "These babies will be fine," she told him. "They will stay with me until they're big enough to emerge." "There was a determination and a grit," George recalled, "an unbelievable will to protect the children. I remember to this day how confident I became because of her."

George burst into tears in the operating room when Jenna and Barbara—named after their grandmothers—were born by cesarean section, premature but healthy. "I realized our life had changed forever," George said, "in a positive way."

∽

AT AGE FORTY, George was "on the road to nowhere," according to his first cousin John Ellis. The story of how George quit drinking—and began going to Bible study—following a hard night's carousing in celebration of his fortieth birthday in 1986 is well known. This was no overnight conversion to sobriety, however, but the result of Laura's many pleas, "after nights that weren't particularly great." But many of his friends think even this was really about his father. "He looked in the mirror and said, 'Someday I might embarrass my father,'" said Joe O'Neill, who was with him when he swore off drinking. "'It might get my dad in trouble.' . . . And boy that was it. That's how high a priority it was. And he never took another drink."

It was as if everything had been cued up for the moment. His name, his parents' vast network and his winning personality opened doors to the moneymen who invested in his oil business, the purchase of the Texas Rangers baseball team and in his political campaigns. Bush may not have been a serious student of much else, but he soon demonstrated that he was an avid student of people. Still smarting after the first campaign, he sought training by Lee Atwater, the "prince of wicked political spin" (in the words of Texas author Bill Minutaglio) of the Republican Party. He would not again fall into the trap of seeming too remote, too elitist, too Yale, too Kennebunkport. When asked how he differed from his dad, George W. answered, "He attended Greenwich Country Day and I went to San Jacinto High School in Midland." Few seemed bothered that the Connecticut-born politician actually attended San Jacinto Junior High for one year before transferring to private schools in Houston and Massachusetts.

When he defeated Texas's popular governor Ann Richards in 1994, Bush first demonstrated what the nation would learn only six years later: that stylistically he was not his father's son. His father's humiliating loss to Bill Clinton and the questions raised about the elder's authenticity opened up wounds inflicted by Hance fourteen years earlier, and accelerated the process by which George W. adopted an assertively different style. Louder, earthier and looser, his affect was closer to Lyndon Johnson than to his father. Culturally a Texan, he is almost as physical—touching, slapping, punching, whispering—as LBJ. In place of the "Johnson lean," George cultivated the "Dubya slouch," in meetings or conferences.

While George polished his populist political style, Laura, seemingly nonpartisan and somewhat detached, became an indispensable political asset. She also provided order in his life, a peaceful space away from the combat zone of politics and a check on his often unwieldy ego. "She's pretty good at keeping me centered," George has said, "and reminding me that I'm not 'it.' " His father agrees: "Golly, she sure can calm him down."

Ann Richards has a single word to describe the wife of the man who ended her political career: "Nurturing." Though Texans expressed a wide spectrum of opinions regarding her husband, Laura received virtually universal praise. In this, as in many other things, the younger Bush seemed to be repeating his father's pattern.

Her apolitical affect was perhaps her strongest political asset. During her tenure as first lady of Texas, she gave very few speeches, sought no public involvement in policy and held few social events. In stark contrast to her counterpart in the White House at the time, she had no qualms about quietly and unobtrusively "standing by her man." "I don't give him a lot of advice," she told Barbara Walters. "I really don't think George wants a lot of advice from me."

George, elected governor at the height of the Whitewater scandal, understood that his wife's traditional approach would win him support from a public weary of the Clintons' personal psychodrama. Laura, he said, was "the perfect wife for a governor," as she kept from "tryin' to butt in and always, you know, compete." His comment spurred a backlash, however, and forced him to acknowledge that he does rely on Laura for advice. In addition to being "a great wife and a good mother," he later said in an interview with *Ladies' Home Journal*, "she's a good adviser, and she's also got very good judgment."

Laura proved adroit at sidestepping press attempts to probe differences between husband and wife. It was widely rumored that she did not share George's enthusiasm for the death penalty, and at a press conference in Houston in the last year of her husband's governorship, a reporter asked her point-blank about whether or not she supported his position on capital punishment. "If I differ with my husband I'm not going to tell *you* about it," she snapped. "Sorry," she added, with a forced smile.

In his quest for the White House, her husband made much of the contrast between Hillary and Laura. She would make a "fabulous first lady," Bush proclaimed. "She cuts right through, through the posturing and positioning," George explained. "America's starved for something. I'm telling you: they're starved for something real. And that's what she brings. She's a real person." The message was clear: Laura would be the un-Hillary in the White House.

∽

ON JULY 31, 2000, Laura Bush went prime-time. With her trademark composure, she stood before the assembled delegates that packed Philadelphia's First Union Center and millions more who watched on television as she opened the convention that would nominate her husband for President.

Her carefully scripted speech demonstrated to the world just how far she had come since her trembling performance on the courthouse steps of Muleshoe. "Okay, that's enough," she began, in a futile attempt to quiet the overzealous reception. "I am honored and I have to say I'm just a little bit overwhelmed. . . ." Never straying from the secure zones of education and family, like all her other speeches, this was more about the melody than the lyrics.

Near the end of her speech, however, Laura inserted a jab worthy of her mother-in-law. She described traveling with her husband and meeting parents and grandparents who would "hold out pictures of their children and then say to George . . . 'I'm counting on you . . . I want my son or daughter to respect the President of the United States of America!'" The delegates loved the not-so-subtle put-down and erupted in whoops and sustained cheers.

She never actually pronounced the names Clinton, Lewinsky or Whitewater. She had learned very well that what she did not say was often more significant than what she did say.

George and Laura fought hard for the presidency, but they did not seem as emotionally invested in the election's outcome as some of their supporters, or, for that matter, Al Gore. "People may not believe that," Laura said of the five weeks it took to determine who won the presidency. "But I knew George and I would be all right either way."

∾

IN JANUARY OF 2001, it seemed likely that George W. and Laura Bush's leadership style and home life would be transferred intact from Austin to Washington. In the first nine months, Laura spent enough time away from the White House to rival Bess Truman's record. Asked about the best advice she had given her husband since he became the leader of the free world, she glibly answered, "Let's see, I don't know. Cut his hair or something. I don't give him a lot of advice."

She seemed even more traditional and less assertive than the tart-tongued Barbara Bush. "[My mother-in-law] is very funny," Laura has said, "very acerbic, very entertaining to listen to. I'm, well, none of those things . . . [Barbara and George W.] both love to needle and they both love to talk." While Barbara Bush communicated her political views with winks and nods, Laura's unthreatening style enables her to be more straightforward. Unlike Barbara, Laura is not feared by White House staffers. From the beginning, she was liked for being just what she claims to be: a traditional wife and mother, a White House anomaly in this or any other time.

Because of her low-key style, few eyebrows were raised when, on January 18, 2001, Laura asserted that she did not think that the 1973 Supreme Court decision declaring a woman's constitutional right to an abortion should be overturned. Her husband supports a constitutional amendment to outlaw abortion, except in cases of rape, incest or danger to the life of the woman.

For the most part, however, Laura stuck to her issues—reading and education—and demurred when pressed to take a policy stand. When a group of women CEOs visited the East Room, she nervously began her remarks by speaking about how Abigail Adams got her laundry done.

Perhaps the most bookish first lady since Abigail Fillmore, to her closest friends she made no bones about where she'd rather be: curled up reading in Crawford, Texas.

For a couple that ran on a platform of restoring dignity to the White House, however, events in the summer of 2001 proved somewhat troubling. Around the same time that Chelsea Clinton was pictured registering for graduate classes in Oxford, the media reported that the first daughters, Jenna and Barbara, faced an Austin magistrate for underage drinking.

ON THE MORNING OF September 11, 2001, Laura was en route to Capitol Hill to testify before the Senate Education Committee. At three minutes past nine, United Airlines Flight 175 ripped into Tower Two of the World Trade Center. It was the second Boeing 767 to hit the Twin Towers that morning.

The President, who had assumed that the first crash had been a tragic accident, sat on a stool and entertained sixteen toddlers at the Emma E. Booker Elementary School in Sarasota, Florida. His Chief of Staff Andrew H. Card, Jr., leaned down and whispered the news into his ear: "A second plane has hit the World Trade Center: America is under attack." Thirty minutes later American Airlines Flight 77 smashed into the Pentagon.

By the day's end, the terrorist attacks claimed the lives of 3,000 people. The world, and the Bush presidency, had changed forever.

"I remember thinking," Laura recalled, "that nothing would ever be the same." First she spoke with her husband, who was at the time on his way back to Washington. Then she called her daughters. Finally, she called her mother, "just for the comfort of her voice." George and Laura spoke twice before noon that day. She calmed the President who seemed ready to tear apart the "tinhorn terrorists" with his bare hands, Texas-style. Once he was back in Washington, George recalled, Laura "never created any sense of alarm in our household, which was great. I mean . . . she was very comforting. The way you see her in public is the way she is in private. She's, you know, calm. She'd occasionally admonish me for getting a little too, you know, overboard on, you know, 'dead or alive.' . . . She thought I could have [been] a little more diplomatic or phrased it differently. But . . . that was just me coming out there."

In the following days, while her husband often seemed barely able to contain his anger—and occasionally choked back tears in public appearances—Laura remained composed, very much a reassuring public figure. She visited burn victims from the Pentagon attacks, appeared on national television and, in sharing her own anguish with the country, struck a chord with the stunned and grieving nation. The day after the attacks, she addressed an open letter to elementary school students: "When sad or frightening things happen, all of us have an opportunity to become better people by thinking about others. . . . I want you to know how much I care about all of you. Be kind to each other, take care of each other and show your love for each other."

She provided a necessary balance to her husband's righteous fury. The President warned the world that America was "fierce when stirred to anger"; the first lady asserted that "we are a kinder nation today." While George talked about smoking "the evil-doers" out of their caves,

Laura counseled the nation's children that, "while there are some bad people in the world, there are many more good people."

Unlike that of her activist predecessors Eleanor and Hillary, Laura's service to the nation comes in simple acts. When she visits classrooms, "Children will sidle up to me and whisper, 'What do you think about what happened?' I'll say 'I'm sad,' and they'll nod and say they are sad too."

She has also served the nation by projecting the strength of her marriage. By reminding Americans of traditional values that seemed suddenly in jeopardy, she steadied and brought comfort. As her husband prosecuted the war on terrorism overseas, Laura soon returned to her normal life. While she frequently mentioned September 11, her public remarks returned to the carefully scripted comments on early childhood and education.

On November 17, 2001, Laura made a little history. In the first Saturday presidential radio address ever delivered in its entirety by a first lady, she fired the first shot in "a worldwide effort to focus on the brutality against women and children by the al-Qaeda terrorist network and the regime it supports in Afghanistan, the Taliban." Her address was short but pulled no punches—describing the "horror" of the Taliban who "pull out women's fingernails for wearing nail polish."

On March 8, 2002, Laura followed up her address with a speech to the United Nations (on International Women's Day) on the status of women in Afghanistan. The quiet small-town Texan who never wanted to be anything but a teacher and housewife ended her speech to the world's largest governing body by calling for "human dignity, private property, free speech, equal justice, education and health care—these rights must be guaranteed throughout the world. Together, the United States, the United Nations and our allies will prove that the forces of terror can't stop the momentum of freedom." The speech might easily have been delivered by her controversial predecessor.

THREE DAYS BEFORE the State of the Union, a *USA Today/CNN*/Gallup poll chose Laura Bush as the most admired woman in America. (Her husband was admired by more Americans than any man since Gallup had begun the poll in 1948.) Though their sky-high approval ratings were a function of the national crisis, they marked a stunning transformation of the most contested presidency in history.

Neither Nancy Reagan nor Hillary Rodham Clinton could have given the President's weekly radio address without political cost to their husbands. Ironically, because Laura does not seem anxious for a public role, she is more easily granted a bully pulpit. Since September 11, 2001, she has emerged as a stabilizing voice in America's national dialogue—something she probably could not have imagined earlier. But the question remains: will she sustain her new role, extend it still further—or slip back into her comfortable, low-profile pre-September 11 existence? The latter seems unlikely—she has proved too valuable a political asset.

NOTES

INTRODUCTION

3 "I never wanted . . ." John Adams letter to Abigail, March 27, 1797, p. 185, *Founding Brothers* by Joseph J. Ellis (New York: Knopf, 2000).

3 "I hope some day . . ." *The Woman in the White House,* Marianne Means (New York: Signet Press, 1963), p. 210.

Presidential Studies Quarterly—Modern First Ladies vol. 20, no. 4 (Fall 1990); *Presidential Studies Quarterly—Reassessments of Presidents and First Ladies* vol. 26, no. 3 (Summer 1996); *First Ladies: The Saga of the Presidents' Wives and Their Power,* vol. 1 (New York: Morrow, 1990), vol. 2 1961–1990 (New York: Morrow, 1991).

Chapter 1
EDITH AND WOODROW WILSON

13 H. W. Brand's *T.R.—The Last Romantic* (New York: Basic Books, 1997), Judy Crichton's *America 1900* (New York: Owl Books, 2000), and Françoise Thebaud's *A History of Women in the West: Toward a Cultural Identity in the Twentieth Century* (Cambridge: Harvard University Press, 1994) were useful in setting the scene for this chapter.

For essential background on the Wilsons I relied on interviews with several key scholars. First among them was the late Professor Arthur Stanley Link, who devoted the better part of his scholarly life to the study of Woodrow Wilson and produced the five-volume collection, *Wilson,* all published by Princeton University Press between 1947 and 1965. I owe thanks to Professor Link for pointing me toward essential scholarship and scholars. Link's Princeton University protégé, Professor Thomas Knock, and Professor John Milton Cooper of the University of Wisconsin were kind and patient in sharing some of their views on both Edith and Woodrow Wilson. Columbia University professors Henry Graff and Alan Brinkley offered historical insights and suggestions on my research and with the manuscript. I am grateful to them all, particularly Professor Brinkley, who was among my first readers and made many helpful suggestions.

Of the many books on the subject, several were invaluable in writing this chapter. August Heckscher's *Woodrow Wilson* (New York: Scribner's, 1991) and Edward Weinstein's *Woodrow Wilson, A Medical and Psycho-*

logical Biography (Princeton University Press, 1981) were the two I relied on most. Many of the key letters of Edith and Woodrow are found in a collection edited by Edwin Tribble, *President in Love—the Courtship Letters of Woodrow Wilson and Edith Bolling Galt* (Boston: Houghton Mifflin, 1981). Throughout the chapter, I also quoted Irwin "Ike" Hood's *Forty-two Years in the White House, The Memoir of White House Chief Usher* (Boston: Houghton Mifflin, 1934). Hood offered a sharply different perspective of Wilson's illness than Edith Wilson's very one-sided account, *My Memoir* (New York: Bobbs Merrill, 1938).

This chapter is also informed by Alden Hatch's *Edith Bolling Wilson—First Lady Extraordinaire* (New York: Dodd, Mead, 1961) and Ishbel Ross's *Power with Grace,* (New York: Putnam, 1975) which represent two subsequent generation's views of this complex woman. Rear Admiral Cary T. Grayson, Edith's co-conspirator in her cover-up, also wrote his own account, *Woodrow Wilson, An Intimate Memoir* (Washington, D.C.: Potomac Books, 1960), which I relied on for the section on the later stage of Wilson's illness. Gene Smith's *When the Cheering Stopped* (New York: Morrow, 1964) is also a valuable account of Wilson's decline. *Woodrow Wilson and the Great Betrayal* by Thomas Bailey (Chicago: Encounter Paperbacks/Quadrangle Books, 1945) backgrounds the political context of the Wilson's marriage.

Throughout this chapter I relied on the *New York Times* archives to tell the story of how Edith manipulated the media from September 1919 until late 1921.

I am grateful to Jenny Lyn Bader for sharing her play, *Petticoat Government,* as well as her acute observations on the indomitable Edith Bolling Galt Wilson. Louis Auchincloss's *Woodrow Wilson* (New York: Penguin Lives, Lipper/Viking Books, 2000), a stylish, astute short biography, confirmed many of my own conclusions about Wilson the man.

Chapter 2
FRANKLIN AND ELEANOR ROOSEVELT

45 The amount of available documentation on the Roosevelts is overwhelming. Doris Kearns Goodwin's *No Ordinary Time—Franklin and Eleanor Roosevelt: The Home Front in World War II* (New York: Touchstone, 1994) is the groundbreaking account of Eleanor and Franklin as wartime couple in the White House. This would be quite a different chapter without Kearns's work. I found Blanche Wiesen Cook's two-volume work entitled *Eleanor Roosevelt* (New York: Viking, 1992, 1999) essential for understanding Mrs. Roosevelt. Joseph Lash's *Eleanor and Franklin* (New York: Norton, 1971) was my bible and touchstone for this chapter. Lash's *Love, Eleanor: Eleanor Roosevelt and Her Friends* (New York: Doubleday, 1982) and *Eleanor Roosevelt: A Friend's Memoir* (New York: Doubleday,

1964) round out and refine the portrait. What Lash and Cook did for Eleanor, Geoffrey C. Ward achieves in his vivid portrayal of Franklin, *A First Class Temperament* (New York: Harper & Row, 1989). Eleanor's own accounts, *This Is My Story, This I Remember, On My Own* and *My Day* (variously published between 1937 and 1961 by Harper & Brothers, New York) are indispensable in forming any clear picture of her astonishing role in our national narrative. No other presidential spouse has left such a record, because none has led such a life.

Eleanor's correspondence offers the freshest and most reliable insights. Her relationship to Lorena Hickock is best understood through their correspondence, *Empty Without You: The Intimate Letters of Eleanor Roosevelt and Lorena Hickock,* edited by Rodger Streitmatter (New York: Free Press, 1998). Eleanor's letters to her daughter, Anna, are collected in *Mother and Daughter: The Letters of Eleanor and Anna Roosevelt,* edited by Bernard Asbell (New York: Coward, McCann & Geoghegan, 1982).

Franklin Roosevelt did not leave much of a personal paper trail. Others have been left to interpret his life. In addition to Lash and Ward, I relied on Robert Ferrell's *The Dying President: Franklin D. Roosevelt, 1944–1945* (Columbia: University of Missouri, 1998) and *Closest Companion—the Unknown Story of the Intimate Friendship between Franklin Roosevelt and Margaret Suckley* (Boston: Houghton Mifflin, 1995) in profiling the final, sad year of the Roosevelt marriage.

I drew on the memories and personal accounts of a number of Roosevelt intimates and associates in writing this chapter. Trude Lash, widow of Joseph Lash and friend of Eleanor, was generous with her time. So were Jane Plakias, William J. Vanden Heuvel, Alan J. Pakula, Arthur Schlesinger, Jr., Raymond Lamontagne and Professor Alan Brinkley. Eleanor's granddaughter Kate Roosevelt Whitney shared a few precious memories of her grandmother. Winthrop Rutherfurd III recalled his step-grandmother, Lucy Mercer Rutherfurd.

No one can hope to penetrate the complex Roosevelt union without spending time at Hyde Park, where Franklin was raised and where Eleanor—before she built her own house, Val Kill—spent her painful early years as his wife. I am grateful to Verne Newton, the director of the Roosevelt Library at Hyde Park, for his hospitality and his guidance, as well as his insights. The bulk of the research material found in this chapter—letters, oral histories and memoranda—are housed in the Roosevelt Hyde Park Library.

45 "No one who ever saw Eleanor . . ." quoted in ER's *My Day*, p. 42. "He might have been happier . . ." *The Autobiography of Eleanor Roosevelt (This I Remember)* (New York: Harper, 1961), p. 279.

47 The story and quotes relating to Eleanor's childhood are drawn from *The Autobiography of ER,* pp. 3–17. Quotations from the letters she wrote Franklin are found in the FDR Library and are reprinted by Lash in *Eleanor and Franklin,* p. 110.

49 "Not only I but you are the luckiest . . ." FDR Library and Lash, *Eleanor and Franklin,* p. 112.

50 "I wondered," she wrote Franklin . . ." Ibid., p. 108.

51 "In the autumn of 1908 . . ." *The Autobiography of ER,* p. 61.

51 "I was perfectly certain . . ." Ibid., p. 75.

52 "It is a little like a drug habit . . ." Ward, *A First Class Temperament,* p. 210.

52 "I am sometimes a little selfish . . ." Ibid., p. 210.

52 "the bottom dropped out . . ." ER letter to Joe Lash, October 25, 1943, FDR Library.

53 "How could she forgive him . . ." author's conversation with ER's granddaughter Kate Roosevelt Whitney.

53 "After that, father and mother . . ." James Roosevelt Oral History, Columbia University Library.

55 Eleanor's political education: based in part on the author's interviews with Trude Lash, William Vanden Heuvel and Arthur Schlesinger, Jr. On Howe's role, see also *The Autobiography of ER,* pp. 123–24, and Blanche Wiesen Cook, *Eleanor Roosevelt,* vol. 1, pp. 282–85.

55 "Dearest Honey . . ." Ward, *A First Class Temperament,* p. 565.

56 "To tell the truth . . ." Roosevelt, *This I Remember,* p. 25.

56 "He was still pretty sick . . ." Frances Perkins Oral History, Columbia University.

57 "Mama made up her mind . . ." *The Autobiography of ER,* p. 117, and *The FDR Memoirs* by Bernard Asbell, p. 235. Also, Roosevelt, *This Is My Story,* p. 336.

57 "[Politics] was a growing bond . . ." Anna Roosevelt Halsted, Oral History.

57 "[Franklin] came to admire . . ." Goodwin, *No Ordinary Time,* p. 118.

58 A wife's job . . . *Good Housekeeping,* August 1930.

58 "I was trying to read to the two youngest . . ." *The Autobiography of ER,* p. 119.

58 "I was beginning to find the political contacts . . ." *This Is My Story,* p. 122.

58 "All the delegates to the national convention . . ." Frances Perkins Oral History.

59 "My Missus and some of her female . . ." Lash, *Eleanor and Franklin,* p. 304.

59 "The demand for Mr. Roosevelt . . ." Ibid., p. 317.

60 "I never did a thing to ask him . . ." Ibid., p. 318.

60 "Now that my husband is actually back . . ." Ibid., p. 320.

60 "Walking was so difficult . . ." Ibid., p. 56.

61 There is little agreement among . . . Elliott Roosevelt and Anna Roosevelt Oral Histories, as well as Goodwin's *No Ordinary Time,* pp. 119–22, and Streitmatter's *Empty Without You,* pp. 335–36, *The Autobiography of ER,* pp. 111–12, *This I Remember,* pp. 29, 114 and 169–70. Asbell, *The FDR Memoirs,* pp. 233–38. See also H. C. Gallagher's *Splendid Deception,* (New York: Dodd, Mead, 1985), pp. 134–41. Also, author's interview with Trude Lash.

62 Eleanor's letters to Joe Lash are found in Joseph P. Lash's *A World of Love: Eleanor Roosevelt and Her Friends* (New York: Doubleday, 1984) and *Love, Eleanor: Eleanor Roosevelt and Her Friends* (New York: Doubleday, 1982).

62 FDR's polio, Lash, *Eleanor and Franklin,* p. 424, and Hugh Gregory Gallagher, *FDR's Splendid Deception,* (New York: Dodd, Mead, 1985), p. 120.

64 *"Did my Eleanor relate . . ."* Roosevelt, *My Day,* p. 41.

64 She asked her husband for a specific . . . Roosevelt, *This I Remember,* p. 76.

64 Eleanor found emotional sustenance . . . See Streitmatter, *Empty Without You.*

65 From the minute Eleanor . . . See Irwin Hoover, *Forty Two Years in the White House* (Boston: Houghton Mifflin, 1934), p. 225.

66 "My first act . . ." Roosevelt, *This I Remember,* p. 164.

66 Life in the Roosevelt White House is based on Martha Gellhorn's Oral History, Goodwin's *No Ordinary Time* and Lash's *Eleanor and Franklin.*

67 It is clear from their choice of companions . . . from Anna Roosevelt Halsted's Oral History.

67 FDR liked his women pliant . . . author's interview with Trude Lash, and Lash, *Eleanor and Franklin,* p. 679.

69 "You don't sleep with someone . . ." Trude Lash to author.

69 "I realize more and more that FDR . . ." Lash, *Love, Eleanor,* p. 242.

69 "Last night . . ." Streitmatter, *Empty Without You,* p. 218.

70 "I've never known a man . . ." *The Autobiography of ER,* p. 159.

70 "Don't upset yourself . . ." Elliott Roosevelt and James Brough, *Mother R— Eleanor Roosevelt's Untold Story* (New York: Putnam, 1977), p. 110.

71 "The bond of their shared history was strong . . ." Roosevelt, *My Day,* p. 44.

71 "Dearest Babs . . ." FDR letters at FDR Library.

71 Roosevelt . . . master of compartmentalization . . . Oral Histories of Anna Roosevelt Halsted, James Roosevelt and Marquis Childs, and author's interviews with Arthur Schlesinger, Jr., and Trude Lash. For more on the "two-camp" White House see Martha Gellhorn Oral History and *My Roosevelt Years* by Norman M. Littell (Seattle: University of Washington Press, 1987), p. 23.

71–3 "Of what was inside him . . . Sis, you see about this . . ." James Roosevelt, Anna Roosevelt Halsted, Elliott Roosevelt Oral Histories.

71 Like other wives of charismatic leaders . . . author's interview with Trude Lash.

73 On the eve of FDR's first fireside chat . . . Roosevelt, *My Day,* p. 85.

73 "To the prisoners of newspapers . . ." Roosevelt, *My Day,* p. 80.

74 "The unemployed are not a strange . . ." Allida M. Black, *Casting Her Own Shadow* (New York: Columbia University Press, 1981), p. 29.

74 "I warned you . . ." David Burnham, *Above the Law* (New York: Scribner's, 1996), p. 271.

74 For Eleanor's role at the convention, see Roosevelt, *This I Remember,* pp. 215–18, and Goodwin, *No Ordinary Time,* pp. 110–36, and press reports from July 19, 1940.

77 "I was conscious of the fact that because I saw . . ." Roosevelt, *My Day,* p. 215.

77 Winston Churchill's letter to his wife is from *Winston and Clementine: The Personal Letters of the Churchills,* edited by Mary Soames (Boston: Houghton Mifflin, 1999), p. 483.

78 Eleanor's letter to her daughter, Anna, is reprinted in Asbell, *Mother and Daughter,* p. 145.

78 "Hustle did you say . . ." November 18, 1942, *London Daily Mail.*

79 A classic Eleanor-Franklin clash . . . "My Day," August 13, 1943; Lash, *Eleanor and Franklin,* p. 216: Goodwin, *No Ordinary Time,* p. 174.

80 After forty years . . . based on Ferrell's *The Dying President; Closest Companion* by Geoffrey C. Ward; and Jim Bishop *FDR's Last Year* (New York: Morrow, 1974). Also, Anna Roosevelt Halsted Oral History.

80 Though unwilling to face up to . . . Lash, *A World of Love,* p. 146.

83 "All right, Franklin . . ." Chester Bowles Oral History.

83 Edith Wilson, who knew something . . . Frances Perkins Oral History.

85 "He might have been happier . . ." Roosevelt, *This I Remember,* pp. 349–51.

86 "We never talked about this . . ." author's conversation with Winthrop Rutherfurd III.

Chapter 3
BESS AND HARRY TRUMAN

88 The core of this chapter is based on Harry Truman's letters to Bess, which are found in *Dear Bess: The Letters from Harry to Bess Truman 1910–1959,* edited by Robert H. Ferrell (New York: Norton, 1983); *Where the Buck Stops: The Personal and Private Writings of Harry S. Truman,* edited by Margaret Truman (New York: Warner Books, 1989); and *Memoirs of Harry S. Truman* (New York: Doubleday, 1956). Also, the author's interviews with Margaret Truman Daniel and Clark Clifford and former White House chief usher Rex Scouten. The following secondary sources helped fill in the background of the Trumans' story: David McCullough's *Truman* (New York: Simon & Schuster, 1992); *Conflict and Crisis* by Robert J. Donovan (New York: Norton, 1977), and *Tumultuous Years: The Presidency of Harry S. Truman 1949–1953,* also by Donovan (New York: Norton, 1982); *Man of the People: A Life of Harry S. Truman* by Alonzo L. Hamby (Oxford: Oxford University Press, 1905); *Bess and Harry: An American Love Story* by Jhan Robbins (New York: Putnam, 1980); *Bess W. Truman* by Margaret Truman (New York: Jove Books/ Macmillan, 1986); *Upstairs at the White House* by J. B. West (New York: Coward, McCann & Geoghegan, 1973).

88 "I never saw a human being . . ." Clark Clifford to the author.

90 Aboard FDR's special funeral train . . . Frances Perkins Oral History.

90 "A woman's place in public . . ." Margaret Truman to author.

95 "Suppose Miss Lizzie . . ." David McCullough's *Truman*, p. 579.

96 "I agree with you that the D.A.R. . . ." This letter is reprinted in *Bess W. Truman*, p. 321.

97 It was more than just midwestern reserve . . . author's interview with Margaret Truman.

97 The story of Truman and the Russian ambassador was related to the author by Clark Clifford.

98 Bess did not even try to mask . . . Millicent Fenwick Oral History, Columbia University.

98 "Bess, think of history . . ." Margaret Truman to author.

99 "Because Harry so valued her . . ." Mary Lasker Oral History, Columbia University.

99 "Though Bess hated life in the . . ." Clark Clifford to author.

100 "She advised that he fire FDR's . . ." Clark Clifford to the author.

101 "The three of us had been . . ." Robbins, *Bess and Harry*, p. 83.

101 Bess Truman never held a single news conference . . . Margaret Truman to author.

103 "Harry and I have been sweethearts . . ." Margaret Truman to author.

Chapter 4
JACQUELINE AND JOHN KENNEDY

104 I am indebted to a great many people for this chapter: Arthur Schlesinger, Jr., Lady Bird Johnson, Benjamin Bradlee, Theodore Sorensen, Richard Reeves, Paul Fay, Jane Stanton Hitchcock, Lisa Drew, Linda Bird Francke, Ambassador Robin Duke, Kitty Hart, George Crile, Clark Clifford, Rex Scouten, William J. Vanden Heuvel and Joe Armstrong all contributed their personal memories of John F. Kennedy and Jacqueline Bouvier Kennedy Onassis. There are a great many serious and not so serious works on the subject of the Kennedys. My job, as well as that of all future Kennedy scholars, has been made considerably easier by the work of Carl Anthony Sferrzza, whose collection of quotes from Kennedy friends and family, *As We Remember Her* (New York: HarperCollins, 1997) was an invaluable source for this chapter. The John Fitzgerald Kennedy Library at Harvard University provided Oral Histories and correspondence and I thank them for their cooperation. See additional sources on pp. 367–68.

104 "I know my husband was devoted to me . . ." Oral History reprinted in Sferrzza, *As We Remember Her*, p. 189.

105 "Since Jack is such a violently independent . . ." Ibid., p. 78.

107 "I only care for the lonely sea . . ." Ibid., p. 7.

108 "I really can't understand why . . ." Kathleen Kennedy's letter to her brother Jack is reprinted in *The Search for JFK* by Joan and Clay Blair, Jr. (New York: Putnam, 1976), p. 281.

109 "She knew instantly . . ." Sferrzza, *As We Remember Her.*

109 "He found his true love too late . . ." Arthur Schlesinger, Jr., to author.

109 "What do you want to talk to my wife about? . . ." Laura Berquist Knebel Oral History, JFK Library.

110 "It was difficult . . ." Sferrzza, *As We Remember Her,* p. 101.

110 The story of JFK's relationship to Pam Turnure was related to the author by Clark Clifford.

110 "I could never describe to you . . ." Jackie's letter to Richard Nixon is from the JFK Library.

110 "She's read every book . . ." Sferrzza, *As We Remember Her,* p. 115.

111 turn on the light . . . *A Hero for Our Time,* Ralph G. Martin (New York: Macmillan, 1983), p. 9.

111 "I wonder how it is with you, Harold . . ." Alistair Horne, *Harold Macmillan,* vol. 2: *1957–1986* (New York: Viking Press, 1989), p. 290.

111 "I could not guess how she felt . . ." Rex Scouten to the author.

112 "The one thing that happens to the President . . ." Jacqueline Kennedy Onassis Oral History at JFK Library and Sferrzza, *As We Remember Her,* p. 182.

112 "I think you are rather like me . . ." Mary Van Rensselaer Thayer, *Jacqueline Kennedy: The White House Years* (Boston: Little, Brown, 1967), p. 33.

113 The punches never stopped . . . author's interview with Raymond Lamontagne.

113 "I don't think he understood women . . ." author's interview with Ben Bradlee.

113 "I have the same feelings about career women that you do . . ." William Lawrence Oral History, JFK Library.

113 "I don't *have to* do anything . . ." author's interview with Robin Duke.

114 I'm not going to go down in the coal mines . . . August Heckscher Oral History, JFK Library.

114 "I want to make this into a grand house . . ." J. B. West, *Upstairs at the White House* (New York: Coward, McCann & Geoghegan, 1973), p. 240.

114 "You know I've never seen so many happy artists . . ." Leonard Bernstein Oral History, JFK Library.

114 Jackie's letter to Kay Halle was made available to the author by Halle's nephew, George Crile.

115 "If Jackie said he had to go . . ." William Walton Oral History, JFK Library.

115 "The Kennedys shared a love of high-level . . ." Laura Knebel Berquist Oral History, JFK Library.

116 "Before the Bay of Pigs . . ." Charles Spalding Oral History, JFK Library.

119 Jackie diverted attention away . . . Michael R. Beschloss, *The Crisis Years, Kennedy and Khrushchev 1960–1963* (New York: HarperCollins, 1992), pp. 182–210.

120 "Few people stayed immune..." author's interview with former White House aide Gwendolyn King.

120 "You know she had a marvelous facility for..." author's interview with Lady Bird Johnson.

121 "You always come to the rescue..." author's interview with Clark Clifford. See also *Counsel to the President* by Clark Clifford with Richard Holbrooke (New York: Doubleday, 1991), p. 363.

122 "Jackie donned what Arthur Schleslinger, Jr., called..." see William Walton and John Carl Warnecke Oral Histories, JFK Library.

122 "We were always trying to get her to do..." August Heckscher Oral History.

123 The first lady's willfulness... author's interview with Robin Duke.

124 "I think the best thing I could do..." *Good Housekeeping,* September 1962.

124 Jacqueline's social ease... author's interview with Ben Bradlee.

125 "You must think of him as this little boy..." Theodore White Papers, JFK Library.

126 "I watched him walk..." Dr. Janet Travell Oral History, JFK Library.

127 Three days later... Beschloss, *The Crisis Years,* p. 477.

127 "This is the first day of the world crisis..." Horne, *Harold Macmillan,* p. 364.

127 "At night after long hours..." Hugh Sidey Oral History, JFK Library.

128 The new closeness did not translate... author's interview with Richard Reeves.

129 "A journalist came into my office..." Pierre Salinger to author.

129 "During the time he was a senator..." Clark Clifford to Richard Holbrooke.

130 "He never wanted them all crowded..." Sferrzza, *As We Remember Her,* p. 193.

131 "There's only one thing I could not bear now..." C. David Heymann, *A Woman Named Jackie* (New York: Birch Lane Press Book, 1989), p. 386.

131 Jackie had seen him sick... Oral History of Janet Lee Bouvier Auchincloss, JFK Library.

132 He wanted her to get better... author's interview with Arthur Schlesinger, Jr.

132 "I miss you very much..." letter of JBK to JFK, JFK Library.

134 "Dear Mr. Chairman President..." JFK Library.

134 "One week later..." Theodore White Papers, JFK Library.

Other books used as background for this chapter:

Bradlee, Benjamin C. *Conversations with Kennedy.* New York: Norton, 1975.

Caroli, Betty Boyd. *First Ladies.* New York: Oxford University Press, 1987.

Collier, Peter, and David Horowitz. *The Kennedys: An American Drama.* New York: Summit Books, 1984.

Dickerson, Nancy. *Among Those Present: A Reporter's View of Twenty-five Years in Washington.* New York: Random House, 1976.

Halberstam, David. *The Best and the Brightest.* New York: Random House, 1969.

Isaacson, Walter, and Evan Thomas. *The Wise Men: Six Friends and the*

World They Made: Acheson, Bohlen, Harriman, Kennan, Lovett, McCloy. New York: Simon & Schuster, 1986.

Johnson, Lady Bird. *A White House Diary.* New York: Holt, Rinehart & Winston, 1970.

MacPherson, Myra. *The Power Lovers: An Intimate Look at Politics and Marriage.* New York: Putnam, 1975.

Manchester, William. *The Death of a President: November 20–November 25, 1963.* New York: Harper & Row, 1967.

O'Donnell, Kenneth P., and David F. Powers, with Joe McCarthy. *"Johnny, We Hardly Knew Ye."* Boston: Little, Brown, 1970.

Schlesinger, Arthur M., Jr. *The Cycles of American History.* Boston: Houghton Mifflin, 1986.

———. *A Thousand Days: John F. Kennedy in the White House.* Boston: Houghton Mifflin, 1965.

Sorensen, Theodore C. *Kennedy.* New York: Harper & Row, 1965.

Sulzberger, C. L. *The Last of the Giants.* New York: Macmillan, 1970.

Thomas, Helen. *Dateline: White House.* New York: Macmillan, 1975.

Travell, Janet. *Office Hours, Day and Night: The Autobiography of Janet Travell, M.D.* New York: World, 1968.

White, Theodore H. *In Search of History: A Personal Adventure.* New York: Warner Books, 1978.

Chapter 5
LADY BIRD AND LYNDON JOHNSON

137 Much of this chapter is based on an extensive interview with Mrs. Johnson. I am also indebted to Michael Beschloss, Professor Alan Brinkley, Robert Caro, Liz Carpenter, Clark Clifford, Liz Smith, Jack Valenti, Harry McPherson, Lynda Bird Johnson, Horace Busby, Katharine Graham, Hal Wingo, Barbara Howar, Charles Guggenheim and Barbara Walters for sharing their impressions and memories of President and Mrs. Johnson. At the LBJ Library in Austin, Texas, Harry Middleton and Betty Tilson gave indispensable and patient assistance. I am grateful to them all, especially Liz Smith, who was tireless in getting me the most important interview—Mrs. Johnson.

There are a number of first-rate studies of both Johnsons that I relied on for background information for this chapter. Among them: Robert Caro's *The Path to Power* (New York: Alfred A. Knopf, 1982) and *Means of Ascent* (New York: Alfred A. Knopf, 1990); Doris Kearns Goodwin's *Lyndon Johnson and the American Dream* (New York: Harper & Row, 1976); Michael Beschloss's *Taking Charge: The Johnson White House Tapes, 1963–1964* (New York: Simon & Schuster, 1997); Robert Dallek's *Flawed Giant: Lyndon Johnson and His Times, 1961–1973* (New York:

Oxford University Press, 1998); *Lyndon, An Oral Biography,* by Merle Miller (New York: Ballantine Books, 1980); and Jan Jarboe Russell's *Lady Bird* (New York: Scribner's, 1999). The Johnsons' own memoirs: Lady Bird's *A White House Diary* (New York: Holt, Rinehart & Winston, 1970), and Lyndon's *The Vantage Point: Perspectives on the Presidency, 1963–1969* (New York: Holt, Rinehart & Winston, 1971) are, of course, essential.

138 Perhaps nothing so clearly . . . based on LBJ's White House tape recordings, provided to the author by the LBJ Library.

139 As Clark Clifford later noted . . . author's interview with Clifford.

139 Lady Bird's sharpest memory . . . author's interview with Mrs. Johnson. See also Lady Bird Johnson, *White House Diary,* p. 6.

139 "I always felt sorry . . ." Lady Bird Johnson to author.

140 "The best day's work . . ." Oral History, LBJ Library.

141 "This morning . . ." this and all other correspondence quoted in this chapter is from the LBJ Library.

141 Lyndon took Lady Bird . . . based on author's interviews with Horace Busby.

142 She was a thirties wife . . . drawn from *Texas Monthly,* August 1999: "Lyndon and Lady Bird, Scenes from a Marriage"; also Caro's *Path to Power,* chapter 25.

144 "It gave me a . . . sort of reassurance . . ." Miller, *Lyndon: An Oral Biography,* p. 120.

146 In truth, Jackie admired . . . Ibid., p. 353.

147 "About five of us reporters . . ." author's interview with Hal Wingo.

148 He ordered director of White House . . . from the White House tapes, LBJ Library.

148 "One thing you've got to remember . . ." Betty Furness Oral History, LBJ Library.

148 In the White House . . . author's interview with Horace Busby.

148 "She was very vigilant . . ." author's interview with Barbara Howar.

148 "It wasn't very romantic . . ." *Among Those Present* by Nancy Dickerson (New York: Random House, 1976), p. 139.

149 "You want to listen for about one minute . . ." White House tapes, LBJ Library, and reprinted in Beschloss's *Taking Charge,* p. 272.

150 "I would stand back and watch Lyndon . . ." unpublished interview of Clark Clifford by Richard Holbrooke.

150 "I recognized it . . ." Lady Bird Johnson to author.

150 "Anybody like you who would . . ." White House tapes, LBJ Library.

151 "Johnson drew no boundaries . . ." author's interview with Rex Scouten.

152 On most mornings . . . author's interview with Jack Valenti.

152 So hungry was Johnson for affection . . . Mary Lasker Oral History, LBJ Library.

153 "One evening in the upstairs residence . . ." author's interview with Clark Clifford.

153 "If you don't want me running around the White House . . ." White House tapes, LBJ Library.

154 Texas congressman Ralph Yarborough . . . author's interview with Harry McPherson.

154 When his wife was away . . . author's interview with Homer Busby.

154 "Unlike most of his predecessors . . ." author's interview with Lady Bird Johnson.

155 Lady Bird's letter to her husband is in the LBJ Library and analyzed by her in *White House Diary,* pp. 137–40 and by Lyndon in his *Vantage Point,* pp. 93–94.

156 The self-pity and the plea for love . . . Beschloss, *Taking Charge,* pp. 527–37.

156 "Beloved . . ." August 25, 1964, LBJ Library, and Lady Bird Johnson, *White House Diary,* p. 192.

156 "In a few words . . ." Lyndon Johnson, *The Vantage Point,* p. 98.

157 Richard Nixon was startled . . . *The Memoirs of Richard Nixon* (New York: Grosset & Dunlap, 1978), p. 272.

158 Katharine Graham of the *Washington Post* . . . Miller, *Lyndon: An Oral Biography,* p. 508.

158 "You read this . . ." White House tapes, LBJ Library, reprinted in *Taking Charge,* p. 251.

158 During the 1964 . . . author's interview with Harry McPherson.

159 In Columbia . . . author's interview with Barbara Howar; also William S. White Oral History, LBJ Library; see also Eric F. Goldman, *The Tragedy of LBJ* (New York: Alfred A. Knopf, 1969), pp. 357–61.

160 As always, Lady Bird . . . Lady Bird Johnson, *White House Diary,* pp. 247–48.

160 "Sometimes it makes me almost angry . . ." *White House Diary,* p. 261.

160 Johnson's aides remember . . . Dallek, *Flawed Giant,* p. 282.

161 He continued to get important legislation passed . . . author's interview with Mrs. Johnson; also Lady Bird Johnson, *White House Diary,* pp. 349.

161 "I had coffee with Lyndon . . ." Ibid., p. 369.

162 Laurence Rockefeller . . . Oral History, LBJ Library.

162 "To see Mrs. Johnson . . ." Shana Alexander, "The Best First Lady," *Life,* December 13, 1968.

162 Stewart Udall . . . Oral History, LBJ Library.

163 "One thing I am sorry about . . ." author's interview with Mrs. Johnson; see also *Austin Statesman,* January 22, 1967, p. 7.

163 "The best thing I can do . . ." *New York Times,* September 10, 1967.

164 "I knew we were going to get into this . . ." White House tapes, LBJ Library.

164 "When five of the most . . ." author's interview with Mrs. Johnson.

165 "I turned off the TV . . ." Lady Bird Johnson, *White House Diary,* p. 521.

165 Eartha Kitt incident described in Ibid., pp. 622–24.

166 "I simply did not want . . ." Ibid., p. 567.

167 "Last night . . ." Ibid., p. 570.

168 "Remember . . . pacing . . ." Ibid., p. 645.

170 As for herself . . . author's interview with Mrs. Johnson.

Chapter 6
PAT AND RICHARD NIXON

171 Julie Nixon Eisenhower, Edward Cox, Henry Kissinger, Peter G. Peterson, David Gergen, Richard Reeves, Professor Henry F. Graff, Nixon White House aides Susan Porter Rose, Patricia Mattson, Diane Sawyer, Gwen King, Penny Adams and Chief Usher Rex Scouten all contributed their time and their memories of Richard and Pat Nixon to this chapter. Several journalists who covered the Nixons were also very helpful, among them: Richard Cohen, Barbara Walters, Helen Thomas, Donnie Radcliffe and Barrie Dunsmore.

There are a great many studies of the Nixon presidency that were essential in providing background for this chapter, including: Nixon's own *Memoirs* (New York: Grosset & Dunlap, 1978); *Richard Nixon: The Rise of an American Politician* by Roger Morris (New York: Henry Holt, 1990); *Pat Nixon: The Untold Story* by Julie Nixon Eisenhower (New York: Simon & Schuster, 1986); *The Haldeman Diaries: Inside the Nixon White House* by H. R. Haldeman (New York: Putnam, 1994); *The White House Years* by Henry Kissinger (Boston: Little, Brown, 1979); *Nixon: The Education of a Politician, 1913–1962* by Stephen E. Ambrose (New York: Simon & Schuster, 1987); *The Lonely Lady of San Clemente: The Story of Pat Nixon* by Lester David (New York: Thomas Y. Crowell, 1978); *Richard Nixon: A Political and Personal Portrait* by Earl Mazo (New York: Harper & Brothers, 1959); *One of Us* by Tom Wicker (New York: Random House, 1991).

171 Pat asked for cottage cheese . . . J. B. West, *Upstairs at the White House* (New York: Coward, McCann & Geoghegan, 1973), p. 356.

172 For a description of the Caracas spitting incident, see Ambrose, *Nixon: The Education of a Politician,* p. 473.

173 "Despite your refusal to let me . . ." This and other correspondence between Richard and Pat Nixon and the account of their courtship is from Julie Nixon Eisenhower's memoir of her mother.

174 He once revealed that his mother . . . Televised interview of Richard Nixon by Frank Gannon, Richard Nixon Library.

174 "If your anger is deep enough . . ." Ken Clawson, "A Loyalist's Memoirs," *Washington Post,* Outlook Section, August 9, 1979.

174 "I can't let my hair down . . ." Stewart Alsop, *Nixon and Rockfeller: A Double Portrait* (New York: Doubleday, 1960), p. 200.

175 "There was no talk of politics . . ." Mazo, *Richard Nixon,* p. 34.

177 "Once I make a decision . . ." Frank Gannon television interview, Richard Nixon Library.

178 "It was the last carefree vacation . . ." Julie Nixon Eisenhower to author.

179 "Dick was sitting in a huge . . ." Wicker, *One of Us,* p. 89.

181 When Pat's old friend . . . Eisenhower, *Pat Nixon,* pp. 171–72.

181 "We don't have as many . . ." Ambrose, *Nixon,* p. 350.

181 "You don't know . . ." Michael Beschloss, *Mayday: Eisenhower, Khrushchev and the U-2 Affair* (New York: Harper & Row, 1986), p. 180.

181 "You probably have never . . ." Eisenhower, *Pat Nixon*, p. 178.

182 Pat almost never complained . . . author's interview with Rex Scouten.

182 "Once you get into this . . ." Mazo, *Richard Nixon*, p. 157.

182 She rarely expressed an opinion . . . Ambrose, *Nixon*, p. 577.

182 She hated reminders of the past . . . David, *The Lonely Lady of San Clemente*, p. 89.

183 "[Pat] saw a stolen election . . ." Eisenhower, *Pat Nixon*, p. 204.

184 Feminist writer Gloria Steinem . . . David, *The Lonely Lady of San Clemente*, pp. 89–90.

186 "I'll have to have a room of my own . . ." West, *Upstairs at the White House*, p. 357.

186 The tone of the Executive Mansion . . . from the Oral History of Constance Stuart, author's interviews with Gwendolyn King, Susan Porter Rose, Patricia Mattson; see also *Haldeman Diaries* as well as David, *The Lonely Lady of San Clemente*, pp. 164–66, and "Pat Nixon's Final Days in the White House" by Helen McCain Smith, *Good Housekeeping*, July 1976.

186 White House memoranda quoted are from the National Archives.

187 Though Nixon tried . . . author's interview with Diane Sawyer.

189 Pett later wrote her . . . Eisenhower, *Pat Nixon*, p. 340.

189 "If she goes . . ." *Haldeman Diaries*, p. 364.

189 "I used to see her in the White House . . ." author's interview with Patricia Mattson.

190 "She told me exactly how she wanted . . ." David, *The Lonely Lady of San Clemente*, p. 145.

190 "A recommendation has been made . . ." White House memo, January 14, 1972, National Archives.

191 "I think it is important . . ." Constance Stuart Oral History, Richard Nixon Library.

191 The one told most frequently . . . *Washington Post* reporter Donnie Radcliffe to the author.

191 "I knew that the road had been hardest . . ." Nixon's *Memoirs*, p. 687.

192 "Her way of dealing with conflict . . ." Julie Nixon Eisenhower to author.

192 "I was not as upbeat as I should have been . . ." Nixon's *Memoirs*, p. 717; also, author's interview with Nixon commerce secretary Peter G. Peterson.

193 "I'm going to relax . . ." author's interview with Gwendolyn King.

194 "I hope I don't wake up . . ." Julie Nixon Eisenhower to the author.

194 "Just tell it . . ." *New York Times*, March 16, 1999.

Chapter 7
BETTY AND GERALD FORD

199 For this chapter I relied on interviews with Betty Ford's press secretary, Sheila Weidenfeld, photographer and Ford family intimate David Ken-

nerly, Rex Scouten, Ford presidential aide Stuart Spencer, Ford White House staffers Patricia Mattson and Gwendolyn King, journalists Donnie Radcliffe, Barbara Walters and Morley Safer. Documentation was furnished by the Gerald R. Ford Library, the University of Michigan, Ann Arbor.

Though I have met and spoken with Mrs. Ford several times in Vail, Colorado, and at a gathering of former first ladies in Bakersfield, California, in October 1996, Mrs. Ford declined to participate in a formal interview. However, her own memoirs, Betty Ford, *The Times of My Life* (New York: Harper & Row, 1978) and *Betty, A Glad Awakening* (Garden City, N.Y.: Doubleday, 1987) are characteristically open and revealing.

201 The quotes from President Ford are found in *A Time to Heal: The Autobiography of Gerald R. Ford* (New York: Harper & Row, 1979).

202 In April 1954 . . . *Washington Post,* April 4, 1954, p. 95.

203 "I'll never forget it . . ." Betty Ford, *The Times of My Life,* p. 123.

204 "In a widely read . . . article . . ." *McCall's,* February 1975.

205 There was a new atmosphere . . . author's interviews with Rex Scouten and Gwendolyn King.

205 The seventies were, of course . . . Winifred D. Wandersee, *On the Move* (Boston: Twayne, 1988), chapter 8.

206 "They were a playful couple . . ." author's interview with David Kennerly.

206 "I kept pushing . . ." Betty Ford, *The Times of My Life,* p. 201.

207 "I went to bed laughing . . ." *Time,* March 3, 1975.

207 "I couldn't understand . . ." *First Lady's Lady* by Sheila R. Weidenfeld (New York: Putnam), p. 357.

207 "Jerry has never . . ." Betty Ford, *The Times of My Life,* p. 206.

207 "As you are well aware . . ." document from Gerald Ford Library.

207 "If she got unhappy . . ." author's interview with Kennerly.

208 In August 1975 . . . author's interview with Morley Safer.

210 "Why should my husband's job . . ." October 25, 1975, Cleveland conference on International Women's Year, transcript in Gerald Ford Library.

212 "I had a great deal of pain . . ." Barbara Walters interview, February 26, 1987.

212 "I had always used alcohol . . ." Barbara Walters interview.

Chapter 8
ROSALYNN AND JIMMY CARTER

215 I am grateful for the extensive interview former first lady Rosalynn Carter granted me. Additional material for this chapter came from interviews with former members of the Carter administration, including Vice President Walter Mondale, Jody Powell, Gerald Rafshoon, Tom Donilon, Pat Caddell, James Johnson, Maxine Isaacs, Richard Holbrooke and Paul Costello. Journalists Sally Quinn, Donnie Radcliffe, Lesley Stahl, and historian Douglas Brinkley gave generously of their time and knowledge, as

did Ambassador Robin Chandler Duke, Clark Clifford, Rex Scouten, Meg Greenfield, Richard Beattie, Linda Bird Francke and President and Mrs. Carter's publisher, Peter Osnos.

Peter G. Bourne's *Jimmy Carter* (New York: Scribner's, 1997), Rosalynn Carter's memoir, *First Lady from Plains* (Boston: Houghton Mifflin, 1984) and Jimmy Carter's *Keeping Faith: The Memoirs of a President* (New York: Bantam Books, 1982) are essential for understanding the Carters. Also, Elizabeth Drew's lengthy *New Yorker* article on the Carter presidency, "In Search of Definition," August, 27, 1979, and James Fallows's, "The Passionless Presidency," *Atlantic Monthly,* September 1979, provided many insights.

217 She was not prepared for what she saw . . . based on the author's interviews with Mrs. Carter and Richard Holbrooke.

218 One of those who helped . . . author's interviews with Pat Caddell and Gerald Rafshoon.

220 "I felt I became independent . . ." author's interview with Mrs. Carter.

220 "I argued, I cried . . ." Rosalynn Carter, *First Lady from Plains,* p. 29.

220 "We're home . . ." Ibid., p. 30.

222 "I don't take defeat easily . . ." author's interview with Mrs. Carter.

223 Few believe he could have been . . . author's interview with Gerald Rafshoon.

224 "I loved the politics and Jimmy never did . . ." author's interview with Mrs. Carter; also Rosalynn Carter, *First Lady from Plains,* p. 122.

224 "I have never seen a political . . ." Bourne, *Jimmy Carter,* p. 345.

225 "How many of you would like to have . . ." *New York Times,* March 20, 1977.

225 "Be kind to us . . ." author's interview with Barbara Walters.

226 Noting awkward lapses . . . author's interview with Ambassador Robin Duke.

227 "Everybody always wants more . . ." Rosalynn Carter, *First Lady from Plains,* p. 177.

227 "But she did not understand . . ." author's interview with Richard Beattie.

228 "Image . . . became a . . ." Rosalynn Carter, *First Lady from Plains,* p. 183.

228 "I found not one word . . ." Ibid., p. 182.

228 "She wanted to be covered . . ." author's interview with Donnie Radcliffe.

228 "We are from Plains . . ." author's interview with Rosalynn Carter.

229 "We were en route to . . ." author's interview with Paul Costello.

230 "If Rosalynn didn't like you . . ." author's interview with Douglas Brinkley.

230 "I have found . . ." *New York Times Magazine,* June 3, 1979.

230 "There was more than a little . . ." author's interview with Mrs. Carter; see also Rosalynn Carter, *First Lady from Plains,* p. 198.

230 "I am closer to the President . . ." *New York Times,* June 6, 1977.

231 "The question raised by . . ." *Newsweek,* June 20, 1977.

231 "The unspoken question behind . . ." *New York Times,* June 15, 1977.

231 Rosalynn brushed off the critics . . . author's interview with Mrs. Carter.

231 "Well, Rosie . . ." *New York Times Magazine,* June 3, 1979.

232 "We used to joke . . ." *Character Above All,* edited by Robert A. Wilson (New York: Simon & Schuster, 1995), p. 184.

232 "I couldn't believe it . . ." Rosalynn Carter, *First Lady from Plains,* p. 175.

233 Each of Carter's aides had . . . Jody Powell to the author.

233 "When I come home very discouraged . . ." *New York Times Magazine,* June 3, 1979.

233 When Carter told longtime . . . Richard Holbrooke to the author.

233 "There's no way I could discuss . . ." Mrs. Carter to author.

233 "I never considered not attending . . ." Rosalynn Carter, *First Lady from Plains,* p. 185.

233 "Rosalynn was the one to point out . . ." author's interview with Jody Powell.

234 "The Begins . . . always seemed . . ." Jimmy Carter, *Keeping Faith,* p. 329.

234 "Waiting for Sadat to arrive . . ." Ibid., p. 328.

235 When Rosalynn was forced . . . Rosalynn Carter, *First Lady from Plains,* p. 281.

235 "The worst thing you could say to Carter . . ." author's interview with Vice President Walter Mondale.

237 Caddell showed Rosalynn a memorandum . . . author's interview with Pat Caddell.

237 "I had majored in social psychology . . ." author's interview with Walter Mondale.

237 "It's not easy for me to accept . . ." Bourne, *Jimmy Carter,* p. 444.

238 Caddell's hoped-for transformation . . . author's interview with Pat Caddell.

238 One of the many ideas tossed out . . . author's interview with Gerald Rafshoon.

239 "I saw real despair there . . ." author's interview with Walter Mondale.

239 "But there he was, running harder . . ." Ibid.

240 Reporters dubbed her the nurse . . . author's interview with Sally Quinn; see also *Washington Post,* July 25, 1979.

241 So Rosalynn set off on another round . . . author's interview with Paul Costello.

241 "All the understandable . . ." Rosalynn Carter, *First Lady from Plains,* p. 365.

243 "What would I have done . . ." *New York Times,* May 12, 1999.

Chapter 9
NANCY AND RONALD REAGAN

244 I am grateful to Nancy Reagan for allowing me to spend an afternoon with her, though she did not wish me to take notes of our conversation. I also wish to thank Kenneth Duberstein, Stuart Spencer, Michael Deaver, Frances FitzGerald, David Gergen, Professor Alan Brinkley, Professor Henry F. Graff, Mike Wallace, Gahl Burt, former Canadian prime minister Brian Mulrooney and Mila Mulrooney, Katharine Graham, Lesley Stahl, Tom Brokaw, Peggy Noonan, Peter G. Peterson, Rex Scouten, Susan Porter Rose, Liz Smith, Mort and Linda Janklow, Sherrie Rollins Westin, and Dr. Mitchell Rosenthal for their time and their willingness to

help me understand the Reagans. Those conversations form the backbone of this chapter.

Ronald and Nancy Reagan have each written memoirs; his, *An American Life* (New York: Simon & Schuster, 1990) was less revealing than hers, *My Turn: The Memoirs of Nancy Reagan* (New York: Random House, 1989). The correspondence between Ronald and Nancy Reagan is reprinted from *I Love You, Ronnie: The Letters of Ronald Reagan to Nancy Reagan* (New York: Random House, 2000).

I have also relied on the following excellent studies of the Reagans: Anne Edwards, *Early Reagan: The Rise to Power* (New York: Morrow, 1987); two works by Lou Cannon, a *Washington Post* reporter who spent many years covering Reagan: *Reagan* (New York: Putnam, 1982) and *President Reagan: The Role of a Lifetime* (New York: Simon & Schuster, 1991); Robert Dallek's *Ronald Reagan: The Politics of Symbolism* (Cambridge: Harvard University Press, 1984); Strobe Talbott, *Deadly Gambits: The Reagan Administration and the Stalemate in Arms Control* (New York: Alfred A. Knopf, 1984); George P. Shultz, *Turmoil and Triumph: My Years as Secretary of State* (New York: Scribner's, 1993); Peggy Noonan's *What I Saw at the Revolution: A Political Life in the Reagan Era* (New York: Random House, 1990); Donald T. Regan, *For the Record: From Wall Street to Washington* (New York: Harcourt Brace Jovanovich, 1988); *Behind the Scenes* by Michael Deaver with Mickey Herskowitz (New York: Morrow, 1987).

244 "[Nancy] was the ignition . . ." Meg Greenfield, *Washington* (New York: PublicAffairs, 2001), p. 216.

244 "Show me an executive . . ." Cannon, *Reagan,* p. 304.

245 "Surround yourself . . ." author's interview with Michael Deaver.

245 "He listened . . ." Regan, *For the Record,* p. 268.

246 "Most of my suggestions . . ." Nancy Reagan, *My Turn,* p. 60.

246 "In some ways . . ." Ronald Reagan, *An American Life,* p. 167.

247 "There's a wall around him . . ." Nancy Reagan, *My Turn,* p. 106.

247 "Janie is a pretty sick girl . . ." *New Yorker,* July 26, 1999.

248 "Don't ask Ronnie for the time . . ." Michael Deaver to the author.

248 "I taught Maureen . . ." Edwards, *Early Reagan,* p. 255.

248 Reagan was on Nancy Davis's . . . Linda Leroy Janklow to the author.

248 "How come you moved in on me . . ." *I Love You, Ronnie,* p. 61.

248 "It nearly killed her . . ." *My Turn,* pp. 69–70.

249 Nancy discovered that . . . *Washington Post,* May 1, 1980, Style, F1.

250 "They look at me . . ." Michael Deaver to the author.

250 The Reagans' love and need . . . *I Love You, Ronnie,* p. 55.

251 "We can preserve for our children . . ." *The Presidents,* Henry F. Graff, editor (New York: Macmillan, 1997), p. 574.

251 In those early days . . . author's interview with former Reagan secretary Nancy Reynolds.

252 Mike Wallace . . . an old friend . . . author's interview with Mike Wallace.

252 Nancy's role as her husband's . . . author's interview with Stuart Spencer.

254 In 1968, Joan Didion . . . *Saturday Evening Post,* June 1, 1968.

254 "Almost two decades later . . ." author's interview with Sally Quinn.

254 "How can you challenge an . . ." *A Time to Heal: The Autobiography of Gerald R. Ford* (New York: Harper & Row, 1979), pp. 333–34.

255 "When one of us has a problem . . ." Ronald Reagan, *An American Life,* p. 167.

255 "Everything began with you . . ." *I Love You, Ronnie,* p. 97.

255 His impressive physical . . . author's interview with Gahl Burt.

255 "I love the whole gang of you . . ." Ibid., p. 160.

255 "But what is really important . . ." Ibid., p. 76.

255 "I never had a real conversation . . ." "Biography of Ronald Reagan," Arts and Entertainment Network.

256 Ronnie called her Mommy . . . author's interview with Nancy Reynolds.

256 "He knows so little . . ." Shultz, *Turmoil and Triumph,* p. 1134.

257 "Ronnie can't be pushed . . ." Anne Edwards, *Early Reagan,* p. 480.

257 "She can smell fear on you . . ." Ed Rollins, *Bare Knuckles and Back Rooms* (New York: Broadway Books, 1996), p. 137.

258 "If I did not hear from her . . ." author's interview with Mike Deaver.

258 "Mrs. Reagan liked to joke . . ." author's interview with Gahl Burt.

258 "Oh, my God . . ." author's interview with Lesley Stahl.

259 "Bush and I would . . ." author's interview with Mike Deaver.

259 "It would be far better . . ." Nancy Reagan, *My Turn,* p. 64.

260 "Ronald Reagan was the most . . ." author's interview with Mike Deaver.

260 Two months into his presidency . . . Ronald Reagan, *An American Life,* p. 269.

260 "Nancy called me . . ." author's interview with Mike Deaver.

261 Reports of Reagan's memory lapses . . . author's interview with Arthur Link.

261 "The contrast between . . ." author's interview with Barrie Dunsmore.

262 "Why wasn't the same thing . . ." *Newsweek,* December 21, 1981.

263 "How do you describe someone . . ." *Newsweek,* December 21, 1981.

263 "I wore white pantaloons . . ." Nancy Reagan, *My Turn,* p. 41.

263 "Nancy had a tropism . . ." author's interview with Peggy Noonan.

264 "I liked Nancy . . ." Katharine Graham to the author.

264 When an aide cautioned . . . Mike Deaver to the author.

265 "There was something likable . . ." Ronald Reagan, *An American Life,* p. 635.

265 "The bureaucrats . . ." Mike Deaver to the author.

265 "He felt that if an American . . ." Peggy Noonan to the author.

265 "Nancy believed . . ." Mike Deaver to the author.

266 "I had a lot of talk with Nancy . . ." *Vanity Fair,* August 1998, and Shultz, *Turmoil and Triumph,* p. 483.

267 Nancy also played a big part . . . author's interview with Kenneth Duberstein.

267 "If . . . I could take back one decision . . ." Nancy Reagan, *My Turn,* p. 312.

268 "I don't think Don Regan . . ." author's interview with Mike Deaver.

269   "By now . . ." Regan, *For the Record,* p. 76.

269   "Apparently Deaver . . ." Ibid., p. 74.

269   "We weren't dealing . . ." Bob Woodward, *Shadow* (New York: Simon & Schuster, 1999), p. 140.

269   "I had to keep trying . . ." Shultz, *Turmoil and Triumph,* p. 868.

270   "Sometimes . . ." Ibid., p. 1133.

271   "Mike, I've got . . ." author's interview with Mike Deaver.

271   "We missed him while he was here . . ." PBS biography of Ronald Reagan ("The American Experience"), 1998.

271   "I think she felt for the kids . . ." author's interview with Dr. Mitchell Rosenthal.

272   "You are remote . . ." Barbara Walters interview on *20/20,* November 17, 1989.

Chapter 10
BARBARA AND GEORGE BUSH

274   Though I have spent time in both Washington, D.C., and New York in President and Mrs. Bush's company, they declined to sit down for formal interviews. For profiling them, I therefore relied on my personal impressions of the couple as well as on interviews with Thomas "Lud" Ashley, Jonathan Alter, Joe Klein, Craig Fuller, Anna Perez, Susan Porter Rose, David Gergen, Lisa Drew, Marlin Fitzwater, Sherrie Rollins Westin, Rex Scouten, Ann McDaniel, Margaret Carlson, Bunny Murdoch, Diane Sawyer, Richard Haas, Peggy Noonan, Roger Ailes, Lesley Stahl, Richard Cohen, Margaret Warner, Donnie Radcliffe, Sally Quinn, former Canadian prime minister Brian Mulrooney and Mila Mulrooney and Barbara Walters.

      Barbara Bush: A Memoir (New York: Scribner's, 1994) and Herbert S. Parmet's very solid biography of George Bush, *George Bush: The Life of a Lone Star Yankee* (New York: Scribner's, 1997), were also important sources; the many others are cited below.

274   "I want you all to take a look . . ." Donnie Radcliffe to the author. See also "Barbara's Backlash" by Marjorie Williams, *Vanity Fair,* August 1992.

276   It was she . . . author's interviews with Bush family friend Lud Ashley, and Peggy Noonan.

276   "Bar's the one . . ." Richard Ben Cramer, *What It Takes* (New York: Vintage Books, 1992), p. 576.

276   "Barbara was always . . ." author's interview with Roger Ailes.

277   "We stopped discussing . . ." Parmet, *George Bush: Lone Star Yankee,* p. 426.

278   "I'll tell you in one sentence . . ." Ann Grimes, *Running Mates: The Making of a First Lady* (New York: Morrow, 1990), p. 54.

278   "All our children were planned . . ." Gail Sheehy, "Is George Bush too Nice to be President?" *Vanity Fair,* February 1987.

278 "I have never felt . . ." This and all the letters quoted in this chapter are published in *All the Best, George Bush* (New York: Scribner's, 1999).

279 "You shouldn't have to tell . . ." Margaret Garrard Warner, "The Wimp Factor," *Newsweek,* October 19, 1987.

279 "Barbara knows how to hate . . ." author's interview with Thomas "Lud" Ashley.

281 "George Bush, and maybe this is a fault . . ." Sheehy, *Vanity Fair,* February 1987.

281 "I can always find . . ." Ibid.

281 "He learned to rely . . ." author's interview with Lud Ashley.

281 "I'd like it . . ." Parmet, *George Bush: Lone Star Yankee,* p. 36.

282 "She's got this great . . ." author's interview with Lud Ashley.

282 "I've always wanted to . . ." Cramer, *What It Takes,* p. 142.

283 "How George loves . . ." *Barbara Bush: A Memoir* (New York: St. Martin's Paperback, 1994) p. 248.

283 Like so many other men . . . Cramer, *What It Takes,* chapters 8 and 9.

284 "One of the reasons . . ." *Barbara Bush: A Memoir,* p. 60.

284 "The day after Robin died . . ." Ibid., pp. 48–50.

284 "I still favor the problem being handled . . ." Lud Ashley to the author.

285 "In a sense it was a matriarchal family . . ." Bill Minutaglio, *First Son: George W. Bush and the Bush Family Dynasty* (New York: Times Books, 1999), p. 57.

285 "She did it all . . ." Grimes, *Running Mates,* p. 58.

286 Bush never quite managed to define . . . *Newsweek,* October 19, 1987.

286 "George Bush never . . ." Sheehy, *Vanity Fair,* February 1987.

286 Nixon came through . . . author's interview with Lud Ashley.

287 "You have two choices . . ." *Barbara Bush: A Memoir,* p. 10.

288 "The Bushes have an . . ." author's interview with Susan Porter Rose.

288 "Although this was planned . . ." *Barbara Bush: A Memoir,* p. 125.

289 She was one of those women . . . This section is based on the author's interviews with Craig Fuller, Susan Porter Rose, Gahl Burt and Bunny Murdoch.

289 "I was very depressed . . ." *Barbara Bush: A Memoir,* p. 144.

291 "*we* became . . ." Cramer, *What It Takes,* p. 152.

291 In 1984 . . . author's interview with Craig Fuller.

292 She learned it . . . *Barbara Bush: A Memoir,* p. 208.

292 "There were times . . ." Grimes, *Running Mates,* p. 186.

292 "There's nothing wrong with . . ." Donnie Radcliffe, *Simply Barbara Bush* (New York: Warner Books, 1989), p. xvii.

293 "As long as Jennifer . . ." author's interview with Craig Fuller; see also Parmet, *George Bush: Lone Star Yankee,* chapter 14.

293 "I decided to raise it . . ." author's interview with Craig Fuller.

294 "She's a wonderful lady . . ." author's interview with Barbara Walters.

294 "Barbara Bush was an ideal . . ." author's interview with David Gergen.

295 "We do things . . ." Radcliffe, *Simply Barbara Bush,* p. 195.

295 "We wanted very much for it . . ." Grimes, *Running Mates,* p. 258.

295 "I am [Nancy's] greatest . . ." *20/20* interview with Barbara Walters, January 20, 1989.

295 Barbara refused to comment . . . author's interview with Anna Perez.

296 "I'm gonna approach my job . . ." *20/20,* January 20, 1989.

296 "I don't think he would . . ." author's interview with Craig Fuller.

296 "She had this way . . ." author's interview with Donnie Radcliffe.

296 "She could cut you down . . ." author's interview with Rex Scouten.

296 Few people who . . . author's interview with Bunny Murdoch.

296 "Vice President Bush . . ." author's interview with Marlin Fitzwater.

297 "I'm not too sure . . ." *Barbara Bush: A Memoir,* p. 228.

297 "She would not . . ." author's interview with Roger Ailes.

297 "Shortly after Bush's . . ." author's interview with Donnie Radcliffe.

298 "Hillary Rodham Clinton is . . ." *Barbara Bush: A Memoir,* p. 228.

298 "I'd always go and see . . ." author's interview with Brian Mulrooney.

299 "So," she said with a hard smile . . . Cramer, *What It Takes,* p. 620.

299 "I've known very few chiefs . . ." author's interview with Roger Ailes.

299 "She picked up that . . ." author's interview with Lud Ashley.

299 "I love John Sununu . . ." *20/20* interview with Barbara Walters, June 26, 1992.

299 Barbara rarely lost . . . Margaret Carlson, "The White Gloves Come Off," *Time,* September 26, 1994.

299 "She is a lovely-looking . . ." *Barbara Bush: A Memoir,* p. 225.

300 "Absolutely . . ." Radcliffe, *Simply Barbara Bush,* pp. 62–63.

300 "Long ago . . ." *Barbara Bush: A Memoir,* p. 292.

300 "George has always . . ." Radcliffe, *Simply Barbara Bush,* p. 59.

302 "The wheels came off . . ." author's interview with Lud Ashley.

303 "I'm sorry Barbara . . ." Jack Germond and Jules Witcover, *Mad As Hell* (New York: Warner Books, 1992), p. 245.

303 The 1992 Republican convention . . . author's interviews with Jonathan Alter and Joe Klein.

303 "Mila [Mrs. Mulrooney] chided Barbara . . ." author's interview with Brian Mulrooney.

Chapter 11
HILLARY AND BILL CLINTON

306 I am grateful to many people for helping me with this chapter: first of all, Hillary Clinton for the interview she gave me in 1997 and for subsequent occasions that enabled me to observe both Clintons in a number of official and unofficial situations. Melanne Verveer, Mandy Grunwald, Donna Shalala, Laura D'Andrea Tyson, George Stephanopoulos, Arthur Schlesinger, Jr., Steven Ricchetti, Paul Begala, Ambassador Tom Siebert, Tom Caplan, Brooke Shearer, Ambassador Derek Shearer, Strobe Tal-

bott, Ruth Goldway, Lisa Caputo, Ambassador Betty King, Ellen Chessler, David Gergen, Margaret Carlson, Joe Klein, Jonathan Alter, Ann Blackman, Sally Quinn, Robert Boorstin, Ann Stock, Maureen White, Steven Rattner, Mike Berman, Vernon and Ann Jordan, David Maraniss, Doug Schoen, Bob Woodward and Lloyd Cutler all gave of their time and their insights. I cannot thank them enough.

There are many—some would say too many—books on the Clintons and the Clinton presidency. Among the ones I found useful are: *First in His Class* by David Maraniss (New York: Touchstone Books, 1995); *Hillary Clinton: The Inside Story* by Judith Warner (New York: Signet Books, 1993); Gail Sheehy's *Hillary's Choice* (New York: Random House, 1999); *All Too Human* by George Stephanopoulos (New York, Boston: Little, Brown, 1999); *On the Edge* by Elizabeth Drew (New York: Simon & Schuster, 1994); *The Seduction of Hillary Rodham Clinton* by David Brock (New York: Free Press, 1996); *Blood Sport: The President and His Adversaries* by James B. Stewart (New York: Simon & Schuster, 1996); *Shadow: Five Presidents and the Legacy of Watergate* by Bob Woodward (New York: Simon & Schuster, 1999); *The Choice* by Bob Woodward (New York: Simon & Schuster, 1996); *The Agenda: Inside the Clinton White House,* also by Bob Woodward (New York: Simon & Schuster, 1994); *Eyewitness to Power: The Essence of Leadership from Nixon to Clinton* by David Gergen (New York: Simon & Schuster, 2000). The best single account of the Clintons' attempted health care reform is *The System: The American Way of Politics at the Breaking Point* by Haynes Johnson and David S. Broder (New York, Boston: Little, Brown, 1997); Jeffrey Toobin's *A Vast Conspiracy: The Real Story of the Sex Scandal That Nearly Brought Down a President* (New York: Random House, 1999); *Behind the Oval Office* by Dick Morris (New York: Random House, 1997); *The Breach* by Peter Baker (New York: Scribner's, 2000); and *Truth at Any Cost* by Susan Schmidt and Michael Weisskopf (New York: HarperCollins, 2000).

306 "Eleanor was strong . . ." author's interview with Arthur Schlesinger, Jr.

306 "Being first lady is a very . . ." author's interview with Hillary Clinton.

308 "Ladies and gentlemen . . ." *New York Times* and the *New York Daily News,* February 7, 2000.

308 "It's Hillary or nobody . . ." Ambassador Tom Siebert to the author, and see also Virginia Kelley, *Leading with My Heart* (New York: Simon & Schuster, 1994), pp. 190–98.

308 "This is a very bonded couple . . ." author's interview with Donna Shalala.

309 "Clinton was the first . . ." George Stephanopoulos to the author.

309 "My boyfriend . . ." Maraniss, *First in His Class,* p. 313.

310 "She was already a perfectionist . . ." Dorothy Rodham to the author.

310 "He thought she was . . ." Brooke Shearer to the author.

310 "Anything Hillary says . . ." Derek Shearer to the author.

310 "If something ever happened . . ." Ann Stock to the author.

311 "She brought discipline . . ." Ruth Goldway to the author.

311 In 1980 . . . Doug Schoen to the author and see also Maraniss, _First in His Class,_ p. 455, and Sheehy, _Hillary's Choice,_ p. 191.

312 "Bill's debt to his wife . . ." based on transcript of January 26, 1992, _60 Minutes_ and author's interview with Steve Kroft.

312 "Her public image is so . . ." Mandy Grunwald to the author.

312 "passionately . . ." Joe Klein to the author.

313 "In my whole life . . ." CNN WorldView transcript of May 7, 2000, John King, reporter.

314 "The same thing . . ." George Stephanopoulos to the author.

314 "All the reporting on Bill Clinton . . ." Mandy Grunwald to the author.

315 "Hillary does not believe . . ." Donna Shalala to the author.

315 "In some ways she was a victim . . ." George Stephanopoulos to the author.

316 "We don't talk about deeply . . ." Dorothy Rodham to the author; see also Sheehy's _Hillary's Choice,_ pp. 318–19.

316 Her pastor . . . Martha Sherrill to the author.

316 "You're lucky to be in my . . ." David Gergen to the author.

317 "They get into arguments . . ." Donna Shalala to the author.

317 The Clintons loved to watch . . . Joe Klein to the author.

317 In December 1998 . . . _Time,_ December 28, 1998–January 4, 1999.

317 "He acts like a baby around her . . ." George Stephanopoulos to the author.

317 "She had a very clear sense . . ." Mandy Grunwald to the author.

318 "They developed an arrogance . . ." Clinton Cabinet member to the author.

319 "Right away . . ." Ann Blackman to the author.

319 "The president was worried . . ." Ambassador Betty King to the author.

319 "It was the first time . . ." Melanne Verveer to the author.

320 "They appointed a woman . . ." Ambassador King to the author.

320 In 1993 health care . . . This portion of the chapter is drawn from conversations with Laura D'Andrea Tyson, David Gergen, Robert Boorstin, Steven Ricchetti and Melanne Verveer as well as Haynes Johnson and David Broder's _The System,_ and Connie Bruck's lengthy _New Yorker_ essay "Hillary the Pol," May 30, 1994.

321 "We needed a talented . . ." Johnson and Broder, _The System,_ p. 9.

321 "We knew it would be easier . . ." Steven Ricchetti to the author.

321 "There were difficult feelings . . ." Melanne Verveer to the author.

321 "People would know I was serious about . . ." Johnson and Broder, _The System,_ p. 101.

321 "I was always wowed . . ." Laura D'Andrea Tyson to the author.

321 "She absolutely thought . . ." Robert Boorstin to the author.

322 "I understood, as many people never tired of telling me . . ." Johnson and Broder, _The System,_ p. 102.

322 " 'H—' began a typical . . ." Ibid., p. 16.

322 I don't care how they do things . . . Bruck, _New Yorker,_ May 30, 1994.

323 One of the few . . . Laura D'Andrea Tyson to the author.

323 The West Wing . . . Robert Boorstin to the author.

324 On September 22, 1993 . . . Melanne Verveer to the author.

324 But Steve Ricchetti . . . Steve Ricchetti to the author.

324 "She was really smart . . ." Laura D'Andrea Tyson to the author.

325 "The reaction was more negative . . ." Bruck, *New Yorker,* May 30, 1994.

325 "Bill and I . . . did not come to Washington . . ." Ibid.

325 "Hillary let the perfect become the enemy of the good . . ." Mandy Grunwald to the author.

325 "There was a chance to get it done . . ." Steven Ricchetti to the author.

325 Rather than reaching out . . . author's interviews with Martha Sherrill and Bob Woodward.

327 As far as Hillary was . . . Mandy Grunwald to the author.

328 "She doesn't treat the stories . . ." Mandy Grunwald to the author.

328 Early in 1995 . . . author's interview with Marian Burros; see also *New York Times,* January 10, 1995, p. 1.

329 The article was, in the words . . . author's interview with Andrew Rosenthal.

330 "Hillary does not waste time . . ." Bruck, *New Yorker,* May 30, 1994.

330 As usual, her husband . . . author's interview with George Stephanopoulos.

330 "I'm very confused by her . . ." author's interview with Donna Shalala.

330 By the spring of 1994 . . . based on interviews with David Gergen, Ann Stock, Robert Boorstin and Joe Klein.

331 "She was adamant . . ." Mandy Grunwald to the author.

331 White House counsel . . . Lloyd Cutler to the author.

331 "She basically lied . . ." Ann Blackman to the author.

332 "No group is more . . ." Bob Woodward to the author.

332 "I'm feeling very . . ." George Stephanopoulos, *All Too Human* (New York, Boston: Little, Brown, 1999), p. 232.

333 "I really believe . . ." Hillary Clinton to the author.

334 "I saw her get off that plane . . ." Joe Klein to the author.

334 "I'm so totally engaged . . ." Hillary Clinton to the author.

334 "It is a violation . . ." transcript of Hillary Clinton's United Nations Conference on Women speech, September 5, 1995, from the White House Office of the First Lady.

335 "I like subterfuge . . ." author's interview with a Dick Morris associate who wished to remain anonymous.

335 Typically, rather than opt . . . author's interview with Joe Klein.

336 "It's not a defined responsibility . . ." Hillary Clinton to the author.

337 "I don't see her as . . ." Donna Shalala to the author.

337 "She was quietly present throughout . . ." Steven Ricchetti to the author.

337 "Hers is an instance of . . ." Melanne Verveer to the author.

338 "Bob, do you think . . ." Toobin, *A Vast Conspiracy,* p. 167.

338 Clinton's oldest friends . . . author's interviews with Ambassador Tom Siebert and Tom Caplan.

339 "His best friend is . . ." author's interview with Derek Shearer.

339 "We all protected the president . . ." author's interview with Donna Shalala.

340 White House correspondent . . . Helen Thomas to the author.

341 "What else can she do . . ." author's interview with George Stephanopoulos.

342 "She blocks it out . . ." author's interview with Mandy Grunwald.

342 "This was not something we talked about . . ." author's interview with Melanne Verveer.

343 First she had to save . . . author's interviews with Steven Ricchetti as well as other close friends of the Clintons who preferred to remain anonymous; see also John F. Harris, "Clinton's Final Run," *Washington Post Magazine,* September 10, 2000.

344 "She had to forgive him . . ." Melanne Verveer to the author.

344 "I believe deeply in . . ." CNN "The World Today," May 14, 1999, "Hillary Rodham Clinton Discusses Her Trip to Macedonia."

345 Following his speech . . . author's interview with Jonathan Alter.

345 In April 1999 . . . transcript of Millennium Evening: "Lessons Learned from a Violent Century," April 12, 1999, the White House, Office of the Press Secretary.

346 "I want independence . . ." Hillary Clinton interview by Lucinda Franks, *Talk,* September 1999.

346 "I am very grateful . . ." transcript of remarks by the president at "Broadway for Hillary Event," October 25, 1999, the White House, Office of the Press Secretary.

346 At 3 A.M. . . . Steven Ricchetti to the author.

347 In February 1992 . . . anonymous interview with White House aide.

347 When, years before . . . David Maraniss, *The Clinton Enigma* (New York: Simon & Schuster, 1999), p. 110.

347 "Everybody that always . . ." John F. Harris, "His Final Run," *Washington Post Magazine,* September 10, 2000.

Chapter 12
LAURA AND GEORGE W. BUSH

351 Interviews and conversations with Tom Bernstein, William Broyles, Jr., Stephen Harrigan, Victor Emanuel and Gregory Curtis—friends and associates of Laura and George W. Bush—helped provide the background for this chapter. *First Son—George W. Bush and the Bush Family Dynasty* by Bill Minutaglio (New York: Times Books, 1999) and *Shrub—the Short But Happy Political Life of George W. Bush* by Molly Ivins (New York: Vintage Books, 2000) were useful, as was *Friday Night Lights* by H. G. Bissinger (New York: Da Capo Press, 2000). Also helpful in understanding George W. Bush's brief life in politics is "The Redemption" by Nicholas Lemann, *New Yorker,* January 31, 2000.

351 "I've always done what . . ." Skip Hollandsworth, "Reading Laura Bush," *Texas Monthly,* November 1996.

351 "I have the best wife . . ." *People,* January 29, 2001.

351 "I hope you will join me . . ." President George W. Bush, State of the Union Address to a Joint Session of Congress, January 29, 2002.

352 "He didn't like it when . . ." Evan Smith, "George, Washington," *Texas Monthly,* June 1999.

353 Midland, built by oil money . . . Bissinger, *Friday Night Lights,* p. 212.

353 "a place where neighbors . . ." "Remarks of Laura Bush Republican National Convention," 2nd Session, July 31, 2000.

353 "I felt very obligated . . ." Ibid.

353 "She would never . . ." Julia Reed Reed, "The Calm Amid the Storm," *Newsweek,* November 22, 1999.

354 "It was a terrible . . ." Frank Bruni, "Quiet Strength: For Laura Bush, a Direction She Never Wished to Go In," *New York Times,* July 31, 2000, p. 1A.

354 "This place . . ." Text of Remarks by President-elect Bush, *Associated Press,* Midland, Texas, January 17, 2001.

354 "Young George . . ." Minutaglio, *First Son,* p. 98.

354 "passing on legacy . . ." Ibid., p. 178.

354 "A lot of people who . . ." Ibid., p. 101.

354 "a very ferocious mother" "The Choice 2000: The Wives," *Frontline,* (PBS video transcript).

354 "My father doesn't have . . ." Minutaglio, *First Son,* p. 117.

355 "George was never . . ." Ibid., p. 87.

355 "I was so uninterested in politics . . ." Ibid., p. 184.

355 "Smitten, I must confess . . ." Myrna Blyth and Nancy Evans, "Fighting for the Family," *Ladies' Home Journal,* November 1, 2000.

356 "The thing that I liked . . ." Minutaglio, *First Son,* p. 184.

356 "I've always done . . ." *Houston Chronicle,* July 20, 1997.

356 "And what do you do . . ." Mark Murray, "A Bush White House: Reading Laura Bush," *National Journal,* October 28, 2000.

356 "darn near collapsed . . ." Bruni, "Quiet Strength."

356 "My daddy and granddad . . ." Lois Romano and George Lardner, Jr., "Young Bush, A Political Natural, Revs Up," *The Washington Post,* July 29, 1999, p. A1.

356 Petrified, she spoke too softly . . . John Hanchette, "Laura Welch Bush: Shy No More," *USA Today,* June 23, 2000.

357 "How was my speech?" . . . Reed, "The Calm Amid the Storm."

357 "These babies will be fine . . ." Ibid.

357 "I realized our life . . ." "Read Her Lips," *CNN* story, debuted on April 8, 2001.

357 At age forty . . . Skip Hollandsworth, "Who Is George W. Bush? Younger. Wilder?" *Texas Monthly,* June 1999.

357 "after nights that weren't particularly . . ." Ibid.

357 "He looked in the mirror . . ." Minutaglio, *First Son,* p. 210.

358 "He attended Greenwich Country . . ." Ivins, *Shrub,* p. xx.

358 "She's pretty good . . ." Lois Romano, "Laura Bush: A Twist on Traditional," *The Washington Post,* May 14, 2000, p. A1.

359 "I really don't think George . . ." "The Real George W. Bush," *ABC News* interview (transcript prepared by Burrelle's Information Services).

359 "the perfect wife . . ." Hanchette, "Shy No More."

359 "she's a good adviser . . ." Blyth and Evans, "Fighting for the Family."

359 "If I differ . . ." Hanchette, "Shy No More."

359 "America's starved for something . . ." Bruni, "Quiet Strength."

360 "People may not believe that . . ." Gregory Curtis, "At Home with Laura," *Time,* January 8, 2001.

360 "Let's see, I don't know . . ." Sarah Wildman, "Portrait of a Lady: How Laura Bush Conquered Feminism," *The New Republic,* August 20, 2001.

360 "[My mother-in-law] is very . . ." Skip Hollandsworth, "Reading Laura Bush," *Texas Monthly,* November 1996.

362 "A second plane . . ." Dan Balz and Bob Woodward, "America's Chaotic Road to War: Bush's Global Strategy Began to Take Shape in First Frantic Hours After Attack," *The Washington Post,* January 27, 2002, p. A1.

362 "I remember thinking . . ." "Remarks by Mrs. Laura Bush," National Press Club, November 8, 2001.

362 "just for the comfort . . ." Susan Page, "The Power Behind the President," *USA Today,* September 25, 2001.

362 "never created any . . ." " 'There Is No Doubt in My Mind. Not One Doubt,' " *The Washington Post,* February 3, 2002, p. A14.

362 "When sad or frightening . . ." Laura Bush, "Elementary School Letter," September 12, 2001.

362 "fierce when stirred . . ." George W. Bush, "Address at the National Cathedral," September 14, 2001.

362 "we are a kinder . . ." "Remarks by Mrs. Laura Bush," National Press Club, November 8, 2001.

363 "while there are some bad . . ." Ibid.

363 "Children will sidle up . . ." Ibid.

363 "a worldwide effort . . ." "Radio Address by Laura Bush to the Nation," Crawford, Texas, November 17, 2001.

363 "horror . . ." Ibid.

363 "human dignity . . ." "Remarks by Mrs. Laura Bush to the U.N. Commission on the Status of Women," March 8, 2002.

363 most admired . . . Laurence McQuillan, "Bush dominates most-admired poll," *USA Today,* January 26, 2001.

ACKNOWLEDGMENTS

Amanda Urban, my friend and the agent for my last four books, started me on this one and offered encouragement and coaxing throughout. I am grateful to Linda Healey, my first editor, who was always available with her usual blend of wisdom, humor and good sense. My editor, Jonathan Segal, proved to be everything an editor should be, and more: encouraging and exacting, intellectually exciting and excited. His tiny, fine script in the margins immeasurably improved the manuscript. My researcher Leslie Powell, a Columbia University scholar in Russian, was there from the beginning and never failed to unearth documents or solve computer crises. I particularly wish to thank historian Benjamin Skinner for his invaluable help in researching and editing the final chapter. Most of all my thanks go to my husband, who sustained me throughout, tirelessly reading and rereading each draft, unflagging in his determination to get the best out of me.

Many others helped me along the way. I wish to thank: Penny Adams, Roger Ailes, Jonathan Alter, Joe Armstrong, Thomas "Lud" Ashley, Jenny Lyn Bader, Richard Beattie, Paul Begala, Mike Berman, Richard Bernstein, Michael Beschloss, Soma Golden Behr (for title inspiration), Ann Blackman, Robert Boorstin, Benjamin Bradlee, Alan Brinkley, Douglas Brinkley, Tom Brokaw, William Broyles, Jr., Susan Burden, Marian Burros, Gahl Hodges Burt, Horace Busby, Barbara Bush, George Bush, Pat Caddell, Tom Caplan, Lisa Caputo, Margaret Carlson, Robert Caro, Liz Carpenter, Jimmy Carter, Rosalynn Carter, Ellen Chessler, Clark Clifford, Hillary Rodham Clinton, Richard Cohen, Joan Ganz Cooney, John Milton Cooper, Paul Costello, Edward Cox, George Crile, Lloyd Cutler, Margaret Truman Daniel, Michael Deaver, Tom Donilon, Lisa Drew, Kenneth Duberstein, Robin Duke, Barrie Dunsmore, Julie Nixon Eisenhower, Paul Fay, Frances FitzGerald, Marlin Fitzwater, Linda Bird Francke, Craig Fuller, David Gergen, Mary Ellen Glynn, Ruth Goldway, Henry F. Graff, Katharine Graham, Meg Greenfield, Mandy Grunwald, Charles Guggenheim, Richard Haas, Kitty Hart, Jane Stanton Hitchcock, Barbara Howar, Maxine Isaacs, Ellen James, Linda Leroy Janklow, Morton Janklow, James A. Johnson, Lady Bird Johnson, Lynda Bird Johnson, Ann Jordan, Vernon Jordan, David Kennerly, Betty King, Gwendolyn King, Henry Kissinger, Joe Klein, Thomas Knock, Steve Kroft, Raymond Lamontagne, Trude Lash, Ellen Levine, Arthur Stanley Link, David Maraniss, Patricia Mattson, Ann McDaniel, Harry McPherson, Harry Middleton, Walter F. Mondale, Brian Mulrooney, Mila Mulrooney, Bunny Murdoch, Verne Newton, Peggy Noonan, Peter Osnos, Alan J. Pakula, Anna Perez, Peter G. Peterson, Jane Plakias, Jody Powell, Sally Quinn, Donnie Radcliffe, Gerald Rafshoon, Steven Rattner, Nancy Reagan, Richard Reeves, Nancy Reynolds, Frank Rich (for special help with my subtitle), Steven Ricchetti, Dorothy Rodham, Susan Porter Rose, Andrew Rosenthal, Dr. Mitchell Rosenthal, Winthrop Rutherfurd III, Morley Safer, Pierre Salinger, Diane Sawyer, Arthur Schlesinger, Jr., Doug Schoen, Rex Scouten, Donna Shalala, Brooke Shearer, Derek Shearer, Martha Sherrill, Tom Siebert, Liz Smith, Ted Sorensen, Stuart Spencer, Lesley Stahl, George Stephanopoulos, Ann Stock, Strobe Talbott, Helen Thomas, Betty Tilson, Laura D'Andrea Tyson, Jack Valenti, William J. Vanden Heuvel, Melanne Verveer, Mike Wallace, Barbara Walters, Margaret Warner, Sheila Weidenfeld, Sherrie Rollins Westin, Maureen White, Kate Roosevelt Whitney, Hal Wingo, Alex Witchel and Bob Woodward.

Photo Credits

Page 13. Woodrow Wilson and Edith Bolling Galt, still unmarried, in Philadelphia, October 9, 1915. © *Bettmann/Corbis*

Page 41. Woodrow and Edith Wilson, March 21, 1920. © *Bettmann/Corbis*

Page 45. The Roosevelts, Easter Sunday, 1941. © *Bettmann/Corbis*

Page 54. Franklin, Eleanor and Sarah Delano Roosevelt, circa 1920. © *Bettmann/Corbis*

Page 72. Franklin and Eleanor Roosevelt, circa 1933. © *Bettmann/Corbis*

Page 88. The Trumans in Kansas City, Missouri, December 30, 1949. © *Bettmann/Corbis*

Page 94. Harry and Bess Truman, April 15, 1942. © *Bettmann/Corbis*

Page 104. The Kennedys leave Otis Air Force Base Hospital in Massachusetts after the death of their son Patrick, August 14, 1963. © *Bettmann/Corbis*

Page 118 Jack and Jacqueline Kennedy with André Malraux, May 11, 1962. © *Bettmann/Corbis*

Page 133. Jacqueline Kennedy and her children, November 25, 1963. © *Bettmann/Corbis*

Page 137. The Johnsons leaving Washington for their Texas ranch, August 25, 1955. © *Bettmann/Corbis*

Page 165. Lyndon and Lady Bird Johnson, May 17, 1966. © *Bettmann/Corbis*

Page 171. The Nixons in Skidway, Georgia, October 12, 1970. © *Bettmann/Corbis*

Page 179. Richard and Pat Nixon, July 12, 1952. © *Bettmann/Corbis*

Page 199. The Fords on their wedding day, October 15, 1948. *Courtesy Gerald R. Ford Library*

Page 213. Jerry and Betty Ford, December 4, 1976. © *Bettmann/Corbis*

Page 215. The Carters on their campaign plane, October 24, 1976. © *Bettmann/Corbis*

Page 242. Jimmy and Rosalynn Carter, December 24, 1980. © *Bettmann/Corbis*

Page 244. The Reagans at their ranch in the Malibu Mountains, California, 1956. © *Bettmann/Corbis*

Page 262. Ronald and Nancy Reagan, September 30, 1982. © *Bettmann/Corbis*

Page 274. The Bushes at the White House on November 4, 1992, before the election results were in. © *Reuters/Corbis-Bettmann*

Page 280. George and Barbara Bush, January 6, 1945. *Courtesy George Bush Presidential Library*

Page 306. The Clintons campaigning in Independence, Missouri, September 7, 1992. © *Reuters/Corbis-Bettmann*

Page 339. Bill and Hillary Clinton, August 14, 2000. © *AFP/Corbis-Bettmann*

Page 351. George W. and Laura Bush on Inauguration Day, 2001. © *Reuters/Corbis-Bettmann*

INDEX

Moore, Virginia, 86
Moran, James P., 342
Morris, Dick, 311, 332, 335
Moyers, Bill, 149, 152, 154, 160, 164
Mulrooney, Brian, 297, 298, 303
Mulrooney, Mila, 303–4
Murdoch, Bunnie, 296
My Turn (N. Reagan), 8, 259

National Mental Health Institute, 99
Naval Academy, U.S., 219–20
Nehru, Jawaharlal, 119
Nessen, Ron, 210
New Deal, 46, 70, 76, 87
Newton, Verne, 367
New York State Bar Association, 197
Niebuhr, Reinhold, 110, 223
Nineteenth Amendment, 10
Nixon, Hannah, 175, 176, 197
Nixon, Julie (Eisenhower), 180, 184,
   191, 192, 193, 194, 196, 197
Nixon, Pat Ryan:
   ambitions of, 175
   early years of, 173–74, 183
   and first lady's role, 185, 190–91,
      194, 195, 206, 207
   hard work of, 185, 190, 191–92,
      194
   and husband's career, 175–76, 177,
      178, 181–82, 183–84, 191, 193,
      194, 195–97, 201
   husband's humiliation of, 179–80,
      186–87, 191, 195, 196–97, 214
   husband's neglect of, 3, 7, 172, 177,
      180, 182, 185, 188–89, 191, 192,
      193–94, 197, 198, 201
   and husband's resignation, 195–97
   illness and death of, 197–98
   independence of, 175
   marriage of, *see* Nixon marriage
   and media, 185, 188–89, 332
   physical appearance and personality
      traits of, 5, 177, 182, 183, 188–90

public image of, 177, 181, 183, 186,
   187, 188–89
public withdrawal of, 5, 180, 182,
   192, 193, 197
travels of, 172, 181, 182, 188–89,
   195
in wife's role, 175–76, 177, 181, 183,
   184, 191–92, 193
Nixon, Richard M.:
   and Bush's career, 285, 286–87
   Checkers speech of, 179–80
   and choice of wife, 9, 173
   and CREEP, 194
   on destiny, 182
   disbarred, 197
   early years of, 91, 173–74
   emotion controlled by, 172, 174–75,
      192, 198
   Ford's pardon of, 201–2, 213
   isolation sought by, 185, 192–94,
      196
   Johnsons and, 158
   Kennedy and, 110
   as lightning rod for others' emo-
      tions, 177, 178–79, 184, 185
   and media, 179–80, 184, 188, 332
   memoirs of, 183, 191, 196
   and mother, 176, 197
   personality traits of, 173, 174–75,
      180, 187, 192, 195, 292, 344
   political advisers to, 177, 185–86,
      193, 239, 285
   political campaigns of, 176–77,
      178–81, 183–84, 185, 192–93,
      194, 198
   political career of, 175, 177, 179–80,
      192, 200, 236
   politics as obsession of, 7, 172, 173,
      175, 176–78, 180, 182, 183–84,
      196, 198
   and Red scare, 176, 177–78, 181
   resignation of, 195–97, 199, 213,
      342
   and tapes, 194, 195